Microaggressions
and Marginality

Microaggressions and Marginality

Manifestation, Dynamics, and Impact

Edited by

Derald Wing Sue

WILEY

John Wiley & Sons, Inc.

This publication is designed to provide accurate and authoritative information in regard to the subject matter covered. It is sold with the understanding that the publisher is not engaged in rendering professional services. If legal, accounting, medical, psychological, or any other expert assistance is required, the services of a competent professional person should be sought.

Designations used by companies to distinguish their products are often claimed as trademarks. In all instances where John Wiley & Sons, Inc., is aware of a claim, the product names appear in initial capital or all capital letters. Readers, however, should contact the appropriate companies for more complete information regarding trademarks and registration.

For general information on our other products and services please contact our Customer Care Department within the United States at (800) 762-2974, outside the United States at (317) 572-3993 or fax (317) 572-4002.

Wiley also publishes its books in a variety of electronic formats. Some content that appears in print may not be available in electronic books. For more information about Wiley products, visit our web site at www.wiley.com.

Library of Congress Cataloging-in-Publication Data:
  Microaggressions and marginality: manifestation, dynamics, and impact/edited by Derald Wing Sue.
    p. cm.
  Includes index.
  ISBN 978-0-470-49139-3 (cloth); 9780470627068 (eMobi); 9780470627198 (ePDF); 9780470627204(ePub)
  1. Aggressiveness. 2. Cross-cultural counseling. I. Sue, Derald Wing.
  BF575.A3M445 2010
  305—dc22
                                                                    2009050972

Printed in the United States of America

V10004692_092018

Contents

Preface

Microaggressions and Marginality: Manifestation, Dynamics, and Impact is the second major text that follows the previous publication of *Microaggressions in Everyday Life: Race, Gender, and Sexual Orientation* (Sue, 2010). Like its predecessor, it represents a major step forward in (1) exploring the psychological dynamics of unconscious and unintentional expressions of bias and prejudice toward socially devalued groups; (2) exploring the numerous manifestations of microaggressions, the harm they engender, and how marginalized groups and individuals cope with them; and (3) expanding the concept of microaggressions beyond simply that of race and the expressions of racism.

It differs, however, in that this recent work invites various experts in their respective fields to present their original research and scholarly works across a broad spectrum of groups in our society who have traditionally been treated as second-class citizens and lesser beings, thereby being marginalized and disempowered. There are separate chapters on racial/ethnic, international/cultural, gender, lesbian/gay/bisexual/transgender (LGBT), disability, class, and religious microaggressions. In the case of racial/ethnic microaggressions, multiple chapters are devoted to specific populations such as African Americans, Latino/a/Hispanic Americans, Asian Americans, Indigenous populations, and biracial/multiracial people.

In less than a decade, research and scholarly theorizing on racial microaggressions have exploded on the scene, especially in the social science literature devoted to topics of implicit bias and subtle racism. With the realization that racial microaggressions reflect the worldviews of perpetrators, such as their ethnocentric assumptions about human behavior, values, biases, and prejudices, it did not take long for other marginalized groups in our society to realize that the manifestation and dynamics of microaggressions could be equally applied to nearly all socially devalued groups. Microaggressions reflect attitudes and beliefs about inclusion/exclusion, superiority/inferiority, healthiness/unhealthiness, and normality/abnormality between groups. While microaggressions include both conscious and unconscious biased beliefs and attitudes, current research reveals that it is the unconscious, subtle, and unintentional expressions that are most damaging and harmful to oppressed groups. Thus, microaggressive research now makes clear that overt expressions of racism, sexism, ageism, and ableism are less problematic than the covert and unconscious manifestations delivered by well-intentioned individuals.

Microaggressions and Marginality: Manifestation, Dynamics, and Impact (1) conceptually organizes the marginalizing experiences of socially devalued groups in our society under an oppression framework, (2) explores and discusses the common dynamics of covert and unintentional biases directed toward them, (3) investigates the detrimental harm perpetrated against these groups, (4) explores possible coping strategies that best allow targets to survive such onslaughts, and (5) recommends what society must do if it is to reduce prejudice and discrimination directed at these groups. What is unique about this text is the devotion of separate in-depth chapters addressing group-specific microaggressions by scholars who are members of these groups or who are working with these populations. This allows readers to compare and contrast the various group-universal and group-specific microaggressions encountered by people of color, women, the poor, religious minorities, gays/lesbians, and so forth. In a number of chapters, groundbreaking research is reported for the first time on group-specific microaggressions.

Part One, "Microaggressions and Marginality," opens with an introductory chapter.

- Chapter 1: "Microaggressions, Marginality, and Oppression: An Introduction" presents the original taxonomy of racial microaggressions that has generated so much interest in understanding the psychological dynamics, manifestation, and impact of unintentional, subtle, and covert forms of racism. In this chapter, the relationship of microaggression, marginality, and oppression applied to all socially devalued groups is proposed as an introduction to the many group-specific chapters to follow.

Part Two, "Racial/Ethnic Manifestation of Microaggressions," is composed of five separate chapters, each dealing with a specific racial/ethnic minority group and/or how microaggressions impact their mental/physical well-being, education, employment, and other endeavors in life.

- Chapter 2: "Black Undergraduates' Experiences with Perceived Racial Microaggressions in Predominately White Colleges and Universities" by Watkins, LaBarrie, and Appio reports an important research study on how Black students experience the numerous racial snubs and invalidations in their day-to-day lives at primarily White institutions. They provide numerous helpful suggestions about what institutions of higher education must do to ameliorate these constant invalidations.

- Chapter 3: "Microaggressions and the Life Experience of Latina/o Americans" by Rivera, Forquer, and Rangel also presents important research on racial microaggressions experienced by Latinos/as in their daily lives. Using a similar qualitative approach as that employed in Chapter 2, these authors go on to describe the types of racial microaggressions this population is most likely to experience and offers possible solutions.
- Chapter 4: "Racial Microaggressions Directed at Asian Americans: Modern Forms of Prejudice and Discrimination" by Lin applies the racial microaggression taxonomy to Asian Americans. The author discusses unique issues that confront this population and compares and contrasts the microaggressions experienced by Asian Americans to those of African Americans and Latinos/as.
- Chapter 5: "The Context of Racial Microaggressions Against Indigenous Peoples: Same Old Racism or Something New?" by Hill, Kim, and Williams indicates how colonialism is a basic part of historic genocide directed toward Indigenous populations throughout the world. They cover various forms of microaggressions directed toward these groups and the harmful effects of them.
- Chapter 6: "Multiracial Microaggressions: Exposing Monoracism in Everyday Life and Clinical Practice" by Johnston and Nadal is among the first scholarly attempts to critically examine the unique and common forms of subtle racism perpetrated against this population. They make helpful suggestions for mental health practitioners who hope to truly understand the life experiences of multiracial clients.
- Chapter 7: "Microaggressions and the Pipeline for Scholars of Color" by Guzman, Trevino, Lubuguin, and Aryan looks at how microaggressions are partially responsible for the lack of faculty of color in institutions of higher education. Throughout the recruitment, retention, and promotion phases, faculty of color encounter significant obstacles in academia. These authors provide possible solutions to this dilemma.

Part Three, "Other Socially Devalued Group Microaggressions: International/Cultural, Sexual Orientation and Transgender, Disability, Class, and Religious," is composed of six chapters that discuss several other socially devalued or marginalized groups in our society. Little doubt exists that international/cultural, gender, sexual orientation, disability, class, and religious microaggressions have historically and continue to be directed toward these specific groups. As a result, the inclusion of these groups will give readers greater understanding of how unintentional biases, prejudices, and discrimination are the result of society's marginalization of those who are socially devalued.

- Chapter 8: "Microaggressions Experienced by International Students Attending U.S. Institutions of Higher Education" by S. Kim and R. H. Kim provides valuable information to colleges and universities about the plight affecting international students and what must be done to make the campus climate truly multicultural.
- Chapter 9: "The Manifestation of Gender Microaggressions" by Capodilupo, Nadal, Corman, Hamit, Lyons, and Weinberg represents another original study aimed at identifying gender microaggressions and their manifestation and impact.
- Chapter 10: "Sexual Orientation and Transgender Microaggressions: Implications for Mental Health and Counseling" by Nadal, Rivera, and Corpus applies the microaggression taxonomy to the LGBT population. They discuss important implications for culturally competent mental health counseling.
- Chapter 11: "Microaggressive Experiences of People with Disabilities" by Keller and Galgay conducts a study of people with disabilities and finds unique insults and invalidations that they experience. They conclude with helpful suggestions about what able-bodied people must do to stop the constant onslaught of disability microaggressions.
- Chapter 12: "Class Dismissed: Making the Case for the Study of Classist Microaggressions" by Smith and Redington is one of the first conceptual pieces to look at how our society treats our less affluent citizens from a microaggressive perspective. While race, gender, and sexual orientation are often discussed in the literature, the power of class discrimination is often overlooked.
- Chapter 13: "Religious Microaggressions in the United States: Mental Health Implications for Religious Minority Groups" by Nadal, Issa, Griffin, Hamit, and Lyons helps readers understand how religious orientation can form the basis of prejudice and discrimination. Not only do they outline a taxonomy of religious microaggressions, but they discuss mental health implications as well.

Part Four, "Microaggression Research," is composed of a final chapter on research.

- Chapter 14: "Microaggression Research: Methodological Review and Recommendations" by Lau and Williams does a superb job in analyzing methodological approaches to microaggression research and issues related to qualitative and quantitative studies and suggests future directions that will prove helpful in strengthening our understanding of this phenomenon. It will arm future researchers with the tools to ask and answer questions about the human condition.

In closing, I wish to acknowledge the help and work of many faculty and graduate students at Teachers College, Columbia University, who have worked with me in producing this volume and the many forthcoming studies on microaggressions. Nearly all contributors are faculty, former doctoral students, current students, or those who have become influenced by them. They represent some of the finest minds in the field, and I am positive they will continue to contribute to the profession.

The important work on racial, gender, sexual orientation, disability, class, religious, and other forms of microaggressions would not have been possible without their energies and efforts. Already, the impact of our work has begun to generate much interest and other scholarly research on this topic. Our work at Teachers College has made us affectionately known as the "microaggression capital of the world." I take pride in this designation but am uncertain how our administration would feel about its possible misinterpretation.

Derald Wing Sue
Editor

About the Editor

Derald Wing Sue is a professor of psychology and education in the Department of Counseling and Clinical Psychology at Teachers College, Columbia University. He has served as president of the Society for the Psychological Study of Ethnic Minority Issues, the Society of Counseling Psychology, and the Asian American Psychological Association. Dr. Sue is an associate editor of *American Psychologist* and continues to be a consulting editor for numerous publications. He is the author of over 150 publications, including 15 books, and is well known for his work on racism/antiracism, cultural competence, multicultural counseling and therapy, and social justice advocacy. Two of his books, *Counseling the Culturally Diverse: Theory and Practice* (Jossey-Bass) and *Overcoming Our Racism: The Journey to Liberation* (John Wiley & Sons), are considered classics in the field. Dr. Sue's most recent research on racial, gender, and sexual orientation microaggressions has been a major breakthrough in understanding how everyday slights, insults, and invalidations toward marginalized groups create psychological harm to their mental and physical health and create disparities for them in education, employment, and health care. A national survey has identified Derald Wing Sue as "the most influential multicultural scholar in the United States," and his works are among the most frequently cited.

Microaggressions
and Marginality

PART I

MICROAGGRESSIONS AND MARGINALITY

CHAPTER 1

Microaggressions, Marginality, and Oppression

An Introduction

DERALD WING SUE

MICROAGGRESSIONS ARE THE everyday verbal, nonverbal, and environmental slights, snubs, or insults, whether intentional or unintentional, that communicate hostile, derogatory, or negative messages to target persons based solely upon their marginalized group membership (Sue et al., 2007). In many cases, these hidden messages may invalidate the group identity or experiential reality of target persons, demean them on a personal or group level, communicate they are lesser human beings, suggest they do not belong with the majority group, threaten and intimidate, or relegate them to inferior status and treatment. While microaggressions are generally discussed from the perspective of race and racism (Pierce, Carew, Pierce-Gonzalez, & Willis, 1978; Solórzano, Ceja, & Yosso, 2000; Sue et al., 2007), any marginalized group in our society may become targets: people of color, women, lesbian/gay/bisexual/transgendered people (LGBTs), those with disabilities, religious minorities, and so on (Sue, 2010).

The most detrimental forms of microaggressions are usually delivered by well-intentioned individuals who are unaware that they have engaged in harmful conduct toward a socially devalued group. These everyday occurrences may on the surface appear quite harmless, trivial, or be described as "small slights," but research indicates they have a powerful impact upon the psychological well-being of marginalized groups (Brondolo et al., 2008; Swim, Hyers, Cohen, & Ferguson, 2001; Szymanski, Kashubeck-West, & Meyer, 2008) and affect their standard of living by creating inequities in health care (Sue & Sue, 2008), education (Bell, 2002), and employment (Purdie-Vaughns, Davis, Steele, & Ditlmann, 2008).

Racial, gender, sexual orientation, disability, class, and religious micro-aggressions deliver hidden demeaning messages that often lie outside the level of conscious awareness of perpetrators. These hidden messages, however, have detrimental impact upon recipients through the contradictory metacommunications they convey. Some sample microaggressions and their hidden meanings are given next (taken from Sue, 2010; Sue & Capodilupo, 2008).

Racial Microaggressions:

- A White man or woman clutches her purse or checks his wallet as a Black or Latino man approaches or passes them. (Hidden message: You and your group are criminals.)
- An Asian American, born and raised in the United States, is compli-mented for speaking "good English." (Hidden message: You are not a true American. You are a perpetual foreigner in your own country.)
- A Black couple is seated at a table in the restaurant next to the kitchen despite there being other empty and more desirable tables located at the front. (Hidden message: You are a second-class citizen and undeserving of first-class treatment.)

Gender Microaggressions:

- An assertive female manager is labeled as a "bitch," while her male counterpart is described as "a forceful leader." (Hidden message: Women should be passive and allow men to be the decision makers.)
- A female physician wearing a stethoscope is mistaken for a nurse. (Hidden message: Women should occupy nurturing and not decision-making roles. Women are less capable than men).
- Whistles or catcalls are heard from men as a woman walks down the street. (Hidden message: Your body/appearance is for the enjoyment of men. You are a sex object.)

Sexual Orientation Microaggressions:

- Students use the term "gay" to describe a fellow student who is socially ostracized. (Hidden message: People who are weird, strange, deviant, or different are "gay.")
- A lesbian client in therapy reluctantly discloses her sexual orientation to a straight therapist by stating she is "into women." The therapist indicates he is not shocked by the disclosure because he once had a client who was "into dogs." (Hidden message: Same-sex attraction is abnormal and deviant.)

- Two gay men hold hands in public and are told not to flaunt their sexuality. (Hidden message: Homosexual displays of affection are abnormal and offensive. Keep it private and to yourselves.)

As indicated previously, microaggressions can be based upon any group that is marginalized in this society. Religion, disability, and social class may also reflect the manifestation of microaggressions. Some of these examples include the following.

- When bargaining over the price of an item, a store owner says to a customer, "Don't try to Jew me down." (Hidden message: Jews are stingy and moneygrubbing.)
- A blind man reports that people often raise their voices when speaking to him. He responds by saying, "Please don't raise your voice; I can hear you perfectly well." (Hidden message: A person with a disability is defined as lesser in all aspects of physical and mental functioning).
- The outfit worn by a TV reality-show mom is described as "classless and trashy." (Hidden message: Lower-class people are tasteless and unsophisticated.)

MARGINALITY AND OPPRESSION

Groups that are marginalized in our society exist on the lower or outer limits of social desirability and consciousness. Whether racial/ethnic minorities, people with disabilities, LGBTs, or women, these groups are perceived negatively, given less status in society, and confined to existing on the margins of our social, cultural, political, and economic systems. The result is often exclusion from the mainstream of life in our society, unequal treatment, and social injustice. The inferior status and treatment associated with marginality are constant, continuing, and cumulative experiences of socially devalued groups. Racial, gender, and sexual orientation microaggressions, for example, are active manifestations of marginality and/or a reflection of a worldview of inclusion/exclusion, superiority/inferiority, normality/abnormality, and desirability/undesirability (Sue, 2003). Because most people experience themselves as good, moral, and decent human beings, conscious awareness of their hidden biases, prejudices, and discriminatory behaviors threatens their self-image. Thus, they may engage in defensive maneuvers to deny their biases, to personally avoid talking about topics such as racism, sexism, heterosexism, and ableism, and to discourage others from bringing up such topics. On the one hand, these maneuvers serve to preserve the self-image of oppressors, but on the other, they silence the voices of the oppressed. In other words, keeping oppression from being acknowledged and enforcing a conspiracy of silence allows oppressors to (1) maintain their innocence (guilt-free) and (2) leave inequities from being challenged (Sue, 2004).

Microaggressions reflect the active manifestation of oppressive worldviews that create, foster, and enforce marginalization. To be confined to the margins of existence in mainstream life is to be oppressed, persecuted, and subjugated; denied full rights of citizenship; imprisoned or trapped to a lower standard of living; stripped of one's humanity and dignity; denied equal access and opportunity; invalidated of one's experiential reality; and restricted or limited as to life choices (Freire, 1970; Hanna, Talley, & Guindon, 2000; Sue, 2004). Oppression can occur through imposition or deprivation. In both cases, they span a continuum from its direct/concrete nature to those with more symbolic or psychological manifestations and from being consciously perpetrated to being unintentional, indirect, and subtle.

IMPOSITION

Oppression by imposition, force, coercion, and duress has been defined by Hanna and colleagues (2000) in the following way: "It is the act of imposing on another or others an object, label, role experience, or set of living conditions that is unwanted, needlessly painful, and detracts from physical or psychological well-being. An imposed object, in this context, can be anything from a bullet, a bludgeon, shackles, or fists, to a penis, unhealthy food, or abusive messages designed to cause or sustain pain, low self-efficacy, reduced self-determination, and so forth. Other examples of oppression by force can be demeaning hard labor, degrading job roles, ridicule, and negative media images and messages that foster and maintain distorted beliefs" (p. 431).

Most of us can immediately recognize the horror and heinous nature of overt and concrete acts of rape (imposition of a penis), torture (imposition of physical and psychological abuse), murder (taking away life), and unjust imprisonment as obvious forms of injustice and unfairness visited upon individuals and groups. Racial hate crimes, for example, are recognized by an overwhelming number of citizens as abhorrent actions that they strongly condemn. They are the actions of White supremacists such as Klan members and Skinheads. Good, moral, and decent folks do not condone such actions. Yet, acts of oppression by imposition or force *through microaggressions* can be many times more harmful to racial/ethnic minorities than hate crimes (Sue, 2010).

The power of microaggressions lies in their invisibility to perpetrators and oftentimes the recipients. The definition of oppression includes imposing "abusive messages" (microaggressions) that both reflect and perpetuate false beliefs about people of color. Those beliefs cause humiliation and pain, reduce self-determination, confine them to lesser job roles and status in society, and deny them equal access and opportunities in education, employment, and health care. Most of the pain and detrimental impact of racism does not come from that of overt racists but from ordinary, normal, decent people who believe in life, liberty, and the pursuit of justice for all. They are unaware of their racial biases and prejudices but act them out in the form of racial microaggressions.

DEPRIVATION

Oppression can also take a second form—that of deprivation. It can be seen as the flip-side of imposition and involves depriving people of desired jobs, an education, health care, or living conditions necessary for physical and mental well-being. Food, clothing, shelter, love, respect, social support, or self-dignity can be wrested from any marginalized group (Hanna et al., 2000). In our history, we once banned the Sioux nation from practicing their spiritual and religious traditions, deprived them of their lands, and took away their dignity as Indigenous people in their own country. Taking away a group's humanity and integrity through forced compliance is a very common practice directed toward marginalized groups. When African American students are told to "calm down" and to speak objectively and without emotion because "emotion is antagonistic to reason" and when Asian Americans are admonished because they are too quiet and nonparticipative in classroom discussions, we are not only imposing Western standards of communication styles upon them but also depriving them of their cultural communication styles. When nursing home attendants address their elderly residents as "sweetie" and "dear," they are unaware of how these microaggressive terms belittle and infantilize the elderly and how they deprive them of their roles as capable and competent adults. "Elderspeak" has been identified as a very harmful and humiliating form of microaggression and can result in a downward spiral for older persons, low self-esteem, withdrawal, and depression (Leland, 2008).

FORMS OF MICROAGGRESSIONS

Microaggressions may take three forms: (1) microassault, (2) microinsult, and (3) microinvalidation (Sue et al., 2007). Figure 1.1 briefly defines each, illustrates their relationship to one another, and lists some common hidden messages/denigrating themes under each category that are directed toward people of color. We use racial microaggressions to illustrate more specifically the forms they take when racism is the primary culprit. Please keep in mind that other marginalized groups either may share or may experience different

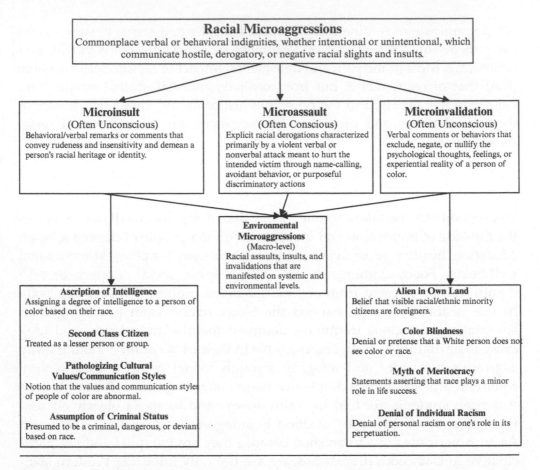

Figure 1.1 Categories and Relationship of Racial Microaggressions. Reproduced from Sue et al. (2007, p. 278).

group-specific themes and hidden messages. Research on gender, sexual orientation, disability, class, and religious microaggressions is needed to identify commonalities and differences that may be directed toward other socially devalued groups.

MICROASSAULTS

Microassaults are conscious biased beliefs or attitudes that are held by individuals and intentionally expressed or acted out overtly or covertly toward a marginalized person or socially devalued group. They differ from the other two forms of microaggressions (to be discussed shortly) in that the perpetrator harbors conscious bias toward an identified and socially devalued group. This bias may be directly and publicly expressed through racist, sexist, or heterosexist statements (using racial epithets or making catcalls toward women, for example) or acted out in any number of ways (preventing a son and daughter from dating or marrying outside of their race, giving second-class service to a woman, and so on). In extreme forms of microassaults, LGBTs may experience teasing and bullying in schools, isolation, physical violence, hate speech, and anti-LGBT legislation.

The case of Matthew Shepard, a gay University of Wyoming student who was tortured, beaten, and tied to a fence to die by two homophobic men, represents extreme acts of hate. Conscious-deliberate bigots generally possess a strong belief in the inferiority of a devalued group and will discriminate when an opportunity arises. Because of strong public condemnation of such undemocratic beliefs and actions, overt expressions of bigotry are most likely to occur when perpetrators feel safe to express their biases and/or they lose emotional control. Social scientists have referred to these forms of overt bigotry as "old-fashioned racism, sexism, or heterosexism" and believe that they have transformed into more disguised, subtle, and less conscious forms (Dovidio & Gaertner, 2000; Salvatore & Shelton, 2007; Sue, 2010; Swim & Cohen, 1997). Interestingly, some research suggests that socially devalued groups may find it easier to deal with old-fashioned forms of bigotry, because no guesswork is involved in discerning the motives of the perpetrator. Unconscious and unintentional bias, however, is ambiguous, and subtle and prejudicial actions are less obvious. As we will shortly see, they create psychological dilemmas for marginalized group members.

MICROINSULTS

Microinsults are also forms of microaggressions, but they differ significantly from microassaults in that they likely occur outside the level of conscious awareness of the perpetrator. These are either interpersonal interactions (verbal/nonverbal) or environmental cues that communicate rudeness, insensitivity, slights, and insults that demean a person's racial, gender, sexual orientation, or group identity and heritage. Microinsults are subtle snubs often unconsciously disguised as a compliment or positive statement directed toward the target person or group. The contradictory communication starts with what appears to be a positive statement but is undermined with an insulting or negative metacommunication.

For example, an African American student who has done outstanding work in his economics class is told by the professor, "You are a credit to your race." On the conscious level, the professor appears to be complimenting the Black student, while on the other hand, the metacommunication contains an insulting message: "Blacks are generally not as intelligent as Whites. You are an exception to your people." This type of microinsult does several things: (1) it disguises a racial bias or prejudicial worldview of the perpetrator; (2) it

allows the perpetrator to cling to the belief in racial inferiority, albeit unconsciously; and (3) it oppresses and denigrates in a guilt-free manner.

Microinsults can take many other forms. For example, they can occur
environmentally. Men who display nude pictures of women from *Hustler* or
Playboy magazines in their places of employment (offices, desks, locker
rooms, etc.) may be unknowingly contributing to sexual objectification.
The hidden message is that women's bodies are not their own and they
exist to service the sexual fantasies of men. The impact is to strip women of
their humanity and the totality of their human essence (intelligence, emotions, personal attributes, and aspirations) and to relegate them to being only
sexual beings. Environmental microaggressions are generally invisible to
those in the majority group but quite visible to those groups most disempowered (Sue, 2010). When a Fortune 400 company displays pictures of its
past CEOs and presidents and they are all White males, there is a powerful
metamessage being communicated to women and employees of color: "You
will not feel comfortable working at this company." "You do not belong
here." "People of color and women do not belong in leadership positions."
"If you choose to stay, your advancement is limited."

MICROINVALIDATIONS

Microinvalidations are similar to microinsults in that they generally occur
outside the level of conscious awareness of perpetrators. However, this form
of microaggression is perhaps the most insidious, damaging, and harmful
form, because microinvalidations directly attack or deny the experiential
realities of socially devalued groups (Sue, 2010). They accomplish this goal
through interpersonal and environmental cues that exclude, negate, or nullify
the psychological thoughts, feelings, beliefs, and experiences of the target
group.

Color blindness, for example, is one of the most frequently delivered
microinvalidations directed toward people of color. It can be defined as an
unwillingness to acknowledge or admit to seeing race or a person's color. Such
an orientation is predicated on the mistaken belief by many Whites that "not
seeing color" means they are unbiased and free of racism. As a result, many
Whites engage in defensive maneuvers not to appear racist by either pretend-
ing not to see color or by actively avoiding any discussions associated with
race (Apfelbaum, Sommers, & Norton, 2008; Bonilla-Silva, 2006). Despite
studies indicating that race and gender are two of the most easily identifiable
qualities seen by people, color blindness and gender blindness inundate our
everyday interactions. "There is only one race: the human race." "When I
look at you, I don't see color." "We are all Americans." "Regardless of your
gender or race, I believe the most qualified person should get the job." Such

statements and their orientation serve to deny the racial, gender, or sexual orientation reality and experiences of these groups. Sue (2010) has suggested that "the denial of differences is really a denial of power and privilege. The denial of power and privilege is really a denial of personal benefits that accrue to certain privileged groups by virtue of inequities." The ultimate denial is a denial that dominant group members profit from the isms of our society and a denial of personal responsibility to take action.

PSYCHOLOGICAL DYNAMICS OF MICROAGGRESSIONS

In a previous publication, Sue and colleagues (2007) identified four major psychological dilemmas or dynamics created by microaggressions directed toward racial groups: (1) the clash of realities between the dominant group and socially devalued group members, (2) the invisibility of unintentional bias and discrimination, (3) the perceived minimal harm of microaggressions, and (4) the catch-22 of responding. The analysis here is being broadened to include a number of different marginalized groups besides that of race.

CLASH OF REALITIES

Studies reveal that culture and group-based experiences (racial, gender, sexual orientation, religious, and class) shape worldviews and influence the perception of reality of various groups (Babbington, 2008; Hanna et al., 2000; Sue, 2010). For example, the racial reality of people of color has been found to be significantly different from that of White Americans (Astor, 1997). Many Whites seem to believe that racism is no longer a significant problem (à la post-Obama race era), while many Blacks continue to report that their lives are filled with constant and continuing experiences of prejudice and discrimination. Women continue to report that sexism keeps them from rising to top managerial positions, that their contributions are not recognized by their male counterparts in the workplace, that they are not promoted when otherwise qualified, and that they encounter the glass ceiling frequently. Men, however, are fond of saying that "competence will rise to the top" regardless of gender and that "you've come a long way, baby."

Such differences in racial, gender, or sexual orientation realities is most pronounced when a significant power differential exists between groups that hold power and those who are most disempowered (Sue, 2003). Whites hold greater power over people of color. Men hold greater power than women. Straights possess greater power than LGBTs, able-bodied people are more likely to have power over those with disabilities, and those with wealth hold greater power over the poor or less affluent. "True power," however, is in a group's ability to define reality (Guthrie, 1998; Hanna et al., 2000; Keltner &

Robinson, 1996). In general, mainstream groups hold the ability to define reality through the tools of education, mass media, and social institutions. When children are taught by parents, the mass media, and schools that LGBTs are sick or deviant, when people of color are portrayed as dangerous and unintelligent, and when women are stereotyped as the weaker sex and less capable in leadership positions, a system of hierarchy and access to privilege and power is established in our society.

Racial, gender, and sexual orientation microaggressions, especially micro-insults and microinvalidations, operate from an imposed reality that is outside the level of conscious awareness when the beliefs, biases, and false assumptions are defined as truth and normative. Thus, if racism, sexism, and hetero-sexism are believed to no longer be a major problem and if normality is based upon White, male, and "straight" standards, then those who differ from them are defined as abnormal and problematic. We have already indicated that microaggressions are reflections of worldviews of inclusion/exclusion and normality/abnormality. When racial microaggressions are delivered by well-intentioned White brothers and sisters, perpetrators are unlikely to be aware of the biased hidden messages they are sending to people of color. Herein lies a major dilemma. If motives and the insulting messages of perpetrators are outside awareness, how do we make the "invisible" visible? In other words, when a clash of racial realities occurs, whose reality is likely to hold sway? Whose reality will be judged to be the true reality? The answer, unfortunately, is that the group who holds the greatest power has the ability to impose reality on less powerful groups.

Let us try to address these questions from the perspectives of both perpetrators and targets using racial microaggressions as an example. In studies dealing with racial microaggressions in the classroom (Sue, Lin, Torino, Capodilupo, & Rivera, 2009), it was found that (1) racial micro-aggressions were often instigators to difficult dialogues on race, (2) students of color could identify and define them quite well, (3) White students had difficulties understanding what they had done or said that was racially offensive, and (4) Whites often became defensive and labeled students of color as "oversensitive" and even "paranoid." Additionally, similar findings regarding White professors were found (Sue et al.). They had great difficulty recognizing racial microaggressions committed by White students; more importantly, they were equally baffled in identifying them when they themselves were the perpetrators!

One common racial microaggression delivered by well-intentioned White teachers can be seen in the following example. Black students often report that when they make a particularly insightful or intelligent comment in class, both White students and White professors act surprised. A common reaction by professors is to compliment the student with a remark such as "That was a most articulate, intelligent, and insightful analysis." On the surface, this is a compliment that many students, regardless of race, should find flattering. Yet, many Black students report being uncomfortable with the remark, and some report being very offended. The hidden racial microaggressive message, they contend, is that it reflects a belief that African Americans generally lack intelligence and are less capable. Thus, when one of them exhibits insight and intellect, it is surprising and unusual. The microaggressive message does two things: (1) it reflects a biased belief that African Americans are less capable than Whites, and (2) it allows the perpetrator to cling to the widespread belief in the inferiority of Blacks, even in the face of contradictory evidence (he or she is an exception).

When targets of microaggressions attempt to point out the offensive nature of remarks and actions from perpetrators, they are told that their perceptions are inaccurate, that they are oversensitive, or that they are paranoid. In other words, they are out of touch with reality. The experiential realities of those in power are imposed upon less powerful groups by denying their perceptions and life experiences. Interestingly, some have asserted or found that those groups who are least empowered have the most accurate assessment of reality (Hanna et al., 2000; Keltner & Robinson, 1996; Sue, 2003). Such a conclusion makes common sense, as those in power do not need to understand disempowered groups to survive or do well, while those without much power must actively discern the mindset and motives of those with power in order to survive. Women in the workforce must understand the thinking of their male counterparts to do well, but the reciprocal is not true for men.

INVISIBILITY OF UNINTENTIONAL BIAS

Research on aversive racism (Dovidio, Gaertner, Kawakami, & Hodson, 2002), subtle sexism (Swim et al., 2001), and heterosexism (Herek, 1998)has shown that socialization and cultural conditioning fosters unconscious biases and misinformation about various marginalized groups in our society; some research even suggests that cultural conditioning can actually connect prejudices to emotions in a neurological manner (Abelson, Dasgupta, Park, & Banaji, 1998). Thus, it is highly possible and even probable that most people have unconsciously inherited the cultural biases of their forebears and that of society.

The concept of aversive racism is central to our understanding of micro-aggressions (Dovidio, Gaertner, Penner, Pearson, & Norton, 2009; Gaertner & Dovidio, 2005). Simply defined, aversive racism is a contemporary form of bias: It is an insidious and less conspicuous form of racism that hides in the assumptions/beliefs/values of well-intentioned people and is difficult to identify in its motivational manifestations. This is especially true when such biases are invisible to perpetrators and are unintentional in nature. According to Dovidio and colleagues, aversive racists truly believe they are nonprejudiced, consciously hold egalitarian values, and would never deliberately discriminate; yet, they are likely to harbor unconscious biases that may result in discriminatory actions. Studies reveal that training and education may be successful in confronting and lessening conscious biases, stereotypes, and preconceived notions but that implicit biases generally remain untouched and unaffected (Boysen & Vogel, 2008).

Because most people experience themselves as good, moral, and decent human beings, they find it difficult to entertain the notion that they may have acted in a racist, sexist, or heterosexist manner. Thus, in addition to holding hidden biases, getting them to confront their prejudices and discriminatory actions threatens their self-image as someone who stands for equality, justice, and respect for everyone. Two layers of resistance are present: (1) the unawareness and unintentionality of their prejudices and discriminatory actions and (2) the need to preserve their self-image as an unbiased and good person. If one's prejudices are unconscious, if one's discriminatory actions are unintentional, and if one's self-image is locked into a belief of one's inherent goodness, the challenges and questions become: How do we make the invisible visible? How do we reach people so that they can become aware of their biases? How do we make people see the harm perpetrated against socially devalued groups in our society? The last question leads us to the third psychological dilemma posed by microaggressions.

PERCEIVED MINIMAL HARM

Even when people acknowledge that they may have made an innocent offensive remark, it is often described as a small slight and the impact is minimized. The recipients of the insults are usually encouraged to "let it go" and "get over it." Such advice, however, is easier said than done and in itself may constitute a microaggression, because it denies the harmful impact and experiential reality of such biases. Indeed, racial microaggressions are often described as banal and minor offenses and as trivial in nature.

Overwhelming evidence exists, however, that far from being trivial, microaggressions have major consequences for marginalized groups. Their cumulative nature and continuing day-in and day-out experience have been found to (1) contribute to a hostile and invalidating campus and work climate (Dovidio et al., 2009; Rowe, 1990; Solórzano et al., 2000), (2) devalue social group identities (Purdie-Vaughns et al., 2008), (3) lower work productivity and educational learning (Salvatore & Shelton, 2007; Sue, 2010), (4) perpetuate stereotype threat (Cardinu, Maas, Rosabianca, & Kiesner, 2005; Steele, Spencer, & Aronson, 2002), (5) create physical health problems (Brondolo, Rieppi, Kelly, & Gerin, 2003; Clark, Anderson, Clark, & Williams, 1999), and (6) assail mental health by creating emotional turmoil, low self-esteem, and psychological energy depletion (Sue, 2010).

Microaggressions are also found to create disparities in health care, education, and employment (Sue, 2010) because they are based upon a biased worldview that is manifested in hiring, retention, and promotion decisions in the workplace; that reduces the quality of education received by students of color, for example; and that may result in lower quality of health care for certain groups. Persons of color, LGBTs, women, people with disabilities, and other marginalized groups are subjected to chronic, continuing, and daily microaggressive stressors from well-intentioned individuals who are unaware of the insults, slights, and demeaning actions they visit upon these groups. Sue (2010) has summarized how microaggressive stress can be manifested through four identifiable pathways:

1. *Biological and physical effects:* Stress has been associated with increased susceptibility to illness and may affect the course of a disease (Keltner & Dowben, 2007; Underwood, 2005). Early studies on the life-change model of stress have found that the accumulation of small changes could be additive and become a potent form of stress equal to the effect of a major catastrophic trauma (Holmes & Rahe, 1967). When these stresses summate and act together, they are strongly correlated with increased illnesses and severity. As we have repeatedly emphasized, race-related, gender-related, and sexual-orientation-related stresses (microaggressions) are anything but insignificant. Women who perceived greater job stress related to bias had higher fibrinogen levels, believed to be correlated with coronary heart disease (Davis, Mathews, Meilahn, & Kiss, 1995); LGBTs who experienced greater levels of microaggressions reported more health-related problems; and it has been shown that race-related stress negatively affects the biological health of persons of color (Brondolo et al., 2008; Clark et al., 1999).

2. *Emotional effects:* Racism, sexism, heterosexism, and other forms of bias directed toward socially devalued groups have been shown to affect their emotional well-being, psychological adjustment, and mental health (Buser, 2009; Moradi, Van den Berg, & Epting, 2009; Utsey & Hook, 2007). Anxiety, feelings of alienation, subjective well-being, and exhaustion may be associated with the experience of group-specific microaggressions (Harrell, 2000; Ponterotto, Utsey, & Pedersen, 2006; Sue, 2010). Depression, for example, has been found to be related to gender (women are more likely to report

these feelings and to exhibit a diagnosable disorder; Strickland, 1992). Gender role conflicts; overt, covert, and subtle sexism; subservient roles to men; and lower sense of self-control have all been suggested as possible causes (Hill & Fischer, 2008; Sue, Sue, & Sue, 2010).

3. *Cognitive effects:* The effects of microaggressions can be classified under three processes: (1) attempts to make meaning of an incident with potential microaggressive overtones, (2) disrupted cognitive processing, and (3) stereotype threat. First, when a microaggressive incident occurs, considerable energy is expended toward attempting to make sense of the situation. (Was this a microaggression? Did what happened really happen? Was this a compliment or a slight? If the latter, how should I respond? If I do, what will be the consequences?) Second, these questions or attempts to understand what has occurred cause cognitive disruption, so the person is unable to focus directly on the task at hand. At work, productivity may be affected, or at school, the student may be less likely to solve problems. Third, stereotype threat may be activated in the mind of the person, leading to lowered performance.

4. *Behavioral effects:* Microaggressions can signal a hostile or invalidating climate that threatens the physical and emotional safety of the devalued group, assails self-esteem, and imposes forced compliance (oppression) upon them. Sue (2010) has summarized five behavioral effects of microaggressions when directed toward marginalized groups: (1) hypervigilance/skepticism (suspiciousness toward the majority group), (2) forced compliance (surviving or being co-opted), (3) rage and anger, (4) fatigue and hopelessness, and (5) strength through adversity. This last behavioral attribute is related to the development of functional survival skills used to negotiate hostile and demeaning microaggressions directed toward the individual or group.

It is clear from an analysis of the harmful and detrimental consequences of microaggressions that marginalized groups in our society suffer biologically, emotionally, cognitively, and behaviorally. Microaggressions are far from banal and insignificant slights; they are oppressive and harmful to the well-being of many groups in our society.

THE CATCH-22 OF RESPONDING TO MICROAGGRESSIONS

Microaggressions, especially microinsults and microinvalidations, place socially devalued group members in an unenviable position of (1) trying to ascertain the motivations behind the actions of perpetrators and (2) deciding whether and how to respond. Since many microaggressions are likely to be delivered unintentionally and their real motives are not conscious to the perpetrator, they are usually filled with double meanings and/or are very ambiguous. On a conscious level, dominant group members who engage in unconscious microaggressions believe they are acting in an unbiased manner, complimenting the target, or making a rationale decision. When a statement such as "I believe the most qualified person should get the job" is made to a female job candidate, the job seeker is caught in a double bind: On the one hand, the statement is valid and reasonable, but on the other hand, experience has shown the woman job hunter that it can be used to justify not hiring women and offering such positions to male candidates. When students of color are seldom called upon by a White professor to answer questions, is this a random act, or is the professor operating from an unconscious assumption that minorities are less likely to have intelligent comments or answers to class problems? The term "attributional ambiguity" has been given to motivational uncertainty in that the motives and meanings of a person's actions are unclear and hazy. Studies suggest that attributional ambiguity depletes psychological energy by diverting attention away from other important tasks (problem solving in classrooms and work productivity in the workplace; Cardinu et al., 2005; Sue, Lin, & Rivera, 2009).

Second, a catch-22 is often induced in the recipient of microaggressions. The conflict involves how to respond to the person when a remark or action conveys a demeaning insult or offense.

In the face of an offensive group-specific comment, the target is placed in a "damned if you do and damned if you don't" situation. That is, if the person does nothing, he or she may suffer from a sense of low self-esteem, a feeling of not being true to the self, and a loss of self-integrity. Yet, to confront the perpetrator or to raise the issue may result in negative consequences. Sue (2010) has observed that most marginalized group members choose or are forced to do nothing. He proposes several reasons for this common reaction.

1. *Attributional ambiguity:* As mentioned, the person is thrown into a very confusing and ambiguous situation, making it difficult to conclude whether an offense has occurred. This is especially true when the perpetrator seems to be a well-intentioned individual.
2. *Response indecision:* Even when a microaggression is obvious to the target, the person may be at a loss as to how best to respond: "If I express anger, the perpetrator will only become defensive." "Should I try a rational approach?" "What is the best way to react and point out its impact upon me?"
3. *Time-limited nature of responding:* In most cases, microaggressions occur quickly and are embedded in the larger context of a communication. The instantaneous nature of microaggressions leaves little time to respond.

By the time a response is considered, the conversation or event may have changed or moved on to something else.

4. *Denying experiential reality:* Many marginalized group members may engage in self-deception and deny that their close neighbor, partner, or friend engaged in an offensive action toward them. In most cases, the person has a need to cling to the belief that the microaggressor does not look down (even unconsciously) upon their race, gender, sexual orientation, and so on.

5. *Impotency of actions:* This is a common reaction—the belief that any action taken will not do any good or will have minimal impact on the microaggressor or situation. Individuals may simply give up or develop a sense of hopelessness. On the other hand, some may simply realize that actions will do little good and desire to conserve their energies and efforts for larger battles.

Ever present in the awareness of marginalized group members is the power differential that generally exists between perpetrators and targets. Should a Latina/o student who is the target of microaggressions from fellow White students or even from the professor raise the issue? In this case, the Latina/o student may be outnumbered in the class by fellow White students who will be unable to see the microaggression; they may become defensive, or they may see the Latina/o student as oversensitive. Additionally, the power differential becomes especially clear if a White professor is involved. Questions and thoughts likely to race through the mind of the student include: "Will the professor be offended?" "Will the professor think less of me?" "Will I get a poor grade in his or her class?" "May be I should just do nothing and let it go."

THE WAY FORWARD: ABOUT THIS EDITED BOOK

All interpersonal interactions that involve race, gender, sexual orientation, religion, class, disability, and so forth may be prone to microaggressions. While the concept of racial microaggressions is not new (Pierce et al., 1978), their impact on academic climates (Solórzano et al., 2000), work sites (Sue et al., 2009), mental health (Sue & Capodilupo, 2008), and the development of a working taxonomy (Sue et al., 2007) has gained high visibility in only recent years. As the understanding of the psychological dynamics of racial microaggressions has developed, many other marginalized groups have begun to translate how microaggressions may be tied to group-specific stereotypes,biases, and misinformation. In the book *Racial Microaggressions in Everyday Life: Race, Gender, and Sexual Orientation*, Sue (2010) summarized and offered a conceptual framework to view how three major sociodemographic groups shared similarities and differences in life experiences related to an ethnocentric, monocultural perspective that socially devalued certain groups in our society.

In this edited book, *Microaggressions and Marginalized Groups in Society*, we attempt to provide a unique cutting-edge text that expands the concepts of microaggressions to include many marginalized groups in our society. It presents the most recent scholarly research and formulations on race, gender, sexual orientation, gender, religion, class, and disability microaggressions. We believe this text will be in high demand for courses in the social sciences, education, and those that are related to topics of marginality, social justice, and prejudice and discrimination.

While much has been written about contemporary forms of racism, sexism, and homophobia, many studies in health care, education, law, employment, mental health, and social settings indicate the difficulty of describing and defining discrimination that occurs via "implicit bias"; it is difficult to identify, quantify, and rectify because of its subtle, nebulous, and unnamed nature. The subtle isms of our society remain relatively invisible and potentially harmful to the well-being, self-esteem, and standard of living of many marginalized groups in society. These daily common experiences of aggression may have significantly more influence on anger, frustration, and self-esteem than traditional overt forms of racism, sexism, and heterosexism. Furthermore, their invisible nature prevents perpetrators from realizing and confronting their own complicity in creating psychological dilemmas for minorities and their role in creating disparities in employment, health care, and education.

The text discusses the manifestation, psychological dynamics, and impact of microaggressions on the well-being of marginalized groups and will elucidate their role in creating disparities in education, employment, and health care. The text is unique because it (1) pulls together in an integrated fashion the relationship of marginality to group-specific microaggressions (race, gender, sexual orientation, class, and religious orientation), (2) contains both conceptual and qualitative research pieces, and (3) allows for comparing and contrasting similarities and differences between and among multiple marginalized groups.

REFERENCES

Abelson, R. P., Dasgupta, N., Park, J., & Banaji, M. R. (1998). Perceptions of the collective other. *Personality and Social Psychology Review, 2,* 243–250.

Apfelbaum, E. P., Sommers, S. R., & Norton, M. I. (2008). Seeing race and seeming racist: Evaluating strategic colorblindness in social interaction. *Journal of Personality and Social Psychology, 95,* 918–932.

Astor, C. (1997). Gallup Poll: Progress in Black/White relations, but race is still an issue. *U.S. Society & Values*. Retrieved February 16, 2007, from http://usinfo.state.gov/journals/itsv/0897/ijse/gallup.htm.

Babbington, C. (2008). Poll shows gap between Blacks and Whites over racial discrimination. Retrieved March 15, 2009, from http://news.yahoo.com/page/election-2008-political-pulse-race-in-america.

Bell, L. A. (2002). Sincere fictions: The pedagogical challenges of preparing White teachers for multicultural classrooms. *Equity and Excellence in Education, 35*, 236–244.

Bonilla-Silva, E. (2006). *Racism without racists: Color-blind racism and the persistence of racial inequality in the United States*. Lanham, MD: Rowman & Littlefield.

Boysen, G. A., & Vogel, D. L. (2008). The relationship between level of training, implicit bias, and multicultural competency among counselor trainees. *Training and Education in Professional Psychology, 2*, 103–110.

Brondolo, E., Brady, N., Thompson, S., Tobin, J. N., Cassells, A., Sweeney, M., et al. (2008). Perceived racism and negative affect: Analyses of trait and state measures of affect in a community sample. *Journal of Social and Clinical Psychology, 27*, 150–173.

Brondolo, E., Rieppi, R., Kelly, K. P., & Gerin, K. W. (2003). Perceived racism and blood pressure: A review of the literature and conceptual and methodological critique. *Annals of Behavioral Medicine, 25*, 55–65.

Buser, J. K. (2009). Treatment-seeking disparity between African Americans and Whites: Attitudes toward treatment, coping resources, and racism. *Journal of Multicultural Counseling and Development, 37*(2), 94–104.

Cardinu, M., Maas, A., Rosabianca, A., & Kiesner, J. (2005). Why do women underperform under stereotype threat? Evidence for the role of negative thinking. *Psychological Science, 16*, 572–578.

Clark, R., Anderson, N. B., Clark, V. R., & Williams, D. R. (1999). Racism as a stressor for African Americans. *American Psychologist, 54*, 805–816.

Davis, M. C., Mathews, K. A., Meilahn, E. N., & Kiss, J. E. (1995). Are job characteristics related to fibrinogen levels in middle-aged women? *Health Psychology, 14*, 310–318.

Dovidio, J. F., & Gaertner, S. L. (2000). Aversive racism and selective decisions: 1989–1999. *Psychological Science, 11*, 315–319.

Dovidio, J. F., Gaertner, S. L., Kawakami, K., & Hodson, G. (2002). Why can't we all just get along? Interpersonal biases and interracial distrust. *Cultural Diversity and Ethnic Minority Psychology, 8*, 88–102.

Dovidio, J. J., Gaertner, S. L., Penner, L. A., Pearson, A. R., & Norton, W. E. (2009). Aversive racism: How unconscious bias influences behavior: Implications for legal, employment, and health care contexts. In J. L. Chin (Ed.), *Diversity in mind and action* (Vol. 3, pp. 21–35). Santa Barbara, CA: Praeger.

Freire, P. (1970). *Pedagogy of the oppressed*. New York: Continuum.

Gaertner, S. L., & Dovidio, J. F. (2005). Understanding and addressing contemporary racism: From aversive racism to the common ingroup identity model. *Journal of Social Issues, 61*(3), 615–639.

Guthrie, R. V. (1998). *Even the rat was White* (2nd ed.). New York: Harper & Row.

Hanna, F. J., Talley, W. B., & Guindon, M. H. (2000). The power of perception: Toward a model of cultural oppression and liberation. *Journal of Counseling and Development*, *78*, 430–446.

Harrell, J. P. (2000). A multidimensional conceptualization of racism-related stress: Implications for the well-being of people of color. *American Journal of Orthopsychiatry*, *70*, 42–57.

Herek, G. M. (Ed.). (1998). *Stigma and sexual orientation: Understanding prejudice against lesbians, gay men, and bisexuals*. Thousand Oaks, CA: Sage.

Hill, M. S., & Fischer, A. R. (2008). Lesbian and heterosexual women's experiences with sexual- and self-objectification. *Counseling Psychologist*, *36*, 745–776.

Holmes, T. H., & Rahe, R. H. (1967). The Social Readjustment Rating Scale. *Journal of Psychosomatic Research*, *11*, 213–218.

Keltner, N. G., & Dowben, J. S. (2007). Psychobiological substrates of Posttraumatic Stress Disorder: Part I. *Perspectives in Psychiatric Care*, *43*, 97–101.

Keltner, D., & Robinson, R. J. (1996). Extremism, power, and imagined basis of social conflict. *Current Directions in Psychological Science*, *5*, 101–105.

Leland, J. (2008, October 7). In "sweetie" and "dear," a hurt for the elderly. *New York Times*. Retrieved from www.nytimes.com/2008/10/07/us/07aging.html?=todayspaper&pagewanted=print.

Moradi, B., Van den Berg, J. J., & Epting, F. R. (2009). Threat and guilt aspects of internalized antilesbian and gay prejudice: An application of personal construct theory. *Journal of Counseling Psychology*, *56*, 119–131.

Pierce, C., Carew, J., Pierce-Gonzalez, D., & Willis, D. (1978). An experiment in racism: TV commercials. In C. Pierce (Ed.), *Television and education* (pp. 62–88). Beverly Hills, CA: Sage.

Ponterotto, J. G., Utsey, S. O., & Pedersen, P. B. (2006). *Preventing prejudice*. Thousand Oaks, CA: Sage.

Purdie-Vaughns, V., Davis, P. G., Steele, C. M., & Ditlmann, R. (2008). Social identity contingencies: How diversity cues signal threat or safety for African Americans in mainstream institutions. *Journal of Personality and Social Psychology*, *94*, 615–630.

Rowe, M. P. (1990). Barriers to equality: The power of subtle discrimination to maintain unequal opportunity. *Employee Responsibilities and Rights Journal*, *3*, 153–163.

Salvatore, J., & Shelton, J. N. (2007). Cognitive costs of exposure to racial prejudice. *Psychological Science*, *18*, 810–815.

Solórzano, D., Ceja, M., & Yosso, T. (2000). Critical race theory, racial microaggressions, and campus racial climate: The experiences of African American college students. *Journal of Negro Education*, *69*(1/2), 60–73.

Steele, C. M., Spencer, S. J., & Aronson, J. (2002). Contending with group image: The psychology of stereotype and social identity threat. In M. Zanna (Ed.), *Advances in experimental social psychology* (Vol. 23, pp. 379–440). New York: Academic Press.

Strickland, B. R. (1992). Women and depression. *Current Directions in Psychological Science*, *1*, 132–135.

Sue, D. W. (2003). *Overcoming our racism: The journey to liberation*. San Francisco, CA: Jossey-Bass.

Sue, D. W. (2004). Whiteness and ethnocentric monoculturalism: Making the "invisible" visible. *American Psychologist, 59*, 759–769.

Sue, D. W. (2010). *Racial microaggressions in everyday life: Race, gender, and sexual orientation*. Hoboken, NJ: John Wiley & Sons.

Sue, D. W., & Capodilupo, C. M. (2008). Racial, gender, and sexual orientation microaggressions: Implications for counseling and psychotherapy. In D. W. Sue & D. Sue (Eds.), *Counseling the culturally diverse: Theory and practice* (5th ed., pp. 105–130). Hoboken, NJ: John Wiley & Sons.

Sue, D. W., Capodilupo, C. M., Torino, G. C., Bucceri, J. M., Holder, A. M. B., Nadal, K. L., & Esquilin, M. (2007). Racial microaggressions in everyday life: Implications for clinical practice. *American Psychologist, 62*, 271–286.

Sue, D. W., Lin, A. I., & Rivera, D. P. (2009). Racial microaggressions in the workplace: Manifestation and impact. In J. Chin (Ed.), *Diversity matters: Education and employment*. Westport, CT: Praeger.

Sue, D. W., Lin, A. I., Torino, G. C., Capodilupo, C. M., & Rivera, D. P. (2009). Racial microaggressions and difficult dialogues in the classroom. *Cultural Diversity and Ethnic Minority Psychology, 15*, 183–190.

Sue, D. W., & Sue, D. (2008). *Counseling the culturally diverse: Theory and practice* (4th ed.). Hoboken, NJ: John Wiley & Sons.

Sue, D., Sue, D. W., & Sue, S. (2010). *Understanding abnormal behavior* (9th ed.). Boston: Wadsworth.

Sue, D. W., Torino, G. C., Capodilupo, C. M., Rivera, D. P., & Lin, A. I. (2009). How White faculty perceive and react to difficult dialogues on race: Implications for education and training. *Counseling Psychologist, 37*, 1090–1115.

Swim, J. K., & Cohen, L. L. (1997). Overt, covert, and subtle sexism. *Psychology of Women Quarterly, 21*, 103–118.

Swim, J. K., Hyers, L. L., Cohen, L. L., & Ferguson, M. J. (2001). Everyday sexism: Evidence for its incidence, nature, and psychological impact from three daily diary studies. *Journal of Social Issues, 57*, 31–53.

Szymanski, D. M., Kashubeck-West, S., & Meyer, J. (2008). Internalized heterosexism. *Counseling Psychologist, 36*, 510–524.

Underwood, A. (2005, October 3). The good heart. *Newsweek*, 49–55.

Utsey, S. O., & Hook, J. N. (2007). Heart rate variability as a physiological moderator of the relationship between race-related stress and psychological distress in African Americans. *Journal of Counseling Psychology, 13*, 250–253.

PART II

RACIAL/ETHNIC MANIFESTATION OF MICROAGGRESSIONS

Black Undergraduates' Experiences with Perceived Racial Microaggressions in Predominately White Colleges and Universities

NICOLE L. WATKINS, THERESSA L. LABARRIE, and LAUREN M. APPIO

A S THE RACIAL-CULTURAL landscape of the United States evolves, racial and ethnic minorities continue to represent a growing percentage of the population. Black people constitute the second-largest racial minority group at 13.4 percent of the U.S. population (U.S. Bureau of the Census, 2008). For the purpose of this chapter, the term "Black" will be used as a racial description to refer to a diverse group of ethnic groups of African descent, including African Americans, Caribbean Americans, Black Latinas/os, and multiethnic individuals who self-identify as Black. The participants in the following study self-identified racially as Black, and their ethnic backgrounds included Caribbean, African, and South and Central American and African American descent. Despite being the second-largest racial group, Black people continue to be disproportionally underrepresented in higher education settings, with only 18.5 percent of Black people earning college degrees (U.S. Bureau of the Census, 2008). While some researchers have focused on college recruitment, enrollment, and retention experiences of Black students (e.g., Feagin, 1992; Gay, 2004), there is a dearth in the research examining the impact of racial microaggressions within the college climate.

We would like to extend a sincere thank you to Sheila V. Graham, Veronica Mitchell, Madonna Constantine, and the inspiring Black undergraduates who shared their stories of disappointment and triumph.

Racism is embedded within a historical context of racial injustice and oppression that is connected to contemporary circumstances, which are maintained through individual and systematic influences (Jones, 1997; Harrell, 2000). Traditional expressions of racism (e.g., Jim Crow laws, cross burnings, lynchings) have evolved into more indirect, covert forms such as racial microaggressions (Constantine & Sue, 2007; Sue & Sue, 2007). While racial microaggressions may be conscious and deliberate, research has focused on subtle and unconscious exchanges (Pierce, Carew, Pierce-Gonzalez, & Willis, 1978), which reveals that many well-intentioned individuals perpetuate racial discrimination without conscious awareness. The commonplace occurrences of racial microaggressions (see Chapter 1 for a taxonomy of racial micro-aggressions) on the surface can appear seemingly minor and innocuous to some (Franklin, 1999); however, these indignities and coded messages communicate racial hierarchy and establish White Eurocentric values as dominant and normative standards for comparison.

White cultural values and norms include the belief in a just world in which good things happen to good people, individualism is valued over collectivism, competition is valued over cooperation, science is separate from religion, logical thought is separate from emotions, verbal communication is valued over nonverbal communication, and the belief is held that hard work will always result in success (Sue & Sue, 2007). While some of these values may resonate with Black students, others may be contradictory to their experiences and cultural traditions, such as encountering a nonjust world of inequality and oppression, relating to a collective Black identity, and valuing emotional expressiveness and nonverbal communication. Indeed, the academic persistence of students of color in higher education has been linked to students' perceptions of cultural congruity within the college environment (Cervantes & Pena, 1988; Gloria & Robinson Kurpius, 1996). As such, Black students may perceive predominantly White institutions (PWIs) as being inhospitable to their racial or cultural values (DeFreece, 1987; Greer & Chwalisz, 2007) and may feel as if they cannot assimilate to or "fit in" with the White majority group.

Unfortunately, Black students often experience significant conflict in trying to maintain identification with their racial and cultural heritage while trying to succeed within White, middle-class values of academia (Gloria & Robinson Kurpius, 1996). In comparison, Black undergraduates attending historically Black colleges and universities report lower levels of minority-status stress (Greer & Chwalisz, 2007) compared to students attending PWIs. Additionally, Black students attending PWIs are likely to report feelings of isolation, alienation, and low cultural congruence (Ponterotto, 1990). Thus, Black students are often relegated to an outsider status within the college climate (Laden, 2004; Twigg, 2005).

Encountering contemporary racism expressed mainly in the form of racial microaggressions, Black students receive explicit and implicit messages that reinforce the message that they are not welcome and will not be integrated into the college community. Moreover, issues of racial and cultural mistrust may essentially deter many Black students from pursuing a college education or impede persistence and success while attending PWIs (Feagin, 1992). Studies further suggest that feelings of isolation and alienation can lead to increased segregation and higher dropout rates for students of color (Cheatham & Berg-Cross, 1992; Feagin, 1992).

Given the prevalence of racism, academic settings are not impervious to the oppressive forces demonstrated by mainstream society (Gay, 2004; Harrell, 2000; Suarez-Balcazar, Orellana-Damacela, Portillo, Rowan, & Andrews-Guillen, 2003); however, there has been limited scientific investigation around experiences with racial microaggressions at PWIs (Solórzano, Ceja, & Yosso, 2000). One college development study surveyed a large, racially diverse sample of college students ($n = 7,347$) and found that students of color reported very different racial realties than their White counterparts (Rankin & Reason, 1998). In fact, students of color typically described the racial climate at their university as "racist, hostile, disrespectful, and less accepting of minority groups," while White students at the same campuses described the racial climates as "non-racist, friendly, and respectful" (Rankin & Reason, 1998, p. 52). These findings suggest that the campus experiences of Black undergraduates often vary greatly from that of their White counterparts.

Arguably, most undergraduates must adjust to the demands of schoolwork, create social networks, manage financial challenges, adapt to new environments, and develop career and personal paths. Nevertheless, students of color face the added stress of combating the considerable strain of dealing with racial microaggressions in addition to adjusting to and persisting within the college environment. The negative psychological implications of racism are documented extensively in the literature (Harrell, 2000; Jones, 1991; Pierce et al., 1978; Rivera, Forquer, & Rangel, Chapter 3 of this volume; Sue et al., 2007).

Findings suggest that racial prejudice and exclusion are racism-related stressors that negatively affect mental and social adjustment for people of color (Dobbins & Skillings, 2000). Negative outcomes associated with racism include diminished self-efficacy, which is characterized by findings around stereotype threat that results from the societal stigma of intellectual inferiority ascribed to Black students that in turn has been shown to negatively impact Black students' school performance (Aronson et al., 1999). In addition, other outcomes of perceived racism in the lives of Black people include poor physical health (e.g., increased blood pressure; Krieger & Sidney, 1996), negative emotional responses (e.g., sadness, anger, frustration, fear, etc.), negative cognitive reactions (e.g., cultural mistrust and hypervigilance; Sue & Sue, 2007), and psychological risks (e.g., increased susceptibility to anxiety, paranoia, and depression; Harrell, 2000).

While existing literature proposes the harmful impact of racial micro-aggressions in the lives of Black people (Franklin & Boyd-Franklin, 2000; Harrell, 2000; Jones, 1997; Pierce, 1995; Solórzano et al., 2000; Sue & Sue, 2007), there remains a scarcity of empirical research investigating the psychological well-being and college adjustment of Black undergraduates in PWIs and the factors that promote resilience. The current study was designed to address some of these gaps in the literature through the qualitative investigation of Black college students' perceptions of (1) racial microaggressions on their college campus, (2) the impact of these microaggressions in their lives, (3) the resilience and coping methods they use to address these microaggressive experiences, and (4) suggestions for the betterment of the university environment.

METHOD

The current study employed a qualitative methodology, consensual qualitative research (CQR), to investigate the underresearched, multifaceted experiences of Black undergraduates and their perceptions of the impact of racial microaggressions in their lives. In general, qualitative methods prioritize lived experiences, social context, and the participants' perspective in contrast to quantitative methods that use researchers' predetermined categories to confirm or disconfirm existent theory (Morrow & Smith, 2000; Spanierman et al., 2008). In particular, CQR has been established as an effective methodology for (1) investigating emerging domains of study (Ponterotto, 2002; Hill, Thompson, & Williams, 1997; Hill et al., 2005); (2) studying racial microaggressions (Kim, Brenner, Liang, & Asay, 2003; Sue et al., 2007); (3) minimizing researcher bias through acknowledging expectations and biases; (4) reaching group consensus with diverse research team members; and (5) using an external auditor to review the work to make sure the participants' words are accurately reflected within the findings.

PARTICIPANTS

Ten self-identified Black undergraduate students from a predominately White northeastern university were recruited through Black student organizations on campus. The selected participants consisted of five men and five women, 18 to 22 years of age, with an average age of 19.3 years (SD = 1.49). A range of academic years was represented among the participants: first-year students (two), sophomores (five), and seniors (three). Participants reported their ethnic backgrounds as African, African American, Bajan American, Black Latino, Haitian American, and Jamaican American. In addition, there were common characteristics among the participants: All self-identified as heterosexual, reported a cumulative grade point average of 3.0 or higher, and identified their family's social economic background as middle class.

RESEARCH TEAM

The four researchers involved in the study were all female: a Black American (senior author), a multiracial American, a White American, and a Black Latina (auditor). Three were doctoral students in counseling psychology, and one was a master's-level clinical psychology student. The primary investigator was trained in diverse research analyses and had experience conducting ethnographic, qualitative, and quantitative research with people of color. Each team member completed a series of CQR training modules hosted by an experienced psychological researcher. In addition, each team member had participated in past research studies on topics such as oppression, diversity, and social justice, which was considered an asset during the conceptualization and analysis of this project.

The central role of researchers within qualitative research methods necessitates the exploration of the researchers' personal values, assumptions, and biases prior to data collection and analysis (Fassinger, 2005). These were identified as the following: (1) Black participants will have experienced racial microaggressions and will be open to speaking about them, (2) Black undergrads will largely find support among peers of color who have had similar experiences with racial microaggressions, (3) Black students will feel compelled to represent their race in both classroom and outside-of-classroom experiences, (4) Black students from predominately White communities will be less aware of and/or may excuse/dismiss or minimize experienced racial microaggressions, (5) Whites will question the validity of their experiences/ reactions to microaggressions based on the perceived intent of the aggressor, and (6) Whites will try to dismiss their experiences as universal to Black people (simply part of our daily struggle) and minimize their impact. As outlined within the CQR process, research team members are encouraged to challenge one another in making interpretations from the actual findings. The goal was to minimize the undue influence of research biases and to elevate the voices of the participants. In addition, the auditor provided another check as an independent reviewer of the data.

MEASURES

A semistructured interview protocol was developed through a review of literature on aversive racism, anecdotal reports, and previous existing research on racial microaggressions (Constantine & Sue, 2007; Harrell, 2000;

Pierce, 1995; Solórzano et al., 2000; Sue et al., 2007). The questions and probes were piloted with four volunteers. The volunteers were all graduate students of color and selected because of their experience, interest, and knowledge of racism and racial microaggressions. During the interviews, the volunteers were asked to provide reactions to the clarity and scope of the questions. Accordingly, the protocol was adjusted based on their feedback.

The resulting interview protocol (see Appendix B) defined the concept of racial microaggressions, shared examples, and prompted participants to share their own personal and witnessed experiences with perceived racial micro-aggressions in the university environment. The final nine questions were intended to (1) generate examples of verbal, behavioral, and environmental racial microaggressions and identify their cognitive, emotional, and behavioral impact; (2) highlight the strategies used to cope with microaggressive expe-riences employed by participants; and (3) access the participants' suggestions for changing the university environment.

PROCEDURES

Prior to the interview, participants signed consent forms and completed a brief demographic questionnaire aimed at obtaining information on race, ethnic background, gender, age, academic year, and socioeconomic status. The interviews ranged in duration from approximately 45 minutes to 2 hours and took place in private, reserved study rooms at the campus library. As compensation, every participant was given a pocket radio with head-phones. In addition, every participant was entered into a lottery for an opportunity to win a $25 gift card. After data collection, one winner was chosen at random. Each interview was audiotaped and then transcribed by members of the research team. Given the sensitive nature of discussing the experience of racial microaggressions, the interviewer was racially matched with the Black participants, because it was believed that racial homogeneity would maximize disclosure and minimize discomfort (Sue, Nadal, et al., 2008).

CQR Data Analysis   Once the interviews were completed, the researchers utilized CQR (Hill, Thompson, & Williams, 1997; Hill et al., 2005) to analyze the data. The data analysis involved five main steps, which are outlined next.

1. Domains   Three of the team members read 8 of the 10 transcripts (two transcripts were removed for the stability check, which will be described in more detail later on) and created a start list of preliminary domains. The identification of broad themes or domains among the transcripts is the first

step used to make meaning from the large amount of data. During this phase, the three team members reached consensus about the start list of domains, and it was sent to the auditor for her input. After questions and issues were raised by the auditor, some of the initial domains were merged and reworded.

2. Core Ideas   The team then organized each transcript by domain and constructed core ideas or abstracts within those domains. Core ideas are brief, succinct summaries of the data within each domain. Within each domain, team members identified transcript quotes used to best illustrate the findings. Consensus was reached among team members regarding the domains and core summaries for the eight transcripts, and the findings were sent to the auditor for review. Once again, feedback from the auditor resulted in clarifying the core ideas and making sure the findings were consistent with the data.

3. Cross-Analysis   Within the cross-analysis phase, the team compared themes across transcripts and clustered each of the core ideas into categories and subcategories. Once categories and subcategories were identified, the transcripts were revisited to assess whether all of the research data was accurately reflected within the resulting domains, categories, and subcategories. After reaching team consensus, the findings were submitted to and reviewed by the auditor for accuracy.

4. Stability Check   Following the completion of the cross-analysis, the two transcripts that were initially removed from the analysis at the onset were brought back and underwent steps 1 through 3. The stability check phase is used to test the consistency of original domains and categories. If no new domains or categories emerge during the analysis of the remaining transcripts, as was the case with this study, data saturation is assumed and the analysis is complete. Alternatively, when new domains or categories arise during the stability check, it is necessary to collect more data to expand the findings, which was not the case for this study.

5. Reporting Findings   Table 2.1 (see Appendix A) was constructed to provide a visual representation of the domains, categories, and subcategories. Although CQR is primarily a qualitative method, it also allows for the quantification of the data through the use of frequency labels. As such, in accordance with guidelines by Hill, Thompson, and Williams (1997) and Hill et al. (2005), categories of data labeled as "general" pertained to 10 cases, "typical" categories applied to 5 to 9 cases, "variant" categories were representative of 2 to 4 cases, and "rare" categories described 1 case.

RESULTS

Ten domains emerged from the analysis. Throughout the following sections, descriptions of the domains, core ideas from each category, and illustrative examples are provided to convey the perceptions and experiences of Black undergraduates at a predominately White university. The CQR frequency labels (e.g., general for 10 cases, typical for 5 to 9 cases, and variant for 2 to 4 cases) are used in the descriptions of the resulting categories. Given the large number of resulting categories, those featured underscore the most salient findings. Refer to Appendix A, Table 2.1, for a comprehensive list of the study's domains, categories, and frequencies.

DOMAIN 1: HIGH-SCHOOL-RELATED EXPERIENCES

This domain pertains to attributes associated with participants' high school experiences, including demographics and experiences of racial microaggressions. While half of participants described their high schools as racially diverse, the other half described them as predominately White. A typical number of participants described experiences in which they felt racially stereotyped and/or experienced racial tension with peers, teachers, and guidance counselors in high school.

DOMAIN 2: UNIVERSITY CAMPUS DEMOGRAPHICS

The demographics of the student body, administration, faculty, and staff on campus were described in this domain. Participants generally described students—and typically described faculty and administrators—on campus as predominately White. The racial stratification of jobs on campus was typically noted, indicating that Black and Latino/a staff are often employed in lower-status positions in comparison to White counterparts.

DOMAIN 3: TRANSITIONS TO NEW ENVIRONMENTS

Domain 3 describes the adjustments Black participants faced upon leaving high school and entering college, along with their expectations about the college environment. A typical number of participants expressed that the racial/ethnic makeup of their high school was dissimilar to college, while a variant number of participants attended predominately White high schools. Among students with a similar high school makeup, one female reported:

I knew what I was getting myself into. It's not that I was shocked and appalled. I mean, appalled, yes, but not shocked.

Participants typically felt disappointed that their college climate was unwelcoming and did not embrace racial diversity.

DOMAIN 4: PERCEPTIONS OF AND REACTIONS TO RACIAL MICROAGGRESSIONS

This domain encompasses participants' responses that describe and define stereotypes associated with being Black, perceptions of and reactions to racial microaggressions, and the balancing of multiple cognitive responsibilities in response to racial microaggressions (e.g., mentally juggling how to befriend a diverse pool of peers without excluding members from one's own race). Refer to Appendix A, Table 2.1, for a snapshot of the rich set of categories and frequencies that emerged within domain 4.

Participants generally described being racially stereotyped and having encountered racism. All participants reported various stereotypes that Black people receive, and three typical stereotype themes emerged: Black people as (1) ignorant or unintelligent; (2) loud, tactless, low class, or "ghetto"; and (3) angry, violent, or criminal.

Participants typically felt that White people did not understand racism or the race-related experiences of people of color because their experiences in society are very different. This perceived lack of understanding is supported by participants' descriptions of the assumptions that White people made about Black people, which was captured by the following six categories.

The first three assumptions occurred at a typical rate: (1) Despite numerous academic accomplishments, participants stated that others attributed their college admission to affirmative action. (2) Among its students and administration, participants also experienced being tokenized by others and considered an expert on topics that deal with racial matters. (3) When participants did not conform to stereotypical behaviors, they were either treated as an exception to the rule or experienced the "Oreo" phenomenon—the assumption that a Black person is trying to "act White" or is "Black on the outside and White on the inside."

The next three assumptions occurred at a variant rate. Participants felt that non-Black students assumed that (4) there was an automatic connection among Black people or an inherent dissimilarity between Black people and people of other races; (5) the Black students were involved in race-based academic support programs, which were noted as creating an "us versus them" dynamic; and (6) people of color were more comfortable with discussing racism as compared to White people.

Participants typically described experiences with subtle racism or racial microaggressions as having a subjective quality, making them difficult to identify and prove, because this form of racism can be unintentional in comparison to more blatant forms of racism (e.g., racial slurs). The following female participant explained that people only reveal so much of their racism, because blatant racism is not politically correct. She went on to describe the forms of racism she experienced as much more subtle verbal and behavioral cues, which expressed the undertone that she was an anomaly or did not belong:

I mean, [overt racism] is not socially acceptable, and so...it might be a little comment or a look or something, but they'll never come out and say, "I hate Black people," or, you know, "I don't think minorities can make it," or, "You people aren't good enough."

Participants generally described various emotional (e.g., sad, uncomfortable, fearful, and angry) and cognitive reactions (e.g., confusion, humor, nervousness, and being silenced) to racism or race-based misunderstandings. The following participant shared her reaction to a traumatic racial incident that occurred on campus in which a student wore a Ku Klux Klan costume during a Halloween social.

I felt very unprepared...to explain my emotions; like, all I knew was, it's wrong. Like, that's just wrong, and I don't understand why it's wrong, but that's upsetting me. And I remember I just started crying, and I was so embarrassed because I...just didn't know how to react, and it just meant so much to me, that one moment, because it was like, I came here to get away from this.

This encounter portrays peer ignorance and insensitivity toward the historical significance of images that represent the racism and oppression faced by Black people in America. In this example, the participant expressed her experience of feeling silenced, invalidated, and distressed. A variant number of participants reported feeling personally responsible for educating others about racism and its consequences and felt that it is necessary to develop an intentional approach (e.g., immediate, sensitive, and direct) when addressing such racism.

Balancing Multiple Cognitive Responsibilities In addition to the reactions previously described, a subdomain was developed to capture the complex reactions participants have had toward racial microaggressions. This subdomain outlines the typical experience of participants feeling as though they must juggle being a representative for Black people, educating others about Black culture, and/or avoiding the perpetuation of Black stereotypes, all while treading lightly about racial matters within interracial friendships. Participants typically felt it was important to evaluate multiple factors to determine whether they should speak out against an exchange that holds racial undertones. These factors include (1) whether the act qualifies as racial prejudice or discrimination, (2) what type of intervention will create a lasting impact, and/or (3) what is at stake. For instance, Black students often have the burden of providing proof of racist intent and may avoid concluding that an act of subtle racism occurred if the intent behind the aggressor's behavior is unclear. Without solid proof, the recipient of the act may be viewed as being overly sensitive, thus perpetuating a racial stereotype. If the participant does address the incident, they feel they must be direct enough in their interaction to be heard and understood and to produce favorable change, all while not jeopardizing diverse friendships or creating a tense environment among peers. Participants also typically reported trying to balance responding to or educating others about racism, while not "overthinking" these incidents or placing too much energy (e.g., "making a big deal," getting offended) on encounters with racial undertones. One participant stated, "I just push it to the side or I don't even want to remember it because it was that bad an experience." When determining whether and how to respond to subtle racism, another participant struggled with not wanting to be perceived negatively by peers, while also not wanting his concerns about racism to be silenced:

> *I am still struggling with it, but it's like, I don't want to be perceived as that "Black power dude" who is always talking about race....But I feel as though I need to break out of that fear, because if I don't, then I'll just be perpetuating the oppression.*

This highlights the double jeopardy that many Black students must attempt to negotiate when deciding whether to voice concerns or educate others to combat racism. The backlash can be that the student becomes the tokenized representative or is dismissed as an emotional Black person. As such, participants typically reported having to manage emotional reactions, such as frustration and sadness, in connection with their experiences with subtle racism. Furthermore, a typical number of participants felt at a loss for how to handle or articulate race-related challenges and often second-guess their responses to racism.

DOMAIN 5: RACE-RELATED EXPERIENCES IN THE CLASSROOM AND WITH FACULTY

This domain includes participant responses that describe classroom and faculty experiences. Participants typically reported experiencing subtle racism, racial tension, and/or discomfort with faculty and students in the classroom. This participant described a White professor who interacted with students of color in a superior manner:

If [my friends] go talk to him [a White professor], he acts one way with them, and then you see him interact with other people. [It's] like, why are you acting that way with my friends—and my friends are all minorities, Blacks especially—and act this way with other students?...Sometimes it's like his whole body language is just, "I am superior," and then when he's talking to other people, he doesn't seem so uptight.

This experience captures a perceived behavioral microaggression of a professor in which the implicit message to Black students is that they are of less-than-equal status to their White peers. A variant number of participants reported that discussions about race in the classroom depend on the professor's discretion and differ by the professor's race. In general, White professors were perceived as avoiding or limiting discussions of race. In comparison, participants experienced that professors of color encouraged discussions of race. One participant contrasts classroom learning experiences with a Black professor with the common classroom experience held by majority White professors on campus:

I took a prose writing class where the professor was Black and...you would have to debate what [the authors] say because it's just so needed, it's good....There were a lot of minorities in the class. So, we would just voice our opinion like we were at a kitchen table or something...as opposed to what you think of as a [university] classroom [where] you keep your composure and you answer with a politically correct response. ... The rest of [the professors] were all White.

This participant describes how Black professors created a classroom environment that was open to in-depth discussions about controversial topics related to race. On the contrary, classroom experiences with White professors were described as only allowing for superficial, politically correct discussions of readings and avoiding in-depth race-related discussions. The implicit message in many predominately White classrooms with White professors was that diverse communication styles and discussions about race were not valued or a part of the normative classroom experience.

Domain 6: Race-Related Experiences with Administrators and Staff

Participants' descriptions of their experiences with administrators and/or staff are described within this domain. A general number of participants experienced subtle racism or expressed being confused by experiences with administrators and/or staff. The following participant describes his negative experiences with a White advisor:

I had an advisor that…was not supportive, made fun of me, and told me most of the time, "Maybe you shouldn't be a doctor." He was White….Every time with him, it was always a negative feeling, and I would always anticipate it.

This verbal and behavioral microaggression signaled to the participant that his advisor does not take his educational goals seriously and maintains a marginal outlook on his potential for academic and career achievement. Notably, participants typically felt that working with administrators and staff (e.g., advisors) who are either people of color or have experience working with students of color was beneficial.

DOMAIN 7: PEER DYNAMICS

This section refers to participants' descriptions of their peer groups and associated interactions with friends and acquaintances on campus. A typical number of participants maintained friendships with mostly other students of color. Participants hypothesized that the makeup of these friendship groups was either a product of similar life experiences, which allow people of color to relate better to one another than to White people, or was typically due to involvement in race-based and/or class-based academic support programs, which was perceived to foster the pervasive feeling on campus that all the Black students seem to know each other and spend time together.

Other participants typically maintained a diverse, interracial group of college friends. Three variant categories describing interracial friendships appeared in this domain. While some participants described feeling at liberty to talk to their White friends about racism, other participants expressed that most friendships with White students on campus were developed in the classroom and that these relationships seem to be more superficial than those with peers of color. Furthermore, bringing up race-related experiences with White or non-Black peers was perceived to be uncomfortable and thus avoided. In addition, a typical number of participants reported being stereotyped, feeling tension, and/or being offended during an interaction with White peers.

Participants noted, at a variant rate, the presence of racial cliques and racial segregation on campus. The differences in the racial attitudes toward Black people held by peers based on their region of origin in the United States or the homogeneity of the communities were typically described among the students. A typical number of participants also noted that there is an experiential difference for Black students on campus who came from predominately White regions compared to those who did not.

DOMAIN 8: INTERSECTIONS OF IDENTITY

Race and racism cannot be explored within a vacuum, because racism is often complicated by membership in other social groups. The intersections of race and racism as they relate to gender, social class, and task balancing are highlighted in the three following subdomains.

Gender Dynamics and Race   This subdomain pertains to experiences related to gender or explicit experiences between the participant and members of the opposite sex. A variant number of participants described a disproportionately higher number of Black females on campus compared to Black males. Thus, Black male participants often experienced being the only Black male in a course, which may place heightened pressure on them to be successful. Participants typically expressed that Black males are frequently seen as academically inferior and/or physically threatening.

A variant number of female participants reported being perceived to be oversexualized and/or portrayed as having an attitude. Participants also noted, at a variant rate, the pervasive social aversion and lower levels of attraction toward the Black physical characteristics (e.g., kinky hair) of Black women. The following quote reveals a participant's feelings that the beauty of Black women is the least valued of all the races and that Black women often feel pressure to alter their physical characteristics: "I feel like when I go out with my friends that aren't Black...I'm just the friend. I am not like one of the girls [men] could be interested in." By being systematically ignored by others when out with friends, in addition to receiving verbal and nonverbal cues that her appearance is different and not attractive, the implicit microaggression is the denigration of Black female physical features. The resulting message is that Black women are not considered desirable and are perceived by men to be less physically appealing than women from other racial/ethnic backgrounds. Furthermore, a variant number of participants stated that Black women were recognized as being the backbone in Black communities and/or stereotyped as working in caretaking occupations, such as nursing.

Social Class and Race   Participants' experiences related to social class background or financial issues are described under this subdomain. At a typical rate, participants linked racial disparities to economic and educational disadvantages. While a variant number of participants reported that Black people utilize scholarships and parental assistance and/or work several jobs to secure funding to afford college, a typical number of participants reported that those from lower socioeconomic status backgrounds, particularly students of color, experience a lack of financial support and face challenges in affording college. In addition, participants typically reported encountering ignorance from White people (e.g., upper class) about the difficulties and barriers people of color face in paying for college, or they are assumed to be working class.

Balancing Multiple Physical Responsibilities Participants typically reported balancing various physical activities (e.g., school, work, campus positions, etc.) or having to take on tasks without support. These tasks include, but are not limited to, balancing multiple jobs, family obligations, and scholastic- and club-related activities. The following participant's remarks demonstrate how her financial needs figured into this balancing act:

> *It's just crazy. Like, all the plans that I had to sit and come up with in my head as to how I'm going to get around this [paying for college]. I'm a certified medical biller and medical administrator, and I'm a medical assistant, and I'm 18 years old. And I got this all done because I'm like, all right, if I do that, to go to medical school you need…some hospital time, and I'm like, I don't have time to go volunteer; like, I'd love to, but I don't have time for that right now. So, I was like, if I do this, then I can work in a hospital and make the money I need to survive but still get the hospital time I need to go to medical school, while I can probably meet a few doctors and make a few connections…and like, just the craziness I've had to go through [to pay for college].*

While it is true that most college students multitask and take on multiple responsibilities, many Black students have the added burden of balancing racism in addition to their hectic academic schedules. In certain instances, students of color maintain a disproportionate number of work, home, and school responsibilities compared to their White peers as a result of pervasive financial needs, family responsibilities, and/or the pressure of overcompensating to avoid perpetuating racial stereotypes.

DOMAIN 9: FACTORS THAT PROMOTE RESILIENCE

Despite the negative psychological impact of microaggressions and other difficulties experienced in the college environment, participants revealed several factors that help them cope. Participants generally described various outlets of support, including family, friends, religious faith, academic support programs, the multicultural center, involvement in clubs, academic leadership positions, and journal writing. Participants typically expressed being inspired by those who work toward change and influence others, including peers, influential alumni, celebrities, and the university's mission. A variant number of participants viewed learning about racial-cultural dynamics and/or living in a diverse community as empowering and felt that these characteristics may decrease campus incidence of racism.

At a typical rate, participants reported rejecting societal messages by using negative encounters with racism as motivation toward achievement of personal and academic success, to prove people wrong, and to inspire future changes. For instance, one participant notes that despite the pervasiveness of racism inside and outside of the university environment, it will not serve as a deterrent in her life: "I mean, I'm going to experience racism in every part of my life, especially...med. school. I'm going to experience it everywhere, so, I mean, it's expected, but it's not going to deter me."

DOMAIN 10: FUTURE EXPECTATIONS FOR THE COLLEGE CAMPUS

Participants shared several suggestions regarding improvements they would like to see for the campus environment, as well as factors they believed would further support a diverse student body. While participants typically stated that the university is promoting diversity and responding to blatant racism, they felt that further improvements were needed in the college environment, such as an increased level of responding to subtle, systematic, and institutional forms of racism. A variant number of participants stated that the university needs greater diversity among its students and administration.

First, participants typically felt that the college should create a better sense of community on campus by promoting interracial dialogues and establishing a climate in which racial-cultural-based events are welcoming to people of all races. Next, participants typically felt that the students on campus often underutilize the cultural programming and campus resources made available on campus. In addition, a variant number of participants felt that all students, regardless of race, need to challenge themselves to talk to and become friends with people outside of their own racial, ethnic, and religious groups. Furthermore, participants typically suggested that the college's first priority should be securing funding and reducing cost of attendance for its students, especially students of color, and that the college should spend less on frivolous expenses (e.g., marketing materials for current students).

DISCUSSION

Scholars have consistently demonstrated the detrimental effects of racial microaggressions in the lives of Black people (Sue & Sue, 2007; Franklin & Boyd-Franklin, 2000; Harrell, 2000; Jones, 1997; Pierce, 1995) and have documented the manifestation of racial microaggressions in the university environment (Gay, 2004; Smith, Allen, & Danley, 2007; Solórzano et al., 2000). The current study builds on this literature by examining (1) college students' perceptions of racial microaggressions on their college campus, (2) the impact of these microaggressions, (3) resilience and coping methods they use to address these microaggressive behaviors, and (4) suggestions for changes in the university environment.

RACIAL MICROAGGRESSIONS ON CAMPUS

This study confirmed that Black college students are experiencing racial micro-aggressions on campus, with White peers, faculty members, administrators, and campus staff being the primary perpetrators of subtle racism. As a group, they frequently encounter negative stereotypes about Black people and mis-conceptions about affirmative action. Specifically, Black people are often characterized as angry, violent, low class, and unintelligent (Sue, Nadal, et al., 2008). Black students receive the message that they are unintelligent primarily through misconceptions of affirmative action status in which their admission into college is attributed to affirmative action initiatives. The as-sumption that Black students' college admission was due solely to affirmative action undermines the intelligence and academic achievements of these stu-dents and further implies that Black college students do not deserve their place as students on campus. These results confirm previous findings that Black students are viewed as hostile, violent, unintelligent, and a "threat to public spaces" (Solórzano et al., 2000, p. 68). Through the expression of these negative racial stereotypes, Black students are repeatedly reminded that they do not belong or are not welcome in the university environment.

Black college students who do not confirm negative Black stereotypes are tokenized and thus viewed as being different from, and implicitly superior to, other Black people. Therefore, while participants were stereotyped against, they were simultaneously seen as exceptions to the negative Black cultural stereotypes. Black college students who are seen as "rare cases of success" are experiencing a subtle form of racism, because their "success" is seen as contrasting with the larger "failure" of Black people as a whole (Solórzano et al., 2000, p. 68). Thus, Black people who do not confirm stereotypes are seen as outliers or tokens, allowing people to continue to espouse stereotypical beliefs in the face of evidence to the contrary.

Even as participants were considered to be token Black students, they were often called upon to be representatives of all Black people during classroom discussions and social conversations, especially about topics related to racial dynamics and racism. Previous researchers have referred to this experience as "spokesperson pressure" (Steele & Aronson, 1995). Because this perspec-tive denies the existence of individual differences in the thoughts, feelings, and behaviors of Black people, it further promotes the existence of group-based negative racial stereotypes. It also thrusts Black students into an ascribed expert status that could cause discomfort, anxiety, and invalidation.

While the discussion of subtle racism was central to the focus of this study, the overlap of gender and racial oppression emerged. Some negative Black stereotypes are differentially applied to Black men and Black women, making their experiences of racism nuanced by their gender identities. Consistent with previous findings that Black male college students routinely report experiences of being viewed as "predators" and "incompetents" (Smith et al., 2007, p. 537), Black male participants faced compounding stereotypes of being considered academically inferior and hypermasculine by peers, teachers, and administrators. Black male students are thus viewed as physically threatening, emotionally restrained, and sexually promiscuous, a cluster of stereotypes which exemplifies how Black men are seen as a threat to public safety by members of the campus community. The stereotypes of Black male hypermasculinity and lack of intelligence act in conjunction most notably when campus police question Black men about their presence on campus (e.g., making requests to see identification for Black male students but not for other students) with the suspicion that these Black men are not likely to be students at the university and must therefore be up to no good.

The many negative stereotypes about Black women reported by participants align with the limited representations of Black womanhood found throughout American history. Specifically, Black female college students are stereotyped as aspiring to work in caretaking professions, such as nursing. Ostensibly, this is not a negative stereotype, as nurses are well-educated and often nurturing people. The oppressive quality of this stereotype reveals itself in light of the "Mammy" image, which is a representation of Black women as self-sacrificing and content in their subservient role as caregivers to White families (West, 1995). Rooted in the slavery era, the Mammy stereotype limits the expectations others have about the careers that Black women are suited to. Thus, Black women with career aspirations that diverge from caretaking roles are met with surprised reactions, which communicate to them that they are stepping out of their expected role in society.

Additionally, because the Mammy is typically depicted as an obese woman with African features, such as dark skin and kinky hair, she is viewed as unattractive, unfeminine, and asexual (West, 1995). Likewise, Black female college students are the targets of messages that communicate to them that they are unattractive and should conform to a White standard of beauty. When responding to these and other derogatory messages, participants felt compelled to avoid perpetuating the stereotype of the "angry Black woman." Indeed, researchers note that the existence of the "Sapphire" stereotype, which represents Black women as aggressive, hostile, and emasculating, is one of the most pervasive in our culture (West, 1995).

Finally, participants recognized instances of environmental or institutional racism on campus, which is defined as the "intentional or unintentional outcomes that result from organizational policies and practices that affect members of racial groups disproportionately" (Carter & Pieterse, 2005, p. 51). For Black college students at a predominately White campus, the lack of racial-ethnic diversity reinforces the message that they are not welcome members of the college community. Further, participants viewed the lack of funding and support for poor students as evidence of institutional racism, because it disproportionately creates barriers for students of color. Participants emphasized that racial disparities in the enrollment and financial support of students of color are representative of the racial discrimination that Black people continue to face on multiple fronts, notably in housing, educational enrichment opportunities, and employment, which accounts for the racial stratification of university jobs and ultimately reinforces a link between race and class in American society.

IMPACT OF RACIAL MICROAGGRESSIONS

Previous research reveals that stress resulting from racism-related experiences has an impact on psychological well-being that is unique from—and at times more powerful than—the impact of other stressful life events (Pieterse & Carter, 2007; Utsey, Giesbrecht, Hook, & Stanard, 2008). As such, Black college students are impacted by racial microaggressions in a multitude of emotional (e.g., sad, angry, and/or anxious) and cognitive ways. An important finding of this study is that Black students expend significant cognitive energy trying to determine the intention behind the microaggression (e.g., whether a person was simply naive or intended to be racist), how to appropriately respond, and the potential cost of such a response, all while trying to avoid perpetuating negative stereotypes about Black people.

When deciding how to respond to a racial microaggression, Black college students generally viewed reacting angrily as an ineffective response, because it would only propagate the stereotype that Black people are angry and aggressive. Conversely, many feel it is their responsibility to address the microaggressor in a direct and sensitive way, in hopes of discussing concerns and clearing up misunderstandings. As a result, Black students exert considerable effort balancing between "being themselves" and the fear that their action will be seen as evidence to further negative expectations of Black people. The process of determining how and whether to respond to a racial microaggression can be exhausting, anxiety provoking, and confusing. Previous literature also highlights that the confusing nature of racial microaggressions causes significant psychological "turmoil," as Black students continuously must question the intention behind perceived racial microaggressions and deal with the resulting negative implications (Sue et al., 2007, p. 335; Sue, Nadal, et al., 2008).

Another significant obstacle Black students may face when dealing with their experiences of racial microaggressions is that these experiences are subtle and ambiguous by definition; thus, they are not always easily recognizable. Therefore, Black students believe that their notion of what constitutes a racial microaggression will not likely be shared by the perpetrator of the microaggression, making the situation difficult to discuss and perhaps impossible to resolve. Another hindrance to communication in these already-tense situations is that White peers, faculty, and administrators are likely unaware of the racial reality that Black college students face. Emerging literature suggests that Black college students and White college students describe their campus racial climate in very different ways (Ancis, Sedlacek, & Mohr, 2000; Rankin & Reason, 1998), such that Black students view their campuses as hostile and unwelcoming to people of color, while White students view these same campuses as friendly and inclusive. However, because White people have the social and cultural power to define the reality of a situation, the racial reality of Black students is deemed invalid or untrue (Sue, Capodilupo, Nadal, & Torino, 2008). Thus, when a Black student is microaggressed against by a White student, faculty member, or staff person, his or her claim that the incident was racially motivated is likely to be minimized by White people, who may lack a critical awareness of racial dynamics on campus and in larger society. Regardless of their intentions, perpetrators of racial microaggressions may unwittingly contribute to Black students' feelings of alienation and devaluation in the university environment.

COPING METHODS AND RESILIENCE

Consistent with findings of past researchers (Plummer & Slane, 1996; Utsey et al., 2007; Utsey, Giesbrecht, et al., 2008), the current study revealed Black college students cope with subtle racism by turning to a number of resources, such as religious and spiritual beliefs and the social support offered by family, friends, and the peers and mentors they meet through their involvement in academic support programs. Specifically, because of their perceived shared experiences with racism, Black college students perceive peers of color as better equipped to relate to each other compared to White peers. As a result, some participants were less likely to seek support from White peers about such matters. However, participants described diverse interpersonal experiences with White counterparts. Some identified White allies as friends and sources of support, whereas other participants detailed their interracial experiences with Whites as superficial and characterized by mistrust.

At times, Black students did not want to "make a big deal" out of their experiences with racial microaggressions; they must "just keep it moving" and try to minimize the impact of racism on their academic achievement. It is possible that these "distancing" coping mechanisms (Plummer & Slane, 1996, p. 306) are used because unlike general stressful life events, racial microaggressions are "pervasive, perpetual, and systematic" (Utsey, Giesbrecht, et al., 2008, p. 58). There are contradicting findings in the literature about the impact of various race-related stress-coping strategies. While the psychological, social, cognitive, and academic costs associated with certain strategies remain unclear, Black college students may find it easier "to let things go" or to accept racial slights rather than expend the energy necessary to challenge them.

Researchers have hypothesized that students of color who grasp the underlying dynamics of racial microaggressions are able to cope more effectively when confronting subtle racism (Sue, Capodilupo, & Holder, 2008). Indeed, the current study reveals that it is empowering for Black college students to live in a racially diverse community, engage with other people of color in their classes, and study racial-cultural dynamics in the classroom. Of note, then, is the finding that White professors often avoid or limit discussions of race and racial-cultural dynamics in the classroom. Given that Black students tend to feel more confident and validated as racial beings when they are encouraged to foster a critical racial consciousness, it follows that White professors' avoidance of these topics is highly disadvantageous to the coping abilities of students of color, as well as to the education of White students, who may unknowingly perpetuate subtle forms of oppression. Additionally, Black students found a great deal of support among faculty of color, particularly professors and advisors, who were more willing to address racial-cultural issues. The many benefits of working with faculty of color highlight how the underrepresentation of faculty of color on campus is all the more injurious in the college experience of Black students, in particular, and all students, in general.

Despite regular experiences with racial microaggressions on campus, Black college students reported being highly motivated to continue to achieve academically. This orientation toward future success has been shown to encourage optimism and resilience in Black people as they confront racism (Utsey, Hook, Fischer, & Belvet, 2008). Feeling encouraged and inspired by influential alumni, celebrities, and their fellow peers, many participants hoped to inspire future change in their respective fields of study and even society as a whole. Ultimately, participants demonstrated that they were resilient in the face of racial microaggressions; in fact, when asked why they continued to pursue their education in an environment where they faced subtle racism regularly, participants reported that dropping out of college was simply not an option for them. Black college students are "survivors" (Smith et al., 2007, p. 573), for they must continue to maintain a strong academic focus while navigating racism in their academic environment.

SUGGESTIONS FOR CHANGES TO THE UNIVERSITY ENVIRONMENT

While most colleges and universities seek to increase the diversity of their student body, participants noted that to reap the full benefits diversity offers, the university must also work to foster a culturally inclusive climate within the campus environment. Because people are naturally drawn to those that share aspects of their personal experience, such as race, culture, religion, beliefs, and personality, the promotion of increased communication between students of diverse backgrounds is essential in reducing intergroup anxiety (Chang, 1999).

To assist students in exploring the nuances and benefits of their diverse campus environment, participants suggested that colleges and universities implement a first-year student experience that includes the exploration of racial-cultural variations within the population as an impetus to get people "out of their shells" and encourage them to interact with students of various cultural backgrounds. While this initiative would be part of a keystone experience, student interactions must be fostered throughout their college experience through ongoing diversity initiatives, such as cultural workshops, residence life programming, and campus dialogues.

FUTURE IMPLICATIONS

The perpetuation of racial microaggressions toward Black students within collegiate settings and their subsequent short-term and long-term impact merits further research. Concurrent with the methodology utilized by CQR, this study invited the participation of a small, highly select group consisting of Black students from a private, urban, predominately White university in the northeastern region of the United States. As such, it is important to exercise caution in generalizing the results of this study to other populations. Replication and extension of the current study is critical to determine the generalizability of the themes identified. Further investigation is necessary to underscore the cognitive, emotional, and psychological outcomes of racial microaggressions and race-related stress. Such research will bring critical knowledge and awareness about the perpetuation and impact of racial microaggressions, and it will help to demystify the confusion and uncertainty that microaggressions often cause for students of color (Sue et al., 2008).

As the study's findings reveal, racial microaggressions can interfere with students' cognitive and affective well-being and contribute to a sense of isolation from peers, faculty, and campus organizations (Cabrera, Nora, Terenzini, Pascarella, & Hagedorn, 1999). Participants described feeling silenced and misunderstood within predominately White environments (e.g., in the residence halls, in class, and on the college campus). In such environments, participants noted that critical conversations about racism and race-related issues and its presence on campus were often skirted. In addition, participants described a sense of discomfort in segregated environments, which were largely perceived as cultivating an air of competition and an "us versus them" dynamic.

Black students also described being taxed by external and internal pressures, on campus and in classroom settings, to educate other students about racial-cultural dynamics, in addition to being tokenized or feeling forced to be a spokesperson for their racial group. Results also revealed that within predominately White environments, Black students are placed into a position in which they feel like they must overcompensate for their race by consciously working to avoid the perpetuation of behaviors that may be perceived as exemplifying social stereotypes. This includes, but is not limited to, internalizing frustration and avoiding conversations about race so as not to be perceived as overly sensitive and feeling like there is limited room for academic missteps in order to avoid being perceived as academically inferior. For these reasons, participants described feeling more at ease and having increased confidence within diverse environments on campus that included the visibility and support of faculty and staff of color. These spaces were reported to engage students within a supportive environment where conversations about race and culture were welcome and valuable lessons could be learned. This finding reinforces the necessity of cultivating an increased representation of student, faculty, and administration of color within predominately White campuses.

CONCLUSION

As this study demonstrates, racial microaggressions are a very real and lived experience for Black undergraduates. To avoid the perpetuation of socially embedded attitudes and behaviors, multicultural training and development programs for college and university personnel must be a mandatory requirement for job training. Guidelines must be created, implemented, and continually evaluated in order to develop effective multicultural trainings and programs to ensure the cultural proficiency of administrators, faculty, school counselors, and other staff at colleges and universities. In addition, knowledge of racial microaggressions and their impact would inform the case conceptualization and treatment implications of mental health practitioners who work with Black undergraduates. Finally, classroom curricula across college departments need to incorporate racial-ethnic dynamics in order to create an awareness, knowledge, and skill base among their students. This process will help prepare the next generation of students for successful entry into a world where all careers are influenced by an increasingly diverse racial-cultural landscape.

REFERENCES

Ancis, J. R., Sedlacek, W. E., & Mohr, J. J. (2000). Student perceptions of campus cultural climate by race. *Journal of Counseling and Development, 78*, 180–185.

Aronson, J., Lustina, M. J., Good, C., Keough, K., Steele, C. M., & Brown, J. (1999). When White men can't do math: Necessary and sufficient factors in stereotype threat. *Journal of Experimental Social Psychology, 35*, 29–46.

Cabrera, A. F., Nora, A., Terenzini, P. T., Pascarella, E., & Hagedorn, L. S. (1999). Campus racial climate and the adjustment of students to college: A comparison between White students and African-American students. *Journal of Higher Education, 70*, 134–160.

Carter, R. T., & Pieterse, A. L. (2005). Race: A social and psychological analysis of the term and its meaning. In R. T. Carter (Ed.), *Handbook of racial-cultural psychology and counseling, Vol. 1: Theory and research* (pp. 41–63). Hoboken, NJ: John Wiley & Sons.

Cervantes, R. C., & Pena, C. (1998). Evaluating Hispanic/Latino programs: Ensuring cultural competence. *Alcoholism Treatment Quarterly, 16*, 109–131.

Chang, M. J. (1999). Does racial diversity matter? The educational impact of a racially diverse undergraduate population. *Journal of College Student Development, 40*(4), 377–395.

Cheatham, H. E., & Berg-Cross, L. (1992). College student development: African Americans reconsidered. In L. C. Whitaker & R. E. Slimak (Eds.), *College student development* (pp. 167–192). Swarthmore, PA: Haworth Press.

Constantine, M. G., & Sue, D. W. (2007). Perceptions of racial microaggressions among Black supervisees in cross-racial dyads. *Journal of Counseling Psychology, 54*, 142–153.

DeFreece, M. T. (1987). Women of color: No longer ignored. *Journal of College Student Personnel, 28*, 570–571.

Dobbins, J. E., & Skillings, J. H. (2000). Racism as a clinical syndrome. *American Journal of Orthopsychiatry, 70*, 14–27.

Fassinger, R. (2005). Paradigms, praxis, problems, and promise: Grounded theory in counseling psychology research. *Journal of counseling psychology, 52*(2), 156–166.

Feagin, J. R. (1992). The continuing significance of racism: Discrimination against Black students in White colleges. *Journal of Black Studies, 22*(4), 546–578.

Franklin, A. J. (1999). Invisibility syndrome and racial identity development in psychotherapy and counseling African American men. *Counseling Psychologist, 27*, 761–793.

Franklin, A. J., & Boyd-Franklin, N. (2000). Invisibility syndrome: A clinical model of the effects of racism on African American males. *American Journal of Orthopsychiatry, 70,* 33–41.

Gay, G. (2004). Navigating marginality en route to the professoriate: Graduate students of color learning and living in academia. *International Journal of Qualitative Studies in Education, 17,* 265–288.

Gloria, A. M., & Robinson Kurpius, S. E. (1996). The validation of the Cultural Congruity Scale and the University Environment Scale with Chicano/a students. *Hispanic Journal of Behavioral Science, 18,* 533–550.

Greer, T. M., & Chwalisz, K. (2007). Minority-related stressors and coping processes among African American college students. *Journal of College Student Development, 48*(4), 388–404.

Harrell, S. P. (2000). A multidimensional conceptualization of racism-related stress: Implications for the well-being of people of color. *American Journal of Orthopsychiatry, 70,* 42–57.

Hill, C. E., Thompson, B. J., & Williams, E. N. (1997). A guide to conducting consensual qualitative research. *Counseling Psychologist, 25,* 517–572.

Hill, C. E., Knox, S., Thompson, B. J., Williams, E. N., Hess, S.A., & Ladany, N. (2005). Consensual qualitative research: An update. *Journal of Counseling Psychology, 52*(2), 196–205.

Jones, J. M. (1991). Psychological models of race: What have they been and what should they be? In J. D. Goodchilds (Ed.), *Psychological perspectives on human diversity in America* (pp. 3–46). Washington, DC: American Psychological Association.

Jones, J. M. (1997). *Prejudice and racism* (2nd ed.). Washington, DC: McGraw-Hill.

Kim, B. S. K., Brenner, B. R., Liang, C. T. H., & Asay, P. A. (2003). A qualitative study of adaptation experiences of 1.5-generation Asian Americans. *Cultural Diversity & Ethnic Minority Psychology, 9,* 156–170.

Krieger, N., & Sidney, S. (1996). Racial discrimination and blood pressure: The CARDIA study of young Black and White adults. *American Journal of Public Health, 86,* 1379 –1378.

Laden, B. V. (2004). Serving emerging majority students. In B. V. Laden (Ed.), *Serving minority populations: New directions for community colleges.* San Francisco, CA: Jossey-Bass.

Morrow, S. L., & Smith, M. L. (2000). Qualitative research for counseling psychology. In S. D. Brown & R. W. Lent (Eds.), *Handbook of counseling psychology* (3rd ed., pp. 199–230). New York: John Wiley & Sons.

Pierce, C. (1995). Stress analogs of racism and sexism: Terrorism, torture, and disaster. In C. Willie, P. Rieker, B. Kramer, & B. Brown (Eds.), *Mental health, racism, and sexism* (pp. 277–293). Pittsburgh, PA: University of Pittsburgh Press.

Pierce, C., Carew, J., Pierce-Gonzalez, D., & Willis, D. (1978). An experiment in racism: TV commercials. In C. Pierce (Ed.), *Television and education* (pp. 62–88). Beverly Hills, CA: Sage.

Pieterse, A. L., & Carter, R. T. (2007). An examination of the relationship between general life stress, racism-related stress, and psychological health among Black men. *Journal of Counseling Psychology, 54,* 101–109.

Plummer, D. L., & Slane, S. (1996). Patterns of coping in racially stressful situations. *Journal of Black Psychology, 22,* 302–315.

Ponterotto, J. G. (1990). Racial/ethnic minority and women students in higher education: A status report. *New Directions for Student Services, 52,* 45–59.

Ponterotto, J. G. (2002). Qualitative research methods: The fifth force in psychology. *Journal of Counseling Psychology, 30,* 394–408.

Rankin, S. R., & Reason, R. D. (1998). Differing perception: How students of color and White students perceive campus climate for underrepresented groups. *Journal of College Student Development, 46,* 43–61.

Smith, W. A., Allen, W. R., & Danley, L. L. (2007). "Assume the position...you fit the description": Psychosocial experiences and racial battle fatigue among African American male college students. *American Behavioral Scientist, 51,* 551–578.

Solórzano, D., Ceja, M., & Yosso, T. (2000). Critical race theory, racial microaggressions, and campus racial climate: The experiences of African American college students. *Journal of Negro Education, 69,* 60–73.

Spanierman, L. B., Oh, E., Poteat, V. P., Hund, A. R., McClair, V. L., Beer, A. M., & Clarke, A. M. (2008). White university students' responses to societal racism: A qualitative investigation. *Counseling Psychologist, 36,* 839–870.

Steele, C. M., & Aronson, J. (1995). Stereotype threat and the intellectual test performance of African Americans. *Journal of Personality and Social Psychology, 69,* 797–811.

Suarez-Balcazar, Y., Orellana-Damacela, L., Portillo, N., Rowan, J. M., & Andrews-Guillen, C. (2003). Experiences of differential treatment among college students of color. *Journal of Higher Education, 74*(4), 428–444.

Sue, D. W., Capodilupo, C. M., & Holder, A. M. B. (2008). Racial microaggressions in the life experience of Black Americans. *Professional Psychology: Research and Practice, 39,* 329–336.

Sue, D. W., Capodilupo, C. M., Nadal, K. L., & Torino, G. C. (2008). Racial microaggressions and the power to define reality. *American Psychologist, 63,* 277–279.

Sue, D. W., Capodilupo, C. M., Torino, G. C., Bucceri, J. M., Holder, A. M. B., Nadal, K. L., & Esquilin, M. (2007). Racial microaggressions in everyday life: Implications for clinical practice. *American Psychologist, 62,* 271–286.

Sue, D. W., Nadal, K. L., Capodilupo, C. M., Lin, A. I., Torino, G. C., & Rivera, D. P. (2008). Racial microaggressions against Black Americans: Implications for counseling. *Journal of Counseling and Development, 86,* 330–338.

Sue, D. W., & Sue, D. (2007). *Counseling the culturally diverse: Theory and practice* (5th ed.). Hoboken, NJ: John Wiley & Sons.

Twigg, C. (2005). *Increasing success for underserved students: Redesigning introductory courses.* Saratoga Springs, NY: National Center for Academic Transformation. Retrieved May 16, 2006, from http://www.thencat.org/Monographs/IncSuccess.htm.

U.S. Bureau of the Census (2008, December). Degrees earned by level and race/ethnicity. In *Statistical abstract of the United States: 2008* (Table 289). Washington, DC: Government Printing Office. Retrieved February 6, 2009, from http://www.census.gov/compendia/statab/tables/09s0289.xls.

Utsey, S. O., Bolden, M. A., Williams, O., III, Lee, A., Lanier, Y., & Newsome, C. (2007). Spiritual well-being as a mediator of the relation between culture-specific coping and quality of life in a community sample of African Americans. *Journal of Cross-Cultural Psychology, 38,* 123–136.

Utsey, S. O., Giesbrecht, N., Hook, J., & Stanard, P. M. (2008). Cultural, sociofamilial, and psychological resources that inhibit psychological distress in African Americans exposed to stressful life events and race-related stress. *Journal of Counseling Psychology, 55,* 49–62.

Utsey, S. O., Hook, J., Fischer, N., & Belvet, B. (2008). Cultural orientation, ego resilience, and optimism, as predictors of subjective well-being in African Americans. *Journal of Positive Psychology, 3,* 202–210.

West, C. M. (1995). Mammy, Sapphire, and Jezebel: Historical images of Black women and their implications for psychotherapy. *Psychotherapy: Theory, Research, Practice, Training, 32,* 458–466.

APPENDIX A: RESULTS TABLE

Table 2.1

Domains, Categories, and Frequencies of Black Undergraduates'
Experiences with Racial Microaggressions

Domain	Category	Frequency
1. High-school-related experiences	Described being racially stereotyped:	Typical
	- Tokenized	Variant
	- Avoided stereotype perpetuation (i.e., could not make errors)	Variant
	Attended a racially diverse HS	Variant
	Attended a predominately White HS	Variant
	Blacks underrepresented in HS honors track	Variant
	White people did not understand dynamics of racism	Variant
2. University campus demographics	Predominately White, with Black students in the minority	General
	Asian students are the largest minority group	Typical
	Faculty and administrators are predominately White	Typical
	Notes racial stratification of jobs on campus	Typical
	Most faculty teaching in race-based ASPs are people of color	Variant
3. Transitions to new environments	Racial/ethnic makeup in HS was dissimilar to college	Typical
	Similar racial/ethnic makeup between HS and college	Variant
	Disappointed college climate was unwelcoming	Typical
	Racism that was more blatant in HS is more subtle in college	Variant
	Feel more connected to college than HS	Variant
	Those from a predominately White HS felt an increased sense of connection to Black students while attending college	Variant
	Interactions with college faculty and staff are as positive or more positive than in HS	Variant
4. Perceptions of and reactions to racial microaggressions	Experienced racial stereotypes and encounters with racism	General
	Depicts emotional/cognitive reactions to racism/misunderstandings	General
	Described racial stereotypes:	Typical
	- Ignorant or unintelligent	Typical
	- Loud, tactless, low class, or "ghetto"	Typical
	- Angry, violent, or criminal	Typical

Note: HS = high school, ASPs = academic support programs.

	Negative stereotyped images of Blacks portrayed in media/statistics	Typical
	White people do not understand racism/ race-related experiences of people of color because their experiences are very different	Typical
	Despite accomplishments, college admission attributed to affirmative action	Typical
	Experienced being tokenized/considered an expert in racial matters	Typical
	Ridiculed for "acting White" or treated as an exception to the rule	Typical
	Subtle racism is difficult to prove and can be unintentional	Typical
	Necessary to use an intentional approach when addressing racism	Typical
	Identifying with Black culture may have a negative impact on career opportunities in predominately White companies/fields	Variant
	Assumed connection between Blacks and dissimilarly with others	Variant
	Assumed involvement in ASPs	Variant
	People of color assumed to be more comfortable discussing racism	Variant
	Felt responsible to educate others about racism/race-related consequences	Variant
	People should be held accountable for use of "N-word" or "colored"	Variant
	No reported direct academic impact of subtle racism	Variant
	Experiences with subtle racism have not been invalidated/minimized	Variant
	Racism likely to occur in White college environments	Variant
4a. Balancing multiple cognitive responsibilities	Juggles being a representative, educating others, avoiding stereotype perpetuation, and maintaining interracial friendships	Typical
	Evaluate multiple factors before responding to race-related exchange	Typical
	Balances responding to racism while not "overthinking" encounters	Typical
	Manages emotional reactions after experiencing subtle racism	Typical
	Unsure/second-guesses how to respond to race-related challenges	Typical
5. Race-related experiences in the classroom and with faculty	Subtle racism and tension with faculty/ students in classroom	Typical

(continued)

Table 2.1
(Continued)

Domain	Category	Frequency
	No subtle racism with faculty/students in the classroom, yet has witnessed or experienced racist behavior	Typical
	Discussions of race in classroom depend on professor's race	Variant
	White professors avoid or limit discussions of race	Variant
	Black professors encourage discussions of race	Variant
6. Race-related experiences with administrators and staff	Experienced subtle racism with administrators/staff	General
	Mentions benefits in working with administrators/staff of color	Typical
	Racial tension from staff of color directed to Black students	Variant
	No experiences of subtle racism with administrators/staff	Variant
	Reports no subtle racism with administrators/staff, yet has encountered individual and institutional racism	Variant
	Frustrated at lack of administrative support for funding efforts to support students of color	Variant
	Subjectivity in defining subtle racism/racist intent of administrators/staff	Variant
7. Peer dynamics	Maintains a diverse group of college friends	Typical
	Friendships consist of mostly people of color	Typical
	Assumption that students of color know each other from ASPs	Typical
	Tension, competition, and self-hatred among students of color	Typical
	Stereotyped/felt tension/offended in interaction with White peers	Typical
	Differences in peers' racial attitudes based on region of origin	Typical
	Notes presence of racial cliques/racial segregation on campus	Variant
	Experiential difference between Black students that come from White neighborhoods and those who do not	Variant
	Most White friendships are superficial/developed in classroom	Variant
	Bringing up race outside of Black peers may be uncomfortable	Variant
	Can talk to White friends about racism	Variant

	Black students create "false consensus" by following trends	Variant
	Describes heterogeneity within racial groups	Variant
8. Intersections of identity		
8a. Gender dynamics and race	Black males portrayed as academically inferior/threatening	Typical
	Fewer Black males on campus than Black females	Variant
	Black males expected to be overly masculine	Variant
	Black women are sexualized/portrayed as having an attitude	Variant
	Black women describe social aversion/lower levels of attraction toward Black physical characteristics	Variant
	Black women labeled as caretakers/working in caretaking fields	Variant
8b. Social class and race	Racial disparities linked to economic/ educational disadvantages	Typical
	Many students of color experience challenges affording college	Typical
	Encounters ignorance from White people about the difficulties and barriers people of color face in financing college	Typical
	Utilize several sources in order to afford college	Variant
8c. Balancing multiple physical responsibilities	Balances various physical activities (e.g., school, work, aid, etc.)	Typical
9. Factors that promote resilience	Outlets of support (e.g., family, friends, religion, etc.)	General
	Influential others who work toward positive change	Typical
	Use negative encounters with racism as motivation to achieve	Typical
	Studying racial-cultural dynamics and living in a diverse community	Variant
	Notes having an internal sense of resiliency that others may not	Variant
10. Future expectations for the college campus	College is promoting diversity, yet more improvements sought	Typical
	Foster an improved sense of community	Typical
	Encourage use of campus resources/cultural event attendance	Typical
	Top priority to secure student funding	Typical
	Increase diversity of student body, faculty, and administration	Variant
	Encourage students to befriend people outside of their in-groups	Variant

APPENDIX B: INTERVIEW PROTOCOL

During this interview, I am going to ask about your personal or witnessed experiences with subtle forms of racism known as *racial microaggressions*.

Racial microaggressions are daily and sometimes fairly minor verbal, behavioral, or environmental injustices that occur to people of color because of their racial or ethnic group membership. And it does not matter whether these injustices are intentional or unintentional. What really matters about these behaviors is that they communicate negative messages to you as a person of color.

Unlike traditional racism (e.g., cross burnings and Rosa Parks's bus boycott days), racial microaggressions can be very subtle, ambiguous, and fuzzy in nature and therefore harder to label. Racial microaggressions can occur in many forms, and some examples include being followed around in a store while shopping because of your race, or even verbal statements that demean or dismiss racial issues or experiences, such as, "I believe the most qualified people should be accepted into the college, and race shouldn't be a part of the college admissions application." Another common racial microaggression might be noticing the absence of Black faculty, Black administrators, or even Black students on your college campus. These are only a few examples; please feel free to discuss anything related to subtle racism or racial micro-aggressions on your campus that comes to mind during this interview.

Although the primary focus of this interview will be on your experiences as a college student, I first want to ask you a couple of questions about your high school experiences.

1. What was the racial composition of your high school? To what extent does your current environment reflect the demographics of your high school?
2. In thinking about some of the stereotypes associated with being Black, how have others on your campus subtly expressed stereotypical beliefs toward you because you are Black? What specific challenges do you face as a Black student with regard to dealing with racial microaggressions or subtle racism?
3. What types of feelings do you have about these experiences? How do you deal with these feelings? With whom do you discuss or share those feelings? When you are discriminated against in subtle ways, what factors determine whether you speak out about those experiences?
4. Please describe specific experiences on your campus in which you felt uncomfortable, disrespected, or unsure about what to think about a comment or nonverbal expression that had racial undertones. In what ways do faculty (i.e., professors and instructors), staff (i.e., advisors,

campus hall directors, security, and other college personnel), other students, and the college environment or programs contribute in both positive and negative ways to your experiences with subtle racism at your institution?

5. How might others have invalidated or disputed your experiences of being discriminated against on your campus? In other words, to what extent and how have others minimized your experiences of subtle racism or racial microaggressions?

6. What effects do you believe the specific experiences of subtle racism at your college or university might have had on you personally? On your academic development in general? On your feeling connected with your university?

7. Despite experiencing challenges with subtle racism on your college campus, what encourages you or motivates you to continue to pursue your college education?

8. In what ways could your college or university do more to promote diversity or to reduce discrimination against people from your racial background?

9. Thank you for sharing your experiences with me today. Is there anything else that you would like to discuss or add to what you have already shared with me?

CHAPTER 3

Microaggressions and the Life Experience of Latina/o Americans

DAVID P. RIVERA, ERIN E. FORQUER, and REBECCA RANGEL

The immigration debate is not only a highly contested policy debate, but one that is highly emotional for many. During conversations on immigration policy, I have often felt uncomfortable because of the draconian measures those against immigration reform support. In characterizing their views, I find that they think because my parents are from another country, I'm not a real American. Further, they tend to associate immigration with "all those Mexicans" that are over-burdening our government.

THIS QUOTE, EXPRESSED by a second-generation Latina, exemplifies one of the many ways in which Latinas/os are made to feel like an *alien in their own land*, or not truly American. The United States has a history of anti-immigration movements and sentiment. Polls taken over the past 20 years suggest that negative opinions concerning immigration have wavered over time, with the largest spike in opinions favoring a decrease in immigration (65%) occurring around the same time as California's passing of Proposition 187 in 1994 (Gallup Poll, 2008). Proposition 187, or the "Save Our State" proposition, was intended to deny government benefits, such as access to basic health care and education, to undocumented immigrants. Proposition 187 was later found to be unconstitutional and reversed (Garcia, 1995). Since then, there have been subsequent rises and falls in opinions regarding immigration; however, a 2008 Gallup Poll reported that 39 percent of Americans favored a decrease in immigration, which is still quite sizeable.

Acknowledgments: We would like to thank Gina C. Torino for serving as the auditor of the data analysis process for this study and Rachel Kim, Suah Kim, and Nicole Watkins for their feedback in preparing this chapter.

Many Latinas/os, regardless of citizenship status, are made to feel like persona non grata in their own country. These anti-immigration messages come from many sources, such as individual communication or via wide-reaching media campaigns. For example, the senior author recently received a forwarded e-mail blaming Latina/o immigration for the current economic recession in the United States. The message accused Latina/o immigrants of leaching health care, education, welfare, and job opportunities from "real" deserving Americans. The message even went on to insinuate that Latina/o immigrants are likely to be criminals and sex offenders. Although unsubstantiated, the message represents one of many unchallenged, daily, stereotypical images portrayed about Latinas/os. As such, this chapter seeks to illuminate the many ways in which this group experiences prejudice and discrimination.

Recognizing that Latinas/os self-identify and can be identified in myriad ways, the following definition is used for the purposes of this chapter. Latina/o refers to an individual living in the United States who identifies racially and/or ethnically as Latina/o or Hispanic or who ethnically and/or racially identifies with people coming from Mexico, Central America, South America, or the Spanish-speaking countries of the Caribbean. This definition of Latina/o was broadly conceptualized to recognize and honor the diverse ethnic and racial experience of Latina/o Americans.

PREJUDICE & DISCRIMINATION AGAINST LATINAS/OS

Despite being one of the fastest growing demographic groups and the largest ethnic group in the United States (U.S. Census Bureau, 2007), Latinas/os continue to overwhelmingly report that discrimination is a problem for them. The National Survey of Latinos (NSL; 2002) revealed that 82 percent of Latina/os believe that discrimination prevents Latinas/os from succeeding in the United States. The NSL further suggests that Latinas/os believe discrimination serves as a barrier in educational attainment and the workplace. Statistics from the U.S. Census Bureau (2008) support this widely held belief through the reporting of disproportionately low numbers of Latina/o high school and college graduates. For example, 8.4 percent of Latina/o Americans 18 years old or older possess a bachelor's degree (U.S. Census Bureau, 2008). This represents the lowest educational attainment rate as compared to non-Latina/o White, Asian, and Black Americans. Additionally, while nearly a full quarter of Latinas/os are employed by the service industry (the largest percentage of any racial group), only 17.8 percent hold professional positions (U.S. Department of Labor, 2008). Given these disparities, it is plausible to hypothesize that there is a relationship between discrimination experienced by Latinas/os and the inequities that they experience in education and the workplace.

Discrimination-related research on Latinas/os has historically been limited; however, there appears to be an upward trend in the amount of attention given to this topic (for a meta-analysis, see Araujo & Borrell, 2006). Although researchers primarily concentrate on adult experiences of discrimination (e.g., Hwang & Goto, 2008; Shorey, Cowan, & Sullivan, 2002), several studies have elucidated the experiences of discrimination for Latina/o youth (e.g., Green, Way, & Pahl, 2006; Rosenbloom & Way, 2004). This suggests that Latinas/os are likely to be the targets of discrimination over the course of their lifetime. Additionally, researchers have gone beyond merely demonstrating that discrimination is a real life problem experienced by Latinas/os and have also investigated the correlates of experienced discrimination (Araujo & Borrell, 2006).

Given that Latinas/os have expressed that they do indeed believe that discrimination is an issue for their community (NSL, 2002), an important area of interest is to understand how discrimination impacts the well-being of this population. In a meta-analysis of research about the mental health correlates of perceived discrimination among Latinas/os, discrimination was correlated with depression and stress (Araujo & Borrell, 2006). Additionally, discrimination has been linked to psychological distress, suicidal ideation, low levels of self-control or personal agency, and low levels of overall well-being (Hwang & Goto, 2008; Moradi & Risco, 2006; Schnieder, Hitlan, & Radhakrishnan, 2000; Shorey et al., 2002). In addition to psychological factors, experienced discrimination has also been linked to higher blood pressure levels in specific Latina/o subgroups, such as Mexican Americans (James, Lovato, & Khoo, 1994). Taken together, these results provide evidence of the harmful impact that discrimination has on the lives of Latinas/os.

Another area of concern concentrates on the predictors of discrimination experienced by Latinas/os. This relatively new line of research suggests that not all Latinas/os have the same experiences with discrimination and addresses the complexity and diversity that exists amongst Latinas/os. For example, the NSL (2002) suggests that Latinas/os differ in their experiences with identity, assimilation, and discrimination. More specifically, the NSL suggests that these differences in experience can be explained by several factors including language fluency, country of origin, physical appearance, and acculturation. A popularly held notion is that skin color is directly related to experiences of discrimination (i.e., darker skin is correlated with an increase in experienced discrimination; Araujo & Borrell, 2006). However, there is evidence to suggest that a darker skin color is not automatically correlated with lower well-being (Lopez, 2008). Instead, it is suggested that ethnic identity may be an indicator of when there is a negative relationship between skin color and well-being, such that Latinas/os higher in ethnic identity have higher levels of self-esteem (Lopez, 2008). This line of research has not only identified potential causes of discrimination for Latinas/os but has also made it clear that substantial variation exists within this group.

It is clear that discrimination is experienced by Latinas/os throughout their lifetime (Hwang & Goto, 2008; Rosenbloom & Way, 2004), negatively affects various aspects of well-being for Latinas/os (James et al., 1994), and can have various predictors based on the inherent diversity of this population (Araujo & Borrell, 2006). However, most studies on prejudice and discrimination against Latinas/os fail to delineate the specific types of discrimination faced by Latinas/os. Instead, it appears that researchers tend to use general conceptualizations of discrimination, often based on Allport's (1954) seminal work on prejudice. Use of these rather loose conceptualizations can possibly explain why the bulk of the research correlating discrimination and well-being focuses on acute discriminatory stressors. These acute stressors are typically intentional in nature, carry major immediate impact, and occur sporadically throughout one's life (Araujo & Borrell, 2006). This somewhat general focus makes it difficult to discern the specific types of discriminatory events experienced by Latinas/os, given the great diversity that exists amongst this group.

Racial Microaggressions and Chronic Stressors

As of recently, the conceptualization of discrimination has widened to include chronic stressors that impact the daily life experience of people of color (Araujo & Borrell, 2006; Harrell, 2000; Sue & Sue, 2008). Chronic discriminatory stressors are typically subtle, unintentional in nature, and occur frequently throughout one's life (Araujo & Borrell, 2006). Although not necessarily a new phenomenon (Pierce, Carew, Pierce-Gonzales, & Willis, 1978), the study of these chronic, race-related stressors and interactions has gained increasing attention by social, educational, and psychological scholars (Dovidio & Gaertner, 2000; Essed, 1991; Solórzano, 1998; Sue, Capodilupo, et al., 2007). Sue and colleagues suggest that these more chronic stressors are more harmful than acute stressors because of their frequent and cumulative nature and refer to them as racial microaggressions. Racial microaggressions are defined as "brief and commonplace daily verbal or behavioral indignities, whether intentional or unintentional, that communicate hostile, derogatory, or negative racial slights and insults that potentially have a harmful or unpleasant psychological impact on the target person or group" (Sue, Capodilupo, et al., 2007, p. 273; see Chapter 1 for a more complete discussion of microaggressions).

Several empirical studies have been conducted that qualitatively investigate the manifestation of microaggressions in the lives of marginalized populations (Capodilupo et al., Chapter 9 in this volume; Keller, Galgay, Robinson, & Moscoso, Chapter 11 in this volume; Nadal, Issa, Griffin, Hamit, & Lyons, Chapter 13 in this volume; Solórzano, 1998; Solórzano, Ceja, &

Yosso, 2000; Sue, Bucceri, Lin, Nadal, & Torino, 2007; Sue et al., 2008). The majority of these studies have classified the types of microaggressions that are experienced by different marginalized populations, such as women, disabled individuals, Asian Americans, and Black Americans. Solórzano (1998) investigated the phenomenon of microaggressions for Latina/o scholars in the context of higher education. Although Solórzano did not classify the various types of microaggressions experienced by Latinas/os, he did show that Latinas/os might experience invisibility, intellectual inferiority, and a sense of not belonging in their role as academic scholars. Additionally, the NSL (2002) suggests that Latinas/os experience subtle forms of discrimination, such as receiving poor service or being treated in a disrespectful manner. Thus far, we have been able to put together from these two studies the types of microaggressions that might be salient in the life experience of Latinas/os. However, no study has qualitatively explored the types of microaggressions experienced by Latinas/os in their daily life.

To date, only two studies have been conducted that classify the various types of racial microaggressions experienced by Asian Americans (Sue, Bucceri, et al., 2007) and Black Americans (Sue et al., 2008). Sue and his colleagues found both differences and similarities in the types of racial microaggressions experienced by these two racial minority groups. Given these findings and the information we currently know about Latinas/os and microaggressions, it is reasonable to expect that Latinas/os, too, will be exposed to microaggressions similar to those of other people of color. Additionally, it is expected that Latinas/os will experience microaggressions that are unique to their experience. Thus, there appears to be a need for further work in describing how microaggressions are experienced in the lives of various marginalized groups, including Latinas/os. In this study, we investigated the phenomenon of racial microaggressions in the lives of Latina/o Americans. It is assumed that Latinas/os do experience microaggressions, based on previous work (NSL, 2002; Solórzano, 1998). Thus, the main goal of this study is to illuminate the type of microaggressions experienced by Latina/o Americans by replicating previous studies on racial microaggressions in the lives of people of color (Sue, Bucceri, et al., 2007; Sue et al., 2008).

METHOD

Qualitative methods are appropriate when researching underinvestigated phenomena (Miles & Huberman, 1994; Morrow & Smith, 2000). To date, qualitative methods have been found to be successful in illuminating the types of microaggressions experienced by people of color (e.g., Solórzano, 2000; Sue et al., 2008; Watkins, LaBarrie, & Appio, Chapter 2 in this volume). Given the exploratory nature of the investigation, a qualitative methodology was used in the current study. Specifically, consensual qualitative research (CQR; Hill, Thompson, & Williams, 1997; Hill et al., 2005) was used because of several unique features of this method. Primarily, CQR requires the use of multiple researchers or judges, an independent auditor to periodically review the work, and the process of consensus to limit the influence of individual bias on the data.

PARTICIPANTS

Participants included 11 individuals from throughout the United States. The sample included 6 women and 5 men, with ages that ranged from 23 to 50. Participants identified racially as White (3), Hispanic (2), Latina (1), Hispanic/Latino (1), Brown (1), Mixed/Indigenous/African/White (1), biracial (1), and not applicable (1). Additionally, participants identified ethnicity as Hispanic (4), Latino (1), Cuban-American (1), Mayan (1), Chicana/White/Native American (1), Puerto Rican (1), Peruvian/Chilean (1), and Mexican-American (1). All participants had earned at minimum a bachelor's degree, and they were employed in various fields, such as higher education, government, and private industry. Additionally, all participants spoke English, and three indicated that Spanish was their first language.

The primary investigator solicited participation through a listserv of Latina/o higher education professionals and a snowball method. Specifically, an e-mail message was sent to the listserv describing the focus and scope of the study and also asking listserv members to forward the message to people who they believed were qualified to participate (i.e., snowballing). The snowball method was used to recruit participants from a variety of work backgrounds. Purposive sampling was used, as it was important to include participants who self-identified as Latina/o or Hispanic and who reported experiencing microaggressions. Participation was voluntary, and no compensation was provided.

RESEARCHERS

The data analysis team was composed of four doctoral students: one Latino American male who served as principal investigator, one Latina American female, and two White American females (one of whom served as the auditor). All team members had prior experience conducting CQR data analysis; thus, minimal training was required. An essential component of CQR is the desire to minimize the subjective influence of the researchers' biases. In an attempt to maintain the integrity of participant voices, CQR researchers begin by clearly stating both their expectations and beliefs before data collection, analysis, and interpretation begin (Hill et al., 1997, 2005). Biases and expectations of the data analysis team included beliefs that Latinas/os microaggressions (1) exist and occur often, (2) may exist "within group" due to power dynamics within the group of Latinas/os, and (3) elicit feelings of anger, powerless, and have a heavy impact on the life of the individual. Furthermore, the researchers hoped that people recognize that Latinas/os microaggressions do exist and Latinas/os are presented with them on a daily basis. Team biases and expectations were revisited at various points throughout the study in an attempt to minimize their impact on the data analysis process.

Measures

Participants were asked to complete a brief demographic questionnaire to gather information regarding their sex, age, race, ethnicity, occupation, highest educational degree obtained, years in the United States, country of origin, residence, and preferred language. A semistructured interview protocol was used to explore participants' experiences of being invalidated and discriminated against because of their race and/or ethnicity (see Appendix A). The protocol was adapted from previous studies investigating the types of microaggressions perceived by people of color (Sue, Bucceri, et al., 2007; Sue et al., 2008).

Procedures

Data was collected through the use of e-mail communication. This method of data collection is gaining popularity in the health field (Hamilton & Bowers, 2006) and has been demonstrated to be appropriate for use with CQR (Kim, Brenner, Liang, & Asay, 2003). Participants engaged in approximately three to five e-mail exchanges with the principal investigator over the course of one week. It was estimated that each participant would spend approximately 15 to 30 minutes on each e-mail communication.

First, participants were e-mailed an informed consent letter explaining the study, their rights of privacy, and a demographic questionnaire. After the primary investigator received consent from the participant, a list of interview questions was sent to the participant. Depending on the need to seek more information and clarification, subsequent e-mail messages were sent and contained follow-up questions to ensure accuracy in the researchers' understanding of the participant responses. Identifying information was removed from the transcripts, and each transcript was assigned a number to sustain confidentiality. Copies of the transcripts were then distributed to each member of the data analysis team. The data was analyzed according to CQR procedures (see the method section in Chapter 2 for a full description of the CQR procedure).

RESULTS

Data analysis revealed eight major domains: (1) ascription of intelligence, (2) second-class citizen, (3) pathologizing communication style/cultural values, (4) characteristics of speech, (5) alien in own land, (6) criminality, (7) invalidation of the Latina/o experience, and (8) other assumed Latina/o attributes. A summary of the domains and categories with corresponding frequencies can be found in Table 3.1. The following frequency labels, as recommended by Hill and colleagues (2005), will be used when describing the domains and categories that emerged from the data: "general," a domain or category endorsed by 10 or 11 participants; "typical," a domain or category endorsed by 6 to 9 participants; "variant," a category endorsed by 2 to 5 participants; and "miscellaneous," a category endorsed by 1 participant.

DOMAIN 1: ASCRIPTION OF INTELLIGENCE

Nine participants described a variety of instances in which their intelligence was questioned or they were assumed to be less qualified. This came in the form of (1) having their accomplishments/qualifications questioned (typical), (2) having their educational success seen as a surprise (variant), (3) being considered an exception to their race/ethnicity when success is achieved (variant), and (4) being talked down to in public (variant).

For instance, a typical response from participants included instances when their *academic qualifications or accomplishments were questioned* or when their academic achievements were attributed solely to affirmative action: "At work superiors have made references to affirmative action suggesting that Latinos and other minorities are not equally qualified." The underlying message here is that Latinas/os are only hired because of their race/ethnicity and are not seen as qualified based on their work experience or accomplishments. Several other participants wrote about receiving messages that Latinas/os were not as qualified for tasks as their White counterparts or were perceived as not being as smart or hardworking: "The most insidious of these came from my high school classmates that told me on a daily basis, 'You can't be Mexican. You're too smart.' Again, the not-so-subtle undertone reads, 'Mexicans are also unintelligent.'" Other school-based examples of Latinas/os having their academic success questioned are exemplified in the following quotes: "In high school, many of my academic accomplishments were questioned because I'm Chicano (e.g., peers telling me, 'You only got into Stanford/the scholarship/etc. because of affirmative action')," and "While I was planning the courses I would take in high school to prepare me for college, my H.S. counselor told me not to apply to Stanford because I 'don't look like the type that spends all her day in

Table 3.1
Summary of Results

Domain	Category	Frequency
Ascription of intelligence	Accomplishments/qualifications questioned	Typical
	Educational success seen as a surprise	Variant
	Exception to race/ethnicity	Variant
	Talked down to in public	Variant
Second-class citizen	Being ignored	Variant
	Being denied goods/receiving differential treatment	Variant
	Excluded	Variant
	Unwelcoming responses	Variant
Pathologizing cultural values/ communication style	Cultural values pathologized	Variant
	Religion	Variant
	Communication style pathologized	Variant
Characteristics of speech	Speaking Spanish	Variant
	Accent	Variant
	Quality of speech	Variant
Alien in own land	U.S. citizenship questioned	Typical
	Latinas/os unwelcomed in United States	Typical
	Negative remarks regarding immigration	Variant
	Assumed undocumented status	Variant
	Language ability questioned	Variant
Criminality	Treated like a criminal	Variant
	Received messages implying illegal activity	Variant
Invalidation of the Latina/o experience	Verbally dismissed	Typical
	Given excuses for negative treatment	Variant
	"You don't look Latina/o"	Miscellaneous
Other assumed Latina/o attributes	Generalizations of Latinas/os	Typical
	Assumed poor	Variant
	Assumed laziness	Variant
	Pathologizing childbearing practices	Variant
	Misidentified ethnicity	Variant
	Drink (alcohol) too much	Miscellaneous

Note: General: 10 to 11 cases; typical: 6 to 9 cases; variant: 2 to 5 cases; miscellaneous: 1 case.

the library.'" The underlying message is that Latinas/os are not intelligent or studious and do not earn admittance to college because of their academic accomplishments.

Three variant categories were also identified. The first of these categories, *educational success seen as a surprise*, was developed from participant statements describing experiences where others were surprised that they went either to college or graduate school, specifically when the institution was a prestigious university. One female participant shared, "I've had people look surprised when they find out I have a master's degree. Also when people find out I was cum laude, they are also surprised." The second category, *exception to race/ethnicity*, was drawn from participants' experience of being told that they were "too smart to be Latina/o" or that it was unusual for a Latina/o to achieve their level of success, sending the message that you cannot be smart *and* Latina/o. And finally, the last category, *being talked down to in public*, describes instances where others "talk down or street" to them, causing some to feel as if lower standards were set for them or that they were treated like they had a mental disability. For example, a male participant shared, "Some people seem to be aggravated by my accent or start talking *very* slowly, as if I had some kind of mental disability."

Domain 2: Second-Class Citizen

Eight participants described experiences where they were treated like second-class citizens, which were described as manifesting in several different ways: (1) being ignored by others, (2) being denied goods or receiving differential treatment, (3) being excluded, and (4) receiving unwelcoming responses from others. These four categories were variant across cases.

The first, *being ignored,* refers to instances where participants were ignored in stores, received less eye contact, or were attended to after White customers. This category is exemplified by the vivid memory a female participant had of shopping with her mom when she was a child: "The customer service rep completely ignored my mom's request for help and bypassed us to attend to a White customer." The message here is that Latinas/os are not seen as deserving of common courtesy or worth being given any type of attention. The second category is related to several participants describing instances about *receiving differential treatment* in stores, which often manifested as being taken less seriously as a consumer in expensive stores, leading to not being treated or given the same amount of attention as White consumers: "Sometimes I notice that employees at government agencies or stores do not treat me as nice as they treat other people who happen to be White." The underlying message is that Latinas/os do not deserve the same type of attention as their White counterparts.

The third category refers to a wide variety of instances where participants described *being excluded* from activities or services. Such instances included being denied opportunities at work, being treated as if they were not a member of the community, and being denied job offers because of their race. And finally, there were several instances when participants *felt unwelcomed by others* because of receiving disdainful looks, hearing derogatory comments, or experiencing indifference from others: "Once we paid, the rep looked at us with disdain, almost as if we weren't allowed to shop there." Such experiences send the message that Latinas/os are not welcome to participate in all spheres of American society.

DOMAIN 3: PATHOLOGIZING CULTURAL VALUES/COMMUNICATION STYLE

Eight participants shared numerous examples of their experiences in which they felt that their culture or values related to their culture were viewed as a deficit. Specifically, values related to religion, communication style, food, dress, and language were identified. The following variant categories emerged from this domain: (1) cultural values pathologized, (2) religion, and (3) communication style pathologized.

Responses indicated several areas of *cultural values that were pathologized*, meaning that the participants received the message that the values of the dominant culture are ideal. Several participants received messages that because the White cultural standards are viewed as the norm, anything that is viewed as non-White is seen as negative, deviant, or not normal. For example, a female participant shared:

> *In my experience, in White families there is a stigma about grown children living with their families. There is a belief that if you live at home it is because you cannot afford any better, or you are mooching off your parents. So, I often find myself having to explain my living situation.*

Another variant category included participants' experience with others making jokes based on *religion* or with being "made fun of for strong belief in religion," sending the message that it is not normal or ideal to have strong religious beliefs. And finally, *communication style pathologized* refers to participants who cited a variety of different instances when they felt that their way of speaking was pathologized. This included instances where they were mocked for using hand gestures while speaking: "White people will sometimes try to mimic very stereotypical hand or body gestures which they attribute to Latinos while talking to me." Additionally, several participants noted individuals commenting on their "Latin temper." One male participant reported:

I am a verbally combative person (a trait I am working on). Now, that means I am constantly getting into debates and heated exchanges with primarily White people....There are a number of people who are allegedly on my side who will tell me that I need to tone it down because I'm just feeding into the stereotype of the "angry Chicano." From my perspective, this is racist in and of itself because the White people I engage with do not have to censor themselves in the same way. That is, if a White man says the exact same words as I do with the exact same tone, he will not be fulfilling a stereotype because he is judged as an individual.

DOMAIN 4: CHARACTERISTICS OF SPEECH

Seven participants provided a depth of negative experiences related to issues of speech and language. The categories represented in this domain include (1) accent, (2) speaking Spanish, and (3) quality of speech. These three categories were variant across cases.

The first category addresses perceptions about *accents*, which refers to instances when participants were accused of having an accent or felt criticized when they were told that they had an accent, receiving the message that having an accent is a deficit. One female participant shared a common experience she has: "Every time a White person states that I have an accent, this implies to me that *only* the 'White way' of speaking is the right way." A second category refers to various issues that were brought up related specifically to *speaking Spanish*. One participant stated that he was teased for speaking Spanish in school, while another felt put down because of language differences, stating, "I remember going down to the subway with my father and having a conversation with him in Spanish. An older woman who was exiting the station yelled out, "You're in America, speak English!" sending the message that it is un-American to speak Spanish.

The final category, *quality of speech*, refers to experiences of receiving negative feedback about various aspects of one's speech, such as being asked to slow their speech or being told that they speak too fast because of their ethnicity. One participant described being made fun of for his speech and has encountered people looking at him strangely and correcting his English pronunciation of certain words: "Many folks say that I speak too fast and it's because of my Cuban nationality." Again, these messages imply that Latinas/os need to adjust the way they speak English in order to be a part of American society.

DOMAIN 5: ALIEN IN OWN LAND

Participants described instances when Latinas/os were made to feel like a "perpetual foreigner" in their own country. The following categories illuminated these experiences: (1) their U.S. citizenship was questioned (typical), (2) they felt Latinas/os were unwelcomed in United States (typical), (3) they experienced negative remarks regarding immigration (variant), (4) they were assumed to have an undocumented status (variant), and (5) their language ability was questioned (variant). All cases were represented in this domain.

In the first typical category, *U.S. citizenship questioned*, many participants shared their experiences of when their citizenship had been questioned. Several participants spoke about being asked how long they have lived in the United States or where they were born. For example, a female shared an example of someone assuming she was from a different country: "Many times when I meet someone they ask me where I am from, so I say Chicago, then they say, 'No, where are you really from?' This happens all the time." Another participant was assumed not to be an American citizen: "Some people ask me if I have a green card even though I'm Puerto Rican." The underlying message here is that Latinas/os must have been born in another country and thus are *less* American.

Latinas/os feeling *unwelcomed in the United States* was the second typical response shared by many participants. Participants discussed messages that they received, ranging from being explicitly told to leave the United States to more subtle messages implying that Latina/o immigrants and their children have no right to be in the United States. The following male participant was told to leave the country because he supported immigrant rights:

> *I am a vocal and active participant in activism supporting immigrant rights. Despite being born in the country, having a father and a grandfather born in the country, I am consistently told when these issues come up, "America—love it or leave it," or "If you hate America so much why don't you just get the fuck out?" (told to me within the last month). The overtones of these comments are that freedom of speech only applies to that speech which makes bigoted people feel comfortable.*

The first variant response refers to instances of hearing *negative remarks regarding immigration,* and in some cases, participants were directly insulted. One participant and his friends were referred to by a derogatory term primarily used against Mexican immigrants who cross the Rio Grande River. He stated, "Once, as I got on the D.C. subway with some Hispanic friends, I overheard a man saying: 'Ah, here come the wetbacks.'" This quote seems to underscore how negatively immigrants are thought of and treated by some individuals. A second variant response, a*ssumed undocumented status,* emerged from a few participants reporting that they had received comments that all Latina/o immigrants are illegal. For example, one participant remarked, "When she said what she did, it felt like an attack on Latinos with an assumption that we are all immigrants but also that all Latino immigrants are illegal and that status of 'illegal' makes someone less than." This quote captures the assumption that all Latinas/os are immigrants and that all Latina/o immigrants are *illegal*, which clearly invalidates the experiences of Latinas/os in the United States.

The third variant response, *language ability questioned*, dealt with others assuming that participants either did not speak English, only spoke Spanish, or were bilingual. The following quote demonstrates the underlying belief held by many Americans that all Latinas/os speak Spanish: "I have had experiences in which people assumed I didn't speak English because I was Latina and therefore preceded to speak to me in a loud voice or use body language when they communicated." The experience of frequently having their language questioned further relegates Latinas/os into the status of *perpetual foreigner* or as people who are not truly American.

Domain 6: Criminality/Assumption of Criminal Status

Six participants described instances in which Latinas/os were assumed to be criminals either because they (1) were treated like a criminal or (2) received messages implying illegal activity. Both these categories were classified as variant responses.

Some participants recalled being accused of shoplifting: "I get differential treatment at stores. Have been followed 2 times to my car by security and asked to show proof of purchase." This quote provides a clear example of how Latinas/os are *assumed to be criminals* and should be closely monitored to make sure they do not steal anything. The following quote again demonstrates how one male participant was treated like a criminal when he congregated with other Latinas/os. Again, the underlying message is that Latinas/os are criminals and should be treated as such:

> When we congregated in mass, we were the subject of increased scrutiny...campus police followed us...and finally had us kneel in the pea gravel with our fingers laced behind our heads until they saw our IDs and determined we were, in fact, students. Their reason for threatening arrest? We were "acting suspiciously."

The second category identified was *receiving messages implying illegal activity*. For example, some participants have been told that Latinas/os smoke marijuana, are violent, urinate in public, are corrupt, and/or are involved in gangs. One participant described her experience of receiving messages that Latino communities are not safe to live in and are assumed to be areas of criminal activity: "I know many folks who have said that they wouldn't live in such and such Latino neighborhood because it is dangerous." Participants also noted their experience of having the way they look or dress correlated with being a gangster, again implying that Latinas/os are associated with criminal activity.

DOMAIN 7: INVALIDATION OF THE LATINA/O EXPERIENCE

Eight participants spoke about feeling invalidated by others through the following forms of communication: (1) having their experience verbally dismissed (typical), (2) being given excuses for negative treatment (variant), and (3) being told they do not look Latina/o (miscellaneous). When asked, participants shared their thoughts and feelings regarding situations in which others invalidated them either through verbal or nonverbal communication.

One typical response was identified as being *verbally dismissed*. Many participants described situations in which they were verbally dismissed by being told that other groups have it worse, they were being "too sensitive," or "that is just life." A female participant was told she was making a big deal out of nothing when she received a racially offensive remark:

> I had a conversation with a male, White co-worker of mine. I had told him about an experience I had had with my Filipino mother-in-law. My mother-in-law saw my legs... and commented that I had "nice Mexican legs." I told my co-worker I was a little insulted by her comment. Why couldn't she have just said that I had nice legs? My co-worker said he hated it when people brought up race/ethnicity into the picture and told me that my mother-in-law just didn't know any better and that I needed to drop it. He suggested that it was me who was making a big deal out of nothing.

The message is that her experience as a Latina is insignificant. Furthermore, the aggressor implies that it is her fault for making a big deal out of this invalidating experience.

One variant response refers to what a few participants described as situations in which people *gave them excuses* for why people treat them negatively. For example, one participant stated: "Sometimes others will say things like 'He didn't really mean what he said,' or 'They didn't know that you were Hispanic,' so I've come to the conclusion that some people are ignorant or just don't know." This quote further demonstrates the invalidating experiences Latinas/os have when individuals minimize the microaggressive incident by giving alternative nonracial or nonethnic reasons for the incident. Additionally, in a miscellaneous response, a male participant felt invalidated because he was told he did not *look* Latina/o or Hispanic. The assumption that Latinas/os cannot have diversity in their physical appearance takes away from the personal experience of being Latina/o. Although this category was underdeveloped, it illustrates the physical diversity inherent in the Latino community and reveals the numerous ways that Latinas/os are invalidated.

DOMAIN 8: OTHER ASSUMED LATINA/O ATTRIBUTES

Finally, every participant shared stereotypes that they believed are generally attributed to Latinas/os. Being assumed poor and lazy, drinking too much, negative assumptions of childbearing practices, and misinterpreted ethnicity were a few of the stereotypes identified by participants. Although we believe that most microaggressions are the manifestation of stereotypes held by the aggressor, the following assumed common Latina/o attributes did not fit into any of the previous domains or categories. Thus, this domain is not a specific type of microaggression experienced by Latinas/os but rather a domain that captures a wide array of microaggressive experiences.

Within this domain, there was one typical response, *generalizations of Latinas/os*, which refers to what many participants described as general stereotypes attributed to Latinas/os such as assuming participants like spicy foods, know how to dance, are hard workers, all look the same, and are made to be a representative of their people. For example, one participant stated, "I have heard so many times 'You all look alike,' or 'Don't your people all do X or Y?' Or something to the effect of 'Isn't that part of your culture?'" Another participant was asked if he came to the United States in a boat because he is Cuban:

> My family is Cuban and although not so much a stereotype, I am usually asked if my family arrived in the United States via boat. Although my family did not arrive via boat (they came by plane in the mid-60s), it is an assumption that is asked of me.

The nuances of the different ways Latinas/os have arrived and settled into the United States are ignored, and generalizations are made that are invalidating to the Latinas/os who experience them. Lastly, a male participant shared an experience in which he was told that all Latinas/os look the same:

> Recently at a meal with several friends, two of five others which were Latino, when the server brought out our food, she gave me and another person the wrong meals. When she switched plates, she remark[ed], "Oh, I am sorry, you all look alike."

The underlying message here is that Latinas/os are not important enough to be seen as individuals.

Four variant responses were identified in this domain. The first, *assumed poor*, refers to instances in which participants had been assumed to be poor or heard general remarks of Latinas/os being poor. A second variant response, *assumed laziness*, corresponds to being told that Latinas/os were lazy and "want things without earning them." The third variant response refers to when people pathologize Latinas/os' *childbearing practices*, assuming that the participants were illegitimate children or children of a teenage mother and believing that Latinas/os have too many children. One female participant shared, "I have also been asked if my parents are married or were they ever married in an effort to find out if I am an illegitimate child." The message here is that Latinas/os are expected to have children out of wedlock, which is considered negative.

The fourth and last variant response, *misidentified ethnicity*, emerged from several participants' experiences of how their ethnicity had been mistaken for another ethnicity. For example, one participant described how she was assumed to be Mexican because she is from Texas:

> *In a town (D.C.) where no one is a true Washingtonian, when people ask me where I am from...and when I tell them Texas, the statement that usually follows is "Oh, so you're Mexican then?" Everyone seems to think that if you're brown and from Texas, you're automatically Mexican.*

This type of experience further invalidates the unique personal experience of being Latina/o.

DISCUSSION AND IMPLICATIONS

The purpose of this investigation was to qualitatively explore experiences of microaggressions in the life experience of Latina/o Americans in order to learn more about the various types of microaggressions perceived by this population. Eight distinct thematic areas were identified from our participants' responses. The content of the responses not only suggests a classification system for illustrating the various types of microaggressions experienced by Latinas/os but also provides evidence for the differences and similarities in the types of microaggressions experienced by the various racial and ethnic minority groups. Additionally, participants often contextualized their experiences with microaggressions, suggesting that various contexts might set the stage for specific types of microaggressions to occur. Thus, there are several implications that can be gleaned from our investigation.

In comparing the types of microaggressions experienced by Latinas/os to those experienced by Asian (Sue, Bucceri, et al., 2007) and Black Americans (Sue et al., 2008), there appear to be similarities and differences in the types of microaggressions experienced by Latinas/os and other racial groups. As is consistent with the similarities in microaggression types that exist between Asian and Black Americans, Latinas/os were found to have experiences in which their intellect was stereotyped, they were treated like second-class citizens, they were assumed to share a common Latina/o experience, and their cultural and communication styles were pathologized. These thematic areas represent stereotypes and assumptions that appear to be common in the life experience of people of color. We suspect that these commonalities are a reflection of the worldview held by the racial majority in which the "different" are relegated to the inferior status, while the majority remain in the superior status.

As was expected, Latinas/os experienced microaggressions that were similar to those experienced by Black Americans and also to those experienced by Asian Americans. Comparable to the experience of Black Americans, Latinas/os also have experiences of being treated like a suspected or outright criminal. Furthermore, Latinas/os also appear to share with Black Americans the experience of being assumed to be inferior to the aggressor. In reference to microaggressive experiences shared with Asian Americans, Latinas/os are also viewed as an alien in their own land and appear to receive messages invalidating their racial experiences.

A major thematic area that appears to be an experience common to Latinas/os as a type of microaggression is being attacked because of speech characteristics. Unlike most other marginalized groups, Latinas/os are most likely to be connected by a single common language, which is Spanish. We suspect that Latinas/os are in part the targets of microaggressions that directly assail their speech because of "English only" initiatives, such as California's Proposition 227, which sought to enforce teaching primarily in English by imposing strict guidelines for the use of bilingual educational programs. Legal scholars suggest that "by attacking non-English speakers, Proposition 227, in light of the historical context and modern circumstances, discriminates on the basis of race by focusing on an element central to the identity of many Latinas/os" (Johnson & Martinez, 2000, p. 1228). The possibility of recognizing a language other than English as a commonly used language in the United States appears to cause apprehension for those who have become accustomed to rely solely on English. These types of wide-reaching political media campaigns make all Latinas/os, as suggested from our results, potential targets of attacks on their speech, regardless of their ability to speak Spanish.

Thus far in the racial microaggression empirical research base (e.g., Sue, Bucceri, et al., 2007; Sue et al., 2008), *microinsults* and *microinvalidations* have been identified as the types of microaggressions commonly experienced by people of color. However, Latinas/os also report being the targets of the third form, known as *microassaults*, as well. A microassault is defined as "an explicit racial derogation characterized primarily by a verbal or nonverbal attack meant to hurt the intended victim through name-calling, avoidant behavior, or purposeful discriminatory action" (Sue, Capodilupo, et al., 2007, p. 274). We do not mean to imply that African Americans and Asian Americans do not experience microassaults but rather that the current context of "the immigration problem" may make it more acceptable for Whites to express their overt biases against Latinas/os. Several examples of microassaults were identified in the data, such as participants who were called or overheard others using derogatory terms, such as *wetback* or *beaner*. Additionally, there were accounts of Latinas/os being forcefully told to leave the country, presumably because of their assumed "illegal alien" status, through statements such as, "Why don't you just get the fuck out?" or through threats to their physical well-being. Other examples of microassaults were present in the form of outright or suspected employment discrimination and negative treatment by law enforcement. This is a noteworthy finding, because the assaultive nature of these interactions not only brings potential for psychological harm and barriers to optimal functioning but also the possibility for physical harm.

Potential implications on the well-being of Latinas/os can be extrapolated by examining the various contexts in which participants reported having shared experiences with microaggressions. As indicated by previous research (Green et al., 2006), Latinas/os experience differential treatment that they attribute to their race or ethnicity throughout their lifetime. Given that the participants were highly educated, all having attained at least a bachelor's degree, it is not surprising that many of their experiences with microaggressions were contextualized in educational settings. The results of our study suggest that experiences with microaggressions during primary and secondary education have both immediate and long-lasting negative effects. For example, some of our participants attributed academic difficulties in college to the lower expectations that were set for them in their early educational experiences. This suggests that the phenomenon of stereotype threat may be operating for Latinas/os who perceive microaggressions assailing their intellect and academic potential (Solórzano, Viallalpando, & Osequera, 2005; Steele, 1997). It is also important to point out that microaggressions committed between teacher and student can heighten the intensity of the impact. This can be attributed to the difference in perceived status between the teacher and student, as Latina/o children might place more weight on what they experience with their teacher as opposed to what they experience with a peer. Latinas/os who are the targets of these types of microaggressions can be set back in their educational and career development due to the internalization of these negative messages.

In addition to experiencing microaggressions in educational settings, our participants also reported experiencing microaggressions in the workplace. These accounts support and are validated by several conceptual and empirical works suggesting that microaggressions and subtle forms of racial discrimination are found in the workplace (Rowe, 1990; Stallworth, McPherson, & Rute, 2001; Sue, Lin, & Rivera, 2009). The microaggressions experienced by Latinas/os in the workplace can manifest in the form of experiencing perceived lower expectations and lack of support from management, being ignored during meetings, and having their cultural practices invalidated. These types of microaggressions can form barriers for Latinas/os in the workplace that lend a hand in creating the racial and ethnic disparities in employment. For example, Latinas/os are well represented in the service industry; however, Latinas/os are vastly underrepresented at the executive and managerial levels of employment (U.S. Department of Labor, 2008). This is a matter of some concern, given the current and projected growth of the Latino community in the United States. Beyond the specific interpersonal types of microaggressions that exist in the workplace, the invisibility of Latinas/os in various professional roles is in and of itself a major environmental microaggression. This sends the message that Latinas/os are not intelligent enough to attain higher status positions and that Latinas/os are only suited for service positions or other undesirable jobs.

The microaggressions Latinas/os perceive in public spaces, such as on the street and in stores or other service industry venues, have the potential for various threats to their well-being. These public forms of microaggressions are perceived in a multitude of ways, such as being the target of racial or ethnic epithets, being followed in a store, or being told not to speak Spanish in public. These microaggressions are often committed in front of other people, which can lead the victim to feel a higher degree of shame. Furthermore, these microaggressions are most likely to occur between individuals who are strangers. Therefore, individuals have to consider the catch-22 effect of responding to microaggressions, which is described as the victim questioning what has just happened to them and weighing the psychosocial costs of responding (Sue, Capodilupo, et al., 2007). Given that some microaggressions committed against Latinas/os are overtly hostile in nature, Latinas/os risk even more potential harm to themselves if they choose to respond. However, if Latinas/os choose not to respond to the aggressor, they lose the opportunity to vent their anger and the opportunity to express the harm of the microaggression to the aggressor. As a result, the cycle of oppression is strengthened and continues to operate when microaggressions go unaddressed. This is especially salient for microaggressions committed in public settings, as there is the potential for a larger audience to be influenced and negatively affected.

It is important that we address some of the limitations inherent in our study. First, due to the nature of qualitative research, we cannot fully generalize the results of our study to fit the experience of the entire Latino community. Given the range of diversity that exists in the Latino community, it is necessary to investigate the experience of microaggressions with other samples of Latinas/os. The results indicate that language and immigration issues play a large role in the types of microaggressions that Latinas/os experience. This being the case, it might be beneficial to investigate the manifestation of microaggressions with individuals who primarily speak Spanish, have an identifiable accent, or are first generation in the United States. Second, our participants represented several geographic areas of the United States; however, there might be differences in the types of microaggressions experienced by Latinas/os based on geographical location. Future research should investigate more closely these potential differences. Third, we did not identify or measure visible racial characteristics of our participants. Other research has indicated that Latinas/os might experience discrimination due to phenotype characteristics (Araujo & Borrell, 2006). Future studies involving Latina/o participants should include measures of skin color and other phenotype characteristics, such as by using self-report, researcher observation, or more scientifically objective measures, such as through the use of a spectrophotometer for skin color assessment (Lopez, 2008).

The results of this study add to the current empirical body of literature that describes the types of microaggressions experienced by marginalized populations. It is quite apparent that microaggressions are present in the social fabric of the United States. However, the specific ramifications of microaggressions in the lives of marginalized people, such as Latinas/os, remain unclear. In order for Latinas/os to be full participants in American society, it is necessary to identify and remove the barriers that are currently preventing Latinas/os from full inclusion. We suggest utilizing qualitative and quantitative research to identify these barriers that serve to maintain sociocultural disparities for Latinas/os. Qualitative research can be used to further build upon the results presented in this chapter, whereas quantitative research is necessary in order to better understand the psychosocial correlates of microaggressions. The ultimate goal for investigating the experience of microaggressions in the lives of Latinas/os is to reduce their harmful effects by increasing overall awareness and decreasing the occurrence of these insidious interactions.

REFERENCES

Allport, G. (1954). *The nature of prejudice*. New York: Doubleday.

Araujo, B. Y., & Borrell, L. N. (2006). Understanding the link between discrimination, mental health outcomes, and life chances among Latinos. *Hispanic Journal of Behavioral Sciences, 28*, 245–266.

Dovidio, J. F., & Gaertner, S. L. (2000). Aversive racism and selective decisions: 1989–1999. *Psychological Science, 11*, 315–319.

Essed, P. (1991). *Understanding everyday racism*. Newbury Park, CA: Sage.

Gallup Poll (2008). *Immigration*. Retrieved May 1, 2009, from http://www.gallup.com/poll/1660/Immigration.aspx.

Garcia, R. J. (1995). Critical race theory and Proposition 187: The racial politics of immigration law. *Chicana/o-Latina/o Law Review, 17*, 118–154.

Green, M. L., Way, N., & Pahl, K. (2006). Trajectories of perceived adult and peer discrimination among Black, Latino, and Asian American adolescents: Patterns and psychological correlates. *Developmental Psychology, 42*, 218–238.

Harrell, S. P. (2000). A multidisciplinary conceptualization of racism-related stress: Implications for the well-being of people of color. *American Journal of Orthopsychiatry, 70*, 42–57.

Hamilton, R. J., & Bowers, B. J. (2006). Internet recruitment and e-mail interviews in qualitative studies. *Qualitative Health Research, 16*, 821–835.

Hill, C. E., Thompson, B. J., & Williams, E. N. (1997). A guide to conducting consensual qualitative research. *Counseling Psychologist, 25*, 517–572.

Hill, C. E., Thompson, B. J., Hess, S. A., Knox, S., Williams, E. N., & Ladany, N. (2005). Consensual qualitative research: An update. *Journal of Counseling Psychology, 52*, 196–205.

Hwang, W., & Goto, S. (2008). The impact of perceived racial discrimination on the mental health of Asian American and Latino college students. *Cultural Diversity & Ethnic Minority Psychology, 14*, 326–335.

James, K., Lovato, C., & Khoo, G. (1994). Social identity correlates of minority workers' health. *Academy of Management Journal, 37*, 383–396.

Johnson, K. R., & Martinez, G. A. (2000). Discrimination by proxy: The case of Proposition 227 and the ban on bilingual education. *U.C. Davis Law Review, 33*, 1227–1276.

Kim, B. S. K., Brenner, B. R., Liang, C. T. H., & Asay, P. A. (2003). A qualitative study of adaptation experiences of 1.5-generation Asian Americans. *Cultural Diversity & Ethnic Minority Psychology, 9*, 156–170.

Lopez, I. (2008). "But you don't look Puerto Rican": The moderating effect of ethnic identity on the relation between skin color and self-esteem among Puerto Rican women. *Cultural Diversity & Ethnic Minority Psychology, 14*, 102–108.

Miles, M. B., & Huberman, A. M. (1994). *Qualitative data analysis* (2nd ed.). Thousand Oaks, CA: Sage.

Moradi, B., & Risco, C. (2006). Perceiving discrimination experiences and mental health of Latina/o American persons. *Journal of Counseling Psychology, 53*, 411–421.

Morrow, S. L., & Smith, M. L. (2000). Qualitative research for counseling psychology. In S. D. Brown & R. W. Lent (Eds.), *Handbook of counseling psychology* (3rd ed., pp. 199–230). New York: John Wiley & Sons.

National Survey of Latinos (2002). *National Survey of Latinos: Summary of findings*. Washington, DC: Pew Hispanic Center; Menlo Park, CA: Henry J. Kaiser Family Foundation. Retrieved March 2, 2009, from http://www.kff.org/kaiserpolls/upload/2002-National-Survey-of-Latinos-Summary-of-Findings.pdf.

Pierce, C., Carew, J., Pierce-Gonzalez, D., & Willis, D. (1978). An experiment in racism: TV commercials. In C. Pierce (Ed.), *Television and education* (pp. 62–88). Beverly Hills, CA: Sage.

Rosenbloom, S. R., & Way, N. (2004). Experiences of discrimination among African American, Asian American, and Latino adolescents in an urban high school. *Youth & Society*, *35*, 420–451.

Rowe, M. P. (1990). Barriers to equality: The power of subtle discrimination to maintain unequal opportunity. *Employee Responsibilities and Rights Journal*, *3*, 153–163.

Schnieder, K. T., Hitlan, R. T., & Radhakrishnan, P. (2000). An examination of the nature and correlates of ethnic harassment experiences in multiple contexts. *Journal of Applied Psychology*, *85*, 3–12.

Shorey, H. S., Cowan, G., & Sullivan, M. P. (2002). Predicting perceptions of discrimination among Hispanics and Anglos. *Hispanic Journal of Behavioral Sciences*, *24*, 3–22.

Solórzano, D. (1998). Critical race theory, race and gender microaggressions, and the experience of Chicana and Chicano scholars. *Qualitative Studies in Education*, *11*, 121–136.

Solórzano, D., Ceja, M., & Yosso, T. (2000). Critical race theory, racial microaggressions, and campus racial climate: The experiences of African American college students. *Journal of Negro Education*, *69*, 60–73.

Solórzano, D. G., Viallalpando, O., & Osequera, L. (2005). Educational inequities and Latina/o undergraduate students in the United States: A critical race analysis of their educational progress. *Journal of Hispanic Higher Education*, *4*, 272–294.

Stallworth, L. E., McPherson, T., & Rute, L., (2001). Discrimination in the workplace: How mediation can help. *Dispute Resolution Journal*, *56*, 35–44, 83–87.

Steele, C. (1997). A threat in the air: How stereotypes shape intellectual identity and performance. *American Psychologist*, *52*, 613–629.

Sue, D. W., Bucceri, J. M., Lin, A. I., Nadal, K. L., & Torino, G. C. (2007). Racial microaggressions and the Asian American experience. *Cultural Diversity and Ethnic Minority Psychology*, *13*, 72–81.

Sue, D. W., Capodilupo, C. M., Torino, G. C., Bucceri, J. M., Holder, A. M. B., Nadal, K. L., & Esquilin, M. (2007). Racial microaggressions in everyday life: Implications for clinical practice. *American Psychologist*, *62*, 271–286.

Sue, D. W., Lin, A. I., & Rivera, D. P. (2009). Racial microaggressions in the workplace: Manifestation and impact. In J. L. Chin (Ed.), *Diversity in mind and in action, Vol. 2: Health, education, and employment contexts* (pp. 157–172). Westport, CT: Greenwood.

Sue, D. W., Nadal, K. L., Capodilupo, C. M., Lin, A. I., Torino, G. C., & Rivera, D. P. (2008). Racial microaggressions against Black Americans: Implications for counseling. *Journal of Counseling and Development*, *86*, 330–338.

Sue, D. W., & Sue, D. (2008). *Counseling the culturally diverse: Theory and practice* (5th ed.). Hoboken, NJ: John Wiley & Sons.

U.S. Census Bureau (2007). *American community survey demographic and housing estimates: 2005–2007.* Retrieved April 17, 2009, from http://factfinder.census.gov/servlet/ADPTable?_bm=y&-geo_id=01000US&-qr_name=ACS_2007_3YR_G00_DP3YR5&-ds_name=&-_lang=en&-redoLog=false&-format=.

U.S. Census Bureau (2008). *Educational attainment in the United States: 2008*. Retrieved April 30, 2009, from http://www.census.gov/population/www/socdemo/education/cps2008.html.

U.S. Department of Labor, Bureau of Labor Statistics (2008). *Household data: Annual averages*. Retrieved April 16, 2009, from ftp://ftp.bls.gov/pub/special.requests/lf/aat11.txt.

APPENDIX A

1. Latinas/os or Hispanics often have experiences in which they are subtly invalidated, discriminated against, and made to feel uncomfortable because of their race and/or ethnicity. In thinking about your daily experiences, could you describe a situation in which you witnessed or were personally subtly discriminated against because of your race and/or ethnicity?
2. What are some subtle ways that people treat you differently because of your race and/or ethnicity?
3. Describe a situation in which you felt uncomfortable, insulted, or disrespected by a comment that had racial or ethnic overtones.
4. Think of some of the stereotypes that exist about your racial and/or ethnic group. How have others subtly expressed their stereotypical beliefs about you?
5. In what ways have others made you feel "put down" because of your cultural values or communication style?
6. In what ways have people subtly expressed that "the White way is the right way"?
7. In what subtle ways have others expressed that they think you're a second-class citizen or inferior to them?
8. How have people suggested that you do not belong here because of your race and/or ethnicity?
9. What have people done or said to invalidate your experiences of being discriminated against?
10. What are some of the ways that you dealt with these experiences?
11. What do you think the overall impact of your experiences has been on your life?

CHAPTER 4

Racial Microaggressions Directed at Asian Americans

Modern Forms of Prejudice and Discrimination

ANNIE I. LIN

RESEARCHERS HAVE DOCUMENTED the transformation of overt racism into more covert forms, making modern manifestations more subtle and difficult to detect (Dovidio & Gaertner, 2000; McConahay, 1986; Sue, 2003). Despite the prolific scholarship and research on racism, racial issues are still perceived in Black and White terms (Young & Takeuchi, 1998). Asian Americans have been largely ignored in discussions of race and racism, despite having experienced a long history of oppression in the United States (David & Lin, 1997). Some speculate that the model minority myth (a belief that Asian Americans are a successful minority group) is partially responsible for excluding Asian Americans from public discourse on race and racism (Delucchi & Do, 1996; Young & Takeuchi, 1998). The purpose of this chapter is to (1) examine reasons for the omission of Asian American perspectives in discussions of racism, (2) discuss contemporary concepts of racial discrimination (one of which is racial microaggressions) and common stereotypes of Asian Americans, (3) describe how racial stereotypes are manifested in racial microaggressions against Asian Americans, and (4) explore the impact racial microaggressions have on Asian American experiences of prejudice and discrimination.

THE MODEL MINORITY MYTH

There is a prevalent belief that Asian Americans are somehow immune to racism and/or have "overcome" their minority status and excel in American society (Kawai, 2005; Min, 1995; Tuan, 1998). As a result, Asian Americans are pervasively viewed as model minorities who have attained the

American dream and thus must experience little to no discrimination (Bell, 1985; Delucchi & Do, 1996; Young & Takeuchi, 1998). Being pitted against the racial plight of other racial minority groups (Hurh & Kim, 1989; Min, 1995; U.S. Commission on Civil Rights, 1986), non-Asian Americans are often skeptical that racism is a part of the Asian American experience (Asamen & Berry, 1987). Those who claim that Asian Americans are successful in attaining the American dream often point to how median family income and employment rates of Asian Americans seem to exceed those found among their White counterparts (Kawai, 2005; Min, 1995; Tuan, 1998).

These income and employment comparisons fail to take into account that Asian Americans tend to have larger numbers of working household members. Further, they are highly concentrated in metropolitan cities, where living standards are higher than the average (Min, 1995). A closer examination shows that individual incomes of Asian Americans remain lower than their White colleagues of comparable education (Min, 1995), and their employment tends to be clustered in low-wage jobs or in lower tiers of white-collar jobs with few promotional opportunities into the management and executive levels of corporations (Cabezas & Kawaguchi, 1988). On the whole, Asian Americans do not possess higher salaries or hold higher positions within a sector, as the model minority myth might imply.

Contrary to popular belief that Asian Americans are immune to discrimination, the history of Asians in America has been fraught with racism and oppression since the fifteenth century (Sue, 1999; Young & Takeuchi, 1998). Having long been the target of racist societal and legislative actions (Sandhu, 1997; Sue & Sue, 2008; Young & Takeuchi, 1998), Asian Americans have been forbidden to relocate, prohibited to own or lease land, and barred from various legal and marriage rights (Sandhu, 1997). Racism was pervasive for early Asian immigrants in every aspect of life: substandard working conditions, lower salary scales, societal stigmatization, anti-Asian harassment, lynching, robberies, and even mass murders (Min, 1995; Sandhu, 1997; Takaki, 1989). Though the Asian American experience with racism is widely documented, many Americans persist in claiming ignorance of these facts or in flatly denying the validity of its existence (Bell, 1985; Delucchi & Do, 1996; Young & Takeuchi, 1998).

It is well documented that overt prejudice and discrimination against Asian Americans continues today (National Asian Pacific American Legal Consortium [NAPALC], 2002; U.S. Commission on Civil Rights, 1986, 1992). The NAPALC (2002) reported that roughly 250 intimidation and threats were targeted against Asian Americans following the September 11 terrorist attacks and that anti-Asian incidents involving assault and threats or intimidation have increased in recent years. Ironically, the model minority myth has brought greater prejudice and discrimination into the Asian American community, invoking dire consequences in its tracks.

Asian ethnic groups that do not conform to the model minority character-istics are often overlooked, rendering the needs of these groups invisible and barring them from funding or governmental compensatory actions for which they would have otherwise qualified. Regardless of their circum-stances, certain Asian groups have been consistently denied funding for social service programs in immigration adjustment, racism-related efforts, affirmative action, and education subsidies of students from low-income families (Hurh & Kim, 1989; Takaki, 1989). Perceiving Asian Americans as excelling in American society may be simultaneously blocking them from receiving the benefits they rightfully deserve. Furthermore, the model minority myth has led to discriminatory admissions quotas and supplemen-tal criteria in limiting the number of Asian American students in elite universities and particular fields (Cabezas & Kawaguchi, 1988; Takagi, 1990). The "overrepresentation" of Asian Americans in school enrollment was considered a "problem" to be resolved through means intended to further disadvantage Asian Americans (Takagi, 1990). Despite its seemingly positive cloak, endorsing the model minority myth fosters overt discrimina-tion against Asian Americans.

SHIFT FROM OVERT TO COVERT FORMS OF RACISM

Aside from overt anti-Asian hate crimes and exclusion from certain minority benefits, Asian Americans also report experiencing subtle forms of discrimi-nation. Literature suggests that contemporary prejudice against Asians is highly covert in nature (Asamen & Berry, 1987; Liang, Li, & Kim, 2004; Sue, Bucceri, Lin, Nadal, & Torino, 2007) and that blatant forms of racism have gradually become more subtle and unconscious in nature (Dovidio & Gaert-ner, 2000; Steele, 1997). Essed (1991) examined these subtle, recurrent forms of discrimination in the everyday lives of racial minorities, emphasizing the experience of being treated with less courtesy and respect and receiving less quality service in public places.

Contemporary forms of racism are considered to be more harmful than blatant old-fashioned racism (Sue, 2003), since people of color report find-ing subtle racism much harder to deal with than traditional overt racism (Dovidio & Gaertner, 1998; Salvatore & Shelton, 2007). Asian Americans may be even more affected and harmed by this new form of discrimination, because they have been culturally conditioned to be sensitive to their social and communication contexts (Leets, 2003). Terms such as "modern racism" (McConahay, 1986), "aversive racism" (Dovidio & Gaertner, 2000), and "racial microaggressions" (Pierce, Carew, Pierce-Gonzalez, & Willis, 1978; Solórzano, Ceja, & Yosso, 2000; Sue, 2003) have been used to describe these subtler forms of racism.

The concept of modern racism was first proposed by McConahay (1986) and asserts that politically conservative Whites can hold egalitarian beliefs and nonracist self-views while preserving negative feelings (hostility, hate) toward Blacks or racial equality in general. Because of society's greater condemnation of racism, however, White Americans are discouraged from blatantly expressing their negative racial sentiments; they will only exhibit racially motivated behaviors under ambiguous situations, where the behavioral or attitudinal norms are unclear. The modern racist, according to McConahay (1986), may believe on a conscious level that they are nonracist and are very sensitive to attributions of prejudice from others. Though they may have a nonracist self-view, their attitudes and beliefs are still very racist in nature. In most cases, modern racists believe (1) discrimination against Blacks no longer exists, (2) Blacks have become too demanding, and (3) their gains are undeserved (McConahay, 1986).

While the concept of modern racism was originally formulated to explain the behavior of conservative Whites, the concept of aversive racism has been used to explain the ambivalent and inconsistent ways in which educated, politically liberal Whites act in situations involving race (Dovidio & Gaertner, 2000). For the aversive racist, if American society is fair and equal and the social climate appears to be more racially accepting, then explicit negative beliefs and attitudes against Blacks (e.g., unconscious fear, uneasiness, discomfort, and disgust) must be inhibited to maintain a racially tolerant front. Due to a fear of exposing their own racist ways, White individuals experience feelings of discomfort toward Blacks, particularly if they endorse liberal egalitarian values. Thus, they will display relatively denigrating, ambivalent, and avoidant behaviors toward Blacks and/or preferential treatment for Whites (Dovidio & Gaertner, 2000). However, these aversive racist behaviors will likely be inhibited until an ambiguous situation arises where nonracial justifications are present and normative guidelines are not. For instance, it would be easier for the aversive racist to hire a White applicant (preferential treatment) when an applicant qualification (the nonracial justification) could be utilized as an excuse, particularly if hiring criteria were not clearly specified (lack of normative guidelines). In fact, aversive racists may even consciously act in pro-Black behaviors in racially biased situations to overcompensate for the conflict between their conscious racially tolerant beliefs and their unconscious racially intolerant feelings (Dovidio & Gaertner, 2000).

RACIAL MICROAGGRESSIONS

Modern racism, aversive racism, and studies on prejudice and discrimination have focused primarily on Black Americans (Swim, Aikin, Hall, &

Hunter, 1995). The focus on African Americans is not surprising, since racism in the United States has traditionally been defined as negative attitudes, opinions, feelings, and behaviors on the part of White Americans against Black Americans (Pettigrew, 1975). Given the past and current treatment of Blacks in the United States, the Black-White dichotomy of issues is understandable. However, research findings for Black Americans cannot be assumed to include and represent the experiences of all people of color, including Asian Americans. Given the unique history of Blacks in America (Griffin, 1996), it is inappropriate to assume that research findings on White attitudes toward Blacks necessarily equate to White attitudes toward other racial groups.

In contrast to the other conceptualizations of contemporary racism, the concept of racial microaggressions has been more inclusive of all people of color. Racial microaggressions have generally been defined as verbal, nonverbal, and/or visual insults directed toward people of color in a subtle, automatic, or unconscious way, often with stunning impact (Sue, 2003; Pierce et al., 1978; Solórzano et al., 2000). The thesis underlying the microaggressive themes, as proposed by Sue and colleagues (2007), appears to be more comprehensive in representing the experiences of all individuals of color, such as ascription of intelligence (i.e., Black/Asian Americans), assumption of criminal status (i.e., Black/Latino/a Americans), alien in own land (i.e., Asian/Latino/a Americans), and denial of individual racism (i.e., all individuals of color; Sue, Capodilupo, et al., 2007).

Initially conceptualized by Pierce and colleagues (1978) and studied by Solórzano and colleagues (2000), the study of racial microaggressions started to gain momentum when Sue and his colleagues (Constantine & Sue, 2007; Sue, Bucceri, et al., 2007; Sue, Nadal, et al., 2008) highlighted the potentially injurious psychological impact of racial microaggressions on targets (Sue, 2003). Though these brief racial exchanges can appear harmless to the perpetrator, they are nonetheless experienced as deeply invalidating and denigrating to people of color. Racial microaggressions can be detected in many everyday encounters. Examples specific to Asian Americans include teachers ignoring the raised hands of Asian American students in classrooms, store cashiers acting surprised at the American accent of the Asian American customer, and airport security personnel screening Asian American passengers with Asian names more thoroughly. Similarly to all people of color receiving such treatment, Asian Americans can experience these microaggressive incidents as a racially personalized affront (Solórzano et al., 2000), incurring a shocking and demeaning effect on the recipients (Sue, 2003).

Verbal instances of racial microaggressions for an Asian American can take form in statements such as "You speak such good English," "But you speak without an accent," and "So, where are you really from?" (Sue, Bucceri, et al., 2007). Many Asian Americans indicate that these statements felt invalidating and marginalizing because they insinuate that Asian Americans are foreigners in their own land (Sue & Sue, 2008). Regardless of being second-, third-, or even fifth-generation Asian American in the United States (Espiritu, 1992; Min, 1995; Omi, 1993), they are still considered as an "illegitimate American" (Tuan, 1998). As one of the most common stereotypes against Asian Americans, being treated according to the "perpetual foreigner" stereotype is an all-too-familiar experience for members of this racial group (Nishi, 1989; Tuan, 1998).

STEREOTYPES

Stereotypes, defined as a set of attitudes and beliefs toward a particular social group (Banaji & Dasgupta, 1998), have been asserted to be the fueling force behind prejudice (Banaji & Greenwald, 1994), and in turn, discrimination (U.S. Commission on Civil Rights, 1986). As such, discrimination has been argued to be rooted in societal stereotypes (Jones, 1997; Lyman, 2000; U.S. Commission on Civil Rights, 1986). A meta-analysis showed implicit attitudes to be better predictors of discrimination than explicitly reported racial attitudes (Poehlman, Uhlmann, Greenwald, & Banaji, 2009), supporting the covert nature of contemporary discrimination. Therefore, conceptually analyzing stereotypes of a particular racial group may shed light on the particular forms of discrimination that this group encounters, such as interracial resentment, antiracial sentiments, hate crimes, and racial microaggressions (Banaji & Dasgupta, 1998; Banaji & Greenwald, 1994; Jones, 1997).

REVIEW OF ASIAN STEREOTYPES

Pervasive Asian stereotypes that have been documented in the literature include model minority, second-class citizen, yellow peril (commonly known as "Asian Invasion"), perpetual foreigner, "all Asians are alike," invisibility, and oversexualization of Asian women. Similarly, much of the historically narrative literature on racism against Asian Americans coincides with the aforementioned stereotypes. For example, the tragic murder of Vincent Chin was due to a Chinese American being mistaken as a Japanese individual. In this instance, the "all Asians are alike" stereotype was so powerfully at work that despite his repeated protests of being mistaken as Japanese, Vincent Chin's killers unleashed on him their rage against Japan for their own loss of jobs. Wen Ho Lee's sworn allegiance to the American government decades earlier did not prevent him from being accused as a spy for the Chinese government, which vividly illustrated the perpetual foreigner stereotype. The internment of thousands of Japanese Americans during World War II provides additional compelling evidence. Interestingly, these popular Asian

Table 4.1

Common Asian American Stereotypes and Racial Microaggressive Themes in Sue, Bucceri, et al. (2007)

Asian Stereotype	Supporting Publications	Racial Microaggressive Themes in Sue, Bucceri, et al. (2007)
Model minority	Cabezas & Kawaguchi, 1988; Min, 1995; Nee & Sanders, 1985; Osajima, 1988; Pittinsky, Shih, & Ambady, 2000; Sue & Okazaki, 1990; Takaki, 1989; Tuan, 1998; Wu, 2002; Yee, 1992	Ascription of intelligence; denial of racial reality
Second-class citizen	DeVos & Banaji, 2005; Kawai, 2005; Taylor & Stern, 1997; Volpp, 2001	Second-class citizenship
Yellow peril/ perpetual foreigner	Kitano & Daniels, 1988; Lee, 2002; Lyman, 2000; Tuan, 1998; Wu, 2002; Yee, 1992	Alien in own land
All Asians are alike	Hurh & Kim, 1989; Takaki, 1989; U.S. Commission on Civil Rights, 1986; Wu, 2002; Yee, 1992	Invalidation of interethnic differences
Invisibility	Sun & Starosta, 2006; Tuan, 1998; Volpp, 2001; Yee, 1992	Invisibility
Oversexualization of Asian women	Espiritu, 1997	Exoticization of Asian women

stereotypes coincide with themes of racial microaggressions against Asian Americans (Sue, Bucceri, et al., 2007). Table 4.1 details the thematic similarities found between the narrative literature on racism against Asian Americans and the Sue, Bucceri, et al. (2007) study. This thematic coincidence further supports a link between stereotypes and prejudicial attitudes, which can lead to more overt discriminatory behaviors (Banaji & Dasgupta, 1998; Banaji & Greenwald, 1994; Poehlman et al., 2009).

RACIAL MICROAGGRESSIONS: SUBTLE RACISM AGAINST ASIAN AMERICANS

Research suggests that different racial groups may experience the effects of racism differently (Crocker et al., 1995, as cited in Crocker & Quinn, 1998) and that some expressions of racism against Asian Americans may be group specific in comparison with other racial groups (Liang et al., 2004; Sue & Sue, 2008; Young & Takeuchi, 1998). Initial empirical evidence for racial microaggressions as a useful construct for different racial groups came from focus group studies with Asian and Black Americans (Sue, Bucceri, et al., 2007; Sue, Nadal, et al., 2008). In a study with Black American participants, themes such as *intellectual inferiority*, *second-class citizen*, *assumption of criminality*, *assumption of inferior status*, *assumed universality of the Black/African American experience*, and *White cultural values/communication styles are superior* emerged (Sue, Nadal, et al., 2008). In contrast, themes of *alien in own land*, *ascription of intelligence*, *exoticization of Asian women*, *invalidation of interethnic differences*, *denial of racial reality*, *pathologizing cultural values/communication styles*, *second-class citizenship*, and *invisibility* arose in the Asian American study (Sue, Bucceri, et al., 2007). In both racial micro-aggression studies, some themes were found in the categories originally proposed by Sue, Capodilupo, et al. (2007), while others were newly emerged themes that were group specific. Some themes appear to be more race specific, in varying degrees, while others seem more universally applicable to all racial groups.

The differential weighting of categories across racial groups may reveal fundamental qualitative differences in how racism and stereotypes are per-petuated against and experienced within each group. For example, Black and Latino/a Americans may experience being mistaken as a criminal (i.e., racial microaggressive category of *assumption of criminality*) more frequently than Asian Americans, while Asian and Latino/a Americans may encounter being treated as non-American *(alien in own land)* at a higher rate than Black Americans. In comparing the two focus group studies on racial microaggres-sions, themes of being exotic, invisible, and intelligent appear to be themes more particular to the Asian American population, while themes related to intellectual inferiority and being unworthy of trust appear to be more specific to Black Americans.

Most Asian American themes could be categorized as either microinsults or microinvalidations in their microaggressive nature, because they are more subtle in content, either conveying rudeness (microinsult) or invalidation of the individual's racial reality (microinvalidation). For example, the themes of *invisibility, exoticization of Asian women, alien in own land,* and *ascription of intelligence* appear to be microinvalidations because all are extremely subtle in negating the experiential reality of the Asian American individual. Many may attempt to defend the legitimacy of these microaggressions by pointing to the vast numbers of Asian foreigners in the United States *(alien in own land)* or the complimentary nature of being perceived as intelligent *(ascription of intelligence)* as justification for their microaggression. The inevitable result of defending such microaggressions is that their psychological impact on Asian Americans are downplayed and often nullified. Under these situations, Asian Americans can feel frustrated and confused if they are presumed to be good in math (i.e., *ascription of intelligence*) when math has never been their forte.

Being constantly perceived as a foreigner can feel very marginalizing for an Asian American (i.e., *alien in own land*), because it conveys the message that the Asian American is not really an American and does not really belong in the United States, though this may be the only country that the individual has ever known. Feelings of helplessness can be evoked in Asian Americans when they are ignored in daily interpersonal interactions and when the entire racial group is not considered for governmental subsidy and assistance (i.e., *invisibility*). As illustrated, even seemingly innocent and "positive" racial microaggressive incidents can induce powerful psychological consequences.

However, some themes may fall into the category of microinsult because they denigrate the individual's racial background. For example, *pathologizing cultural values/communication styles* is a theme that appears more blatantly in demeaning the racial heritage of Asian Americans, because it can be a direct communication to the Asian American that the Asian way is not accepted in American society. Devaluation of Asian American cultural values can occur when teachers tell Asian American students that direct eye contact or vocal participation in the classroom is the only acceptable classroom behavior in conveying interest and engagement, even though these values may directly contradict values taught in the Asian American's upbringing.

Due to the subtle nature of racial microaggressions, this conceptual way of understanding contemporary racism against Asian Americans may be particularly useful. The model minority deception has plagued many Americans, even some Asian Americans, as they buy into this myth and report believing that Asian Americans do not encounter racism (Asamen & Berry, 1987; Delucchi & Do, 1996) or that the racism they encounter is minimal (Ruggiero & Taylor, 1997). One study found Asians to have a greater tendency than Blacks in minimizing discrimination in order to maintain a sense of control over their life events (Ruggiero & Taylor, 1997). In fact, Asian Americans who were aware of their experience with discrimination have noted the unintentional nature of racism that they frequently receive from non-Asians. Perhaps the need to maintain a sense of control over their lives (Ruggiero & Taylor, 1997) and the subtlety of their experienced racism (Tuan, 1998) also contributed to the general lack of awareness of racism against Asian Americans. Particularly given the pervasiveness and "positive tone" of Asian American stereotypes and the subtle nature of racism against this group, prejudice and discrimination against Asian Americans may be more covert, internalized, easily justified, and prone to result in future microaggressive encounters.

IMPLICATIONS OF RACIAL MICROAGGRESSIONS

Current scholarship and research on covert racism support the assertion that regardless of the intentions of the perpetrator, these subtle acts of discrimination can significantly harm the victims in a myriad of ways (Solórzano et al., 2000; Sue, Bucceri, et al., 2007; Sue, Nadal, et al., 2008). It has been stressed that encountering such incidents can have a striking and demeaning effect on the recipients (e.g., Sue, 2003). Due to the covert, automatic, and unconscious nature of racial microaggressions (Solórzano et al., 2000), individuals may engage in racially microaggressive behaviors without conscious awareness (Sue, 2003). Because White American racial worldviews and cultural stereotypes are often unconsciously embedded in racial microaggressions, many well-intentioned individuals do not detect the harm in racial microaggressions or even perceive them as a form of prejudice and discrimination. However, when these individuals unconsciously express attitudes of White American superiority or in-group favoritism through racial microaggressions, the recipients of racial microaggressions may feel inferior or invalidated.

MENTAL HEALTH

There is a paucity of studies on the effects of subtle racism, particularly those that are representative of various racial groups (Delgado & Stefancic, 1992; Johnson, 1988; Lawrence, 1987). However, existing research on overt racism shows that the subjective experience of discrimination may invoke a devastating effect on one's physical and mental health (Klonoff, Landrine, & Ullman, 1999; Williams, Neighbors, & Jackson, 2003). In addition, perceived subtle racism has been found to be associated with greater negative emotional reactions than when the injustice is blatant (Motoike, 1995). Studies have found everyday occurrences of discrimination to be positively associated with distress, depression, and generalized anxiety (Cress & Ikeda, 2003; Kessler, Mickelson, & Williams, 1999; Taylor & Turner, 2002) and subtle, recurring discrimination to be inversely related to life satisfaction (Broman, 1997; Essed, 1991).

Interestingly, Asian Americans are still perceived as model minorities who have succeeded in society, and as such, it is believed that they do not face obstacles such as prejudice and discrimination. Some have argued that even seemingly positive stereotypes can have devastating consequences when transferred into discriminatory behaviors (Lin, Kwan, Cheung, & Fiske, 2005; U.S. Commission on Civil Rights, 1986). Unsurprisingly, studies on psychological correlates of racism have found perceived discrimination to be negatively associated with well-being (Lee, 2003) and subjective competence (Ying, Lee, & Tsai, 2000), while positively associated with anxiety, depression, suicidal ideation, and psychological distress for Asian Americans (Hwang & Goto, 2008; Lee, 2003).

A survey of the literature reveals only a few published studies that focus specifically on racial microaggressions and their effects on various groups (Constantine, 2007; Constantine & Sue, 2007; Pierce, 1995; Solórzano et al., 2000; Sue, Bucceri, et al., 2007; Sue, Capodilupo, & Holder, 2008; Sue, Capodilupo, et al., 2007; Sue, Nadal, et al., 2008). Solórzano and colleagues (2000) reported that microaggressions result in self-doubt, frustration, sense of isolation, and negative racial climates for Blacks (Solórzano et al., 2000). Sue, Capodilupo, and colleagues' (2007) study described the potential rupture in therapeutic alliance between a White counselor and a client of color through occurrences of racial microaggressions in a counseling dyad. Similarly, Constantine and Sue (2007) found White supervisors perpetrating racial microaggressions to be detrimental to Black counseling trainees, the supervisory relationship, and even the clients of color that were being seen by the trainees (Constantine, 2007; Constantine & Sue, 2007). Pierce (1995) has noted that the cumulative effects of racial microaggressions may result in "diminished mortality, augmented morbidity, and flattened confidence" (p. 281). Investigators of racial microaggressions concluded that the potential psychological effects of racial microaggressions are particularly devastating because of their subtle and ambiguous nature. An even more negative psychological outcome could be suggested for Asian Americans in micro-aggressive encounters due to the role of social approval in their self-esteem development, as dictated by Asian cultural values (Crocker et al., 1995, as cited in Crocker & Quinn, 1998). Accordingly, feelings of confusion, pain, anger, shame, inferiority, and loneliness have been associated with this subtle form of racism for Asian Americans (Tuan, 1998). Given the many seemingly positive Asian American stereotypes and the subtle nature of discrimination against Asian Americans in the United States and Asian cultural values, it can be concluded that the cumulative potential effects of racial microaggressions on Asian Americans can be particularly distressing and demoralizing.

EDUCATION

Studies have shown that unlike blatant old-fashioned racism, contemporary subtle forms of prejudice and discrimination can impede cognitive functioning and performance (Banaji & Greenwald, 1994; Salvatore & Shelton, 2007; Steele, 1997). One particular study on prejudice found ambiguous racial prejudice to significantly interfere with task performance that required attention and concentration from the participants (Salvatore & Shelton, 2007). In another study, participants exhibited decreased task performance when having to cope with aversive racism versus overt racism, suggesting that participants find subtler forms of discrimination to impede cognitive functioning (Dovidio & Gaertner, 1998). Steele's study (1997) on stereotype threat also shows that simply the reminder of a negative stereotype of the participant's group membership can adversely affect an individual's academic performance.

As an aggregate, these results highlight how subtle prejudice and discrimination, such as racial microaggressions, can negatively impact students in academia by interfering with their cognitive processes, thereby hindering their learning and academic performance. For example, when an Asian American student's raised hand is repeatedly ignored by the instructor (i.e., *invisibility*), the student may feel invisible, diminished in self-esteem, and discouraged in speaking up next time. On the other hand, if the Asian American student does not verbally participate as frequently as other non-Asian students and receives a lower grade as a result, despite considerable efforts exerted in written work (i.e., *pathologizing cultural values/communication styles*), the Asian American student may begin to feel a lack of control in directing and attaining success in his or her academic path.

Being automatically tracked for a career in math or science (i.e., *ascription of intelligence*) by the school counselor without consideration of personal interest or academic performance may compromise the sense of competency and agency within the Asian American student. Given the Asian cultural value of compliance to authority figures, the Asian American student may feel conflicted between personal preference and respecting the opinion of a professional authority. As a result, academic performance may suffer due to a lack of personal interest or ability in the tracked career. Whether the microaggression is perpetrated by instructors or fellow classmates, the Asian American student's learning and academic performance may be impeded when a great portion of their cognitive energy is directed toward coping with microaggressions rather than absorbing the curriculum.

EMPLOYMENT

Researchers and scholars have also found that subtle forms of prejudice and discrimination can be harmful to employees of color in the workplace (Deitch et al., 2003; Rowe, 1990; Stallworth, McPherson, & Rute, 2001). Because racial microaggressions and other forms of subtle racism may not be easily identified and justified, they often exacerbate the unequal opportunities that already exist in the world of work (Sue, Lin, & Rivera, 2009). Scholars suggest that occupational segregation and glass ceilings are actually created and maintained through subtle discrimination (Rowe, 1990; Stallworth et al., 2001). Additionally, when the racial microaggression is perpetrated by a superior, the power differential inherent in the professional relationship may further hinder the employee of color to speak out for fear of retribution (Rowe, 1990). Others also speculate that encountering subtle prejudice in the workplace can impair performance and reduce productivity (Franklin, 2004; Hinton, 2004; Rowe, 1990) through diverted mental energy as they process the ambiguous prejudice and discrimination (Salvatore & Shelton, 2007).

Racial microaggressions may demoralize an Asian American employee and reduce his or her professional productivity in many ways. Being asked where the Asian American is from (i.e., *alien in own land*) or receiving the message that Asian cultural values or communication styles are not suitable for the American workplace *(pathologizing cultural values/communication styles)* can induce feelings of alienation and marginalization. Consequently, the Asian American professional may lack a sense of belonging at work, thus reducing a sense of ownership of position and responsibilities and ultimately diminishing work performance. Being assumed that one is smart and competent (i.e., *ascription of intelligence*), for example, may place undue pressure on the Asian American employee to perform and may result in performance anxiety and reduced productivity. Given the complexity of workplace dynamics, racial microaggressions experienced in the professional realm may prove to be inordinately challenging for the Asian American in the workplace.

CONCLUSION

In sum, it is clear that (1) racism is part of the Asian American experience, (2) the model minority myth has obfuscated the reality of racism for Asian Americans, (3) Asian Americans experience contemporary racism through racial microaggressions, (4) racial microaggressions against Asian Americans are created through stereotypes that American society has formed against this racial group, and (5) racial microaggressions have deleterious effects on Asian Americans. The question becomes, what do we do now?

Studies have suggested the most effective way to lessen discriminatory attitudes, prejudicial behaviors, and unconscious bias is through acquiring awareness or raising consciousness (Banaji & Dasgupta, 1998; Son Hing, Li, & Zanna, 2002). Perhaps due to its unconscious nature, overt specific instruction not to engage in subtle prejudice and discrimination would not be helpful in reducing racial bias (Banaji & Dasgupta, 1998). Instead, the first step is to make the "unconscious conscious" (Banaji & Greenwald, 1994) by allowing "mental (cognitive and motivational) resources to overrule the consciously unwanted but unconsciously operative response" (p. 70). Thus, an in-depth examination of racial microaggressions and their effects may be one way to make the "invisible visible" (Sue, 2003). Social psychologists examining prejudice and racial bias suggested that simply having the knowledge and awareness of possessing biases as well as their sources of influence would help people to minimize the occurrence of prejudice (Banaji & Dasgupta, 1998).

Though the scientific community has begun to empirically validate the concept of racial microaggressions for all people of color, different facets of racial microaggressions have yet to be examined. Without extensive empirical research and documentation to better understand racial microaggressions, the potential threats that they pose and the psychological costs of their manifestations can be easily dismissed (Solórzano et al., 2000). Similarly, anecdotes, narratives, and qualitative literature on racism against Asian Americans support the existence of prejudice and discrimination and the subtle form that racism may take for Asian Americans. However, there has been little systematic investigation into the experience of racial microaggressions for Asian Americans. To date, there has only been one empirical study conducted on racial microaggressions experienced by Asian Americans (Sue, Bucceri, et al., 2007). Given the model minority myth and other stereotypes that Asians encounter in American society, it is imperative to elucidate the extent of such bias and discrimination from the perspective of the recipients of racial microaggressions in order to combat this contemporary form of discrimination. An accurate and in- depth understanding of how Asian American stereotypes function to fuel and maintain the covert ways of racial microaggressions, as well as their affects on the lives of Asian Americans, may help to bring greater insight and appreciation for the Asian American experience of racism.

REFERENCES

Asamen, J. K., & Berry, G. L. (1987). Self-concept, alienation, and perceived prejudice: Implications for counseling Asian Americans. *Journal of Multicultural Counseling and Development*, 15, 146–160.

Banaji, M. R., & Dasgupta, N. (1998). The consciousness of social beliefs: A program of research on stereotyping and prejudice. In V. Y. Yzerbyt, G. Lories, & B. Dardenne (Eds.), *Metacognition: Cognitive and social dimensions* (pp. 157–170). Thousand Oaks, CA: Sage.

Banaji, M. R., & Greenwald, A. G. (1994). Implicit stereotyping and prejudice. In M. P. Zanna & J. Olson (Eds.), *The psychology of prejudice: The Ontario Symposium* (Vol. 7, pp. 55–76). Hillsdale, NJ: Erlbaum.

Bell, D. A. (1985, July 15). The triumph of Asian-Americans: America's greatest success story. *New Republic*, 22, 24–32.

Broman, C. L. (1997). Race-related factors and life satisfaction among African Americans. *Journal of Black Psychology*, 23, 36–49.

Cabezas, A., & Kawaguchi, G. (1988). Empirical evidence for continuing Asian American income inequality: The human capital model and labor market segmentation. In G. Y. Okihiro, S. Hune, A. A. Hansen, & J. M. Liu (Eds.), *Reflections on shattered windows: Promises and prospects for Asian American studies* (pp. 144–164). Pullman: Washington State University Press.

Constantine, M. G. (2007). Racial microaggressions against African American clients in cross-racial counseling relationships. *Journal of Counseling Psychology, 54,* 1–16.

Constantine, M. G., & Sue, D. W. (2007). Perceptions of racial microaggressions among Black supervisees in cross-racial dyads. *Journal of Counseling Psychology, 54,* 142–153.

Cress, C. M., & Ikeda, E. K. (2003). Distress under duress: The relationship between campus climate and depression in Asian American college students. *NASPA Journal, 40,* 74–97.

Crocker, J., & Quinn, D. (1998). Racism and self-esteem. In J. L. Eberhardt & S. T. Fiske (Eds.), *Confronting racism: The problem and the response* (pp. 169–187). Thousand Oaks, CA: Sage.

David, G., & Lin, J. (1997). Civil rights and Asian Americans. *Journal of Sociology and Social Welfare, 24*(1), 3–24.

Deitch, E. A., Barsky, A., Butz, R. M., Chan, S., Brief, A., & Bradley, J. C. (2003). Subtle yet significant: The existence and impact of everyday racial discrimination in the workplace. *Human Relations, 56,* 1299–1324.

Delgado, R., & Stefancic, J. (1992). Images of the outsider in American law and culture: Can free expression remedy systemic social ills? *Cornell Law Review, 77,* 1258–1297.

Delucchi, M., & Do, H. D. (1996). The model minority myth and perceptions of Asian-Americans as victims of racial harassment. *College Student Journal, 30,* 411–414.

DeVos, T., & Banaji, M. R. (2005). American = White? *Journal of Personality and Social Psychology, 88,* 447–466.

Dovidio, J. F., & Gaertner, S. L. (1998). On the nature of contemporary prejudice: The causes, consequences, and challenges of aversive racism. In J. L. Eberhardt & S. T. Fiske (Eds.), *Confronting racism: The problem and the response* (pp. 3–32). Newbury Park, CA: Sage.

Dovidio, J. F., & Gaertner, S. L. (2000). Aversive racism and selective decisions: 1989–1999. *Psychological Science, 11,* 315–319.

Espiritu, Y. L. (1992). *Asian American panethnicity.* Philadelphia, PA: Temple University Press.

Espiritu, Y. L. (1997). *Asian American women and men.* Thousand Oaks, CA: Sage.

Essed, P. (1991). *Understanding everyday racism.* Newbury Park, CA: Sage.

Franklin, A. J. (2004). *From brotherhood to manhood: How Black men rescue their relationships and dreams from the invisibility syndrome.* Hoboken, NJ: John Wiley & Sons.

Griffin, J. H. (1996). *Black like me.* New York: Signet.

Hinton, E. L. (2004, March/April). Microinequities: When small slights lead to huge problems in the workplace. *DiversityInc,* 79–82.

Hurh, W. M., & Kim, K. C. (1989). The "success" image of Asian Americans: Its validity, and its practical and theoretical implications. *Ethnic and Racial Studies, 12,* 512–537.

Hwang, W.-C., & Goto, S. (2008). The impact of perceived racial discrimination on the mental health of Asian Americans and Latino college students. *Cultural Diversity and Ethnic Minority*, *14*, 326–335.

Johnson, S. (1988). Unconscious racism and the criminal law. *Cornell Law Review*, *73*, 1016–1037.

Jones, J. M. (1997). *Prejudice and racism* (2nd ed.). Washington, DC: McGraw-Hill.

Kawai, Y. (2005). Stereotyping Asian Americans: The dialectic of the model minority and the Yellow Peril. *Howard Journal of Communications*, *16*, 109–130.

Kessler, R. C., Mickelson, K. D., & Williams, D. R. (1999). The prevalence, distribution, and mental health correlates of perceived discrimination in the United States. *Journal of Health and Social Behavior*, *40*, 208–230.

Klonoff, E. A., Landrine, H., & Ullman, J. B. (1999). Racial discrimination and psychiatric symptoms among Blacks. *Cultural Diversity and Ethnic Minority Psychology*, *5*, 329–339.

Lawrence, C. (1987). The id, the ego, and equal protection: Reckoning with unconscious racism. *Stanford Law Review*, *39*, 317–388.

Lee, B. T. (2002). Liars, traitors, and spies: Wen Ho Lee and the racial construction of disloyalty. *Asian American Policy Review*, *10*, 1–16.

Lee, R. M. (2003). Do ethnic identity and other-group orientation protect against discrimination for Asian Americans? *Journal of Counseling Psychology*, *50*, 133–141.

Leets, L. (2003). Disentangling perceptions of subtle racist speech: A cultural perspective. *Journal of Language and Social Psychology*, *22*(2), 145–168.

Liang, C. T. H., Li, L. C., & Kim, B. S. K. (2004). The Asian American racism-related stress inventory: Development, factor analysis, reliability, and validity. *Journal of Counseling Psychology*, *51*, 103–114.

Lin, M. H., Kwan, V. S. Y., Cheung, A., & Fiske, S. T. (2005). Stereotype content model explains prejudice for an envied outgroup: Scale of anti-Asian American stereotypes. *Personality and Social Psychology Bulletin*, *31*, 34–47.

Lyman, S. M. (2000). The "Yellow Peril" mystique: Origins and vicissitudes of a racist discourse. *International Journal of Politics, Culture and Society*, *13*, 683–747.

McConahay, J. B. (1986). Modern racism, ambivalence, and the Modern Racism Scale. In J. F. Dovidio & S. L. Gaertner (Eds.), *Prejudice, discrimination and racism* (pp. 91–126). Orlando, FL: Academic Press.

Min, P. G. (Ed.). (1995). *Asian Americans: Contemporary trends and issues*. Thousand Oaks, CA: Sage.

Motoike, P. T. (1995). The effect of blatant and subtle discrimination on emotions and coping in Asian American university students. *Dissertation Abstracts International Section A: Humanities and Social Sciences*, *55*(12-A), 3789.

National Asian Pacific American Legal Consortium (2002). *Backlash: When America turned on its own*. Washington, DC: Author.

Nee, V., & Sanders, J. (1985). The road to parity: Determinants of the socioeconomic achievements of Asian-Americans. *Ethnic and Racial Studies*, *8*, 75–93.

Nishi, S. M. (1989). Perceptions and deceptions: Contemporary views of Asian Americans. In G. Yun (Ed.), *A look beyond the model minority image: Critical issues in Asian America* (pp. 3–10). New York, NY: Minority Rights Group, Inc.

Omi, M. (1993). Out of the melting pot and into the fire: Race relations policy. In Leadership Education for Asian Pacifics, Inc. (LEAP) Asian Pacific American Public Policy Institute & the University of California–Los Angeles Asian-American Studies Center (Eds.), *The state of Asian Pacific America: Policy issues to the year 2020* (pp. 199–214). Los Angeles, CA: Editors.

Pettigrew, T. F. (1975). *Racial discrimination in the United States*. New York: Harper & Row.

Pierce, C. (1995). Stress analogs of racism and sexism: Terrorism, torture, and disaster. In C. Willie, P. Rieker, B. Kramer, & B. Brown (Eds.), *Mental health, racism, and sexism* (pp. 277–293). Pittsburgh, PA: University of Pittsburgh Press.

Pierce, C., Carew, J., Pierce-Gonzalez, D., & Willis, D. (1978). An experiment in racism: TV commercials. In C. Pierce (Ed.), *Television and education* (pp. 62–88). Beverly Hills, CA: Sage.

Pittinsky, T. L., Shih, M., & Ambady, N. (2000). Will a category cue affect you? Category cues, positive stereotypes and reviewer recall for applicants. *Social Psychology of Education, 4,* 53–65.

Poehlman, T. A., Uhlmann, E., Greenwald, A. G., & Banaji, M. R. (2009). Understanding and using the Implicit Association Test: III. Meta-analysis of predictive validity. *Journal of Personality and Social Psychology, 97,* 17–41.

Rowe, M. P. (1990). Barriers to equality: The power of subtle discrimination to maintain unequal opportunity. *Employee Responsibilities and Rights Journal, 3,* 153–163.

Ruggiero, K. M., & Taylor, D. M. (1997). Why minority group members perceive or do not perceive the discrimination that confronts them: The role of self-esteem and perceived control. *Journal of Personality and Social Psychology, 72,* 373–389.

Salvatore, J., & Shelton, J. N. (2007). Cognitive costs of exposure to racial prejudice. *Psychological Science, 18,* 810–815.

Sandhu, D. S. (1997). Psychocultural profiles of Asian and Pacific Islander Americans: Implications for counseling and psychotherapy. *Journal of Multicultural Counseling and Development, 25,* 7–22.

Solórzano, D., Ceja, M., & Yosso, T. (2000). Critical race theory, racial microaggressions, and campus racial climate: The experiences of Black American college students. *Journal of Negro Education, 69,* 60–73.

Son Hing, L. S., Li, W., & Zanna, M. P. (2002). Inducing hypocrisy to reduce prejudicial responses among aversive racists. *Journal of Experimental Social Psychology, 38,* 71–78.

Stallworth, L. E., McPherson, T., & Rute, L. (2001). Discrimination in the workplace: How mediation can help. *Dispute Resolution Journal, 56,* 35–44, 83–87.

Steele, C. M. (1997). A threat in the air: How stereotypes shape intellectual identity and performance. *American Psychologist, 52,* 613–629.

Sue, D. W. (2003). *Overcoming our racism: The journey to liberation.* San Francisco, CA: Jossey-Bass.

Sue, D. W., Bucceri, J. M., Lin, A. I., Nadal, K. L., & Torino, G. C. (2007). Racial microaggressions and the Asian American experience. *Cultural Diversity and Ethnic Minority Psychology, 13,* 72–81.

Sue, D. W., Capodilupo, C. M., & Holder, A. M. (2008). Racial microaggressions in the life experience of Black Americans. *Professional Psychology: Research and Practice, 39*, 329–336.

Sue, D. W., Capodilupo, C. M., Torino, G. C., Bucceri, J. M., Holder, A., Nadal, K. L., & Esquilin, M. (2007). Racial microaggressions in everyday life: Implications for clinical practice. *American Psychologist, 62*, 271–286.

Sue, D. W., Lin, A. I., & Rivera, D. P. (2009). Racial microaggressions in the workplace: Manifestation and impact. In J. L. Chin (Ed.), *Diversity in mind and in action, Vol. 2: Disparities and competence: Service delivery, education, and employment contexts* (pp. 157–172). Santa Barbara, CA: Praeger.

Sue, D. W., Nadal, K. L., Capodilupo, C. M., Lin, A. I., Torino, G. C., & Rivera, D. P. (2008). Racial microaggressions against Black Americans: Implications for counseling. *Journal of Counseling and Development, 86*, 330–338.

Sue, D. W., & Sue, D. (2008). *Counseling the culturally diverse: Theory and practice*. Hoboken, NJ: John Wiley & Sons.

Sue, S. (1999). Asian American mental health: What we know and what we don't know. In W. J. Lonner (Ed.), *Merging past, present, and future in cross-cultural psychology: Selected papers from the Fourteenth Congress of the International Association for Cross-Cultural Psychology* (pp. 83–89). Exton, PA: Swets & Zeitlinger.

Sun, W., & Starosta, W. J. (2006). Perceptions of minority visibility among Asian American professionals. *Howard Journal of Communications, 17*, 119–142.

Swim, J. K., Aikin, K. J., Hall, W. S., & Hunter, B. A. (1995). Sexism and racism: Old-fashioned and modern prejudices. *Journal of Personality and Social Psychology, 68*, 199–214.

Takagi, D. Y. (1990). From discrimination to affirmative action: Facts in the Asian American admissions controversy. *Social Problems, 37*, 578–592.

Takaki, R. (1989). *Strangers from a different shore: A history of Asian Americans*. Boston: Little, Brown.

Taylor, C. R., & Stern, B. B. (1997). Asian-Americans: Television advertising and the "model minority" stereotype. *Journal of Advertising, 26*, 47–61.

Taylor, J., & Turner, R. J. (2002). Perceived discrimination, social stress, and depression in the transition to adulthood: Racial contrasts. *Social Psychology Quarterly, 65*, 213–225.

Tuan, M. (1998). *Forever foreigners or honorary Whites? The Asian ethnic experience today*. Piscataway, NJ: Rutgers University Press.

U.S. Commission on Civil Rights. (1986). *Recent activities against citizens and residents of Asian descent*. Washington, DC: Author.

U.S. Commission on Civil Rights. (1992). *Civil rights issues facing Asian Americans in the 1990s*. Washington, DC: Author.

Volpp, L. (2001). "Obnoxious to their very nature": Asian Americans and constitutional citizenship. *Citizenship Studies, 5*, 57–71.

Williams, D. R., Neighbors, H. W., & Jackson, J. S. (2003). Racial/ethnic discrimination and health: Findings from community studies. *Racial/Ethnic Bias and Health, 93*, 200–208.

Wu, F. H. (2002). *Yellow: Race in America beyond Black and White*. New York: Basic Books.

Yee, A. H. (1992). Asians as stereotypes and students: Misperceptions that persist. *Educational Psychology Review, 4,* 95–132.

Ying, Y.-W., Lee, P. A., & Tsai, J. L. (2000). Cultural orientation and racial discrimination: Predictors of coherence in Chinese American young adults. *Journal of Community Psychology, 28,* 427–442.

Young, K., & Takeuchi, D. T. (1998). Racism. In L. C. Lee & N. W.S. Zane (Eds.), *Handbook of Asian American psychology* (pp. 401–432). Thousand Oaks, CA: Sage.

CHAPTER 5

The Context of Racial Microaggressions Against Indigenous Peoples

Same Old Racism or Something New?

JILL S. HILL, SUAH KIM, and CHANTEA D. WILLIAMS

ADDRESSING RACIAL MICROAGGRESSIONS within Indigenous communities requires knowledge and understanding of the relevant historical, cultural, and social contexts that have influenced these communities, as well as their relationships with the dominant culture, for more than half a millennium. A very brief historical description of colonization and its calamitous effects within Indigenous communities is provided. We then connect this history to more modern manifestations of ongoing colonization and resulting detrimental effects within Indigenous communities, including the perpetuation of racial microaggressions. Additionally, we offer preliminary observations regarding contemporary Indigenous Peoples' experiences of racial microaggressions. Finally, we provide recommendations for exploring this area with Indigenous communities in ways that promote liberation as well as knowledge for the evolving nature of colonization.

We use several terms throughout this chapter to describe Indigenous Peoples, with the full understanding that the act of labeling or naming can, in itself, be a racial microaggression. Indeed, an official definition of Indigenous Peoples is quite challenging due to the tremendous diversity that exists across nations and communities, along with the unique challenges and issues they face. For the purpose of this chapter, *Indigenous Peoples* refers to those "who have experienced the imperialism and colonialism of the modern historical period....They remain culturally distinct, some with their native languages and beliefs still alive. They are minorities in territories and states over which they once held sovereignty" (Smith, 2005, p. 86). In referring to Indigenous Peoples and communities, we have attempted to be sensitive to context in our use of terms that have been traditionally used or preferred by various Indigenous groups, *in general*. For example, we use terms such as Native American, American Indian, Alaska Native, Aboriginal Australian, Indigenous Australian, and Maori to generally describe the Indigenous Peoples of North America, Australia, and Aotearoa (New Zealand). While we do not explicitly refer to any specific Indigenous nation or community, we certainly acknowledge and assert the rights of all Indigenous nations and communities to self-definition.

IMPACT OF COLONIALISM

From first contact—indeed, some have argued that even prior to that time (see Newcomb, 2008)—Indigenous Peoples have been perceived and represented as a "problem" to be dealt with by ruthlessly violent colonizing forces of domination and subjugation. In the New World, such forces metastasized through religious oppression, forced assimilation, systems of government developed in colonized lands, and applications of papal law that served to further subdue and nearly annihilate Indigenous Peoples and dispossess them of land and other material resources. Anishinaabeg activist and scholar Winona LaDuke reminds us that

> *xenophobia and a deep fear of Native spiritual practices came to the Americas with the first Europeans. Papal law was the foundation of colonialism; the Church served as handmaiden to military, economic, and spiritual genocide and domination. Centuries of papal bulls posited the supremacy of Christendom over all other beliefs, sanctified manifest destiny, and authorized even the most brutal practices of colonialism. Some of the most virulent and disgraceful manifestations of Christian dominance found expression in the conquest and colonization of the Americas.* (2005, p. 12)

HISTORIC LOSS AND TRAUMA

Many Indigenous scholars have documented the devastating history of colonialism and colonization for Indigenous Peoples across the world. The ruinous effects of this history within Indigenous communities linger, manifested not only in the losses of language, customs, rituals, sacred knowledge, and culture (Duran & Duran, 1995; Duran, Firehammer, & Gonzalez, 2008; Gone, 2008; Hill, Pace, & Robbins, 2010; Smith, 1999), but also more obviously in the overwhelming disparities in physical health outcomes between Indigenous communities and the majority culture. For example, in the United States, American Indian and Alaska Native Peoples die at alarmingly higher rates than other Americans from tuberculosis, alcoholism, diabetes, homicide, suicide, motor vehicle crashes, and unintentional injuries (Indian Health Service [IHS], 2006). Additionally, American Indian and Alaska Natives' life expectancy rates are lower than all other Americans', while the infant mortality rate for these same communities is significantly higher (IHS, 2006).

Indigenous Peoples of North America have also suffered from another calamitous force: *historical trauma* (Yellow Horse Brave Heart, 1998, 2003), also known as the *soul wound* (Duran, Duran, Yellow Horse Brave Heart, & Yellow Horse-Davis, 1998; Duran et al., 2008). The authors define these synonymous concepts as "cumulative emotional and psychological wounding, over the lifespan and across generations, emanating from massive group trauma experiences" (Yellow Horse Brave Heart, 2003, p. 7) and the experience of "some form of historical trauma that continues to cause confusion and suffering in the present" (Duran et al., 2008, p. 288). This inherited legacy of trauma and unresolved grief, through generations of systemic oppression, has engendered residual psychological, physiological, and social harm (Belcourt-Dittloff & Stewart, 2000). The historical losses of Indigenous Peoples meet the United Nations' definition of genocide (Yellow Horse Brave Heart & DeBruyn, 1998).

The effects of historical trauma and the soul wound are not unique to the Indigenous Peoples of North America, however; these are effects of colonialism and colonization. Similarly, Aboriginal Australians have endured centuries of colonization, genocidal practices, dispossession of land, dislocation, and a range of discriminatory actions at both individual and systemic levels (Mellor, 2003; Raphael, Delaney, & Bonner, 2007). Indeed, Indigenous Australians also experienced negation and suppression of their cultural practices and traditional knowledge by the majority Australian culture (Halloran, 2004). One of the greatest traumatic assaults on Aboriginal Australian communities in the twentieth century, however, was

> the Government's White Australia Policy and an explicit strategy of indigenous assimilation through forced removal of children from their family of origin and placement with Europeans. This latter strategy, referred to as the Stolen Generations, undermined and destabilized Aboriginal social structures, and was perhaps the most critical assault on Aboriginal culture, as it removed a central mode of cultural practice, and thus, transmission. (Halloran, 2004, p. 5)

Contemporary Indigenous Australians experience significantly more negative health outcomes when compared to the Australian population as a whole. For example, infant mortality rates are more than double the rate of the national population; Indigenous Australians' life expectancy is nearly 20 years lower compared to the general population; and for all age groups and all causes of death, the death rate among Aboriginal Australians is higher compared to the national average (Australian Bureau of Statistics, 2001, 2002, as cited in Mellor, 2003, pp. 58–59).

The Maori of Aotearoa (New Zealand) were colonized in much the same way as the Indigenous Peoples of North America and Australia and have experienced similar outcomes. For example, Maori were also dispossessed of their language, cultural practices, and land base. They were additionally subjugated to the assimilative policies of the British Crown government manifested through different vehicles: for example, compulsory educational policies and practices. Researchers have directly linked disparities in health outcomes experienced by Maori, such as poorer life expectancy rates, higher rates of mortality due to cardiovascular disease, cancer, respiratory disease, and injury, to historical and contemporary forms of colonialism and racism (Durie, 1994; Howden-Chapman & Tobias, 2000; Robson, 2004). For these reasons, Sue (2010) asserts that American Indians, Alaska Natives, and other Indigenous Peoples are uniquely ill-fated; unlike racial/ethnic groups that immigrated to the United States, Australia, or New Zealand and struggled to obtain equal resources, Native Peoples, Indigenous to their lands, had their rights and resources stolen from them and have been forced to endure resultant catastrophic effects for generations. Anthropologist John Ogbu (1978), in describing racial dynamics within the United States, termed these individuals as involuntary or "caste-like" minorities.

MODERN RACISM

While we have identified land dispossession, assimilating and culturally invalidating educational agendas, and genocidal practices as part of the traumatic events responsible for the historic loss and soul wound, these events are still happening around the world to Indigenous communities. Overdrawn disputes and legal hurdles over land claims and the resistance to systematically implementing multicultural and bilingual education are ongoing struggles for Indigenous communities in the United States and abroad. Across the world, genocide is still occurring (i.e., Africa, Central America, South America). Moreover, and to further encapsulate the experiences of Indigenous Peoples, proponents of theories of modern racism suggest that racial discrimination has taken a new form in the United States and elsewhere, one that is more subtle and pervasive in its regularity than old-fashioned racism: racial migroaggressions.

RACIAL MICROAGGRESSIONS

The theory of racial microaggressions as proposed by Sue and colleagues (2007) contends that marginalized groups in the United States endure everyday slights and insults that individually and/or systemically denigrate people of color. While emergent studies conducted with persons of African, Latino/a, and Asian descent within the United States have demonstrated that racial microaggressions cause substantial psychological distress and harm, to date, no investigations have examined how racial microaggressions manifest in the experiences of Indigenous Peoples.

MICROINSULTS AND MICROINVALIDATIONS

According to microaggression theory, microinsults include subtle snubs and espouse hidden messages of derogation oftentimes unknown to the perpetrator but insulting to the victim nonetheless (Sue et al., 2007). They describe microinvalidations as behaviors and communications that nullify the thoughts, feelings, and experiential reality of a person. These microaggressions are often fueled by unconsciously or consciously operating stereotypes of a particular group. In the case of American Indians and Alaska Natives, some commonly held negative images or stereotypes include being alcoholics, uneducable, savages, primitive, superstitious, and uncivilized (Sue, 2003). Sue (2010) also contends that Native Americans' lifestyles, including cultural values, customs, spirituality, language, and worldview, are invalidated in their everyday lives. Even worse, these lifeways and thoughtways are pathologized by the majority culture (Trimble, Scharrón-del Río, & Hill, in press). While some current attitudes toward Native Americans remain negative, some expressions of these attitudes may be less explicit, to an extent, than they have been in the past.

In Australia, covert group racism may exist in which the subtle derogation of Indigenous people is a normative and shared social activity among well-meaning White non-Indigenous Australians (Ngarritjan Kessaris, 2006). The author contends that racism toward Aboriginal Australians has become normalized because of the societal structures and practices that are in place (e.g., colonization and cultural dominance), and this casual racism has gone unnoticed by its perpetrators. Examples of a collective racism include historical misrepresentations in textbooks, entitlements felt by White Australians to speak about Aboriginal Australians in their presence and with authority, inquiry into Indigenous culture without discretion, and expectations placed on Aboriginals to be experts on their culture. The innocence with which these statements are made by White Australians toward Aboriginal Australians reflects the ignorance and perceived nonmalevolence White individuals feel about their actions. The frequency, unpredictability, and cumulative effects of these insults are the most troubling, as they often occur in the workplace and in classrooms, where these statements typically go unchallenged (Ngarritjan Kessaris, 2006).

EXAMPLES OF RACIAL MICROAGGRESSIONS

Recent research in the experiences of Indigenous people with racism offers examples of discrimination that support the original taxonomy of racial microaggressions proposed by Sue and colleagues (2007). In a study of experienced racism reported by Aboriginal Australians, the author described examples of behavioral racism that reflected the subtle quality of racial microaggressions, including ignoring, staring, avoidance, patronization, segregation, and denial of identity (Mellor, 2003). These manifestations are reflective of attitudes that endorse Indigenous Peoples and other people of color as "second-class citizens," a theme proposed by Sue and colleagues (2007). Preliminary findings from a study conducted by the authors of this chapter adhere to other themes in the current microaggression taxonomy proposed by Sue and colleagues (2007). For example, one participant stated:

> At times I feel as though there is an assumption by non-Indigenous people that Indigenous people are not very intelligent. I have been in situations whereby non-Indigenous people have said to me that they were not aware of the amount of knowledge I had (in particular in the areas of admin/finance). Whilst there was never a direct comment about my Aboriginality in these situations, I find this to be a very covert form of racism.

This example reflects the theme of "ascription of intelligence" in which people of color are often assumed to have inferior intelligence compared to White individuals.

The following example not only exhibits beliefs that Indigenous people are assumed criminals or social deviants, but it also reflects the covert racism that goes unchecked and is collectively accepted by those in the dominant culture:

> Staff and students laughing at a student's comments at a student society function where a student in the opening welcome speech stated that he apologized that Indigenous people couldn't make it tonight to give a "welcome to country," as they are all too drunk down on the riverbank to make it. I was shocked to see all students and colleagues laughing at this. Upon lodging a formal complaint, both an Indigenous student and I became known as problems and troublemakers.

Another participant experienced having his cultural values and communication style pathologized because they ran counter to those of the majority culture; he experienced an explicit expectation that he assimilate to the dominant culture:

> When I misunderstand the way something was said and ask people to paraphrase, sometimes they say things like "'Your kind' shouldn't be here if you can't understand

what we are saying." I get a lot of comments in regards to my using nonverbals in my communication. If I mention my cultural values, they either make jokes about it or they try and use me as the "token" Indigenous person, so I guess it is sometimes best to keep your thoughts to yourself.

Because of the often-unconscious quality of racial microaggressions, prejudicial attitudes may not surface in perpetrators' self-reports. For example, in a study of university students' racial attitudes toward American Indians that utilized a series of vignettes, students reported generally positive views of American Indians, with the exception of one scenario in which an American Indian student received free health care (Ancis, Choney, & Sedlacek, 1996). However, the authors caution that the positive regard for American Indians reported in this study may reflect national trends toward political correctness in the 1980s and 1990s and promotion of favorable, albeit narrow, depictions of American Indians in the media. The negative response that perceived free health care for American Indians elicited can suggest that there is some opposition toward systemic efforts at racial equality and what may be considered as "unearned benefits" (Ancis et al., 1996).

In our preliminary results, one participant stated, "When I won a university medal for teaching excellence, a non-Indigenous staff member said to me that the university must have needed to improve its equity statistics; hence they gave me an award." This illustration also reflects the theme of "myth of meritocracy" in which people of the dominant culture believe that marginalized peoples receive undeserved rewards due to their race or ethnicity. These results suggest that the reality of systemic inequalities are not actively explored or critically evaluated in college classrooms and in mainstream society.

ENVIRONMENTAL MICROAGGRESSIONS

Along with the covert racism and prejudice experienced by this population at the interpersonal level, Indigenous Peoples also sustain more macrolevel insults based on racial prejudice. Most evident are the institutional practices that continue to marginalize this group through health care disparities and unequal employment and educational opportunities. Although health data for American Indians and Alaska Natives, Aboriginal Australians, and Maori exhibit disproportionately high morbidity and mortality rates, members of these groups remain largely underserved and underrepresented in medical and mental health services.

The macrolevel racism experienced by Aboriginal Australians in one qualitative study was described as being more diffuse, anonymous, and intangible (Mellor, 2003). Examples included a collective lack of concern for Indigenous people, a selective view of history in mainstream society, the dominating nature of the White culture, misinformation about Indigenous people, and its perpetuation in the media. The author also described the pervasiveness of cultural dominance—Western culture in Australia—in denying the right or opportunity for Aboriginal people to practice aspects of their own culture. Aboriginal Australians also disproportionately experienced selective application of laws, regulations, and punishments. Furthermore, this study found that media perpetuated stereotypes of Aboriginals as drunks, dirty, destructive, and unable to live in Western-style housing (Mellor, 2003).

The depictions of American Indians in the media have historically been stereotypical, usually representing members of this group as "savages." Moreover, American Indians have usually been relegated into three dominant images: the generic Indian, the Indian as "other," and the good/bad Indian (Berkhofer, 1978). The generic Indian image homogenizes American Indians into one entity without regard to the natural heterogeneity of their cultures, physical features, traditions, and values among individuals and the different tribes. The Indian as the "other" depiction reflects the idea that Indians exist as an opposition or contrast to the dominant White culture, which effectively dehumanizes them. This relates to what was previously mentioned as the act of labeling as a racial microaggression. Said (1978) describes the process of maintaining positional superiority—that is, the enactment of centuries-old Euro-American traditions of imperialism, power, construction of knowledge and discourse, and representation of the other. According to Smith (1999), "These ideas are predicated on a sense of Otherness. They are views which invite a comparison with 'something/someone else' which exists *on the outside,* such as the oriental, the 'Negro,' the 'Jew,' the 'Indian,' the 'Aborigine' " (p. 32). Finally, the good/bad Indian represents a dichotomous view of American Indians as either subservient, friendly, and noble savages or as degraded individuals who have succumbed to society's transgressions, such as drinking (Berkhofer, 1978).

American Indians as historic relics have also been featured prominently in media representations, where they have been depicted as artifacts of a romanticized colonial era, thus not having a place in modern times. These depictions further the idea that American Indians are "second-class citizens," outside of mainstream culture, social deviants, and homogenized, as reflected by the mentality that "they are all the same." Furthermore, in a study of present-day portrayals of American Indians in the news and an examination of the covert manner in which they were invalidated, the authors found that American Indians were "silenced" through lack of direct quotes from individuals (Miller & Dente Ross, 2004). Rather, their experiences were told by a narrator who defined their culture in Anglo-American terms, placing American Indians as "they" and not "us."

MICROASSAULTS

In the microaggression taxonomy, microassaults are offenses committed against marginalized groups that most closely resemble traditional racism and other discriminatory actions meant to harm and demean individuals and groups (Sue et al., 2007). While Indigenous Peoples encounter everyday subtle slights that disparage their racial-cultural background, we cannot ignore the fact that they continue to face overt prejudices and racist acts driven by intent to harm physically, psychologically, socially, and culturally. In the qualitative study of interviews with Aboriginal Australians on their experiences with racism previously mentioned, the author found that racism toward participants occurred in four categories: verbal and behavioral racism at both individual and institutional levels, discrimination, and macrolevel racism (Mellor, 2003). Verbal racism included name-calling and general derogatory remarks. There was a strong emphasis on skin color in verbal manifestations of racism. These expressions consisted of racialized terms such as the use of "Blackness" and "colored people," in addition to the use of overtly racist verbal harassments. Participants also reported hearing other remarks that they believed had racist connotations through sarcasm and teasing. These verbalizations ranged from childhood teasing to police harassment. Other forms of verbal racism included both overheard and deliberate comments, comments that were meant to be hurtful, intimidation, threats, and jokes and jeers. The examples that were provided were overt in nature and reported as undoubtedly racist by the participants. They also described their perpetrators as freely perpetuating harmful stereotypes and exhibiting racism.

In our preliminary findings, an American Indian participant also recalled an instance in which he was deliberately assaulted because of his race.

> *In my first year of teaching here, as I was teaching the course with heavy emphasis on the injustices suffered by Native Americans historically, a small group of students decided that I had been being "un-American" and "anti-American" for illustrating several historical injustices. So, a small group of friends that lived in the Diversity in Education dormitory decided to "teach me a lesson." On Halloween, a male student and female student disrupted my course's exam by doing a war whoop as [the male student] ran down the stairs "dressed as an Indian," all bought from the Dollar Store, shooting me with rubber suction-cupped arrows, telling me to "go back to my own country."*

This instance illustrates microassaults driven by the attitude that American Indians are considered aliens in their own land and that their traditional values can be blatantly disrespected. It also suggests an environmental microaggression in which Native regalia is misappropriated and reproduced, then sold at the Dollar Store, thereby commercializing and demeaning an entire culture.

MASCOTS

One of the most obvious expressions of racial microaggressions is the portrayal of Native Americans as mascots by sports teams, in advertisements, and in other forms of media (e.g., cartoons and movies) within the United States. The use of Native Americans as mascots by sports teams is a long-held tradition embraced by collegiate teams, such as the University of North Dakota's Fighting Sioux, and national sports teams, such as the Washington Redskins and the Cleveland Indians' Chief Wahoo (Fryberg, Markus, Oyserman, & Stone, 2008; Sue, 2010). These entities typically claim that their use of Native American representations as mascots is intended to honor American Indians. During games, mascots portraying American Indians are often seen riding horses up and down the sideline of sporting events, mimicking a tomahawk chop, or yelling or imitating perceived Native rituals (e.g., war chants or dances).

The use of Native Americans as mascots is a blatant form of discrimination that is commonly seen in modern American society. Such forms of discrimination and racism historically experienced by members of other oppressed groups within the United States have been largely eradicated from the mainstream, whereas the one-dimensional image of American Indians as warriors or savages continues to be seen even today. This remains a widely controversial and contested issue within the United States. American Indian mascots like Chief Wahoo (the mascot for the Cleveland Indians) and Chief Illiniwek (retired mascot of the University of Illinois at Urbana-Champaign) are misrepresentations of Native cultural values and traditions (Fryberg et al., 2008). These and similar caricatures provide an extremely limited view of American Indians. In their research on the consequences of the use of American Indian mascots and other prevalent images/representations of American Indians on the self-concept of American Indian students, Fryberg and colleagues (2008) found that students experience negative effects in the areas of self-esteem, community worth, and possible selves. The authors conclude that the use of American Indian mascots is harmful for the group caricaturized by the mascots, because in such contexts, there are typically few alternative representations or characterizations of American Indians. Such evidence suggests how the use of American Indian mascots significantly detracts from the overall personal and academic success of Native American students. To counter and reduce the negative effects of these types of representations, the authors (Fryberg et al., 2008) suggest either eliminating the use of American Indian mascots altogether or developing and institutionalizing a broader, more appropriate, and more accurate array of social representations of American Indians.

EFFECTS OF RACISM AND COPING

Since we have all experienced aggression at some point in our lives, it is not hard to imagine and empathize with some of the feelings of anger, shame, inferiority, increased vulnerability, and decreased sense of safety that some of our previously cited examples describe as resulting from these events. Nevertheless, unless we are part of a marginalized and oppressed group, it might be difficult to understand the effect that systematic discrimination and microaggressions can have on our integral well-being (physical, mental, emotional, interpersonal, and spiritual). The experience of racism, discrimination, and oppression has noxious effects on our individual and collective well-being, as we discuss below.

HEALTH AND WELL-BEING

The experience of racism has been linked with significant deleterious health effects (Carter, 2007; Durie, 1994; Robson, 2004). Among Indigenous communities, the experience of racism within the context of colonization has created similar detrimental consequences and effects across nations and continents. Similar to American Indians and Alaska Natives, Aboriginal Australians and Maori have poor health outcomes, high infant mortality rates, higher rates of unemployment and imprisonment, and live in poorer living conditions than their non-Indigenous counterparts (Mellor, 2003; Robson, 2004).

The psychological well-being of Indigenous Peoples is also compromised. In a study of depressive symptoms among American Indians located in the upper Midwest, the authors found that perceived discrimination was strongly associated with depressive symptoms and that engagement in cultural practices buffered some of the negative effects of discrimination (Whitbeck, McMorris, Hoyt, Stubben, & Lafromboise, 2002). Those who reported experiencing discrimination were twice as likely to score above threshold for depressive symptoms; nevertheless, engaging in cultural practices at above-average levels reduced this likelihood by 29 percent. Such practices included speaking their Indigenous language, going to powwows, and participating in other traditions. Thus, the stronger the ties to the Indigenous culture, the more protective these practices were from high levels of depressive symptoms. The authors suggest that American Indians with low involvement in cultural practices may not experience the protective benefits of cultural identification and belongingness. Considering Western institutional initiatives and expectations for Indigenous persons to "Whiten" or acculturate and the level to which participating in cultural practices is directly or subtly discouraged, the health landscape for Indigenous individuals and communities becomes even more grim. Indeed, distress caused by discrimination could make Indigenous individuals further withdraw from their own communities.

In an examination of the coping styles employed by Indigenous Australians in the face of racism, responses appeared to be situation specific and ranged from attempts at protecting the self, maintaining self-control, and confronting the racism (Mellor, 2004). Responses toward protecting the self included acceptance, withdrawal, resignation, or avoidance of future contact; cognitive reinterpretation of the event; using social supports; attempts to achieve to prove worthiness; and attempts to make their children stronger in response to the same fate. Efforts at self-control among Indigenous Australians included ignoring the incident, containing their reactions, and imagining ideal responses toward the perpetrator. Confronting the racism included educating the perpetrator, contesting the racism, asserting one's rights, asserting one's ethnic identity, taking control, using external supports from authorities, and seeking revenge (Mellor, 2004). Similar responses have been reported elsewhere with other oppressed groups (Carter, 2007). The author suggested that future research should explore the adaptive and maladaptive effects of these coping styles and whether they mitigate racist situations and the psychological impact or exacerbate them (Mellor, 2004).

APPROACHING RESEARCH

The need for further research within Indigenous communities is undisputed: More needs to be known not only about the effects of racism, oppression, and microaggressions, but also about resiliency and protective factors to these circumstances. Nevertheless, research has often been a source of trauma and exploitation and a vehicle of colonization to many Indigenous communities (Smith, 1999; Trimble, Scharrón-del Río, & Bernal, in press; Trimble, Scharrón-del Río, & Hill, in press). Thus, it is necessary that we are mindful of how the needed research will approach these communities: Researchers need to be aware of the historical and political context, both past and present, in which the research will take place. This awareness cannot be a passive process: It involves constant self-reflection and a commitment not to perpetuate past and present histories of oppression within Indigenous communities.

ENGAGEMENT WITH DIFFICULT KNOWLEDGE

Anecdotal experiences of Indigenous scholars and researchers, including those of the first author, suggest that non-Indigenous colleagues and under-graduate and graduate students are generally unaware of the sociopolitical and historical factors that have oppressed, shaped, and marginalized Indig-enous communities and nations. This "unknowing," undoubtedly an artifact of colonialism and contemporary expression of White privilege, must be countered as well as resisted within the field as well as in society in general. Some scholars refer to this countering/resistance process as part of decolonization (Grande, 2007; Smith, 1999, 2006) and/or conscientization (Freire, 1972; Duran, 2006; Duran et al., 2008; Smith, 2003), which are not reserved solely for the colonized (Tuck & Fine, 2007; White, 2006). Non-Indigenous persons should be aware that this requires deep emotional reflection, competent supervision, and commitment to engage fully with difficult, often painful knowledges.

Trimble (2010) reminds us that

> culture and ethnicity matter, but they did not seem to matter enough in the history of the development of psychology....Culture and ethnicity matter so much that it behooves the investigator to spend considerable time with an ethnocultural group of interest to learn about the deep cultural elements of one's lifeways and thoughtways and how they contribute to social and psychological character. (p. 151)

In the case of Indigenous Peoples, part of these deep cultural elements to which Trimble refers include not only the experiences and effects of imperialism, colonialism, and colonization, but also, perhaps more importantly, the aspects of culture that foster survival, resilience, and vitality. In the face of over-whelming oppression spanning more than half a millennium, what are the cultural elements responsible for survival, resilience, and vitality within Indigenous communities?

LIBERATION AND NEW FORMS OF COLONIZATION

Historically, Indigenous communities have justifiably viewed research as another blunt instrument of colonization rather than as an effective tool to assert rights of sovereignty and self-determination (Smith, 1999, 2005). Duran and colleagues (2008) encourage professionals in the field to take a liberatory approach in working with Indigenous Peoples; this approach requires coun-selors and other professionals "to undertake a serious self-examination of the impact of their privileged position in society that often leads them to ignore many of the injustices that underlie clients' soul wounds and psychological distress" (p. 289). The process of conducting research with Indigenous groups requires similar efforts at self-examination as well as an explicit understanding of the sociopolitical and historical context of Indigenous communities. Duran and colleagues (2008) advocate the use of qualitative research methods in all research endeavors with Indigenous groups, as these methods have been found to be more congruent with Indigenous ways of knowing than quantitative methodologies. Further, the authors view qualitative strategies as an ideal vehicle for liberating the field from traditional and purely Western or positivistic scientific methods of inquiry that have perpetuated the spread of culturally biased information.

We also advocate the use of qualitative methodologies in examining the effects of both old-fashioned racism as well as more modern forms of racism as expressions of colonization. For Indigenous Peoples, it is clear that blatant expressions of racism remain, whether through omissions and misrepresentations in educational curricula or on display at sporting events televised for national audiences. Sanctioned by society, these expressions continue to cause substantial harm to Indigenous Peoples. Further, while more subtle forms of racism do exist, it is important to note that colonization has evolved, and with it, different forms of racism. However, the goals of the new colonization remain the same as the old. Maori scholar Graham Hingangaroa Smith (1994) argues that for Indigenous Peoples, colonization has changed form in the neoliberal context in ways that are frequently economic (see LaDuke, 1999, 2005). This is clearly viewed in terms of globalization and exportation of capitalism. These forms of racism should also be explored and disrupted within Indigenous communities.

In exploring, identifying, and disrupting both old and new forms of racism as tools of colonialism, Indigenous scholars and researchers have suggested that on the local level, approaches to research in Indigenous communities must be congruent with the aims of liberation, self-determination, and the right of Indigenous nations and communities to sovereignty (Duran et al., 2008; Smith, 2005). Indeed, a shift has occurred within Indigenous communities in this area. Smith (2005) reminds us that "more recently…indigenous researchers have been active in seeking ways to disrupt the 'history of exploitation, suspicion, misunderstanding, and prejudice' of indigenous peoples in order to develop methodologies and approaches to research that privilege indigenous knowledges, voices, experiences" (p. 87).

CONCLUSION

While it is abundantly clear that much remains to be achieved in terms of raising the consciousness of the members of dominant social groups regarding the social, political, cultural, and historical contexts unique to

Indigenous Peoples, nations, and communities, there is evidence of systemic progress. For example, in 2005, the American Psychological Association (APA), citing significant research evidence of the psychological harm associated with the use of American Indian mascots to American Indian people, adopted a resolution that recommended and supported the immediate retirement of American Indian mascots, symbols, images, and personalities by schools, colleges, universities, athletic teams, and organizations (APA, 2005).

On September 13, 2007, the United Nations General Assembly adopted the Declaration on the Rights of Indigenous Peoples (Resolution 61/295); 144 states voted in favor of the declaration, while 4 opposed it: Australia, Canada, New Zealand, and the United States (United Nations Permanent Forum on Indigenous Issues, 2007). While the declaration is nonbinding, it is the most comprehensive statement ever developed concerning the rights of Indigenous Peoples. In 2009, the Australian government reversed its original opposition and endorsed the declaration.

These, as well as the other examples described in this chapter, are significant reflections of what individuals, institutions, and society have done and indeed must continue to do to advocate for and allow equal access and opportunity for the liberation of Indigenous Peoples across the globe. The shifts occurring within nations and communities, academic institutions, and various levels of government—the results of generations of Indigenous struggle and resistance—are evidence of the ongoing decolonization and transformation of Indigenous Peoples to reclaim and assert their rights to self-determination and sovereignty, even in the face of the ever-changing forces of neocolonialism. Indeed, it is through the processes of recovering and revitalizing Indigenous languages, lifeways, cosmologies, ceremonies, ontologies, epistemologies, and methodologies that the horrific wounds of colonialism will begin to heal.

REFERENCES

American Psychological Association (APA). (2005). *APA resolution recommending the immediate retirement of American Indian mascots, symbols, images, and personalities by schools, colleges, universities, athletic teams, and organizations.* Washington, DC: Author.

Ancis, J. R., Choney, S. K., & Sedlacek, W. E. (1996). University students' attitudes toward American Indians. *Journal of Multicultural Counseling and Development, 24,* 26–36.

Belcourt-Dittloff, A., & Stewart, J. (2000). Historical racism: Implications for Native Americans. *American Psychologist, 55,* 1166–1167.

Berkhofer, R. (1978). *The White man's Indian.* New York: Vintage Books.

Carter, R. T. (2007). Racism and psychological and emotional injury: Recognizing and assessing race-based traumatic stress. *Counseling Psychologist, 35*, 13–105.

Duran, E. (2006). *Healing the soul wound: Counseling with American Indians and other Native peoples.* New York: Teachers College Press.

Duran, E., & Duran, B. (1995). *Native American postcolonial psychology.* Albany: State University of New York Press.

Duran, E., Duran, B., Yellow Horse Brave Heart, M., & Yellow Horse-Davis, S. (1998). Healing the American Indian soul wound. In Y. Danieli (Ed.), *International handbook of multigenerational legacies of trauma* (pp. 341–354). New York: Plenum.

Duran, E., Firehammer, J., & Gonzalez, J. (2008). Liberation psychology as the path toward healing cultural soul wounds. *Journal of Counseling & Development, 86*, 288–295.

Durie, M. (1994). *Whaiora: Māori health development.* Auckland, New Zealand: Oxford University Press.

Freire, P. (1972). *Pedagogy of the oppressed.* Harmondsworth, U.K.: Penguin.

Fryberg, S. A., Markus, H. R., Oyserman, D., & Stone, J. M. (2008). Of warrior chiefs and Indian princesses: The psychological consequences of American Indian mascots. *Basic and Applied Social Psychology, 30*, 208–218.

Gone, J. P. (2008). Mental health discourse as Western cultural proselytization. *Ethos, 36*, 310–315.

Grande, S. (2007) Red pedagogy: Indigenizing inquiry or, the un-methodology. In N. K. Denzin & M. D. Giardina (Eds.), *Ethical futures in qualitative research: Decolonizing the politics of knowledge* (pp. 133–143). Walnut Creek, CA: Left Coast Press.

Halloran, M. J. (2004, July). *Cultural maintenance and trauma in Indigenous Australia.* Paper presented at the 23rd Annual Conference of the Australia and New Zealand Law and History Society, Perth, Western Australia.

Hill, J. S., Pace, T. M., & Robbins, R. R. (2010). Decolonizing personality assessment and honoring Indigenous voices: A critical examination of the Minnesota Multiphasic Personality Inventory-2. *Cultural Diversity and Ethnic Minority Psychology, 16*, 16–25.

Howden-Chapman, P., & Tobias, M. (Eds.). (2000). *Social inequalities in health: New Zealand, 1999.* Wellington, New Zealand: Ministry of Health.

Indian Health Service. (2006, January). *Facts on Indian health disparities.* Washington, DC: Author.

LaDuke, W. (1999). *All our relations: Native struggles for land and life.* Cambridge, MA: South End Press.

LaDuke, W. (2005). *Recovering the sacred: The power of naming and claiming.* Cambridge, MA: South End Press.

Mellor, D. (2003). Contemporary racism in Australia: The experiences of Aborigines. *Personality and Social Psychology Bulletin, 29*, 474–486.

Mellor, D. (2004). Responses to racism: A taxonomy of coping styles used by Aboriginal Australians. *American Journal of Orthopsychiatry, 74*, 56–71.

Miller, A., & Dente Ross, S. (2004). They are not us: Framing of American Indians by the *Boston Globe. Howard Journal of Communications, 15*, 245–259.

Newcomb, S. T. (2008). *Pagans in the Promised Land: Decoding the doctrine of Christian discovery*. Golden, CO: Fulcrum Publishing.

Ngarritjan Kessaris, T. (2006). About being Mununga (Whitefulla): Making cover group racism visible. *Journal of Community and Applied Social Psychology, 16*, 347–362.

Ogbu, J. U. (1978). *Minority education and caste: The American system in cross-cultural perspective*. San Diego, CA: Academic Press.

Raphael, B., Delaney, P., & Bonner, D. (2007). Assessment of trauma for Aboriginal people. In J. P. Wilson & C. T. Tang (Eds.), *Cross-cultural assessment of psychological trauma and PTSD* (pp. 337–358). New York: Springer.

Robson, B. (2004). *Economic determinants of Māori health and disparities: A review for Te Ropu Tohutohu i te Hauora Tumatanui*. Wellington, New Zealand: Public Health Advisory Committee of the National Health Committee.

Said, E. (1978). *Orientalism*. London: Vintage Books.

Smith, G. H. (1994). Maori culture for sale. *Polemic, 4*, 33–40.

Smith, G. H. (2003, November–December). *Kaupapa Māori theory: Theorizing Indigenous transformation of education and schooling*. Symposium conducted at the New Zealand Association for Research in Education (NZARE)/Australian Association for Research in Education (AARE) Joint Conference, Auckland, New Zealand.

Smith, L. T. (1999). *Decolonizing methodologies: Research and Indigenous Peoples*. New York: Zed Books.

Smith, L. T. (2005). On tricky ground: Researching the Native in the age of uncertainty. In N. K. Denzin & Y. S. Lincoln (Eds.), *The SAGE handbook of qualitative research* (3rd ed., pp. 85–107). Los Angeles, CA: Sage.

Smith, L. T. (2006). Choosing the margins: The role of research in Indigenous struggles for social justice. In N. K. Denzin & M. D. Giardina (Eds.), *Qualitative inquiry and the conservative challenge* (pp. 152–171). Walnut Creek, CA: Left Coast Press.

Sue, D. W. (2003). *Overcoming our racism: The journey to liberation*. San Francisco, CA: Jossey-Bass.

Sue, D. W. (2010). *Microaggressions in everyday life: Race, gender and sexual orientation*. Hoboken, NJ: John Wiley & Sons.

Sue, D. W., Capodilupo, C. M., Torino, G. C., Bucceri, J. M., Holder, A. M. B., Nadal, K. L., & Esquilin, M. (2007). Racial microaggressions in everyday life: Implications for practice. *American Psychologist, 62*, 271–286.

Trimble, J. E. (2010). The principled conduct of counseling research with ethnocultural populations: The influence of moral judgments on scientific reasoning. In J. G. Ponterotto, J. M. Casas, L. A. Suzuki, & C. M. Alexander (Eds.), *Handbook of multicultural counseling* (3rd ed., pp. 147–161). Los Angeles, CA: Sage.

Trimble, J., Scharrón-del Río, M.R., Bernal, G. (in press). The itinerant researcher: Ethical and methodological issues in conducting cross-cultural mental health research. In D. C. Jack & A. Ali (Eds.), *Cultural perspectives on women's depression: Self-silencing, psychological distress and movement to voice*. New York: Oxford University Press.

Trimble, J. E., Scharrón-del Río, M. R., & Hill, J. S. (in press). Ethical considerations in the application of cultural adaptation models with ethnocultural populations. In

G. Bernal & M. M. Domenech Rodriguez (Eds.), *Cultural adaptations: Tools for evidence-based practice with diverse populations*. Washington, DC: American Psychological Association.

Tuck, E., & Fine, M. (2007). Inner angles: A range of ethical responses to/with Indigenous decolonizing theories. In N. K. Denzin & M. D. Giardina (Eds.), *Ethical futures in qualitative research: Decolonizing the politics of knowledge* (pp. 145–168). Walnut Creek, CA: Left Coast Press.

United Nations Permanent Forum on Indigenous Issues (2007). *United Nations Declaration on the Rights of Indigenous Peoples* (A/RES/61/295). Retrieved October 30, 2009, from http://www.un.org/esa/socdev/unpfii/en/declaration.html.

Whitbeck, L. B., McMorris, B. J., Hoyt, D. R., Stubben, J. D., & LaFromboise, T. (2002). Perceived discrimination, traditional practices, and depressive symptoms among American Indians in the upper Midwest. *Journal of Health and Social Behavior*, 43, 400–418.

White, C. J. (2006). Humbling and humble research: A modest witnessing. In N. K. Denzin & M. D. Giardina (Eds.), *Qualitative inquiry and the conservative challenge* (pp. 215–223). Walnut Creek, CA: Left Coast Press.

Yellow Horse Brave Heart, M. (1998). The return to the sacred path: Healing historical trauma and historical unresolved grief response among the Lakota through psychoeducational group intervention. *Smith College Studies in Social Work*, 68, 287–305.

Yellow Horse Brave Heart, M. (2003). The historical trauma response among Natives and its relationship with substance abuse: A Lakota illustration. *Journal of Psychoactive Drugs*, 35, 7–13.

Yellow Horse Brave Heart, M., & DeBruyn, L. M. (1998). The American Indian holocaust: Healing historical unresolved grief. *American Indian and Alaska Native Mental Health Research*, 8, 60–82.

CHAPTER 6

Multiracial Microaggressions

Exposing Monoracism in Everyday Life and Clinical Practice

MARC P. JOHNSTON and KEVIN L. NADAL

MULTIRACIAL PEOPLE HAVE been part of the history of the United States for centuries, as exemplified by the term *mulatto* first appearing in the 1850 U.S. Census (Morning, 2003). Despite this history, the year 2000 marked the first Census that allowed respondents to check more than one box for their racial identification, yielding 57 possible multiple-race identities based off of 6 main racial categories (Morning, 2003). Thus, Census 2000 was a critical state-issued marker for U.S. society's validation and acceptance of the growing multiracial community, as it offered an opportunity for the government, educational systems, and media to become aware of the number of various multiracial demographics in the United States (DaCosta, 2007). In addition to the U.S. Census's inclusion of multiraciality, issues concerning multiracial persons have also been a topic of interest in academia, as exemplified by a multidisciplinary surge in research and theory around multiracial identity, as well as surrounding political and social issues concerning multiracial persons (Shih & Sanchez, 2009). Additionally, the recent election of a biracial, African American-identified president has brought issues surrounding race and politics to the forefront (e.g., Thomas & Jackson, 2008), including issues surrounding multiraciality (e.g., Navarro, 2008) and "postracial" America (e.g., Lee, 2008). However, while the experiences of multiracial individuals seem to have gained much more popularity in academic and social arenas, little attention has been given to multiracial people's experiences with racism or discrimination.

There are reasons that may partially explain why there is a dearth of literature examining multiracial individuals' experiences with racism. First, perhaps multiracial persons are assumed to experience only racism that is similar to monoracial individuals. For example, a biracial Black/White individual may be perceived only as Black and may experience racism accordingly. Second, the existing literature on multiracial people tends to focus primarily on identity and internal struggles in "choosing" between their multiple racial backgrounds (e.g., Poston, 1990) instead of examining race-related experiences within a monoracially designed society. Finally, because racism has become more subtle and covert and "old-fashioned racism" (e.g., hate crimes, blatant discrimination, racial slurs) has decreased (Nadal, 2008; Sue, Capodilupo, et al., 2007), individuals (both multiracial and monoracial) may have a more difficult time in identifying racism and may not recognize when subtle discrimination occurs.

This phenomenon of racism becoming more subtle and covert has been given the name "racial microaggressions" and has become more pervasive in the fields of psychology and education (e.g., Nadal, 2008; Solórzano, Ceja, & Yosso, 2000; Sue, Capodilupo, et al., 2007). Racial microaggressions are defined as "brief and commonplace daily verbal, behavioral, or environmental indignities, whether intentional or unintentional, that communicate hostile, derogatory, or negative racial slights and insults to the target person or group" (Sue, Capodilupo, et al., 2007, p. 273). These experiences occur daily, are commonplace, and are often invisible to the perpetrator of the microaggression because of unconscious bias (e.g., Banaji & Greenwald, 1994), an overall lack of awareness of racial issues (Sue, Capodilupo, et al., 2007), or both. Microaggressions may be invisible to the victims (or recipients) as well, as subtle insults or put-downs cannot always be attributed to the victim's race. As a result, recipients of microaggressions often feel a catch-22 of whether or not to respond to the microaggression. If they do respond and address the enactor of the microaggression, the interaction may lead to psychological stress or potential physical threat. If they choose not to respond, they may perseverate about the incident and feel psychological distress for not voicing their concern (Nadal, in press). Feeling the weight of these cumulative, everyday microaggressions has been shown to have detrimental psychological impacts on people of color (e.g., Sue, Bucceri, Lin, Nadal, & Torino, 2007; Sue, Capodilupo, & Holder, 2008; Sue, Nadal, et al., 2008).

Sue, Capodilupo, and colleagues (2007) have proposed a taxonomy of racial microaggressions consisting of several categories including micro-assaults (namely, conscious or explicit verbal and behavioral interactions), microinsults (unintentional demeaning actions or remarks about one's racial heritage), and microinvalidations (actions that invalidate a person's racial reality). Several types of microaggressions fall within each category. A Latina/o person being angrily told to "go back where you came from" could be identified as a microassault. Microinsults may include an African American person being told with surprise that she or he is "very articulate" or an Asian American person being assumed to be good at math and science. A person of color being told that "racism doesn't exist" or that she or he "complains about racism too much" are illustrations of micro-invalidations. These few examples of microaggressions have been well documented in counseling practice and everyday life (see Sue, Capodilupo, et al. for a review).

While most of the research on microaggressions has focused on race and racism, others have expanded notions to include microaggressions based on gender (e.g., Nadal, 2010; Capodilupo et al., Chapter 9 in this volume), sexual orientation or transgender status (e.g., Nadal, 2008; Nadal, Rivera, & Corpus, Chapter 10 in this volume), ability (e.g., Keller & Galgay, Chapter 11 in this volume), and religion (Nadal, 2008; Nadal, Issa, Griffin, Hamit, & Lyons, Chapter 13 in this volume). Microaggression taxonomies for all of these oppressed groups are created, following the original taxonomy on microaggressions. This framework on microaggressions presents a compelling way to view the everyday lives of multiracial people, whose experiences have been excluded by previous research on racial microaggressions targeting students of color (Solórzano, Allen, & Carroll, 2002), African Americans (Solórzano et al., 2000; Sue, Capodilupo, & Holder, 2008; Sue, Nadal, et al., 2008), Asian Americans (Sue, Bucceri, et al., 2007), and Latina/o Americans (Rivera, Forquer, & Rangel, Chapter 3 in this volume; Solórzano, 1998). Some of these studies (e.g., Sue, Bucceri, et al., 2007) may have included multiracial participants but do not explicitly identify them as multiracial persons, or they focus solely on participants' general experiences with race and not on their specific race-related experiences as multiracial persons.

The lack of inclusion of multiracial people has been a common thread in discussions on race and racism (Spickard & Daniel, 2004; Wijeyesinghe, 2001). This exclusion may be an example of a microaggression itself, sending an indirect message that multiracial persons' experiences with racism are minimal when compared to their monoracial counterparts (Root, 1990). Excluding multiracial people from the scholarship on racial microaggressions may stem from a longer history of *monoracism*, or what this article defines as a social system of psychological inequality where individuals who do not fit monoracial categories may be oppressed on systemic and inter-personal levels because of underlying assumptions and beliefs in singular, discrete racial categories. Thus, it is important to recognize that previous studies on microaggressions may not be representative for multiracial people, because their potentially unique experiences have been excluded from such studies.

Furthermore, multiracial people may be targets of "traditional" racial microaggressions (or microaggressions based on perceptions of one's race or phenotype as a person of color) in addition to multiracial microaggressions, which are daily verbal, behavioral, or environmental indignities, whether intentional or unintentional, enacted by monoracial persons that communicate hostile, derogatory, or negative slights toward multiracial individuals or groups. For example, if a biracial Asian/Latino man is treated as inferior or receives substandard service, it may be because of his general ascribed status as a person of color and not necessarily due to his multiracial heritage. At the same time, this individual may also hear messages from his family that he is "not Asian enough" or "not Latino enough," which would be considered a microaggression based on his multiracial status. Accordingly, multiracial microaggressions involve individuals' mixed-heritage status and are experienced by multiracial persons of any racial makeup or phenotype.

This chapter disscusses different types of multiracial microaggressions and is divided into three major sections. The first part reviews the literature on the experiences of multiracial people and theorizes how the lens of microaggressions can be applied to multiracial individuals. The second part provides a taxonomy of multiracial microaggressions, citing themes, examples of such themes, and the messages that are conveyed with each. Finally, the third part discusses implications of multiracial microaggressions and provides recommendations for professional practice and future empirical research.

THE CHANGING FACE OF RACE AND RACISM

At the foundation of the concept of multiracial microaggressions is an understanding of the changing face of racism in the United States. Racism has been defined as "a system of advantage based on race and supported by institutional structures, policies, and practices that create and sustain benefits for the dominant white group, and structure discrimination, oppression, and disadvantage for people from targeted racial groups" (Bell, 2007, p. 117). Many scholars have theorized and documented that racism in the United States has been transformed from more old-fashioned or blatant forms of racist incidents to more subtle and covert forms (Dovidio, Gaertner, Kawakami, & Hodson, 2002; McConahay, 1986; Nadal, 2008; Sears, 1988; Sue, Capodilupo, et al., 2007). While documenting and understanding racism in its multiple forms is important for progressing toward equality, there has been less focus on better understanding how the use of rigid racial categories can be considered the "very basis of racism" (Spickard, Fong, & Ewalt, 1995, p. 581). A recent growth of research on the fluid nature of racial categorization (e.g., Doyle & Kao, 2007; Harris & Sim, 2002: Hitlin, Brown, & Elder, 2006) contends that racial identification is not fixed for both monoracial and multiracial individuals. However, there is still a common belief in the essentialist nature of discrete racial categories, which is related to the aforementioned definition of monoracism. As a result of this systemic understanding of racial categories, multiracial persons may experience subtle forms of discrimination in institutional settings and in their everyday interactions.

In order to better understand monoracism, it may be helpful to look at the theory of genderism, or "an ideology that reinforces the negative evaluation of gender non-conformity or an incongruence between sex and gender" (Hill & Willoughby, 2005, p. 534). Bilodeau (2009) expands genderism further and defines it as "a social system of structural inequality with an underlying assumption that there are two, and only two genders" (p. 54). Bilodeau's study on transgender students' experiences in higher education used Queer Theory to understand which variables made college campuses unsafe for transgender students and found the underlying system of the gender categories themselves to be oppressive toward transgender and gender non-conforming persons. These findings on genderism can be translated to the theory of monoracism in that individuals who do not fit monoracial categories may be oppressed on systemic and interpersonal levels. This can be exemplified by previous literature demonstrating that multiracial persons often receive direct or indirect messages to "choose" between their multiple racial identities (e.g., Root, 1990) or feel marginalized (e.g., Stonequist, 1937). The message that is conveyed to multiracial persons is that being monoracial is the norm or ideal and that being multiracial is substandard or different.

THE MULTIRACIAL EXPERIENCE

It is vital to review literature on the multiracial experience as a basis for conceptualizing multiracial individuals' experiences with microaggressions. The next sections outline research on multiracial identity and experiences, multiracial persons' experiences with racism and discrimination, and others' perceptions of multiracial people, which inevitably influence monoracial individuals' likelihood of enacting multiracial microaggressions.

MULTIRACIAL IDENTITY AND EXPERIENCES WITH RACISM

A large body of research on multiracial persons focuses on identity development through one of four approaches: the problem, equivalent, variant, and ecological approaches (Rockquemore, Brunsma, & Delgado, 2009; Thornton & Wason, 1995). *The problem approach* (e.g., Stonequist, 1937) relied on a foundational belief that being a multiracial person presents a problematic social position that generally ends in tragedy. Building on stage models of Black racial identity development (e.g., Cross, 1971), *the equivalent approach* treated Black and White multiracial individuals as equivalent to monoracial Black people, due largely to identity politics after the 1960s civil rights and Black power movements (Rockquemore et al., 2009). *The variant approach* conceptualized multiracial people as their own distinct group, worthy of being studied in unique ways (e.g., Poston, 1990). Lastly, *the ecological approach* (e.g., Root, 1996b; Renn, 2004; Rockquemore, 1999) focused scholarly attention to the contextual influences surrounding identity development rather than the particular identity outcomes.

An example of this ecological approach in the practical setting of higher education is Renn's (2004) ecological model for understanding the identity of mixed-race college students through five "identity patterns." These patterns include *monoracial identity* (choosing only one racial category to identify with), *multiple monoracial identities* (choosing to identify with both racial backgrounds), *multiracial identity* (choosing a term that reflects a multiracial identification, such as "biracial" or "mixed"), *extraracial identity* (opting out of racial categorization by refusing to identify according to such categories), and *situational identity* (identifying differently based on the situations the person is placed in). Renn's patterns, which reflect other models posited by researchers (e.g., Kilson, 2001; Rockquemore & Brunsma, 2002; Wallace, 2001), are important to consider due to the complex nature of racial identity, which is often influenced by other people's reactions to the multiracial person's identity (e.g., Root, 1990; Wijeyesinghe, 2001). These "reactions," or verbal remarks and behavioral actions, are common outlets in which multiracial microaggressions may occur.

Although many studies have focused on the impact of racism on specific racial/ethnic populations, including African Americans, Native Americans, Latinas/os, and Asian Americans (see Sue & Sue, 2008 for a review), few studies have focused on multiracial individuals' experiences with racism. Root (1990) found racism to have an impact on the identity development of multiracial people, stating, "It is the marginal status imposed by society rather than the objective mixed race of biracial individuals which poses a severe stress to positive identity development" (p. 188). However, this racism primarily dealt with a common understanding of racial discrimination based on monoracial status as a person of color. For instance, when a multiracial person who looks phenotypically Black is called the "N-word," she or he is experiencing racial discrimination that may be due to her or his racial appearance.

Some previous studies have documented the hardships and discrimination faced by multiracial individuals, including a lack of social recognition (Nakashima, 1996), isolation and disapproval from extended family (e.g., Root, 1998), exclusion from neighborhood and community (Kerwin

& Ponterotto, 1995; Kerwin, Ponterotto, Jackson, & Harris, 1993), and social isolation (Brown, 1995; Gaskins, 1999). In a review of empirical studies related to psychological outcomes and multiracial individuals, Shih and Sanchez (2005) revealed that 19 out of 28 qualitative studies found their participants feeling predominately positive about their multiracial identity and a relatively high comfort level in dealing with issues relating to their racial identity. Conversely, they also found 14 studies that revealed negative experiences related to racial identity of multiracial individuals. These negative cases dealt largely with a person's inability to develop and define their racial identity. With respect to peer relations, Shih and Sanchez's review also revealed some changes over time in the patterns relating to social acceptance and rejection, with more of the recent studies (from the mid-1990s) documenting social acceptance, which they suggest may be a reflection of changes in the social attitudes of the larger U.S. society regarding race relations. These societal changes may not just affect how multiracial individuals perceive their experiences and identities but may also influence the focus that researchers take on their studies.

In an exploratory study on the issues and experiences of multiracial college students, Nishimura (1998) documented students' experiences growing up with families that negated race as an issue (e.g., being told "color doesn't matter"), but students felt that was unrealistic, because "race was an ever-present issue" (p. 48). In relation to experiences with racism, one student recalled being called a "zebra" in second grade and described it as his first experience with racism. While the other findings from Nishimura's study relate to multiracial students' struggles with identity and feelings of subtle pressure from peers to choose a racial identity, it cannot be distinguished whether these feelings were self-imposed or were reactions to verbal or behavioral actions by peers. Further examining external pressure, Townsend, Markus, and Bergsicker (2009) used an open-ended survey asking multiracial participants to describe a situation where their biracial identity caused them tension and pressure to identify monoracially. Out of their 59 respondents (representing 16 Black/White, 23 Asian/White, and 20 Latino/a/White students), 16.9 percent provided situations that were coded into the category of "racism, prejudice, racial stereotyping." Many more of their respondents mentioned situations involving appearance (28.8%) and dealing with demographic forms (23.7%) forcing the individual to identify with one race. Although the study reports minimal experiences related directly to racism and racial discrimination, it may be hypothesized that multiracial persons may experience subtle, everyday, and covert forms of discrimination. Such instances may be harder to clearly identify as racism, giving more validity to the theoretical argument for using microaggressions to analyze multiracial individuals' experiences with racism.

In a recent dissertation on the identity development of multiracial people, Jackson (2007) found that all of her participants described experiences with racism and discrimination. These were described as being direct (e.g., being called a racial slur) or indirect (e.g., overhearing a racially denigrating joke). While the majority of direct experiences involved being called a racial slur, most were traditionally monoracial slurs (e.g., being called a "Chink" or the "N-word"), while others described specific examples related to their multi-racial background (e.g., being called an "Oreo"). Phenotype is hypothesized to play a major role in racial discrimination, as Root (2001) found that multiracial individuals who were of mixed Asian and Black heritage faced more racism than others who were of mixed Asian and White heritage. Conversely, another study by Brackett and colleagues (2006) found that multiracial White/Black students experienced more prejudice compared to their monoracial Black and monoracial White peers. These findings suggest that not fitting into other people's conceptions of racial categories may lead to experiencing more racial discrimination.

PERCEPTIONS OF MULTIRACIAL PEOPLE

While reviewing multiracial individuals' self-perceived experiences with dis-crimination is important, empirical studies on how others view multiracial people provide an understanding of the monoracist biases, attitudes, and stereotypes (both conscious and unconscious) that may lead to multiracial microaggressions. Building upon previous studies that found others held beliefs that biracial children were socially awkward and ostracized in social settings (Jackman, Wagner, & Johnson, 2001) and that biracial children may have problems with social acceptance (Chelsey & Wagner, 2003), Sanchez and Bonam (2009) examined the potential effects of biracial identity disclosure on evaluator perceptions. In their first two studies, Sanchez and Bonam found that biracial (Black/White and Asian/White) applicants were perceived as being less warm and sometimes less competent when compared to monoracial White and minority (Black and Asian, respectively) applicants. The biracial applicants were also viewed as less qualified for minority scholarships than monoracial minorities. Despite the aforementioned examples of phenotype mediating racial discrimination (e.g., Root, 1990, 2001), Sanchez and Bonam's (2009) findings prove discrimination can occur without any phenotypic cues, leading to negative ratings, perceptions, and assumptions of inferiority of multiracial persons. Moreover, the findings suggest that biracial people who disclose their biracial identity (e.g., on application forms) may be more vulnerable to more negative evaluations than monoracial White or minority individuals, providing a new way of viewing multiracial people's struggle with answering the "race question" on demographic forms.

Examining public representations of multiracial people also offers insight into how they are perceived by others. Thornton (2009) analyzed the question of multiraciality from both predominantly White and Black newspapers and found major differences in views and opinions about mixed-race persons. White newspapers held the new multiracial movement as a symbol of a positive move toward the end of racism and a color-blind society. Conversely, Black newspapers reported the multiracial movement as a threat to the African American community's fight for continued civil rights, largely arguing that mixed Black-White individuals assert a multiracial identity as a way to try to "escape" from Blackness. This threat of potential discrimination or exclusion from a multiracial person's respective communities may lead to some multiracial individuals choosing (whether consciously or unconsciously) to identify with monoracial labels (Shih and Sanchez, 2009). Thus, the large body of research on how multiracial people identify still holds importance in exposing the influences of monoracism on multiracial people.

TOWARD A TAXONOMY OF MULTIRACIAL MICROAGGRESSIONS

Root (2003) provides a list of common issues and experiences of racially mixed people. These "50 experiences" evolved from a questionnaire she developed during a study on biracial siblings from 1996 to 1997. This list provides a comprehensive (though not exhaustive) understanding of commonly (though not unanimously) experienced verbal, behavioral, or environmental actions that often aim to negatively slight multiracial individuals. Because of Root's long history of studying multiraciality from personal, theoretical, and empirical perspectives (see Root, 1990, 1992, 1996a, 1996b, 1998, 2001, 2003), this theoretical chapter uses her list of experiences as a starting point for a taxonomy of multiracial microaggressions.

There are several themes that emerge from Root's (2003) list of 50 experiences. One theme includes being excluded or made to feel isolated. For example, a multiracial person being told "You aren't Black, Latina/o, Asian, Native...enough" or being treated differently by relatives because of being multiracial both send the indirect message that she or he is inferior to monoracial people. Other experiences relate to the exoticization of multiracial people, or the idea that a multiracial person's race can be objectified by monoracial people. Examples include being told "You look exotic" or hearing "Mixed-race people are so beautiful or handsome." Other experiences relate to when others deny a person's multiracial reality. For instance, the experience of a biracial Black/White person being accused of "acting or wanting to be White" implies that the person is not allowed to act/be White, even if that is part of his or her heritage. Related to this idea are a group of experiences that assume a person is monoracial. Examples include people saying things in a multiracial person's presence that they might not say if they knew how that person racially identified or having your mother assumed to be your nanny or babysitter. Another theme that emerged was the pathologizing of a multiracial person's identity or experiences. This occurs when multiracial people are viewed as psychologically abnormal, like the common adage "But what about the children?" in response to common problematic views of the products of interracial marriages (Childs, 2006). The assumption is that multiracial people are confused about their identity or have a harder time figuring it out than others.

Given the well-documented experiences of multiracial individuals, we propose a taxonomy of multiracial microaggressions, or microaggressions based on multiracial status, which send hostile, derogatory, or negative messages toward multiracial persons. Examples of multiracial microaggressions from everyday life (see Table 6.1) and in clinical practice (see Table 6.2) are included. Based on the literature on multiracial persons' feelings of "otherness" (e.g., Root, 1990; Weisman, 1996), being forced to choose (e.g., Buckley & Carter, 2004; Hall, 1992; Herman, 2004; Townsend et al., 2009), and overall experiences with racism (e.g., Jackson, 2007), there were five categories of microaggressions identified: (1) exclusion or isolation, (2) exoticization and objectification, (3) assumption of monoracial or mistaken identity, (4) denial of multiracial reality, and (5) pathologizing of identity and experiences. Re-examining Root's (2003) "Issues and Experiences of Racially Mixed People" and combining with other studies on the experiences of multiracial people, the following section provides further details and examples of the types of microaggressions that multiracial people may face based on their multiracial status or identity.

Category 1, *exclusion or isolation*, occurs when multiracial persons are made to feel excluded or isolated based on their multiracial statuses. Several subthemes might fall within this category, including (1) questioning authenticity, (2) the endorsement of a monoracial society and norms, and (3) the second-class status and treatment of multiracial people. It is common for multiracial people to be *questioned on their authenticity*, which is exemplified by being told "You aren't (insert race here) enough." This is a common experience for many multiracial people and can be viewed as exclusionary; the indirect message sent is that someone is different or substandard because she or he isn't monoracial. Some examples of types of microaggressions that fall under the subtheme of *endorsement of a monoracial society and norms* include demographic forms and applications that ask for a single race. Answering the "race question" on such forms is a common thread of multiracial experiences (Townsend et al., 2009), but it can also be viewed as an environmental microaggression. The institution or individual who is

Table 6.1
Examples of Multiracial Microaggressions in Everyday Life

Theme	Example	Message
Exclusion or isolation: occurs when a multiracial person is made to feel excluded or isolated based on their multiracial status	A multiracial person is told "You have to choose; you can't be both."	You are not being authentic, because you don't fit.
	A multiracial person has difficulty filling out a form that asks for a single race only.	You do not fit monoracial society's norms.
	A multiracial person is not accepted by grandparent(s) or relatives because of their parents' interracial relationship.	You have a second-class status because of your multiracial identity.
Exoticization and objectification: occurs when a multiracial person is dehumanized or treated like an object	A multiracial person is asked "What are you?"	You are not normal, and it is okay for me to ask you about it.
	A multiracial person is told "Mixed-race people are so beautiful."	Your features are exotic and beautiful and can be sexually objectified.
	A multiracial person is told "We all will be like you someday."	You are the poster child for a post-racial society or the "racialized ideal."
Assumption of monoracial identity (or mistaken identity): occurs when multiracial people are assumed or mistaken to be monoracial (or a member of a group they do not identify with)	A multiracial person witnesses comments others might not say if they knew how the person identified racially.	Everyone in the group must be monoracial; it's okay to make comments about other groups.
	A multiracial person's mother is assumed to be a nanny or babysitter, or father is assumed to be an older boyfriend.	You must not be related to either one of your parents because you do not look like them.
Denial of multiracial reality: occurs when a multiracial person is not allowed to choose their own racial identity	A multiracial person is subjected to competition over "claims" from different racial or ethnic groups.	How you choose to identify does not matter; it's about who claims you.
	A multiracial person is accused of "acting or wanting to be White."	You're not allowed to act White, even if that is part of your heritage.
Pathologizing of identity and experiences: occurs when multiracial people's identities or experiences are viewed as psychologically abnormal	A multiracial person overhears someone say "All multiracial people have issues."	If you identify as multiracial, you must be confused about your identity.
	A multiracial person is told "You are a mistake."	Interracial families are not normal and must be because the mother accidentally got pregnant.

Table 6.2
Examples of Multiracial Microaggressions in Clinical Practice

Theme	Example	Message
Exclusion or isolation: occurs when a multiracial client is made to feel excluded or isolated based on his/her multiracial status	A multiracial Asian/Black client is asked "Why are you here?" when attending an Asian American community mental health center.	You do not belong.
Exoticization and objectification: occurs when a multiracial client is dehumanized or treated like an object	When a multiracial client discusses low self-esteem with her physical appearance, a counselor responds, "But your looks are so exotic!"	You are not the norm.
Assumption of monoracial identity (or mistaken identity): occurs when multiracial clients are assumed or mistaken to be monoracial (or members of a group they do not identify with)	A counselor speaks to a multiracial Asian/White client in Spanish.	Your physical appearance doesn't match what it should.
Denial of multiracial reality: occurs when a multiracial client is not allowed to choose his/her own racial identity	A monoracial therapist tells a multiracial client that her experiences with race are "probably all in her head."	Your experiences aren't valid.
Pathologizing of identity and experiences: occurs when multiracial clients' identities or experiences are viewed as psychologically abnormal	A counselor constantly brings up racial issues in therapy to a multiracial client, despite its not being the presenting problem.	Your confusion about your identity must impact your mental well-being.

gathering this information (e.g., college admissions, research surveys, etc.) is unconsciously endorsing a monoracial society, leaving multiracial people to feel excluded or isolated. Also related to exclusion and isolation are the ways that multiracial people are treated that make them feel isolated based on a perceived *second-class status*. This happens broadly when multiracial people might be well liked by their peers but kept at a distance in intimate relationships (Root, 1990). However, the more common experience in second-class status relates to family relationships. For instance, a multiracial person cut off by grandparent(s) or relatives because of being a product of an interracial relationship (Root). This second-class treatment sends the message to multiracial people that they do not fit in society (or even their family) and are therefore excluded.

Category 2, *exoticization and objectification*, occurs when a multiracial person is dehumanized or treated like an object. The ubiquitous experience of being asked "What are you?" (e.g., Gaskins, 1999) is a prime example of potentially making multiracial persons feel dehumanized and abnormal, with a person's phenotype usually playing a significant role in these types of microaggressions (Wijeyesinghe, 2001). Several subthemes emerged within this category, including microaggressions that (1) put race on display, (2) objectify multiracial people sexually, or (3) use multiracial people as the "poster children" for the future, or in other terms, objectifying multiracial people as the "racialized ideal." The idea of *putting race on display* relates to the fact that a multiracial person's self-disclosure is viewed as a public event (Buckley & Carter, 2004) in which others feel entitled to ask multiracial people questions about their background that would not normally be asked of nonmultiracial people. Another subtheme is when multiracial people are *objectified sexually*. Being told "You look exotic" or "All mixed-race people are so good-looking" are common experiences that denigrate multiracial people (particularly women) and treat them as sexualized objects (Root, 1990). Similarly, a monoracial person may say "I want to marry someone of another race so that I can have beautiful babies," which further exoticizes multiracial persons and values only their physical appearance. Such biases may be the result of another subtheme of *multiracial people as the "racialized ideal."* Being told "You have the best of both worlds" or hearing someone say "Everyone will be multiracial one day" objectifies multiracial people as the poster children of a post-racial society. Moreover, in an era of anti–affirmative action legislature and ballot initiatives, multiracial people have been used in the arguments against "checking race boxes," which have been described as being "demeaning to the growing millions of our citizens who are multiracial or multiethnic" (Fryer & Loury, 2005, p. 150).

Category 3, *assumption of monoracial identity (or mistaken identity)*, occurs when multiracial people are assumed or mistaken to be monoracial (or a member of a group they do not identify with). Related to the previous examples of endorsing a monoracial society and norms, people often make assumptions that everyone around them is monoracial. For instance, a biracial Asian/White person may be with a group of White people and witness comments (e.g., racial jokes, slurs, etc.) that are made about Asian people because the others do not know the biracial person's heritage. The message is that everyone is monoracial and it is okay to make negative comments about other groups. These microaggressions often result when others view a multiracial person with one of their parents and make assumptions about their relationships. For example, a biracial Latino/White child is seen with his Latina mother, and his friends assume the mother is a nanny or babysitter, or a biracial Black/White young woman is seen with her

White father, who is assumed to be an older boyfriend. The message is that they must not be related because monoracial heritage is the norm and family members must be of the same race.

Category 4, *denial of multiracial reality and experiences*, occurs when multiracial persons are not allowed to choose their own racial identities. This category differs from the previous category on assumptions of a monoracial identity in that the enactor of the microaggression is usually aware of the multiracial person's mixed heritage. Despite this awareness, in these microaggressions, multiracial people are still denied the freedom to create their own multiracial reality. This may happen when a multiracial person is subjected to people of different racial groups competing to "claim" the multiracial person for their own group. Comedian Dave Chappelle brought this idea to public attention during his "racial draft" skit on *Chappelle's Show*, where Black and Asian groups competed to claim Tiger Woods for their own groups (Bell-Jordan, 2007). Although in the skit the fictional Tiger Woods is ecstatic about finally being "part of a race" (Bell-Jordan, p. 82), the real-life implications send a message to multiracial people that it does not matter how they choose to identify but rather that the power comes from the community or family who claims the individual. This is supported by previous literature, which has supported that multiracial people "find themselves continually defined by people other than themselves" (Spickard, 2007, p. 394). Another example of this type of microaggression is a multiracial person who is accused of "acting or wanting to be White." The message to that person is that she or he is not allowed to act or be White, even if that is part of the person's heritage. Allowing multiracial people to identify however they want has been posited as a right (Root, 1996a), and the denial of that chosen identity has been demonstrated to have negative effects on a multiracial person's motivation and self-esteem (Townsend et al., 2009).

Category 5, *pathologizing of identity or experiences*, occurs when multiracial persons' identities or experiences are viewed as psychologically abnormal. This category is similar to Sue, Capodilupo, and colleagues' (2007) *pathologizing of cultural values or communication styles* but targets a person's multiracial identity itself (or any experiences related to being multiracial), regardless of one's cultural values or communication styles. This idea relates to the stereotype of the "tragic mulatto" caught between racial groups and destined to fail (see Mafe, 2008; Raimon, 2004) or the "marginal man" theory (see Park, 1928; Stonequist, 1937), which viewed a biracial person as living in-between two distinct peoples (races) but never being fully accepted by either group. The legacies of these archetypes and theories perpetuate conceptions that a multiracial person (usually Black/White) is faced (or will be faced) with so many obstacles in which she or he must live life at the margins or end in tragedy. There are two subthemes emerging under this category: (1) psychopathology and (2) family pathology. Examples of psychopathology microaggressions include a multiracial person overhearing someone say "All multiracial people have issues" or a counselor or psychologist who constantly brings up racial issues in counseling sessions, despite the multiracial person's presenting problems not stemming from racial issues. The messages in these examples are that multiracial people are confused about their identity, and that confusion manifests itself in their mental well-being. Examples of family pathology microaggressions include a multiracial person being told "You were a mistake" or asked "How did that happen?" (in response to their heritage). The messages that are sent are that interracial relationships (and multiracial children) are wrong and abnormal. Furthermore, being the product of an interracial union may also be viewed as deviant. For instance, if the person has a White father and an Asian mother, outsiders may assert the father had an "Asian fetish." These families are viewed as being atypical, sending messages that being multiracial is inferior or unacceptable.

DISCUSSION

The proposed taxonomy of multiracial microaggressions aligns with the previous literature on monoracial microaggressions in a number of ways. First, similar to previous microaggression research, many of these microaggression incidents may be unconscious to the enactor in that she or he may not realize the impact that her or his statements or behaviors may have on the recipient. In fact, many of these statements may be intended to be compliments, and the enactor of such microaggressions may not understand why a multiracial person would be upset or offended. For example, telling a multiracial person that she or he is exotic may be intended to send a message that one is physically attractive. However, when such words are used, multiracial individuals may feel objectified or dehumanized in that they are only being recognized for their physical appearances. These experiences of objectification align with research on Asian Americans (see Sue, Bucceri, et al., 2007), women (see Capodilupo et al., Chapter 9 in this volume), and Lesbian, Gay, Bisexual, Transgender, and Queer (LGBTQ) persons (see Nadal et al., Chapter 10 in this volume), who often report anger, frustration, or resentment when they feel objectified. These unconscious and unintentional biases can be exemplified with many of the other multiracial microaggression categories as well, including denying multiracial identity and experiences or assumption of monoracial identity.

Similarly, the proposed taxonomy on multiracial microaggressions includes the same types of microaggressions that were proposed with racial

microaggressions: (1) microassaults, (2) microinsults, and (3) microinvalidations. When multiracial persons are told by a monoracial person that "all
multiracial people have issues" or when a grandparent refuses to interact
with her or his multiracial grandchild, the enactors of such microaggressions
are likely conscious of their biases and their actions. While their behaviors
may not be physically assaultive or threatening, such acts can be viewed as
microassaults and may have damaging mental health impacts on their
recipients. Microinsults occur when multiracial individuals are indirectly
insulted through statements and behaviors (e.g., when a multiracial person's
racial heritage is put on display by consistently being asked "What are
you?"). Although these inquiries may seem innocuous, hearing them on a
regular basis is something that monoracial persons may not experience,
which may result in a unique type of stress for multiracial people. Finally,
examples of microinvalidations may include instances when multiracial
persons are told that their experiences with race are not as difficult as
they are for monoracial people of color; such statements deny the reality
of multiracial persons and may also cause psychological distress for the
recipients.

Additionally, multiracial microaggressions may be similar to previously
identified microaggressions in that the recipients may have difficulty in
recognizing microaggressions when they occur. Previous literature has found
that monoracial people of color, women, and LGBTQ persons may struggle
with recognizing when microaggressions occur (see Nadal, 2008, 2010; Sue,
Capodilupo, & Holder, 2008; Sue, Capodilupo, et al., 2007 for a review).
Nadal (in press) cites an internal process that recipients of microaggressions
may experience in which individuals may ask themselves the following
questions after they experience a potential microaggression: (1) Did this
microaggression really occur? (2) Should I respond to this microaggression?
(3) How should I respond to this microaggression? The first question
transpires when an individual first recognizes that a microaggression may
have occurred. Some microaggressions may be easier to recognize than others.
For example, being told "You are not Black enough" may be easier to label as a
microaggression than situations where multiracial persons are treated like a
second-class citizen (e.g., feeling that they are being treated differently than
monoracial peers). The latter exemplifies incidents where it may be difficult to
pinpoint such behavior as being race related, thus making it harder to label as
a multiracial microaggression.

Secondly, when experiencing a microaggression, the individual must
decide whether she or he should address the microaggression incident. For
example, in the aforementioned examples, the individual may wonder if
confronting the enactor of the microaggression would lead to defensiveness,
an argument, or tension in his/her interpersonal relationship. Accordingly,

they may feel more able to address a microaggression with a loved one than they would with a stranger on the street or an acquaintance (Nadal, in press). Finally, the third question entails the decision of how the person will address an enactor of a microaggression. In some cases, the microaggression recipient may choose to approach the enactor in a calm and collected way in order to prevent a hostile or negative argument; however, in other cases, the recipient may feel the need to be more direct, emotional, or straightforward with her or his response (Nadal, 2010).

It is hypothesized that microaggressions experienced by multiracial persons may also influence one's identity development and coping mechanisms. As aforementioned, Renn (2004) outlined five "identity patterns" for multiracial persons, including (1) monoracial identity, (2) multiple monoracial identities, (3) multiracial identity, (4) extraracial identity, and (5) situational identity. Perhaps multiracial individuals may develop these identity patterns or statuses as a way of coping with the microaggressions that they experience on a regular basis. For example, when a multiracial Latino/White man is excluded by individuals of one of his heritages (e.g., Latino peers or family members tell the multiracial individual that he is "not Latino enough"), it is possible that this individual may reject his Latino heritage and develop a monoracial White identity (e.g., "I'm only White") or an extraracial identity (e.g., "I don't identify with any race"). Conversely, another multiracial individual experiencing the same types of microaggressions may assert a monoracial Latino/a identity (e.g., "I'm only Latino/a") in that she or he may try to "act more Latino/a" in order to avoid being rejected or excluded in the future. Multiracial microaggressions may also lead to a situational identity pattern in that individuals may learn to adapt to particular group or cultural norms or "pass" within particular racial groups in order to prevent experiencing microaggressions in the future.

IMPLICATIONS FOR THEORY, RESEARCH, AND CLINICAL PRACTICE

There are several implications that this taxonomy on multiracial micro-aggressions has on theory, research, and clinical practice. First, including multiracial microaggressions into the literature is necessary in order to understand the ways in which microaggressions impact individuals of all oppressed groups, particularly multiracial persons and other subgroups who are often ignored or overlooked. Multiracial persons are becoming an increasingly larger population in the United States, and it becomes an ethical responsibility to further incorporate this population into the dis-course on multicultural and race-related issues. Future research on micro-aggressions must include multiracial and monoracial persons' experiences, citing the similarities and differences that are faced by individuals of both groups. Further studies may employ both qualitative and quantitative methods to examine the influences of microaggressions on multiracial persons. It may be beneficial to empirically support how multiracial micro-aggressions may impact an array of mental health variables, such as self-esteem, identity development, psychological distress, and other psychological disorders.

Furthermore, training programs of psychology and other helping professions must include multiracial issues in multicultural competence models. First, psychologists and other practitioners must become knowledgeable about the experiences of multiracial persons by understanding the psychological stressors that mixed-race people may experience by virtue of belonging to one or more racial groups. Practitioners must be specifically informed about the experiences and psychological outcomes of multiracial microaggressions in order to prevent these from occurring in clinical settings. Second, counselors and clinicians must be aware of multicultural dynamics that may occur in psychotherapy settings, particularly with monoracial-multiracial dyads. When monoracial practitioners interact with their clients, they must be conscious of the ways in which their monoracial identities may influence their biases, assumptions, and attitudes about multiracial persons, while recognizing the privilege that they have as monoracial individuals. By exposing multiracial microaggressions in everyday interpersonal interactions (and particularly in clinical settings), it is anticipated that such monoracism in systems, institutions, and relationships may be minimized, promoting positive mental health of all multiracial persons.

REFERENCES

Banaji, M. R., & Greenwald, A. G. (1994). Implicit stereotyping and prejudice. In M. P. Zanna & J. M. Olson (Eds.), *The psychology of prejudice: The Ontario Symposium* (Vol. 7, pp. 55–76). Hillsdale, NJ: Erlbaum.

Bell, L. A. (2007). Overview: Twenty-first century racism. In M. Adams, L. A. Bell, & P. Griffin (Eds.), *Teaching for diversity and social justice* (2nd ed., pp. 117–122). New York: Routledge.

Bell-Jordan, K. E. (2007). Speaking fluent "joke": Pushing the racial envelope through comedic performance on *Chappelle's Show. Performance Research, 12*(3), 74–90.

Bilodeau, B. L. (2009). *Genderism: Transgender students, binary systems and higher education.* Saarbrücken, Germany: VDM Verlag.

Brackett, K. P., Marcus, A., McKenzie, N. J., Mullins, L. C., Tang, Z., & Allen, A. M. (2006). The effects of multiracial identification on students' perceptions of racism. *Social Science Journal, 43,* 437–444.

Brown, U. M. (1995). Black/White interracial young adults: Quest for racial identity. *American Journal of Orthopsychiatry, 65,* 125–130.

Buckley, T. A., & Carter, R. T. (2004). Biracial (Black/White) women: A qualitative study of racial attitudes and beliefs and their implications for therapy. *Women & Therapy, 27*(1/2), 45–64.

Chelsey, G. L., & Wagner, W. G. (2003). Adults' attitudes toward multiracial children. *Journal of Black Psychology, 29*, 463–480.

Childs, E. C. (2006). Black and White: Family opposition to becoming multiracial. In D. L. Brunsma (Ed.), *Mixed messages: Multiracial identity in the color-blind era* (pp. 233–246). Boulder, CO: Lynne Rienner Publishers, Inc.

Cross, W. E. (1971). The Negro-to-Black conversion experience: Toward a psychology of Black liberation. *Black World, 20*, 13–27.

DaCosta, K. M. (2007). *Making multiracials: State, family, and market in the redrawing of the color line*. Stanford, CA: Stanford University Press.

Dovidio, J. F., Gaertner, S. L., Kawakami, K., & Hodson, G. (2002). Why can't we all just get along? Interpersonal biases and interracial distrust. *Cultural Diversity and Ethnic Minority Psychology, 8*, 88–102.

Doyle, J. M., & Kao, G. (2007). Are racial identities of multiracials stable? Changing self-identification among single and multiple race individuals. *Social Psychology Quarterly, 70*(4), 405–423.

Fryer, R. G., Jr., & Loury, G. C. (2005). Affirmative action and its mythology. *Journal of Economic Perspectives, 19*(3), 147–162.

Gaskins, P. (1999). *What are you? Voices of mixed-race young people*. New York: Holt.

Hall, C. C. I. (1992). Please choose one: Ethnic identity choices for biracial individuals. In M. P. P. Root (Ed.), *Racially mixed people in America* (pp. 250–264). Newbury Park, CA: Sage.

Harris, D. R., & Sim, J. J. (2002). Who is multiracial? Assessing the complexity of lived race. *American Sociological Review, 67*, 614–627.

Herman, M. (2004). Forced to choose: Some determinants of racial identification in multiracial adolescents. *Child Development, 75*, 730–748.

Hill, D. B., & Willoughby, B. L. B. (2005). The development and validation of the Genderism and Transphobia Scale. *Sex Roles, 53*(7/8), 531–544.

Hitlin, S., Brown, J. S., & Elder, G. H., Jr. (2006). Racial self-categorization in adolescence: Development and social pathways. *Child Development, 77*, 1298–1308.

Jackman, C. F., Wagner, G. W., & Johnson, J. T. (2001). The Attitudes toward Multiracial Children Scale. *Journal of Black Psychology, 27*, 86–99.

Jackson, K. F. (2007). Beyond race: Examining the cultural identity of multiracial individuals. *Dissertation Abstracts International, Section A: Humanities and Social Sciences, 68*(5-A), 2172.

Kerwin, C., & Ponterotto, J. G. (1995). Biracial identity development. In J. G. Ponterotto, J. M. Casas, L. A. Suzuki, & C. M. Alexander (Eds.), *Handbook of multicultural counseling* (pp. 199–217). Thousand Oaks, CA: Sage.

Kerwin, C., Ponterotto, J. G., Jackson, B. L., & Harris, A. (1993). Racial identity in biracial children: A qualitative investigation. *Journal of Counseling Psychology, 40*, 221–223.

Kilson, M. (2001). *Claiming place: Biracial young adults in the post-civil rights era*. Westport, CT: Bergin & Garvey.

Lee, J. (2008). A post-racial America? Multiracial identification and the color line in the 21st century. *Nanzan Review of American Studies, 30*, 13–31.

Mafe, D. (2008). Self-made women in a (racist) man's world: The "tragic" lives of Nella Larson and Bessie Head. *English Academy Review, 25*(1), 66–76.

McConahay, J. B. (1986). Modern racism, ambivalence, and the Modern Racism Scale. In J. F. Dovidio & S. L. Gaertner (Eds.), *Prejudice, discrimination and racism* (pp. 91–126). Orlando, FL: Academic Press.

Morning, A. (2003). New faces, old faces: Counting the multiracial population past and present. In L. I. Winters & H. L. DeBose (Eds.), *New faces in a changing America: Multiracial identity in the 21st century* (pp. 41–67). Thousand Oaks, CA: Sage.

Nadal, K. L. (2008). Preventing racial, ethnic, gender, sexual minority, disability, and religious microaggressions: Recommendations for promoting positive mental health. *Prevention in Counseling Psychology: Theory, Research, Practice and Training, 2*(1), 22–27.

Nadal, K. L. (2010). Gender microaggressions: Implications for mental health. In M. A. Paludi (Ed.), *Feminism and Women's Rights Worldwide, Volume 2: Mental and Physical Health* (pp. 155–175). Santa Barbara, CA: Praeger.

Nadal, K. L. (in press) Responding to racial, gender, and sexual orientation microaggressions in the workplace. In M. Paludi, E. DeSouza, & C. Paludi, Jr. (Eds.), *The Praeger handbook on workplace discrimination: Legal, management, and social science perspectives*. Westport, CT: Praeger.

Nadal, K. L., Issa, M. A., Leon, J., Wideman, M., Meterko, V. M., & Wong, Y. (2010). *Sexual orientation microaggressions: A qualitative study*.

Nakashima, C. L. (1996). Voices from the movement: Approaches to multiraciality. In M. P. P. Root (Ed.), *The multiracial experience: Racial borders as the new frontier* (pp. 79–97). Thousand Oaks, CA: Sage.

Navarro, M. (2008, March 31). Who are we? New dialogue on mixed race. *New York Times*. Retrieved July 6, 2009, from http://www.nytimes.com/2008/03/31/us/politics/31race.html#.

Nishimura, N. J. (1998). Assessing the issues of multiracial students on college campuses. *Journal of College Counseling, 1*, 45–53.

Park, R. E. (1928). Human migration and the marginal man. *American Journal of Sociology, 33*, 881–893.

Poston, W. S. C. (1990). The biracial identity development model: A needed addition. *Journal of Counseling and Development, 69*, 152–155.

Raimon, E. A. (2004). *The "tragic mulatta" revisited: Race and nationalism in nineteenth-century antislavery fiction*. New Brunswick, NJ: Rutgers University Press.

Renn, K. A. (2004). *Mixed race students in college: The ecology of race, identity, and community*. Albany: State University of New York Press.

Rockquemore, K. A. (1999). Between Black and White: Exploring the biracial experience. *Race and Society, 1*, 197–212.

Rockquemore, K. A., & Brunsma, D. L. (2002). *Beyond Black: Biracial identity in America*. Thousand Oaks, CA: Sage.

Rockquemore, K. A., Brunsma, D. L., & Delgado, D. J. (2009). Racing to theory or retheorizing race? Understanding the struggle to build a multiracial identity theory. *Journal of Social Issues*, 65(1), 13–34.

Root, M. P. P. (1990). Resolving "other" status: Identity development of biracial individuals. *Women and Therapy*, 9, 185–205.

Root, M. P. P. (Ed.). (1992). *Racially mixed people in America*. Newbury Park, CA: Sage.

Root, M. P. P. (1996a). A bill of rights for racially mixed people. In M. P. P. Root (Ed.), *The multiracial experience: Racial borders as the new frontier* (pp. 3–14). Thousand Oaks, CA: Sage.

Root, M. P. P. (1996b). The multiracial experience: Racial borders as the significant frontier in race relations. In M. P. P. Root (Ed.), *The multiracial experience: Racial borders as the new frontier* (pp. xii–xxviii). Thousand Oaks, CA: Sage.

Root, M. P. P. (1998). Experiences and processes affecting racial identity development: Preliminary results from the Biracial Sibling Project. *Cultural Diversity and Mental Health*, 4, 237–247.

Root, M. P. P. (2001). Factors influencing the variation in racial and ethnic identity of mixed-heritage persons of Asian ancestry. In T. K. Williams-Leon & C. L. Nakashima (Eds.), *The sum of our parts: Mixed heritage Asian Americans* (pp. 61–70). Philadelphia, PA: Temple University.

Root, M. P. P. (2003). Issues and experiences of racially mixed people. In M. P. P. Root & M. Kelly (Eds.), *The multiracial child resource book: Living complex identities* (pp. 132–134). Seattle, WA: Mavin Foundation.

Sanchez, D. T., & Bonam, C. M. (2009). To disclose or not to disclose biracial identity: The effect of biracial disclosure on perceiver evaluations and target responses. *Journal of Social Issues*, 65(1), 129–148.

Sears, D. O. (1988). Symbolic racism. In P. A. Katz & D. A. Taylor (Eds.), *Eliminating racism: Profiles in controversy* (pp. 53–84). New York: Plenum.

Shih, M., & Sanchez, D. T. (2005). Perspectives and research on the positive and negative implications of having multiple racial identities. *Psychological Bulletin*, 131, 569–591.

Shih, M., & Sanchez, D. T. (2009). When race becomes more complex: Towards understanding the landscape of multiracial identity and experiences. *Journal of Social Issues*, 65, 1–11.

Solórzano, D. (1998). Critical race theory, racial and gender microaggressions, and the experiences of Chicana and Chicano scholars. *International Journal of Qualitative Studies in Education*, 11, 121–136.

Solórzano, D., Allen, W., & Carroll, G. (2002). Keeping race in place: Racial microaggressions and campus racial climate at the University of California, Berkeley. *UCLA Chicano/Latino Law Review*, 23 (Spring), 15–112.

Solórzano, D., Ceja, M., & Yosso, T. (2000). Critical race theory, racial microaggressions, and campus racial climate: The experiences of African American college students. *Journal of Negro Education*, 69, 60–73.

Spickard, P. R. (2007). What must I be? Asian Americans and the question of multiethnic identity. In M. Zhou & J. V. Gatewood (Eds.), *Contemporary Asian*

America: A multidisciplinary reader (2nd ed., pp. 393–407). New York: New York University Press.

Spickard, P. R., & Daniel, G. R. (Eds.). (2004). *Racial thinking in the United States: Uncompleted independence.* Notre Dame, IN: University of Notre Dame Press.

Spickard, P. R., Fong, R., & Ewalt, P. L. (1995). Undermining the very basis of racism: Its categories. *Social Work, 40,* 581–584.

Stonequist, E. V. (1937). *The marginal man: A student in personality and culture conflict.* New York, NY: Russell & Russell.

Sue, D. W., Bucceri, J. M., Lin, A. I., Nadal, K. L., & Torino, G. C. (2007). Racial microaggressions and the Asian American experience. *Cultural Diversity and Ethnic Minority Psychology, 13*(1), 72–81.

Sue, D. W., Capodilupo, C. M., & Holder, M. B. (2008). Racial microaggressions in the life experience of Black Americans. *Professional Psychology: Research and Practice, 39,* 329–336.

Sue, D. W., Capodilupo, C. M., Torino, G. C., Bucceri, J. M., Holder, A. M., Nadal, K. L., & Esquilin, M. (2007). Racial microaggressions in everyday life: Implications for counseling. *American Psychologist, 62*(4), 271–286.

Sue, D. W., Nadal, K. L., Capodilupo, C. M., Lin, A. I., Torino, G. C., & Rivera, D. P. (2008). Racial microaggressions against Black Americans: Implications for counseling. *Journal of Counseling & Development, 86,* 330–338.

Sue, D. W., & Sue, D. (2008). *Counseling the culturally diverse* (5th ed.). Hoboken, NJ: John Wiley & Sons.

Thomas, D. A., & Jackson, J. L., Jr. (2008). Politics and the shifting boundaries of Blackness. *Transforming Anthropology, 16,* 93–94.

Thornton, M. C. (2009). Policing the borderlands: White- and Black-American newspaper perceptions of multiracial heritage and the idea of race, 1996–2006. *Journal of Social Issues, 65,* 105–127.

Thornton, M., & Wason, S. (1995). Intermarriage. In D. Levinson (Ed.), *Encyclopedia of marriage and the family* (pp. 396–402). New York: Macmillan Publishing.

Townsend, S. S. M., Markus, H. R., & Bergsicker, H. B. (2009). My choice, your categories: The denial of multiracial identities. *Journal of Social Issues, 65,* 185–204.

Wallace, K. R. (2001). Relative/outsider: The art and politics of identity among mixed heritage students. Westport, CT: Ablex.

Weisman, J. R. (1996). An "other" way of life: The empowerment of alterity in the interracial individual. In M. P. P. Root (Ed.), *The multiracial experience: Racial borders as the new frontier* (pp. 152–164). Thousand Oaks, CA: Sage.

Wijeyesinghe, C. L. (2001). Racial identity in multiracial people: An alternative paradigm. In C. L. Wijeyesinghe & B. W. Jackson (Eds.), *New perspectives on racial identity development: A theoretical and practical anthology.* New York: New York University Press.

CHAPTER 7

Microaggressions and the Pipeline for Scholars of Color

FERNANDO GUZMAN, JESUS TREVINO,
FERNAND LUBUGUIN, and BUSHRA ARYAN

I NSTITUTIONS OF HIGHER learning are beginning to acknowledge that one of the hallmarks of a great university is a diverse community of scholars, staff, and students dedicated to the preparation of leaders who can live and work in highly pluralistic and complex environments (Bowen & Bok, 1998). As such, institutions of higher learning across the United States continue to expend tremendous resources and efforts to diversify and recruit, retain, and promote more students, staff, and faculty of color into the system of higher education.

In pursuit of campus diversity, one area that has received extra attention over the last several decades is the recruitment and retention of talented scholars of color. For the purpose of this chapter, the term "scholars of color" refers to both doctoral students of color and faculty of color. With respect to faculty of color, research in higher education continues to suggest that the presence of Native American, Latino/a, African American, and Asian American professors exposes students to different perspectives, new and innovative courses, and new and engaging pedagogies (Turner, 2002). Moreover, faculty of color also provide mentoring and role models for both majority and minority students. It is also clear that as majority or White faculty retire, institutions of higher education will increasingly look to recruit faculty of color to replace them (Turner, 2002). The factors just outlined speak loudly about the importance of working toward increasing the presence of faculty of color in the academy.

The Status of the Pipeline

To obtain a better understanding of why there is a need to increase the number of scholars of color, one merely needs to look at the status of the "educational pipeline" for scholars of color, the standard metaphor for the educational journey and progress of people of color as they achieve academically (Ryu, 2008). The total number of doctoral degrees conferred in 2005 was slightly over 56,000. In examining degrees earned by race and ethnicity, out of the total doctoral degrees awarded, Whites earned 29,144 (51.9%), African Americans earned 2,889 (5.1%), Hispanics earned 1,740 (3.1%), Asian Americans earned 2,996 (5.3%), and American Indians earned 214 (0.4%). Taken as a whole, U.S. domestic graduate students of color earned approximately 14 percent of the total doctoral degrees conferred in 2005.

The data for faculty tells a similar story. According to the *Chronicle of Higher Education* Almanac Issue for 2008 to 2009 ("The Nation," 2008), there were a total of 675,624 teaching personnel in the academy, including professors, associate professors, assistant professors, instructors, lecturers, and other teaching professionals. In considering race and ethnicity, approximately 109,964 (16.27%) were African American, Hispanic, Asian American, and American Indian. By rank, racial/ethnic professors numbered 20,856 compared to 145,936 White faculty. African American, American Indian, Asian American, and Hispanic associate professors numbered 22,429 compared to 112,507 White associate professors. The data indicate that the majority of racial/ethnic teaching personnel are located at the assistant professor level, with a total of 31,253. In contrast, there were only 11,157 White assistant professors.

Understanding the low number of scholars of color in the pipeline requires an examination of the challenges that this group faces as they pursue their doctoral degrees, apply for academic positions, and work toward tenure (Padilla, 2003). The literature is replete with barriers and obstacles in the perilous journey that people of color encounter on their way to becoming members of the academy (Aronson & Swanson, 1991; Carter, Pearson, & Shavlik, 1996; Turner, 2002; Turner, 2007). Many of these hazards work to discourage scholars of color from entering and persisting in academia. These range from the lack of mentoring to hostile classroom climates to bias in the tenure review process. And while these factors and others are detrimental to the recruitment and retention of faculty of color, one set of barriers impacting scholars of color that has not received much attention from researchers are racial microaggressions.

Racial Microaggressions

Over the last several decades, the theories and research on contemporary racism suggest that overt expressions of racism have been replaced by more subtle behaviors and actions that lead to the degradation and continued marginalization of people of color (Sue et al., 2007; Williams, 2000). It has been found that this type of prejudice and discrimination manifests itself in unconscious ways and beliefs, often by Whites who believe that they are racially sensitive, liberal, and nonracist (Goodman, 2001; Wise, 2008). Microaggressions are defined as subtle verbal, nonverbal, and visual insults and invalidations directed toward people of color from well-intentioned Whites who respond in both an automatic and unconscious fashion (Solórzano, Ceja, & Yosso, 2000). More specifically, microaggressions occur in everyday interactions between people who represent different groups and convey powerful yet subtle derogatory messages about the subordinate status of marginalized groups. When directed at people of color, these are known as racial microaggressions.

INCLUSIVE EXCELLENCE

Within the context of higher education, racial microaggressions can be theoretically grounded and understood using the inclusive excellence (IE) model, which many U.S. colleges and universities are beginning to utilize to drive their diversity and inclusiveness agendas. The IE concept was developed by the Association of American Colleges and Universities (2002) when it commissioned a set of scholarly papers focusing on the theory and practice of inclusive excellence (Milem, Chang, & Antonio, 2005). Inclusive excellence is about the transformation of our institutions of higher learning by embedding inclusiveness into all aspects and processes of a college or university.

Specific to the focus of this chapter, the IE model consists of several dimensions that have implications for contextualizing microaggressions and their impact on scholars of color: history, compositional diversity, campus intergroup relations and climate (e.g., behavioral and psychological), organizational diversity, and social influences. The model posits that these five dimensions impact the inclusiveness or exclusiveness of the campus (Milem et al., 2005).

1. The historical dimension of the IE framework suggests that an institution's past regarding to what extent it has included or excluded diverse populations impacts the diversity and inclusiveness of a campus. At many colleges and universities, there are still numerous practices, traditions, artwork, norms, and other institutional aspects that send discriminatory and offensive messages to people of color (e.g., stadiums named after slave owners, race-themed parties, degrading racial mascots/symbols for college sports teams, and discriminatory financial aid policies).

2. Compositional diversity speaks strictly to the practice of conceptualizing and pursuing diversity as a number only. That is, many colleges and universities think of diversity as the pursuit of a certain number of people from specific groups that need to be represented on campus. Thus, diversity is reduced to a number that incidentally, the majority finds problematic, because they believe that it is fueled by affirmative action policies, which in turn leads to the recruitment of undeserving and unqualified people. Consequently, faculty, staff, and students of color are constantly bombarded by microaggressions suggesting that their presence on campus is the direct result of a program that promotes mediocrity and incompetence.

3. The corollary to compositional diversity is campus climate. That is, once compositional diversity (e.g., a critical mass) is achieved on campus, what is the status of the climate for diversity and campus intergroup relations? Are students interacting with each other? Are there acts of insensitivity including microaggressions being committed against members of different racial groups? Is the institution welcoming to people from diverse groups? The research in higher education suggests that colleges and universities continue to struggle with less-than-ideal climates for diversity, filled with negative experiences for individuals from multicultural groups.

4. Organizational diversity involves the structural pieces of an institution that promote or discourage inclusiveness (Milem et al., 2005). Policies, procedure, departments, high-level leadership, marketing, communications, finances, and hiring practices are but a few of the organizational dimensions that influence the inclusiveness of a college or university.

5. Finally, societal factors are incidents or issues that occur outside the institution but spill onto the campus. These include debates about social issues (e.g., affirmative action, immigration, globalization), political events (e.g., elections), tragedies (e.g., September 11), and other phenomena that are discussed, debated, or ignored in classes, residence halls, programs, and offices. How these issues are handled on a college campus can determine whether members of diverse communities feel welcome or alienated on campus.

In considering racial microaggressions and the IE model, it is clear that the former can contribute to exclusive and unwelcoming campus environments and can impact inclusiveness and diversity across each of the five IE domains. Over the last several decades, researchers have produced numerous examples of microaggressions related to the history of institutions, compositional diversity, campus climate, organizational diversity, and societal factors. With respect to the focus of this chapter, racial micro-aggressions manifest themselves at different points of the educational pipeline. That is, given that the pipeline is integrally connected to U.S. higher education, it stands to reason that whether one is pursuing a doctoral degree, applying for a faculty position, or working toward tenure, one will encounter microaggressions all along the journey (Sue et al., 2007). These microinsults and invalidations serve to discourage and wear down scholars of color. In the end, it is clear that if we are to increase the number of faculty of color entering the academy, we must gain a greater understanding of the barriers that prevent us from achieving this goal; in particular, racial microaggressions.

MICROAGGRESSIONS ALONG THE PIPELINE

In this chapter, the authors examine microaggressions that scholars of color experience in relation to three parts of the pipeline: doctoral experiences, applying for faculty positions, and pursuing tenure. Using Sue and colleagues' (2007) model for classifying microaggressions, the focus will be on identifying specific examples of microinsults and microinvaldiations that scholars of color experience on their journey to becoming part of the professoriate. In identifying the microaggressions, the authors draw on several resources. First, we draw on the literature examining the experiences of people of color as they move along the pipeline. Much has been written about the challenges that scholars of color confront between the points of pursuing a doctoral degree and achieving tenure. However, while the literature does not specifically label the barriers as microaggressions, many of the documented challenges are in fact and can be defined as such. Second, we also draw on the valuable experiences and insights of the authors.

The lead author (Fernando Guzman) has seven years of experience working as a multicultural talent scout to recruit graduate students of color and faculty of color into the academy, which serves as a critical source for identifying the challenges to and opportunities for diversifying the academy. Moreover, he has extensive experience working with doctoral students and search committees, negotiating contracts, retaining junior faculty, and supporting faculty of color as they undergo the tenure process. We also draw on the 20 years of experiences and knowledge of the second author (Jesus Trevino) as a senior diversity officer with valuable experience in implementing IE at both a large, public, research one institution and a small, private university. From the third author (Fernand Lubuguin), we draw on his experiences as a faculty member of color who is currently working toward tenure and who teaches in the field of counseling psychology. Finally, the chapter benefits from the contributions of a graduate woman of color (Bushra Aryan) who is pursuing her doctoral degree in higher education and conducting research on the experiences of doctoral students of color; in particular, women of color.

In the following section, we identify specific microaggressions directed at scholars of color along the pipeline. We begin with cataloging the incidents and comments experienced by graduate students of color. Next, we present examples of microaggressions that scholars of color have encountered while beginning to look for academic positions. Here, we identify those insults and invalidations ranging from those encountered while visiting a campus and interviewing for positions to the job offer and contract negotiations. Finally, in the last section, microaggressions that scholars of color experience while working toward tenure are presented.

In approaching this section, the reader should keep several ideas in mind. First, the microaggressions presented (in quotes) are simply examples of some of the microinsults and invalidations that have been reported in the literature. The authors believe that these represent only the tip of the iceberg and that readers can and will probably recount numerous and different microaggressions. Second, some of the microinsults and invalidations identified in the section on search committees would not necessarily be said directly to a candidate of color. Rather, these comments have been expressed to the lead author as a faculty recruiter working with search committees.

DOCTORAL EXPERIENCES

In addition to the everyday challenges of pursuing a doctoral degree, doctoral students of color experience specific microaggressions. This section focuses on those incidents.

DISCOURAGEMENT

"You are not cut out for doctoral work. You may want to try some other career. Are you sure you want to go on for a Ph.D.? You can make a good living with a master's degree." For many graduate students of color, the journey in pursuit of a doctoral degree begins with words designed to discourage them from beginning the process (Chesler and Crowfoot, 2000). They often report that they were advised early on by faculty and college advisors not to pursue a doctoral degree. Undergirding these statements of discouragement are the beliefs and assumptions that people of color are not talented or skilled enough to make it through a doctoral program.

QUESTIONING ABILITY AND QUALIFICATIONS

"You speak and write very well, despite being from Mexico." Graduate students of color often find that their academic skills, abilities, and experiences sometimes come as a surprise to members of the majority or are distorted, highlighted, and used against them. The previous microaggression is one that is directed at Latino/a students; however, plenty of examples can be found of similar comments referring to African Americans, Native Americans, and Asian Americans. The message suggests that a student of color is surprisingly talented, despite not being born or raised in the United States, which is a false assumption, and that the group to which he or she belongs is not capable of producing high quality academic work. One student shares,

> *Exacerbating this self-doubt and pressure to represent my entire ethnic group were rumblings among some White students in the program that I was admitted into the program primarily because I was Latino and not for my intellectual capabilities, nor my potential to be an effective counseling psychologist.* (Herrera, 2003, p. 117)

"We are calling to go over your qualifications for the doctoral program. We just want to make sure that you accomplished everything that you wrote down in your application." Graduate students of color also report that the authenticity of their qualifications and accomplishments are constantly challenged by both faculty and fellow students. These range from follow-up phone calls placed to students of color after they have turned in their doctoral program applications in which the applicant's accomplishments are scrutinized to responses that suggest disbelief about the academic and professional experiences of students of color.

"If you are going to make it in this doctoral program, let me give you some advice: You need to speak well and write well. You need to act professionally. Come to class on time." In addition to the microaggressions discussed previously, some graduate students of color have reported being scolded by faculty in their program about their behavior, skills, and talents, the quality of their work, and their overall demeanor. The message to the students is full of demeaning assumptions about the lack of professionalism, abilities, and personal behavior.

"Congratulations on getting accepted to the Ph.D. program. Let me recommend as your advisor that you start with some master's-level courses to nail down your fundamentals. Also, here is a list of academic support services on campus." In addition to being lectured on professional behavior, one of the issues that graduate students of color often confront is low expectations from White faculty members regarding their skills and abilities.

Often, these manifest themselves as encouragement to take lower-level courses as a way of improving their abilities. Low expectations are based on false assumptions that leave the students shocked and dismayed.

"When we have class discussions, you are too theoretically aggressive. Lighten up." On the other hand, being an extremely bright and intelligent graduate student of color sometimes becomes a liability. Many doctoral students of color have reported being sanctioned for engaging in deep theoretical discussions with professors and other students. Often, professors get frustrated and place a pejorative label on the behavior (e.g., "You are too aggressive in your thinking; tone it down"). Instead of using the student's intelligence as a strength, it is used to remind the student that they are out of line (e.g., intellectually elitist) and need to conform to their role as a student.

"Fellow students are complaining that you appear to be angry, particularly during class discussions. What is going on?" Closely tied to this quote are the perceptions held by Whites that people of color are angry with them. Unfortunately, this stereotype plays out when graduate students of color are passionately engaged in classroom discussions. More specifically, some doctoral students of color are accused of behaving and speaking in an angry manner. To remedy the situation, a faculty member is often recruited to "chat" with the student of color to point out that there is a communication problem and that fellow students are complaining about her or his attitude in class. For the most part, the accusations are false and are specifically related to the misperception of passion as anger by Whites.

ASSUMING ETHNIC/RACIAL EXPERTISE

"We need you to explain to us why Asian Americans are quiet and unassuming." Assumptions about the expertise regarding the groups to which they belong and the dynamics of race and ethnicity in the United States play out in the doctoral experience for graduate students of color.

One assumption that members of the majority often make is that all graduate students of color are experts on every aspect of the groups to which they belong (Chesler and Crowfoot, 2000). Thus, by this assumption, every Native American can comment at any moment about any aspect (e.g., economics, history, psychology, sociology, health) of over 500 tribes that reside in the United States. Three issues arise as a result of the incorrect assumption of ethnic/racial expertise. First, assuming that graduate students of color are experts on anything related to their groups is a direct contradiction of the belief that they are not intelligent, talented, and gifted for doctoral work. Second, graduate students of color often report fatigue from the assumption that they know everything and from constantly being asked to represent their group and educate the majority. Third, members of the majority take no responsibility for educating themselves and instead opt to rely heavily on people of color to educate them.

"I know that this is the third committee this year that I have asked you to serve on, but I need the student-of-color perspective." Given the assumption of racial/ethnic expertise, graduate students of color often find themselves serving on too many committees and task forces for the department or university (Castellanos & Jones, 2003). Faculty and administrators overtax the time and energy of the few students of color that have been recruited and admitted into a doctoral program. Most students of color agree that some service is positive and are willing to serve in order to support their department. However, service becomes a burden when they are asked to serve on too many initiatives while taking classes, writing papers, working, and undertaking many other student responsibilities, especially when their majority peers do not carry these additional duties.

"Can we interview you for our class project on poverty?" Graduate students of color also express frustration over being asked to serve as a "class project." That is, other students will ask a graduate student of color if they are willing to be interviewed for a class assignment examining poverty, race, education, or other sociological phenomena. The students of color often report feeling like exotic subjects to be studied and to have their lives publicly examined and/or problematized.

ACADEMIC INVALIDATION

"Your literature review should draw primarily from European writers who have most of the theories in this area." Graduate students of color often report that their academic work is constantly challenged and invalidated by majority faculty and students. They often encounter microaggressions related to their literature reviews, databases, methodology, and sources.

Some graduate students of color report that on occasion, White faculty have suggested to them that most of the literature review for their work should come from European/Western writers and sources. Faculty who push for the use of Western writers possess the worldview that all knowledge and great works have been produced by European or Western philosophers, artists, writers, economists, and other academicians. Moreover, the belief is that people from Latin America, Asia, Africa, and other parts of the world have not contributed to the world knowledge base and therefore are to be excluded from research, papers, theses, and dissertations. In the end, the European worldview is supported, and non-European worldviews are invalidated.

"Don't use the National Chicano Survey for your study. I don't think it is good data." Graduate students of color also report that their advisors sometimes discourage them from using local or national databases that are specific to people of color. The Inter-University Consortium for Political and Social Research's National Chicano Survey at the University of Michigan or other databases that specialize in people of color are perceived to be flawed; therefore, doctoral students of color are discouraged from using them, feeding back to the narrowly defined and exclusive canon previously described.

"You used a sample of 2,000 African Americans. How generalizable are your results? I have concerns about the validity of your findings." Despite using adequate sample sizes and other appropriate statistical measures, the methodology of graduate students of color sometimes comes under intense scrutiny and suspicion. When used by majority students, the methodology is supported as a sound approach. Yet, when students of color use the same methodology, it somehow becomes flawed and dubious.

"You are primarily using sources written by scholars of color. I think your work will not be as strong. Try to vary your sources." Using too many sources from scholars of color is touted as a deficit, and graduate students of color are discouraged from the practice. The publications, research, and journals of scholars of color all come under suspicion regarding their quality, rigor, and the soundness of the research.

SOCIAL NETWORKING AND INVOLVEMENT

"Don't hang out with graduate students of color. Don't segregate yourself." Research on involvement and engagement in college by students suggests that those students who are involved in their collegiate experience tend to have higher levels of persistence, graduation, and a multiplicity of other positive outcomes. However, for some graduate students of color, specific types of involvement such as ethnic/racial student groups and social justice activism are portrayed as detrimental to their experience (Herrera, 2003), whereas other experiences (e.g., volunteering to help the department) are encouraged.

Social support networks such as the African American Graduate Students Association or the Asian Graduate Student Social Workers Organization can contribute to the persistence and graduation of graduate students of color. Despite the research supporting the beneficial effects of social support networks, Latino/a, Asian, Native American, and African American graduate students are sometimes discouraged from participating in ethnic organizations that are negatively portrayed as forms of self-segregation.

"You are wasting time being an activist, addressing issues, and trying to reform the department. Your time would be better spent working on your academic work." Graduate students of color are often discouraged from addressing issues of social justice (Chesler and Crowfoot, 2000). The message they receive is that "despite the fact that there are issues of inequality and discrimination in our department, you are wasting time being an activist." In a nutshell, this is the message that graduate students of color receive when they tackle issues of diversity in their department or college. Stated differently, the students are told to stay in the role of being a student and to not "rock the boat."

"We know that there is a lack of diversity in the department. Can you help us by going out to visit some of the local colleges and recruiting undergraduates to apply to our program?" In contrast to the involvement activities discussed previously, graduate students of color are often asked or encouraged to serve as volunteers for a department or college. This is particularly true in the area of recruitment of students of color. Doctoral students of color are often asked to become volunteer recruiters for what is essentially the responsibility of paid staff or faculty members. Thus, in addition to pursuing a doctoral degree, the students are asked to do extra, unpaid work to assist the department in diversifying the student body.

ETHNIC/RACIAL INVALIDATION

"You are different from other minorities. You don't look ethnic!" Graduate students of color have a multitude of intersecting identities. It is important to recognize the within- and between-diversity of Latinos/as, Native Americans, Asian Americans, and African Americans. Nevertheless, despite this fact, White faculty, students, and staff often comment that some graduate students of color do not look like members of their group (Allport, 1954). The message is that people of color look a certain way and that the graduate student of color who is the target of the comment does not look like or belong to an ethnic group (Aguirre, 2000).

APPLYING FOR FACULTY POSITIONS

One of the dynamics along the pipeline for scholars of color is applying for faculty positions. In this section, we explore numerous microaggressions directed at individuals pursuing academic positions.

RECRUITMENT, SEARCH STRATEGIES, AND JOB DESCRIPTIONS

"We advertised in the *Chronicle of Higher Education* and the local newspaper. It's not our fault that people of color did not apply for the position." One of the barriers in recruiting faculty of color is the perception of members of search committees that they simply have to advertise academic positions, and by virtue of some advertising, people of color will apply. This is a simplistic and naive position that history has proved does not lead to diverse hiring pools. Nevertheless, the majority of searches in U.S. higher education operate under these assumptions that lead to minimal or no change in the diversity of faculty. Diversifying the faculty is a complicated, multidimensional, action-oriented, daily, and long-term process that requires resources and full-time staff for success.

"You're suggesting that we modify the job description to include a statement about diversity. What does a position in finance have to do with diversity? I don't get it." Inclusive excellence is about embedding diversity into all aspects of the institution, including job descriptions. It is also about shifting the responsibility for inclusiveness to everyone at the institution (Milem et al., 2005). Nevertheless, the current campus diversity models impact the search process, because some departments and search committees believe that diversity has very little to do with them. To be effective in recruiting faculty of color, search committees will have to embed diversity into all aspects of the process (Smith, Turner, Osei-Kofi, & Richards, 2004; Turner, 2002).

"She is Asian, a graduate of Harvard, and being recruited by a lot of other universities. We will never be able to get her to come to our university. I don't think we should waste our time trying to recruit her." Often, departments fail to diversify their hiring pools because they become self-defeating in recruiting candidates of color (Smith, Wolf, & Busenberg, 1996; Turner, 2002). In essence, candidates are eliminated before they are even considered for a position. Stated differently, recruitment decisions are undertaken on behalf of candidates of color that essentially dismiss them from the process.

SEARCH COMMITTEES

"Why do we have to have racial diversity on the committee? We have expertise on the committee and are very capable of reviewing applications for this position." The attitude expressed in this comment is often the sentiment of search committees as they begin the process of identifying candidates for a faculty position. The literature is clear about the importance of having a diverse search committee for the success of attracting and hiring faculty of color (Smith et al., 2004). Turner (2002) strongly recommends that search committees be as diverse as possible. She states that

> by involving people with different points of view or by bringing in a fresh face, the chair can ensure that multiple perspectives and fresh ideas are brought to bear in evaluating candidates. Also, people of color, whether administrators or faculty, should have a presence on the committee. One scholar of color, an endowed professor, emphasizes the importance of a diverse search committee. Be sure that there are

respected and highly visible people of color [who are committed to hiring of minorities] on the committee. (p. 13)

CAMPUS VISIT

"I know that the digital projector that we ordered for the colloquium didn't work well. Nevertheless, her presentation was horrible." One of the salient issues that emerges during a candidate's campus visit is the hosts' carelessness in being attentive to the space, technology, and other presentation needs of candidates of color. A digital projector that does not work properly can ruin the presentation of a candidate. Hosting the candidates' colloquium in an old room can also influence the candidates' performance and possibly the impressions of members of the selection committee. First, there is no need for equipment failure when someone can easily check in advance the adequacy of the equipment. Second, inattentiveness to these issues may also send messages to the candidates of color about the value of diversity to the institution. Of course, presentation and space issues affect all candidates. However, it becomes extremely crucial when recruiting candidates of color. Microaggressions are committed when the candidates of color are eliminated from the process by blaming them for a poor presentation rather than the search committees taking responsibility for their failure to be attentive to the details of the campus visit.

PROTOCOL

"Hey folks, thank you for coming to this colloquium. This is Tracey, who will speak for about 30 minutes. Then, we will open it up for questions. Take it away, Tracey." It is good professional protocol to introduce all candidates, no matter their racial background or gender, properly and with their titles. However, candidates of color and women often report that protocol is violated when campus hosts do not introduce them using their doctoral title and are flippant about their academic background. The message, whether deliberate or unconscious, is one of disrespect and serves to devalue the accomplishments of these candidates.

ETHNIC/RACIAL INSULTS

"It will be great having you as a colleague, because you can tell us where all the great Mexican restaurants are in town." This is one example of racial insults that candidates of color are often subjected to during their visit to campus. Embedded in the message are degrading stereotypes and assumptions about the candidates and the added value that they bring to the academy. It may also signal to the candidate about what to expect in the way of professional and interpersonal relations if they accept a position with the department and institution.

CANDIDATE SELECTION

"Yes, she is a highly qualified Native American scholar and can be successful in our department. But I have serious doubts that she will ever leave her current position and accept the job at our institution. We should go with the second candidate." Highly qualified candidates of color are often dismissed in the final candidate selection process using superfluous and irrelevant criteria. Thus, instead of extending a job offer to the candidate, they are dismissed in favor of other candidates based on speculation and unfounded assumptions.

REVERSE QUOTA

"We hired a South Asian faculty member two years ago. Isn't that enough? Why do we have to hire another person of color?" Hiring more than one faculty of color into a department is often turned into a problem by search committees that results in not hiring additional faculty of color. In the end, diversity becomes a burden and a liability against hiring additional candidates of color in what essentially amounts to a "reverse quota." Padilla and Chavez (1995) refer to this phenomenon as the "one-slot-for-minorities hiring rule" (p. 11). Moreover, search committees that impose such quotas fail to realize how difficult it is to recruit people of color and the opportunities squandered when they limit themselves to one faculty of color, which further tokenizes the one person of color in the department.

FIT

"I am just not sure that she is a good fit for our department. I didn't like her attitude and dress." The concept of "fit," of who is compatible with faculty in a department, is often used to dismiss and not hire candidates of color. In describing this phenomenon, Turner (2002) suggests that search committees have a penchant for hiring faculty who resemble the faculty who are already in the department. Danowitz-Sagaria (2002) describes the tendency to hire people who look like "us" as an evaluative filter. She writes:

> Candidates were screened for professional behavior, leadership and decision-making style, as well as their fit and image within an administrative unit and/or university. This filter evolved throughout searches as thresholds were established for all candidates

or when one candidate exhibited characteristics or behaviors judged desirable by a
search chair or committee member. The standards applied were often vague, value-
laden, class-, culture-, or ideologically based. (p. 687)

In sum, fit can often carry a message about the language, appearance, communication style, and other personal attributes that selection committees and hiring authorities find valuable and attractive in a candidate (Chesler & Crowfoot, 2000; Danowitz-Sagaria, 2002). Often, candidates of color are not hired under the guise that they do not fit in the department.

JOB OFFER/NEGOTIATING CONTRACT

"We really value diversity and want to diversify our faculty. However, the faculty in the department have low salaries, so we can't offer you a higher salary than them. It just wouldn't be fair." Candidates of color often report that colleges and university representatives often give mixed messages about the value of diversity during contract negotiations. On the one hand, the diversity is touted during the visit as a valuable goal of the institution. On the other hand, the compensation packages that are offered to scholars of color do not reflect this philosophy. Granted, compensation of faculty is a complicated process involving a multiplicity of factors. However, there are plenty of cases where White candidates have received generous packages justified by the perceived value of their contributions to the department. Conversely, there are also cases in which equally qualified candidates of color are offered less because their value and contributions to the institutions are devalued.

PURSUING TENURE

The pursuit of tenure is the end goal for some faculty. However, in considering scholars of color, the process can be challenging in different ways than for majority faculty. Some of the challenges are microaggressions, which are explored further in the following section.

TEACHING

"Two of your students came to see me as the chair of the department with complaints about your teaching. They are upset about your in-class comments regarding White privilege. What are you doing to these students? How are the other 35 students doing? I am concerned." Faculty of color often receive complaints by majority students, particularly about their teaching. Research has demonstrated that faculty of color and women faculty sometimes receive lower teaching evaluations than other faculty, especially when they teach courses on diversity (Davalos, 1999). For the most part, these courses challenge the students' perceptions of racial, ethnic, and gender dynamics and the privileges attached to those social identities. In pushing the students to think critically about these issues, some students become contentious, disagree, become argumentative, and file complaints with the chair of the department. In addressing the issue, faculty of color often report that the chair automatically takes the side of the students instead of listening to the faculty member to learn about the situation. The concern is that these evaluations will be taken into consideration during the tenure review process.

ACADEMIC SEGREGATION

"We assigned you to teach three of our diversity courses. I think you will really enjoy teaching them. Good luck." Pre-tenure faculty of color report that they are academically segregated when it comes to diversity in a department (Aguirre, 1995). Teaching courses is a good example. Faculty of color often report that they are assigned to teach all of the multicultural-related courses in a department. The message in this action is that White faculty are not responsible for diversity and that these courses are the domain of faculty of color. Moreover, studies have shown that these are some of the most difficult, contentious, and emotionally draining courses. Teaching about differences, power, privilege, and oppression is extremely challenging work (Adams, Bell, & Griffin, 1997). As stated previously, student evaluations for these courses are often negative and can affect tenure for faculty of color.

RESEARCH

"You shouldn't publish in ethnic/racial journals, because that is not going to get you tenure. You should publish in mainstream publications that are reputable. Also, don't do research on people of color. It is too narrow and does not really contribute to the field." Scholars of color report that their research on race and ethnicity is often devalued by White faculty colleagues (Gregory, 1999; Turner & Myers, 2000). In addition, journals that are devoted to race and ethnicity are devalued by White faculty colleagues, and junior faculty of color are told not to publish in them (Chesler & Crowfoot, 2000). Specifically, early on, many pre-tenure faculty of color are advised not to publish research in, for example, the *Journal of Chicana/o Studies* or the *Journal of African American History*, because the work will not count or will be valued less toward tenure.

SERVICE

"Don't get involved with ethnic/racial campus or community organizations and groups. It will not get you tenure." Campus and community service has always been controversial in relation to tenure. Faculty in general are told that service is an important part of the tenure process. Nevertheless, there is much research that suggests that research and publications carry an over-preponderance of weight when it comes to tenure. For faculty of color, campus and community service to ethnic/racial communities is often not an option. For reasons ranging from a commitment to social justice to collectivism and care for communities of color, faculty of color are called upon to mentor students of color and majority students, serve on diversity committees, participate and support community agencies, join ethnic/racial campus groups, address issues of discrimination, and many other service activities (Canul, 2003). In addition to all of these volunteer efforts, faculty of color have to teach, undertake research, and publish. Nevertheless, in the end, many of these activities are discounted in the tenure process.

DIVERSITY TAXATION

"I know that you are serving on the university-wide diversity committee. So, I hate to ask you to set up and run a diversity committee that will examine issues of diversity in the department, but will you do it?" While faculty of color are discouraged from campus and community service involving ethnic/racial constituencies and organizations, administrators are not shy about recruiting them to do service within and outside the department. This is particularly true when it comes to diversity work (e.g., "We need the minority perspective") but also applies to other activities related to the department (e. g., new-student orientation, search committees, recruiting students of color; Smith et al., 1996; Torres-Guzman, 1995). In the end, service to the department is often not considered in the tenure process (Aguirre, 2000).

TENURE

"You wrote two books on racism, five articles in refereed journals, and three chapters in edited books. That is all good for possibly getting tenure, but your teaching evaluations are not that great." The literature on the experiences of faculty of color chronicles a multiplicity of issues that emerge in attempting to achieve tenure. Discrimination, politics, and nebulous tenure standards and guidelines are but a few of the issues that mar the academic career path of many faculty of color (Padilla & Chavez, 1995). Often, faculty of color are held to higher and different standards.

IMPLICATIONS

The microaggressions presented in this chapter and found all along the educational pipeline have implications in a number of areas. First, inclusive excellence is a process designed to transform colleges and universities into institutions that embrace and value the presence and contributions of all sexual orientations, Latinos/as, African Americans, differently abled people, all genders, Asian Americans, Native Americans, and many other groups found on college campuses. Clearly, microaggressions mitigate against the implementation and fulfillment of IE by contributing to hostile and unwelcoming environments. This in turn contributes to the loss from or the failure to recruit to the pipeline scholars of color, which diminishes the goal of inclusive excellence.

Second, the large number of faculty who are slated to retire in the near future makes the recruitment of faculty of color an opportunity and a timely and pressing issue. Given the changing demographics with more students of color accessing higher education, it is clear that in order to find replacements for those retiring professors, we will have to educate, train, and draw from the population of scholars of color. In turn, this suggests that success in this area will depend on the improvement of the pipeline and movement of scholars of color into the ranks of the faculty. The literature on the recruitment and retention of scholars of color suggests that there are numerous barriers that they confront on the path to becoming tenured faculty members (Castellanos & Jones, 2003; Padilla & Chavez, 1995). These challenges include a multiplicity of microaggressions that erode the likelihood of yielding a significant cadre of faculty of color. Thus, we must make an effort to rid the pipeline of microaggressions, improve the journey, and increase the number of scholars of color pursuing academic careers.

Finally, microaggressions are antithetical to our notions of social justice, equality, equity, and a whole host of other democratic values. That is, most institutions of higher learning explicitly espouse values and goals regarding the improvement of and care for human diversity. Yet, racial insults and invalidations contradict these ideals and augment in a variety of ways the distance and inequalities between us and our fellow human beings. Discrimination, oppression, prejudice, and all genres of inequalities are manifestations of processes that expose an inconsistency between our institutions' ideal and actual values. Given that they are part of and support an entire system of oppression and privilege (Adams et al., 1997), the same holds true for microaggressions.

Given that microaggressions in academia are perpetuated by well-intentioned, good people who do so unconsciously—as opposed to bigoted individuals—addressing and eliminating these acts of insensitivity will be challenging (Adams et al., 1997). Nevertheless, there are a number of action steps and strategies that can be taken, and in the following section, we propose several recommendations.

As is the case with most human problems, awareness is the first step in the process of reducing or eliminating microaggressions. By contributing to the literature and examining microaggressions directed at scholars of color, the authors hope that this is a beginning point for becoming aware of the existence and dynamics of microaggressions in the academy. To address microaggressions in the graduate school experience, discussions and readings about microaggressions should be disseminated at and introduced in graduate-student orientations by faculty and staff. The more that faculty and students know about microinsults and microinvalidations, the more that they will be empowered to think about and address them.

Addressing microaggressions that occur while scholars of color are applying for academic positions will require working with those who play a role in the recruitment of candidates of color and in search committees (Turner & Myers, 2000). Representatives of human resource departments and equal opportunity units need to incorporate information about microaggressions and their negative impact on the recruitment of multicultural talent into their work with search committees. The goal is to disseminate information and educate others who play a role in the recruitment pipeline about the destructive nature of racial insults and invalidations.

Microaggressions and their impact on the tenure process need to be addressed by educating and training tenure committees. Deans and department chairs could host campus workshops for all faculty to understand how microaggressions work against scholars of color in the tenure review process. One area with which tenure committees need to become familiar involves the journals that publish the work of faculty of color. A common grievance (i.e., microaggression) often heard from members of tenure committees involves being unfamiliar with ethnic/racial scholarly publications such as *Atzlan*, the *Journal of Chicano/a Studies*, and the *Journal of the National Association of Black Social Workers*. In the end, this lack of familiarity leads to the disqualification or omission of valuable research conducted by scholars of color who are engaged in the tenure review process. Here, library staff could be enlisted to help faculty become familiar with these important journals as a way to accurately assess the work of scholars of color.

In addition to institutional-level interventions just discussed, addressing microaggressions at the individual level will be required for effective and lasting change. Obviously, the interventions will differ between those who commit microaggressions—White faculty and students—and those who are subjected to them—scholars of color.

Formal diversity trainings are a conventional and acceptable means of promoting awareness and understanding of microaggressions. White faculty and students will have to be educated about and trained in microaggressions, including the concepts of White privilege and modern aversive racism. Since the manifestations of aversive racism are generally subtle and unconscious, improving personal understanding and self-awareness requires more than merely acquiring knowledge. In addition, the person's ability, openness, and willingness to discuss racism and diversity must also be developed.

Building on the heightened awareness and understanding of White faculty, the amelioration of microaggressions can be further advanced by White faculty working toward becoming allies to faculty of color. White faculty who become allies can utilize their privilege to speak out and support their colleagues of color, particularly in circumstances when microaggressions have occurred. Creating cadres of allies can be a powerful means of addressing microaggressions.

Addressing microaggressions in relation to the pipeline will also require specific training of scholars of color designed to improve their understanding of academia and thereby encourage their participation. One particular program that has met with some success is the University of Denver's "Promoting Multicultural Excellence in the Academy," a national summer institute designed to address the underrepresentation of faculty of color and women in academia. The institute assists participants in clarifying their goals with respect to pursuing a faculty career and provides doctoral students of color and women with the necessary information to prepare them for faculty positions in higher education. As a part of the institute, participants are exposed to examples of racial microaggressions that they will encounter on their journey toward becoming faculty and how to successfully address them. In the end, more of these programs will be required if we are to diversify the academy.

CONCLUSION

This chapter on microaggressions and the challenging journey that scholars of color traverse along the pipeline toward academia initiates the process of exposing specific examples of microinsults and microinvalidations directed at people of color as they complete doctoral degrees, apply for academic positions, and pursue tenure. It is imperative for many compelling reasons that microaggressions be addressed, exposed, and ameliorated. This is especially true if we are to increase the number of scholars of color and diversify the academy. The work presented in this chapter is limited, given that the authors relied heavily on the literature and personal experiences rather than a full-blown study designed to systematically examine racial microaggressions. Future research must focus on systematic studies, both quantitative and qualitative, that specifically examine the microaggressions that scholars of color experience on their journey into academia. Studies that focus on the perpetrators of microaggressions and the motivations behind the insults and invalidations would be helpful. Moreover, studies attempting to determine how to prevent and educate about microaggressions would contribute greatly to the literature.

This chapter represents a beginning point in exposing and understanding racial microaggressions directed at scholars of color. Addressing micro-aggressions will improve the pipeline and allow for an increase in the recruitment and retention of faculty of color.

REFERENCES

Adams, M., Bell, L. A., & Griffin, P. (1997). *Teaching for diversity and social justice: A sourcebook.* New York: Routledge.

Aguirre, A. (1995). A Chicano farmworker in academe. In R. V. Padilla & R. C. Chavez (Eds.), *The leaning ivory tower: Latino professors in American universities* (pp. 17–27). Albany: State University of New York Press.

Aguirre, A. (2000). Women and minority faculty in the academic workplace [Special issue]. *ASHE-ERIC Higher Education Report, 27*(6).

Allport, G. W. (1954). *The nature of prejudice.* Reading, MA: Addison-Wesley.

Aronson, A., & Swanson, D. L. (1991). Graduate women on the brink: Writing as "outsiders within." *Studies Quarterly, 19*(3/4), 156–173.

Association of American Colleges and Universities. (2002). *Greater expectations: A new vision of learning as a nation goes to college.* Washington, DC: Author.

Bowen, W. G., & Bok, D. (1998). *The shape of the river: Long term consequences of considering race in college and university admissions.* Princeton, NJ: Princeton University Press.

Canul, K. H. (2003). Latina/o cultural values and the academy: Latinas navigating through the administrative role. In J. Castellanos & L. Jones (Eds.), *The majority in the minority: Expanding the representation of Latina/o faculty, administrators and in higher education* (pp. 167–175). Sterling, VA: Stylus Publishing.

Carter, D., Pearson, C., & Shavlik, D. (1996). Double jeopardy: Women of color in higher education. In C. S. V. Turner, M. Garcia, A. Nora, & L. I. Rendon (Eds.), *Racial and ethnic diversity in higher education: ASHE reader series* (pp. 460–464). Boston: Pearson Custom Publishing.

Castellanos, J., & Jones, L. (2003). *The majority in the minority: Expanding the representation of Latina/o faculty, administrators and students in higher education.* Sterling, VA: Stylus Publishing.

Chesler, M. A., & Crowfoot, J. (2000). An organizational analysis of racism in higher education. In the Association for the Study of Higher Education (ASHE) & C. Brown (Eds.), *ASHE reader on organization and governance in higher education* (5th ed., pp. 436–469). Boston: Pearson Custom Publishing.

Danowitz-Sagaria, M. A. (2002). An exploratory model of filtering in administrative searches. *Journal of Higher Education, 73*(6), 677–710.

Davalos, K. (1999). *Literature review on teaching diversity material in United States: Understanding students' behavior, evaluations, and women and ethnic minority faculty with recommendations for Loyola Marymount University.* Unpublished paper, Loyola Marymount University, Los Angeles, CA.

Goodman, D. J. (2001). *Black women in the academy.* New York: University Press of America.

Gregory, S. T. (1999). *Promoting diversity and social justice: Educating people from privileged groups.* Thousand Oaks, CA: Sage.

Herrera, R. (2003). *Notes from a Latino graduate student at a predominantly White university.* In J. Castellanos & L. Jones (Eds.), *The majority in the minority: Expanding the representation of Latina/o faculty, administrators and in higher education* (pp. 111–125). Sterling, VA: Stylus Publishing.

Milem, J., Chang, M. J., & Antonio, A. L. (2005). *Making diversity work on campus: A research-based perspective.* Washington, DC: Association of American Colleges and Universities.

Padilla, R. V. (2003). *Barriers to accessing the professoriate.* In J. Castellanos & L. Jones (Eds.), *The majority in the minority: Expanding the representation of Latina/o faculty, administrators and in higher education* (pp. 179–204). Sterling, VA: Stylus Publishing.

Padilla, R. V., & Chavez, R. C. (1995). *The leaning ivory tower: Latino professors in American universities.* Albany: State University of New York Press.

Ryu, M. (2008). *Minorities in higher education 2008: Twenty-third status report.* Washington, DC: American Council on Education.

Smith, D. G., Turner, C. S., Osei-Kofi, N., & Richards, S. (2004). Interrupting the usual: Successful strategies for hiring diverse faculty. *Journal of Higher Education, 75*(2), 133–160.

Smith, D. G., Wolf, L. E., & Busenberg, B. E. (1996). *Achieving faculty diversity: Debunking the myths.* Washington, DC: Association of American Colleges and Universities.

Solórzano, D., Ceja, M., & Yosso, T. (2000). Critical race theory, racial microaggressions, and campus racial climate: The experiences of African American college students. *Journal of Negro Education, 69*(1/2), 60–73.

Sue, D. W., Capodilupo, C. M., Torino, G. C., Bucceri, J. M., Holder, A. M. B., Nadal, K. L., & Esquilin, M. (2007). Racial microaggressions in everyday life: Implications for clinical practice. *American Psychologist, 62*(4), 271–286.

The nation: Number of full time faculty members by sex, rank, and racial and ethnic group, Fall 2005. (2008). *Chronicle of Higher Education, 55*(1), 24. Retrieved April 2, 2009, from http://chronicle.com/weekly/almanac/2008/nation/0102402.htm.

Torres-Guzman, M. E. (1995). *Surviving the journey.* In R. V. Padilla & R. C. Chavez (Eds.), *The leaning ivory tower: Latino professors in American universities* (pp. 53–65). Albany: State University of New York Press.

Turner, C. S. V. (2002). Women of color in academe: Living with multiple marginality. *Journal of Higher Education, 73*(1), 74–93.

Turner, C. S. V. (2007). Pathways to the presidency: Biographical sketches of women of color first. *Harvard Educational Review*, 77(1), 1–38.

Turner, C. S. V., & Myers, S. M., Jr. (2000). *Faculty of color in academe: Bittersweet success*. Boston: Allyn & Bacon.

Williams, L. (2000). *It's the little things: Everyday interactions that anger, annoy, and divide the races*. San Diego, CA: Harcourt, Inc.

Wing, A. K. (Ed.). (2003). *Critical race feminism: A reader* (2nd ed.). New York: New York University Press.

Wise, T. (2008). *White like me: Reflections on race from a privileged son*. Brooklyn, NY: Soft Skull Press.

PART III

OTHER SOCIALLY DEVALUED GROUP MICROAGGRESSIONS:

International/Cultural, Sexual Orientation and Transgender, Disability, Class, and Religious

CHAPTER 8

Microaggressions Experienced by International Students Attending U.S. Institutions of Higher Education

SUAH KIM and RACHEL H. KIM

T HE UNITED STATES continues to be a preferred destination for international students seeking educational opportunities abroad, despite some decline in enrollment following the terrorist attacks of September 11, 2001. In the 2007 to 2008 academic year, the number of international students attending American colleges and universities experienced a 7 percent increase, reaching a record high of 623,805 students (Institute of International Education [IIE], 2008)—the biggest growth since 9/11. The majority of international students to the United States are from Asian countries (61%), with Canada (4.7%), Mexico (2.4%), Turkey (1.9%), and Saudi Arabia (1.6%) rounding out the top 10 countries of origin. Most international students enroll in graduate programs in business, engineering, and the sciences (IIE, 2008). With these increasing numbers, international students offer clear benefits to American institutions: (1) They can enhance campus diversity by contributing different perspectives in classrooms that improve appreciation for other cultures. (2) Their research and academic work adds global perspectives and talents that help make the United States competitive in international markets, such as in business, education, and scientific discovery. (3) Their presence also provides American students and educators opportunities to interact with those from other countries, which can facilitate cross-cultural sensitivity and understanding.

As international students continue to establish a growing presence on American campuses, there is increasingly more research on examining acculturation, psychological well-being, adjustment, and support services for this population (e.g., Frey & Roysircar, 2006; Poyrazli & Grahame, 2007;

Wadsworth, Hecht, & Jung, 2008; Wilton & Constantine, 2003). Most studies report psychological distress due to difficulties in socializing with American peers, communicating with professors or advisors, and adjusting to different classroom norms and activities (Essandoh, 1995; Hsieh, 2007; Swagler & Ellis, 2003); perceived discrimination (Constantine, Kindaichi, Okazaki, Gainor, & Baden, 2005; Lee & Rice, 2007; Schmitt, Spears, & Branscombe, 2003; Spencer-Rodgers, 2001); and most notably, stressors related to language proficiency (Mori, 2000; Swagler & Ellis, 2003). Although this research implores university personnel to develop greater awareness of issues that international students face, much of the onus for change is placed on international students to adjust to life in their host country by adopting intercultural competence (Lee & Rice, 2007). However, many difficulties lie in less-than-friendly campus and classroom environments that can hinder the educational process.

International students' experiences with discrimination had been conceptualized from a neoracism perspective, which contends that prejudicial attitudes and behaviors are attributed to cultural differences rather than race alone (Lee & Rice, 2007). This contemporary form of racism was popularly rationalized as an attempt to preserve national identity and the values of the dominant culture. Direct (i.e., overt) and indirect (i.e., covert) types of neoracism were evident in institutional practices and interactions with faculty and American peers. Interestingly, international students reported experiencing discomfort and inhospitality but had some difficulty pinpointing the precise source of these feelings, perhaps due to the subtlety of the insults. Conceptually, it appears that international students are encountering microaggressions that are similarly experienced by other marginalized groups in the United States.

Racial microaggressions are subtle verbal, nonverbal, or environmental slights and indignities that are intentionally or unintentionally committed toward people of color (Sue, Capodilupo, et al., 2007). Oftentimes, the perpetrator is unaware that she or he has committed such acts, and the target is left to wonder about the intent, the veracity of the insults, and the proper reaction and its consequences. The daily occurrences of these microaggressions may cumulatively denigrate people's identities in more subversive and harmful ways than blatant forms of racism (Sue, 2003). While international students are able to identify overt acts of prejudice, their internalized "outsider" status in a host country may lead them to underrate the subtle slights and indignities that they experience from their American classmates, teachers, and the educational system as a whole. Furthermore, understanding microaggressions committed against American students of color, though seemingly similar, may shade the nuances experienced by non-White international students and the unique insults they face in a country where multicultural sensitivity often excludes them. This chapter examines microaggressions that might be experienced by international students attending colleges in the United States. Implications of this review have significant bearings on education, counseling practices, student services, and global relations, as many of these international students return home or continue to work abroad.

MICROAGGRESSIONS

The themes identified in this chapter were adapted from the taxonomy that was first proposed by Sue, Capodilupo, and colleagues (2007) and incorporate findings from research on the experiences of international students (see Table 8.1). The difficulties international students face appear

Table 8.1
Examples of Microaggressions Experienced by International Students in U.S. Higher Education

Theme	Location	Microaggression	Message
Classroom ascription of intelligence	Classroom	An international student is perceived as unintelligent because of an accent.	You are unintelligible and unintelligent.
		An international student's silence is interpreted as being incompetent.	You have nothing valuable to contribute to the class.
Pathologizing cultural values/ communication styles	Social	"You should be more assertive."	Assimilate to the dominant culture.
	Classroom	Professors give poor participation grades to international students because of their lack of active questioning and commenting.	You need to speak up in class in order to receive a positive evaluation.
Invalidating international issues and perspectives	Curriculum	Curriculum is insensitive to international issues, and dialogues on issues pertaining to international students are discouraged.	The "American way" is the right way.
	Classroom	Professors do not seek or validate input of international students.	Your perspective is irrelevant.
Assumption of homogeneity	Social, classroom, institution	A Taiwanese international student is mistaken to be from China.	You are all the same.
Exclusion and social avoidance	Social and classroom	Professors and domestic peers reference American pop culture, tell jokes, and	You do not belong.

(continued)

Table 8.1
(*Continued*)

Theme	Location	Microaggression	Message
		use slang during class discussions.	
		International students are not included in social gatherings with American peers.	You are rejected from our group.
Invisibility	Social	American peers ignore international students or do not acknowledge their presence In hallways and classrooms.	You are unnoticeable.
	Classroom	American peers dismiss ideas of international students during group projects/discussions.	You have nothing productive to contribute to the group.
		Professors call on American students more frequently.	Your contribution to the class is insignificant.
Environmental and systemic microaggressions	Institution, educational system	New-student orientations do not include acclimation to an environment different from their home country, including adjusting to climate, urban/rural/ suburban settings, classroom expectations, food, housing, and use of public transportation.	Your needs are not important enough to address on a systemic level.
		There is a lack of funding for international students, and they are prohibited from working off campus or being a part-time student.	You may study here because you are an economic boon to our country. So, do not take away our jobs or use other resources.
		Preferential treatment is given to American students for teaching assistantships.	You are incompetent in presenting ideas clearly.
		There are exhaustive barriers to visa obtainment.	You are not welcome here.
		International students' use of certain chemicals in labs is barred, or such students are removed from research projects.	You are a terrorist.

to exist in three domains: social interactions, classrooms, and campus institutions. Social interactions include those between international students and American students and faculty; classrooms include course curricula and class dynamics; and campus institutions include university policies and organizations that govern or serve the student body. A common thread in each of these domains is the language barrier. Attaining English proficiency in itself is a significant stressor in studying in the United States (Dao, Lee, & Chang, 2007; Mori, 2000; Poyrazli & Grahame, 2007; Sumer, Poyrazli, & Grahame, 2008; Swagler & Ellis, 2003). The majority of research purports that language proficiency is also a primary source of perceived discrimination (Constantine et al., 2005; Lindemann, 2005; Poyrazli & Lopez, 2007; Spencer-Rodgers, 2001). Thus, the microaggressions presented in this chapter are predominantly experienced by international students whose native language is not English.

THEME 1: ASCRIPTION OF INTELLIGENCE

Research on racial microaggressions experienced by Black and Latino Americans suggests an ascription of intelligence that attributes to them lower intelligence and competence than Whites (Sue, Capodilupo, & Holder, 2008). However, Asian Americans often experience the reverse bias, where they are perceived to have greater intelligence, particularly in math and the sciences (Sue, Bucceri, Lin, Nadal, & Torino, 2007). These racial microaggressions toward people of color may have a fine distinction from those experienced by international students.

With international students, specifically those whose first language is not English, there appears to be an ascription of unintelligence from others. Asian international students in particular, despite their race and the assumption of intelligence ascribed to Asian Americans, are sometimes presumed to have lesser intelligence. Much of this attitude derives from perceived accents and language and communication deficits. In qualitative and quantitative studies, international students—Asians in particular—often reported sensing an assumption of unintelligence from their peers and professors because their accents were deemed unintelligible and/or because they were silent in class discussions (Hsieh, 2007; Swagler & Ellis, 2003). Consequently, some international students felt the need to work harder to obtain good grades in order to challenge this view (Hsieh, 2007). This pressure to achieve high grades became a significant stressor, and students went to great lengths to earn credibility for their intelligence (e.g., paid for English language tutoring, purchased both English and native language versions of textbooks; Lee & Rice, 2007). Therefore, when professors and students dismiss comments and questions from international students by stating "I don't understand you" or by simply ignoring them, the underlying message received by international students may be "You are unintelligent."

THEME 2: PATHOLOGIZING CULTURAL VALUES/COMMUNICATION STYLES

The increasing diversity in American classrooms makes communication and discourse between students and teachers challenging without adequate understanding of the cultural dynamics in place. The classroom environment can be disempowering when American peers and instructors maintain a cultural homogeneity to which international students are pressured to assimilate. This implicit standard could lead international students to internalize self-deficient identities when they are unable to conform to the dominant culture (Hsieh, 2007); they might believe that they lack competency as a student. These differences can be particularly difficult for international students as they face some unexpected classroom norms such as active participatory styles, seminar formats, oral presentations, group work, role-playing, term papers, and egalitarian teacher-student relationships. International students must then fit into a narrow standard of student behaviors in order to succeed (Pedersen, 1991).

Thus, how international students are expected to express themselves in class could be incongruous to how they perceive themselves as students, because classroom norms and behaviors previously shaped by their home cultures are violated (Wadsworth et al., 2008). For example, international students who are unaccustomed to expectations for active classroom participation can develop an identity gap between who they should be (i.e., vocal participants) and who they are (i.e., quiet notetakers), which can reduce educational satisfaction. However, even if international students wish to become more active in discussions, the responsibility for change is placed solely on them without recognizing that classroom climates often do not support their voices (Hsieh, 2007).

Many international students find that their cultural values are in conflict with American social norms. For example, some students report difficulties with egalitarian student-teacher and student-advisor relationships and prefer indirect communications and behaviors that respect the hierarchy they are familiar with in their home countries (Essandoh, 1995; Hyun, Quinn, Madon, & Lustig, 2007; Mori, 2000). Thus, American professors may negatively evaluate international students who avert their eyes when speaking to them and who do not speak up in class. Interactions with American peers are also difficult for international students because of conflicting cultural norms. Some students have trouble relating to certain social aspects of American college culture such as "partying" and the open expression of sexuality (Lee & Rice, 2007). Moreover, American ideas of friendship can be impermanent, and certain colloquialisms such as "Let's hang out," "I'll give you a call," or "Come over anytime" may be taken as sincere interest when they are often used to convey mere friendliness and are not genuine invitations to follow through (Mori, 2000). In some instances, these statements may be misinterpreted for romantic gestures.

Because of the need to negotiate these new social norms and language differences, international students frequently fear being misunderstood or perceived negatively and may thus interact less with American peers (Swagler & Ellis, 2003). In view of this, American students hold stereotypic views of international students and in one study labeled them as secluded, lost, insular, handicapped, psychologically distressed, and socially inhibited (Spencer-Rodgers, 2001). American students in this study also sensed that international students kept to themselves. However, these stereotypes validated international students' fears of discrimination, and in fact, their perception of shared mistreatment from host nationals increased identification with other international students and away from the majority group (Schmitt et al., 2003). Thus, professors and students alike disregard the conflicting norms international students face and often pathologize cultural values and communication styles with little consideration to their own contributions to the silencing and isolation of international students.

THEME 3: INVALIDATION OF INTERNATIONAL ISSUES AND PERSPECTIVES

American classrooms can be disempowering to international students when there is a failure to acknowledge international issues (e.g., global perspectives) or to value their input in class discussions. One standpoint is that Whiteness operates in classrooms to oppress students of color. Whiteness can be described as a set of practices that assumes privilege, acts as a reference point for determining the social location of others (i.e., racializing others), and perpetuates inequities in resources, interactions, and social climates (Diangelo, 2006). In a study that observed the production of Whiteness in a classroom, White students were affirmed on several levels when the professor responded to their participatory styles, questions, and comments and supported their research interests. Moreover, the professor unwittingly approved these students' disregard for the perspectives of their international peers by simply allowing it without challenge, even when the class discussion was international in nature (Diangelo, 2006). American students and professors inadvertently work in concert to invalidate international students not only when they do not incorporate their input into the discussions but also when this failure goes unnoticed. In this study, White students acknowledged the presence of Asian American students by greeting them at the start of class, and these students of color were also able to enjoy the classroom banter that ensued, while the international students were excluded from this camaraderie (Diangelo, 2006). In this way, the author argued that international students of color were located at a lower rung in the pedagogical ladder than American students of color.

In one qualitative study, some international students reported a lack of support for their voices in the classroom and feared negative reactions or ignorant comments about their countries (Poyrazli & Grahame, 2007). Because international students are a numerical minority in the classroom, they may find it difficult to dissent or offer alternative views, even when they speak about their own cultures. In another study, some students found that professors asked about their cultures, only to then counter them by drawing on their own academic knowledge (Lee & Rice, 2007), which not only invalidated these students' experiential realities but also relayed the message to American students that this behavior was acceptable.

The perspectives of international students are not only ignored when their contribution to discussions are summarily rejected but also when the curriculum is insensitive to international issues, despite some institutions' professed commitment to multiculturalism. For example, course curricula often prize American ideals such as capitalism, competition, individualism, and independence. Without a more balanced view of socioeconomic values that includes global perspectives and with the dismissal of international perspectives, students may be left with the message that "the American way is the right way." This attitude may be evidenced by some American students' ethnocentric view of American superiority and their disinterest in international issues including world affairs as well as the concerns and opinions of their international peers (Diangelo, 2006; Hsieh, 2007; Pedersen, 1991). Such a classroom climate undermines the intercultural learning that begot foreign student exchange programs in the first place.

Theme 4: Assumption of Homogeneity

Despite the evident heterogeneity of international students, as they came from nations around the globe, there was a consensual stereotype held by American students in one study that they were a homogenous group and were negatively connoted as "foreign" (Spencer-Rodgers, 2001). What's more, even though international students were unquestionably deemed as "not American," they were still subjected to the racial categorizations of American stereotypes (Lee & Rice, 2007). That is, because of skin color, some international students were classified into racialized groups in the United States (e.g., African American, Latino/a American, Asian American) that they shared little cultural similarities with. These students then had to learn the stereotypes that were associated with their arbitrarily assigned racial groups, which might eventually leave them feeling negatively about their own cultural identities (Lee & Rice, 2007). Since international students usually originate from majority statuses in their home countries and are unaccustomed to American manifestations of racism, this exposure can be remarkably unsettling.

In a study of American students' attitudes toward international students, international students were also often summed up into one entity that was largely considered socially and culturally maladjusted (Spencer-Rodgers, 2001). In actuality, the term "international students" encompasses many different cultures, and students' experiences of life in the United States may be different, depending on various factors (Fouad, 1991). Most observably, students from both non-Western and non-English-speaking countries perceived more discrimination than students from countries such as Europe, Canada, New Zealand, and Australia (Lee & Rice, 2007; Poyrazli & Lopez, 2007; Sodowsky & Plake, 1992). However, intercultural differences exist among students from the same region such that not all African, Asian, and North and South American students experience identical difficulties and needs as other students from the same continents. Nevertheless, not only are international students often confused for other ethnicities, but they may also be thrust into services and events that group international students together without sensitivity to cultural norms (e.g., gender segregation) and the sociopolitical dynamics between their home countries (e.g., nations in conflict). Therefore, this assumption of homogeneity denies ethnic and individual differences that may insult and nullify the unique identities of international students.

THEME 5: EXCLUSION AND SOCIAL AVOIDANCE

While some studies showed that greater acculturation was associated with lower stress and higher educational satisfaction (Wadsworth et al., 2008; Wilton & Constantine, 2003), acculturation could be hindered by various social factors that were essential to the process. Acculturation of international students to the host culture occurs at both the individual and sociocultural levels, including adoption of colloquial language, fashion, and eating habits; familiarization with popular culture; and forging relationships with host nationals. However, international students often feel excluded both inside and outside the classroom, and in fact, American students may also avoid their international peers. Some international students feel excluded from classroom discussions because of communication barriers and social norms. For example, international students reported difficulties in understanding the fast speech, jokes, and slang of their American professors and peers (Poyrazli & Grahame, 2007). They also felt unable to join in on conversations about American popular culture including sports, politics, and other topics (Swagler & Ellis, 2003). This unspoken assumption that all students will understand the American idiosyncrasies that underlie classroom discourse and social situations conveys the hidden message that international students do not belong.

In a study of American students' beliefs and stereotypes of international students, American peers reported moderately positive views of them as "brave" and "courageous" for studying abroad but held negative beliefs that were significantly associated with prejudicial attitudes and social avoidance (Spencer-Rodgers, 2001). In fact, international students reported being excluded from study groups and were rarely invited to social gatherings by American peers (Lee & Rice, 2007). American students described international students as naive, bewildered, socially maladjusted, and insular (Spencer-Rodgers, 2001) and negatively evaluated accented English, except that of Western Europeans (Lindemann, 2005). Thus, although international students may want and attempt to make friendships with American students, they must work against the negative stereotypes that these students have previously developed. International students already feel like outsiders, and their insecurities are exacerbated by this social avoidance, leaving them feeling lonely, isolated, and rejected by host peers.

THEME 6: INVISIBILITY

International students also report feeling invisible in classrooms and in interactions with American students. Asian Americans similarly described experiences of being overlooked, particularly on issues of race, which implied that they were not a racial group that experienced discrimination (Sue, Bucceri, et al., 2007). Likewise, multiculturalism in the United States and within educational settings may not include concerns of international students (Diangelo, 2006), as exemplified in Theme 3. Thus, international students may experience similar microaggressions with their American counterparts of color. However, international students' accounts of invisibility indicated a distinct disregard of their presence. Specifically, international students reported being ignored, talked over, and dismissed when working in group projects with American students (Hsieh, 2007; Lee & Rice, 2007). Although invisibility is not intentionally committed against international students by Americans, this effect may be an unfortunate byproduct of the insidious microaggressions described in Themes 1 through 5. That is, the pervasiveness of these slights may have socialized American students and educators to systematically and automatically neglect the mere existence of international students. This nonverbal microaggression can be exemplified in professors who do not call on international students who wish to participate in class discussions and in American peers who fail to acknowledge international students in hallways and classrooms (Diangelo, 2006). The implicit messages of these snubs are that international students are unnoticeable and insignificant.

THEME 7: ENVIRONMENTAL AND SYSTEMIC MICROAGGRESSIONS

Since the terrorist attacks of September 11, it had become more difficult for international students to obtain F-1 student visas to the United States. The drop in enrollment of international students following this incident was most accounted for by those coming from the Middle East. New legislation and regulatory practices had been implemented to increase homeland security, and international students had become persons of scrutiny since it was determined that one of the 9/11 terrorists entered the United States on a student visa. The USA PATRIOT Act of 2003 and other legislations not only created hurdles to visa obtainment but also imposed restrictions on privacy, employment, areas of study, and license procurement (Urias & Yeakey, 2009). Specifically, student records could be court ordered without consent during terrorist investigations. Universities must also comply with regulations to extensively screen "high-risk" students and scholars through photograph and fingerprint matching against a terrorist database and to continuously track entry and exit of these individuals (Urias & Yeakey, 2009). Furthermore, any individual from a "State Sponsor of Terrorism" as designated by the U.S. Department of State could be denied visas, despite a lack of evidence of terrorist activity. The Patriot Act also defines "restricted persons," which include international students, who are barred from using certain chemicals, materials, and equipment in laboratories or research studies (Urias & Yeakey, 2009). One wonders, were similar restrictions placed on White males following the Oklahoma City bombing—the deadliest terrorist attack on U.S. soil pre-9/11?

These regulations mostly impact students from the Middle East, Muslims, and scholars in the physical sciences, as demonstrated by declines in their enrollment immediately following 9/11 (Urias & Yeakey, 2009). For others, the new hurdles delay visa obtainment, payroll placement, and driver's license and Social Security number procurements, as more paperwork is required. Although some argue that these new legislations increase domestic security, others contend that they are largely ineffectual and only perpetuate the notion that America is unwelcoming to nonnationals. Because of university compliance to these rules, many international students have begun to view international student affairs offices as regulatory monitors and not resources of support for adjustment-related concerns. Some students have sensed an assumption of criminality (Urias &

Yeakey, 2009) similar to that experienced by Black Americans (Sue et al., 2008) and Latino/a Americans (Rivera, Forquer, & Rangel, 2009) but with the nuanced suggestion that they may threaten the nation's security. At a systemic level, these regulations convey the message that international students are not welcome in this country.

At an institutional level, environmental microaggressions might also manifest in a lack of culturally relevant resources, an inhospitable campus climate, and little structural support for international students. In fact, many international students reported a lack of culturally relevant resources and guidance such as new-student orientations that met their specific needs (Poyrazli & Grahame, 2007; Wilton & Constantine, 2003). A significant stressor was navigating the infrastructure of urban settings including public transportation and housing that were new to some international students (Poyrazli & Grahame, 2007). However, student orientations often exclude these needs when they welcome new students. Although international students experienced many stressors while studying in the United States, research suggested an underutilization of counseling services (Essandoh, 1995; Frey & Roysircar, 2006; Hyun et al., 2007). At the same time, the cultural values and beliefs held by most international students were often in direct conflict with the traditional American concept of mental health, and counselors are too often untrained or insensitive to these differences (Essandoh, 1995; Mori, 2000). These institutional slights may convey the message that the needs of international students are not important enough to address and that they are one portion of the student body that can be ignored.

The greatest number of students comes from Asia, including India, China, South Korea, and Japan, because of their strong economies, a growing middle class, and an assumption by recruiters that Asians will be able to pay their way without aid (McClure, 2009). In the 2007 to 2008 academic year, international students as a whole dispensed over $15.5 billion to the U.S. economy in tuition costs and living expenses (NAFSA, 2008). Because of this major monetary contribution, international students are often viewed as economic commodities—consumers of an American education—and less attention is paid to their adjustment, well-being, and educational satisfaction (Lee & Rice, 2007). In reality, international students reported that financial problems were a significant stressor (Hyun et al., 2007).

International students do not qualify for many fellowships that are usually exclusive to U.S. citizens, and thus, financial support must come from the university, the academic department, and their own resources. Financial support for graduate students typically comes in the form of research and teaching assistantships, which can not only relieve financial burdens but also provide opportunities for professional growth. However, some international students found themselves disproportionately assigned to research assistantships, while both research and teaching assistantships were preferentially offered to American students (Lee, 2007; Pedersen, 1991). There was an assumption that international students would be unable to present ideas clearly because of perceived language deficiencies (Pedersen, 1991). What's more, some international students experienced penalties for voicing these inequities and were stripped of their graduate funding without explanation, while American peers negotiated their finances with impunity (Lee & Rice, 2007). Federally, international students are also restricted from working off campus and are allowed fewer working hours than American students. These institutional policies, attitudes, and associated behaviors toward international students send the message that they may only reside in the United States to study and may not take away jobs and resources that are categorically reserved for Americans.

IMPLICATIONS

Research on international students can offer valuable insight into ways to improve the educational system and student services that could result in students having a more positive experience while studying in the United States. Although international students report difficulties outside of school and face discrimination at a societal level, we have focused this chapter on their experiences in the educational setting. This section proposes strategies that can be implemented in the classroom, in campus resources, and at the institutional level to enhance the lives of international students on American college campuses.

FOR EDUCATORS: CLASSROOM, CURRICULUM, AND INTERPERSONAL STRATEGIES

Educators ought to become aware of the many difficulties that international students face in the classroom. Firstly, professors should become more sensitive to the language barriers and cultural norms that might impede effective communication and understanding among international students, American students, and professors themselves. Professors could refrain from making jokes or American cultural references without explaining them and discourage the use of slang, if possible. Professors should also consider the disempowering nature of the classroom that could silence international classmates instead of assuming that their silence is a cultural idiosyncrasy. They should consider the discomfort some international students feel toward classroom activities that require oral participation. Professors might abstain from requiring this activity, use other methods to evaluate classroom participation (e.g., accept written reactions to discussions), or provide support and assistance to those students who would like to develop this skill.

Secondly, educators should incorporate global perspectives into their curriculum as appropriate so that students could be exposed to broader issues than what is known domestically. For example, professors might incorporate theories, concepts, and cultural mores taught and practiced in other countries into their curriculum. They might also encourage their students to think more critically about American, Western, or culturally dominant ideas and consider their relevance or applicability to other nations and cultures. This might also allow international students to feel that they could contribute to the classroom discussion by sharing their own worldviews. It is then imperative that professors incorporate international students' input into the discourse and support their voices. Professors should also encourage American students to integrate ideas offered by international students into their evolving thoughts. Allowing for this exchange of ideas promotes mutual learning between American students and international peers and their understanding of multiculturalism.

Thirdly, professors should recognize the unequal power dynamics between American students and international students in the classroom, largely by virtue of English proficiency. For example, in group projects, this power differential might make the voices of international students less heard and more powerless. Because group projects are usually evaluated on oral presentation, an international student who is deemed as having "substandard" English ability will often be marginalized in the group and assigned a minor speaking role, which can enable a deficient self-perception (Hsieh, 2007). Therefore, instructors might actively assign willing international students to lead their groups.

Lastly, educators who advise students should be sensitive to the needs of their international advisees. International students who had functional relationships with advisors were less likely to report emotional or psychological distress (Hyun et al., 2007). Therefore, it is important for advisors to be attuned to the unique needs of international students and to be sensitive to cultural differences between them. Many international students expect and prefer hierarchal relationships with their professors and advisors. As such, educators in these roles should try to assume this dynamic and accept formal communications and offer direct advice when needed. Advisors should also be aware of the financial needs of their international advisees and might advocate for stable funding and assistantships.

For Campus Resources: Culturally Sensitive and Needs-Specific Counseling Strategies

Concerns of international students should be addressed not only during their period of stay in the United States but also before they arrive and after they leave (Lin & Yi, 1997). Before arrival, it is important for the school to prepare students by sending essential information to reduce anxiety and possible cultural shock. This may include sending information regarding housing (availability, off-campus options) and financial requirements (cost of tuition, health insurance) of the institution. Because international students are required to assume studies full time, they need to provide evidence of financial support from their home country.

Once international students arrive on campus, it is important to continue to assist students as they adjust to the United States in a way that strikes a healthy balance between the new culture and their own cultural identities. For example, counselors can take part during orientation and collaboratively work with the international students' office to meet the needs of students. It is important for counselors to be visible and to take an active role in making themselves available to the students, whether it is going to different ethnic association clubs or attending events that are hosted by international students' offices. It is vital for academic institutions to develop creative and effective ways to market services offered at the counseling center and to devise outreach programs that are culturally appropriate (Hyun et al., 2007; Yi, Lin, & Kishimoto, 2003).

International students are found to underutilize counseling centers when compared to U.S. ethnic and racial minority students (Hyun et al., 2007; Nilsson, Berkel, Flores, & Lucas, 2004). Because they may manifest their emotional distress through their physical symptoms, it is important to network with medical professionals on campus and in the community to effectively address the psychological needs of international students. Psychological well-being also may decline within the first four months of their stay in the United States; thus, effective orientation and support programs should reach out to these students early on (Cemalcilar & Falbo, 2008). International students who sought counseling presented with concerns about depression, assertiveness, academic major, and anxiety. International students not only face issues common to all undergraduate and graduate students, but they also have to cope with additional stressors and experience lower adjustment than domestic peers (Hechanova-Alampay et al., 2002).

In order to help manage the psychological stressors of international students, counseling centers should design appropriate programs and interventions specifically for this population. It is important to conduct ongoing assessments to determine the nature and the types of programming that will be most helpful in meeting the needs of international students. Furthermore, in order to effectively work with international students, counselors should develop their own cultural self-awareness as an essential component of training. One obstacle to international students in using counseling services is the shortage of culturally knowledgeable and sensitive counselors (Mori,

2000). Therefore, bicultural, bilingual personnel can be valuable sources of consultation on a variety of cultural issues. For example, outreach programs conducted by older international students could be provided for newly arrived international students in which common reactions to language, cultural barriers, and issues such as loneliness, stress, and anxiety could be shared and discussed amongst peers (Nilsson et al., 2004).

As the number of international students continue to grow, it is important to address the issue of training future counselors and psychologists in working with international students. It becomes imperative that counselor trainees be adequately trained to provide culturally competent and sensitive counseling services to the international student population (Jacob, 2001). Counselor trainees should not only be up to date with current literature and cultural trends that are specific to this population but should also be open to interpersonal interactions, which can help promote awareness and knowledge and develop culturally sensitive skills (Jacob, 2001). Counselors and trainees should also focus on continuing to examine any personal biases, assumptions, or stereotypes that may impede effective work with international student populations.

Counselors and counselor trainees need to be aware that traditional notions and methods of counseling may not be familiar to international students. Alternative ways of counseling may be more beneficial to individuals who come from cultures that place less emphasis on verbal expression (Komiya & Eells, 2001). For example, psychoeducational programs should frame counseling as a learning opportunity rather than as "mental health" services. Furthermore, use of more direct approaches such as cognitive and behavioral interventions that focus less on emotional expression may also be more appropriate for some international students who may view the counselor as the expert. Other interventions can include stress- or time-management workshops that focus on issues such as how to balance home life and school and maintain healthy relationships with family and friends (Yi et al., 2003). It is also important not only to educate international students about the symptoms of anxiety and depression but also to provide ready access to services so that international students may react more proactively to perceived stressors (Hayes & Lin, 1994).

A study found that international students expected counseling to involve advice giving, with the expectation that counselors provide structure and direction in solving problems. In contrast, international students found both the nondirective/client-centered approach and the directive/problem-solving approach in counseling to be helpful (Yau, Sue, & Hayden, 1992). Regarding counselor preferences, counselors who demonstrated cultural competence on social influence variables of expertness, attractiveness, and trustworthiness were perceived more favorably by Asian international students than counselors who did not (Zhang and Dixon, 2001). Therefore, in order to establish rapport and trust when working with international students, counselors should be aware of their own competency and limits.

One study created a support group for Asian international students in order to address issues specific to Asian women (Carr, Koyama, & Thiagarajan, 2001). The goal of the group was to ease the students' adjustment to the U.S. culture, provide culturally sensitive counseling, normalize members' experience, and increase effective coping skills in a safe and supportive environment. The group facilitators encouraged group members to express feelings in their first language, and the participants and group leaders were able to help translate the information or ideas to other group members when language became an obstacle. Through anonymous feedback forms, the international students enjoyed speaking English without fear of judgment and appreciated the opportunity to express their feelings and have them validated by others. Another study looked at utilizing workshops that focused on improving English to draw in students from Taiwan (Swagler and Ellis, 2003). Using ways to build confidence and reduce communication anxiety and other psychological aspects of speaking English in a neutral setting helped students address their concerns. It is important to keep in mind that international students are not a homogenous group, and program development should take place with recognition that within-group differences exist among international students.

FOR INSTITUTIONS: POLICY AND SYSTEMIC CHANGES

Colleges and universities enrolling international students should have a clearly stated policy on goals and objectives of the international education program at the institution. Insofar as institutions continue accepting students from abroad, it is recommended that they continue to work toward equitable treatment of them and be sensitive to their needs. For example, institutional budgeting and planning should reflect support for international students such that funding is available to adequately assist these students and provide resources that are equipped to accommodate for them. Not only should finances go toward alleviating tuition costs, but they should also fund outreach programs, tutoring, hiring competent personnel, and implementing support services as they often do for domestic students.

Institutions should also be responsible for training and informing faculty and administrative staff on the needs of international students such as adjustment concerns in studying in the United States and in negotiating conflicting cultural norms in the classroom. Colleges and universities must also demonstrate sensitivity to cultural needs including social, religious, dietary, and housing issues (Pedersen, 1991). They might even consider advocating for change at a national level to lift exhaustive barriers to student visa obtainment and employment restrictions that are placed on international students. Finally, if international students experience injustice from professors, students, or campus policies, there should be an advocate in place to address their concerns. All in all, institutions should uphold a standard of responsibility toward all their students.

DISCUSSION

In recent years, international students have steadily entered the United States to obtain an education outside of their home countries. International students' desire to study here and institutions' acceptance of them promotes the growing notion of internationalization. In its truest form, this phenomenon is an act of diplomacy—an appreciation of intercultural exchange and interdependence between nations. However, the experiences of international students described in this chapter reflect a globalization of education where they are more likely treated as units of national revenue. This implicit attitude is apparent not only because of the obvious lack of funding and the restrictions on employment but also because little is done to welcome them. The disparities in their treatment from American students are often subtle and unintentional and thus difficult to detect and address.

However, since the study of microaggressions has grown, international students are included among those who have been marginalized in this country. Their identities have been invalidated, minimized, and pathologized; they also have been ignored, rejected, and unsupported, both at interpersonal and institutional levels. Many of the problems they face are due to indirect verbal and nonverbal acts of discrimination that disregard their cultural values, communication styles, and experiential realities. If institutions are to continue enrolling international students, acceptance of them should not end with their admission. Instead, these colleges and their personnel must continually address the needs of international students, expose inequities and prejudices, and consciously institute an environment of support and understanding.

A limitation of this review of the literature is that because of the heterogeneity of international students as a group, the findings reported in this chapter reflect the most commonly reported microaggressions. Thus, this report could be enhanced by giving more specificity to insults that are experienced differentially by gender, acculturation level, ethnicity, religion, and so forth. Instead, this chapter gives a general overview of the experiences of international students in the United States, and future research should study experiences of international students and examine the theoretical framework of microaggressions against them. To observe the lasting impact of these occurrences, further research should also be conducted on international students who return to their home countries. If these students develop and maintain a negative perception of the United States due to their experiences here, the positive global relations that are expected from the internationalization movement may be ruptured. Our hope is that this research will not only validate the experiences of international students but also entreat educators, administrators, counselors, students, and institutions to implement change.

REFERENCES

Carr, J. L., Koyama, M., & Thiagarajan, M. (2001). A women's support group for Asian international students. *Journal of American College Health, 52,* 131–134.

Cemalcilar, Z., & Falbo, T. (2008). A longitudinal study of the adaptation of international students in the United States. *Journal of Cross-Cultural Psychology, 39*(6), 799–804.

Constantine, M. G., Kindaichi, M., Okazaki, S., Gainor, K. A., & Baden, A. L. (2005). A qualitative investigation of the cultural adjustment experiences of Asian international college women. *Cultural Diversity and Ethnic Minority Psychology, 11,* 162–175.

Dao, T. K., Lee, D., & Chang, H. L. (2007). Acculturation level, perceived English fluency, perceived social support level, and depression among Taiwanese international students. *College Student Journal, 41*(2), 287–295.

Diangelo, R. J. (2006). The production of Whiteness in education: Asian international students in a college classroom. *Teachers College Record, 108*(10), 1983–2000.

Essandoh, P. K. (1995). Counseling issues with African college students in U.S. colleges and universities. *Counseling Psychologist, 23*(2), 348–360.

Fouad, N. A. (1991). Training counselors to counsel international students: Are we ready? *Counseling Psychologist, 19,* 66–71.

Frey, L. L., & Roysircar, G. (2006). South Asian and East Asian international students' perceived prejudice, acculturation, and frequency of help resource utilization. *Journal of Multicultural Counseling and Development, 34,* 208, 222.

Hayes, R. L., & Lin, H. (1994). Coming to America: Developing social support systems for international students. *Journal of Multicultural Counseling & Development, 22,* 7–16.

Hechanova-Alampay, R., Beehr, T. A., Christiansen, N. D., & Van Horn, R. K. (2002). Adjustment and strain among domestic and international student sojourners: A longitudinal study. *School Psychology International, 23,* 458–474.

Hsieh, M. (2007). Challenges for international students in higher education: One student's narrated story of invisibility and struggle. *College Student Journal, 41*(2), 379–391.

Hyun, J., Quinn, B., Madon, T., & Lustig, S. (2007). Mental health need, awareness, and use of counseling services among international graduate students. *Journal of American College Health, 56*(2), 109–118.

Institute of International Education (IIE) (2008). International students at U.S. campuses at all-time high. Retrieved March 30, 2009, from http://opendoors.iienetwork.org/?p=131590.

Jacob, E. J. (2001). Using counselor training and collaborative programming strategies in working with international students. *Journal of Multicultural Counseling & Development, 29,* 73–88.

Komiya, N., & Eells, G. T. (2001). Predictors of attitudes toward seeking counseling among international students. *Journal of College Counseling, 4,* 153–160.

Lee, J. J. (2007). Neo-racism toward international students. *About Campus, 11*(6), 28–30.

Lee, J. J., & Rice, C. (2007). Welcome to America? International student perception of discrimination. *Higher Education, 53,* 381–409.

Lin, J. G., & Yi, J. K. (1997). Asian international students' adjustment: Issues and program suggestions. *College Student Journal, 31,* 473–479.

Lindemann, S. (2005). Who speaks "broken English"? US undergraduates' perceptions of non-native English. *International Journal of Applied Linguistics, 15*(2), 187–212.

McClure, A. (2009). International students still flock to U.S. *University Business, 12*(1), 11.

Mori, S. C. (2000). Addressing the mental health concerns of international students. *Journal of Counseling & Development, 78,* 137–144.

NAFSA: Association of International Educators (2008). International students contribute $15.54 billion to U.S. economy. Retrieved April 14, 2009, from http://www.nafsa.org/public_policy.sec/international_education_1/eis_2008.

Nilsson, J. E., Berkel, L. A., Flores, L. Y., & Lucas, M. S. (2004). Utilization rate and presenting concerns of international students at a university counseling center: Implications for outreach programming. *Journal of College Student Psychotherapy, 19,* 49–59.

Pedersen, P. B. (1991). Counseling international students. *Counseling Psychologist, 19,* 10–58.

Poyrazli, S., & Grahame, K. M. (2007). Barriers to adjustment: Needs of international students within a semi-urban campus community. *Journal of Instructional Psychology, 34*(1), 28–45.

Poyrazli, S., & Lopez, M. D. (2007). An exploratory study of perceived discrimination and homesickness: A comparison of international students and American students. *Journal of Psychology, 141*(3), 263–280.

Rivera, D. P., Forquer, E. E., & Rangel, R. (2009). Microaggressions and the life experience of Latina/o Americans. In D.W. Sue (Ed.), *Microaggressions and marginalized groups in society: Race, gender, sexual orientation, class and religious manifestations.* Hoboken, NJ: John Wiley & Sons.

Schmitt, M. T., Spears, R., & Branscombe, N. R. (2003). Constructing a minority group identity out of shared rejection: The case of international students. *European Journal of Social Psychology, 33,* 1–12.

Sodowsky, G. R., & Plake, B. S. (1992). A study of acculturation differences among international people and suggestions for sensitivity to within-group differences. *Journal of Counseling & Development, 71,* 53–59.

Spencer-Rodgers, J. (2001). Consensual and individual stereotypic beliefs about international students among American host nationals. *International Journal of Intercultural Relations, 25,* 639–657.

Sue, D. W. (2003). *Overcoming our racism: The journey to liberation.* San Francisco, CA: Jossey-Bass.

Sue, D. W., Bucceri, J., Lin, A. I., Nadal, K. L., & Torino, G. C. (2007). Racial microaggressions and the Asian American experience. *Cultural Diversity and Ethnic Minority Psychology, 13*(1), 72–81.

Sue, D. W., Capodilupo, C. M., & Holder, A. M. B. (2008). Racial microaggressions in the life experience of Black Americans. *Professional Psychology: Research and Practice, 39*(3), 329–336.

Sue, D. W., Capodilupo, C. M., Torino, G. C., Bucceri, J. M., Holder, A. M. B., Nadal, K. L., & Esquilin, M. (2007). Racial microaggressions in everyday life: Implications for clinical practice. *American Psychologist, 62,* 271–286.

Sumer, S., Poyrazli, S., & Grahame, K. (2008). Predictors of depression and anxiety among international students. *Journal of Counseling and Development, 86,* 429–437.

Swagler, M. A., & Ellis, M. V. (2003). Crossing the distance: Adjustment of Taiwanese graduate students in the United States. *Journal of Counseling Psychology, 50,* 420–437.

Urias, D., & Yeakey, C. C. (2009). Analysis of the U.S. student visa system: Misperceptions, barriers, and consequences. *Journal of Studies in International Education, 13*(2), 72–109.

Wadsworth, B. C., Hecht, M. L., & Jung, E. (2008). The role of identity gaps, discrimination, and acculturation in international students' educational satisfaction in American classrooms. *Communication Education, 57*(1), 64–87.

Wilton, L., & Constantine, M. G. (2003). Length of residence, cultural adjustment difficulties, and psychological distress symptoms in Asian and Latin American international college students. *Journal of College Counseling, 6,* 177–186.

Yau, T. Y., Sue, D., & Hayden, D. (1992). Counseling style preference of international students. *Journal of Counseling Psychology, 39,* 100–104.

Yi, J. K., Lin, J.-C. G., & Kishimoto, Y. (2003). Utilization of counseling services by international students. *Journal of Instructional Psychology, 30,* 333–342.

Zhang, N., & Dixon, D. N. (2001). Multiculturally responsive counseling: Effects on Asian students' ratings of counselors. *Journal of Multicultural Counseling and Development, 29,* 253–262.

CHAPTER 9

The Manifestation of Gender Microaggressions

CHRISTINA M. CAPODILUPO, KEVIN L. NADAL, LINDSAY CORMAN, SAHRAN HAMIT, OLIVER B. LYONS, and ALEXA WEINBERG

JUST AS ACTS of racism and ethnic discrimination have become more covert and subtle in a changing U.S. society that admonishes blatant racism, so, too, has the nature of sexism changed. Whereas overt and blatant sexism refers to harmful and unfair treatment of women that is intentional, visible, and unambiguous (Swim & Cohen, 1997), subtle or covert sexism is hidden or unnoticed because it is built into cultural and societal norms (Swim & Cohen, 1997). For example, a male CEO may endorse a belief in gender equality and thus may adhere to hiring practices and promotion policies that are not biased against women. However, a closer examination of his actual behavior reveals that he routinely attends sporting events and dinners with lower-ranking male employees and that this increased contact differentially impacts his evaluation (and thus promotion) of male workers over similarly positioned female workers. The CEO most likely does not intend to discriminate against his female employees. In fact, if questioned, he may explain that female employees do not seem to have an interest in attending sporting events, that the events are social and not work related, or that these conversations outside of the workplace do not influence promotion decisions.

Although there has been significant progress in women's rights since the Nineteenth Amendment and the Civil Rights Act were passed, both overt sexism and subtle discrimination based on gender are still widespread (Swim & Cohen, 1997; Swim, Hyers, Cohen, & Ferguson, 2001). For example, in 2008, the Equal Employment Opportunity Commission received 11,648 charges of sexual harassment filed by women (2,219 charges were filed by men). It has also been suggested that at least 60 percent of women in the United States experience some form of sexual harassment in the workplace but do not report these incidents, either because they do not meet legal criteria for harassment or due to personal and psychological reasons. Thus, published reports about sexual harassment (and other forms of sexism) are unlikely to reflect accurate rates of occurrence.

Clearly, the dynamics of subtle sexism are intricate and complicated, yet few studies have investigated this phenomenon (Benokraitis, 1997). The literature that does exist suggests that subtle sexism invalidates women, dismisses their contributions and accomplishments, and limits their effectiveness in social and professional settings (Benokraitis, 1997; Nielsen, 2002; Watkins et al., 2006). Women's experiences with sexism have also been found to lead to a myriad of psychological stressors including a decrease in comfort and self-esteem and feelings of anger and depression (Swim et al., 2001). Some empirical studies have supported that the objectification of women is associated with depression, low self-esteem, sexual dysfunction, eating disorders, and body image issues (Fredrickson & Roberts, 1997; Hill & Fischer, 2008; Kozee, Tylka, Augustus-Horvath, & Denchik, 2007).

A recent body of research has identified a phenomenon that is related to subtle sexism: microaggressions. Microaggressions are defined as "brief and commonplace daily verbal, behavioral, or environmental indignities, whether intentional or unintentional, that communicate hostile, derogatory, or negative racial slights and insults toward members of oppressed groups" (Nadal, 2008, p. 23). Like previous studies on sexism, microaggressions have been found to lead to an array of difficult emotions (e.g., frustration, anger, sadness), as well as to have negative mental health consequences for those who are the recipients of such discrimination (Sue, Bucceri, Lin, Nadal, & Torino, 2007; Sue, Nadal, Capodilupo, Torino, Lin, & Rivera, 2008). However, most research on microaggressions has focused primarily on racial interactions and has failed to examine the ways that subtle forms of discrimination may have an impact on other oppressed groups, including women (Nadal, 2008). Thus, the current study seeks to understand the experiences of gender microaggressions from the perspective of women.

LITERATURE REVIEW

In order to understand gender microaggressions, it is important to examine the literature involving various forms of sexism: everyday sexism, sexual harassment, objectification theory, and benevolent and hostile sexism. Reviewing previous research on sexism allows for an opportunity to recognize how gender microaggressions may differ from other manifestations of sexism. For example, Nadal (2010) cites that one of the main ways that gender microaggressions differ from other forms of subtle sexism is that gender microaggressions can be categorized into three categories: gender micro-assaults, gender microinsults, and gender microinvalidations. Gender micro-assaults resemble the "old-fashioned" form of sexism in which individuals speak and behave in blatantly sexist ways. For example, a microassault may include a man calling a woman a "bitch" or a "whore" (Nadal, 2008). Microinsults are behaviors and statements that are often unintentional and convey a negative message about women. For example, when a teacher only calls on male students over female students in the classroom, the message is sent that men are more intelligent or more important than women (Sue & Capodilupo, 2008). Microinvalidations are unintentional verbal statements that negate women's thoughts or feelings. A gender microinvalidation may be demonstrated by a group of male coworkers who consistently go out after work together but do not invite a female coworker, assuming she would not be interested in the sports they watch (Sue & Capodilupo, 2008).

A similar concept to gender microaggressions is the phenomenon of everyday sexism, which can be defined as the subtle forms of sexism that women experience on a daily basis (Swim et al., 2001). One qualitative study found that female college-student participants reported one to two impactful experiences of sexism a week, which reflected the following three categories: (1) traditional gender role stereotypes and prejudice, (2) demeaning and derogatory comments and behaviors, and (3) sexual objectification (Swim et al., 2001). Examples of traditional gender role stereotypes included men saying "It's not my job to wash dishes" or a woman being told by her husband "not to worry her pretty little head about these complex insurance issues." Examples of demeaning and derogatory comments and behaviors included men using demeaning labels such as "bitch" or "chick" and making derogatory, sexist jokes. Examples of sexual objectification included men making direct comments about a female participant's physique, as well as threats of sexual contact and catcalls. Participants reported psychological impacts such as decreased comfort and self-esteem, as well as feelings of anger and depression (Swim et al., 2001).

Similar experiences of everyday sexism were found in a study of adolescent girls (Leaper & Brown, 2008) who reported sexism mainly being related to academics (e.g., having their math and science abilities questioned) and/or athletics (e.g., being teased about their athletic ability). Participants discussed multiple incidents that included being called demeaning names, receiving unwanted romantic attention, and being taunted about their physical appearance. Taken collectively, these findings support research that informed the Schedule of Sexist Events (SSE)—a measure that assesses perceived frequencies of sexist discrimination (see Klonoff & Landrine, 1995; Matteson & Moradi, 2005). Three subscales have emerged from the SSE that mirror the categories reported by female participants in studies by both Swim and colleagues (2001) as well as Leaper and Brown (2008): (1) sexist degradation and its consequences (e.g., being called a sexist name), (2) unfair sexist events at work/school (e.g., being denied a raise, promotion, or tenure at work), and (3) unfair treatment in distant and close relationships (e.g., being treated unfairly by people in helping jobs; Matteson & Moradi, 2005). Initial studies using the SSE find that 99 percent of a female sample ($n = 633$) experienced sexism at some point in their life, while 97 percent of the sample experienced sexism in the past year (Klonoff & Landrine, 1995).

Other concepts aligned with gender microaggressions include research on covert or subtle sexism (see Swim & Cohen, 1997; Swim et al., 2001; Swim, Mallett, & Stangor, 2004). Given that it is not politically correct in today's climate to endorse beliefs that women are inferior, a man who perpetuates subtle sexism is one who publicly claims that men and women are equal, yet would never vote for a female presidential candidate or assumes that an authority figure (e.g., supervisor, author, or medical doctor) would be a "he" without knowing their gender (Nadal, 2010; Swim et al., 2004). Subtle sexism, while often unintentional, still perpetuates gender stereotypes and status differences (Swim et al., 2004) similar to gender microaggressions. Given the research on subtle sexism, the psychological impact of gender micro-aggressions can potentially be felt just as deeply as encounters with blatant and overt sexism (Sue & Capodilupo, 2008).

Understanding objectification theory can be beneficial in understanding specific types of gender microaggressions. Objectification theory can be defined as "a framework for understanding the experiential consequences of being female in a culture that sexually objectifies the female body" (Fredrickson & Roberts, 1997, p. 173). Studies indicate that women who reported high instances of being gazed at also reported viewing themselves on appearance-based terms (i.e., self-objectification; Kozee et al., 2007; Hill & Fischer, 2008), while more direct objectification (e.g., catcalling or name-calling) and assaults (e.g., rape or physical abuse) lead to more direct adverse psychological issues such as depression, sexual dysfunction, eating disorders, and body image issues (Fredrickson & Roberts, 1997; Hill & Fischer, 2008).

Finally, research on benevolent and hostile sexism may help to understand the types of attitudes that may lead to gender microaggressions. Benevolent sexism is defined as "a subjectively favorable, chivalrous ideology that offers protection and affection to women who embrace conventional roles" (Glick & Fiske, 2001, p. 109). Conversely, hostile sexism is defined as "antipathy toward women who are viewed as usurping men's power" (Glick & Fiske, 2001, p. 109). These types of attitudes may lead to unconscious forms of sexism toward women. For example, as an act of benevolent sexism, a man may believe that he is being a gentleman in carrying a heavy box for a woman or paying for her dinner; however, the message that may potentially be conveyed to the woman is that she is not capable of doing things herself. An act of hostile sexism may include calling a female authority figure a "bitch" or telling a woman that she complains about sexism too much. These attitudes or ideals may manifest as gender microaggressions. For example, a man who is benevolently sexist may assume a woman to hold traditional gender roles, while a man who enacts hostile sexism may belittle the authority of a woman in a leadership role (Nadal, 2010).

TAXONOMY OF GENDER MICROAGGRESSIONS

Gender microaggressions are defined as brief and commonplace daily verbal, behavioral, and environmental indignities that communicate hostile, derogatory, or negative sexist slights and insults toward women (Nadal, 2010). These microaggressions can manifest consciously or unconsciously, in the sense that perpetrators may not realize that their statements or behaviors may send negative and psychologically harmful messages toward women. In the case of all microaggressions, the impact of being on the receiving side can cause emotional or physical discomfort, confusion, or even more significant mental health problems (Nadal, 2008; Sue, Bucceri, et al., 2007; Sue, Capodilupo, et al., 2007; Sue, Nadal, et al., 2008).

A proposed taxonomy of gender microaggressions has been introduced and discussed by several researchers. The original taxonomy on microaggressions was introduced by Sue and Capodilupo (2008) and included various ways that microaggressions may impact members of oppressed groups (namely people of color, women, and lesbian, gay, bisexual, and transgender [LGBT] persons). Six themes specifically involved gender and included (1) *sexual objectification*, (2) *second-class citizen*, (3) *assumptions of inferiority*, (4) *denial of the reality of sexism*, (5) *assumptions of traditional gender roles*, and (6) *use of sexist language*. Nadal (2010) extended the taxonomy by adding two additional themes: (7) *denial of individual sexism* and (8) *environmental microaggressions*.

The first category of gender microaggressions is *sexual objectification*, which occurs when a woman is treated as a sexual object. For example, a man who catcalls a woman while she walks down the street or a male stranger placing his hands on a woman's hips as he passes reduces a woman to being viewed only as an object. The second category is *second-class citizen* and occurs when men are given preferential treatment over women (Sue & Capodilupo, 2008), such as a female employee being passed up for a job promotion, though she is equally as qualified as her male coworker. Nadal (2010) labels this category as *invisibility*, with examples including a male CEO not knowing the names of his female employees while knowing the names of the male employees, sending the message that women are not as important as men. The third category is *assumptions of inferiority*, which takes place when a woman is assumed to be less competent than men (either physically or intellectually). For example, when a woman is carrying boxes and a man decides to help by grabbing the boxes without her permission, he sends a message that she is not physically strong. An example of the fourth category, *denial of the reality of sexism*, transpires when a man tells a woman that she is exaggerating about how many times a day she gets catcalled on the street.

The fifth category, *assumptions of traditional gender roles*, occurs when an individual assumes that a woman should uphold traditional gender roles (e.g., a career-oriented 40-year-old woman is asked why she never had any children). The sixth category is *use of sexist language*, which occurs when language is used to demean a woman, such as by calling a female coworker "sweetie" or "honey." The seventh category is *denial of individual sexism*, which is when a man denies his own gender biases or prejudices. For example, an employer who says "I treat men and women the same," although he doesn't know the names of his female employees, describes someone who denies that he is capable of being sexist (Nadal, 2008). Finally, the last category is *environmental microaggressions*, which are macrolevel aggressions that occur on the systemic and environmental level. Examples of this category could be systemic issues (e.g., the fact that women get paid less than men or that the majority of university professors in a department are male) or environmental (e.g., when a corporation has pictures of the board of directors of the company featuring all men; Nadal, 2010).

METHOD

As the purpose of the current investigation is to gain a deeper understanding of women's experiences of gender microaggressions, a qualitative method was used to collect and analyze data. Qualitative inquiry is particularly appropriate when the phenomenon of study has received little empirical attention (Morrow & Smith, 2000). Focus group methodology, in particular, allows for exploration of a new area of investigation (Krueger & Casey, 2008) and creates a scope for members of disenfranchised groups to frame their accounts (Fine, 1992). In focus groups, participants are encouraged to share their perspective and point of view without necessarily coming to consensus (Krueger & Casey, 2008), providing an integrated description of the phenomena of study. The group discussion is conducted several times with similar types of participants (i.e., women) to allow researchers to identify patterns and themes (Krueger & Casey, 2008). In the current investigation, directed content analysis was used to systematically classify, code, and categorize data into themes.

PARTICIPANTS

In an effort to obtain a diverse sample, participants were recruited both from the community and from local universities via various means of solicitation. Flyers were posted at several community organizations and dormitories for women. E-mail requests were also sent to women's interest groups and relevant student organizations. Participants were also solicited from the Research Experience Program at a large public university in a northeastern metropolitan area in which Psychology 101 students are required to participate in research studies on campus as part of their grade. In order to participate in the study, individuals only needed to identify as women.

A total of 12 women participated in the study, forming three focus groups. Each focus group consisted of an average of four participants. The women ranged in age from 18 to 43 (mean age: 25) and identified as White ($n = 4$), Asian ($n = 4$), Latina ($n = 3$), and Black ($n = 1$). Seven of the women indicated that they are heterosexual, while five did not report their sexuality. With regard to religion, the women identified as Catholic ($n = 4$), Christian ($n = 2$), and Jewish ($n = 2$). Four women did not report their religion. The majority of the participants were students ($n = 10$), three of whom were international students.

RESEARCHERS

The research team was comprised of one Asian male professor, one White female doctoral student, and two White females, one Black female, and one White male, all of whom were master's students. A crucial aspect of qualitative inquiry involves identifying the researchers' biases and assumptions, as these can potentially influence the data collection and analysis process (Fassinger, 2005). As such, the research team met prior to data collection and again before analyzing the data to freely discuss their assumptions and beliefs. Among these were beliefs that (1) participants would be able to easily generate examples of gender microaggressions; (2) the nature of microaggressions would be different for women of different ages, racial/cultural backgrounds, and sexual orientation; and (3) a disproportionate number of microaggressions would involve women's physical appearance.

MEASURE

A questionnaire assessing participants' age, ethnicity, sexual orientation, religion, level of education, years in the United States, and occupation was used to collect demographic information. A semistructured protocol (see Appendix A) was also used to collect focus group data. The protocol consisted of 12 questions that probed for examples of microaggressions (e.g.,

"Think about a time when you may have been discriminated against because of your gender. Describe the scenario as best as you can"). Follow-up questions were asked to inquire about interpretations of the event (e.g., "How did you understand that?"), as well as reactions to the event (e.g., "How did you feel when it happened?"). While many of the protocol questions were informed by the gender microaggressions taxonomy discussed earlier (Nadal, 2010; Sue & Capodilupo, 2008), open-ended questions were also utilized (e.g., "What are your experiences with subtle sexism?") to afford an opportunity to discuss microaggressive events that may not be captured by the taxonomy.

PROCEDURES

Research participants were assigned to one of three focus groups based on their location (i.e., women from the community participated at one location versus university students at another location) and availability. No financial compensation was offered. A definition of microaggressions was provided for participants. Each focus group lasted approximately 75 minutes and was conducted by a three-person team: a facilitator and two observers, all of whom were female. The role of the facilitator was to lead the discussion while the observers noted participation details, nonverbal behaviors (e.g., head nodding, smiling, laughing), and group dynamics (Krueger & Casey, 2008). The facilitator and observers convened for approximately 30 minutes once the group had concluded to process their experience, including personal reactions, emergent themes, social climate, and any problematic issues.

The focus groups took place in two locations: an enclosed private room at a community center and an enclosed private room at a university in the northeast. Before the formal interviewing started, participants indicated agreement to be audiotaped and to participate in the research via consent forms. The duration of the focus group as well as the debriefing session between facilitator and observer was audiotaped and then transcribed verbatim (with identifying information removed). Once transcription was complete, all tapes were destroyed. The transcripts were checked for accuracy by both the facilitator and the observer prior to data analysis.

A directed content analysis was used to qualitatively analyze the data. The goal of a directed approach to content analysis "is to validate or extend conceptually a theoretical framework or theory" (Hsieh & Shannon, 2005, p. 1281). The aim of the present study is to validate (or extend) the gender microaggressions taxonomy (Nadal, 2010; Sue & Capodilupo, 2008). Using the taxonomy, the research team members worked independently to identify key concepts or variables as the initial coding categories (Hickey & Kipping,

1996). Next, the research team met as a whole and developed initial definitions of the eight categories (i.e., *second-class citizen, assumption of inferiority*, etc.) identified in the gender microaggressions taxonomy (Nadal, 2010; Sue & Capodilupo, 2008). Each individual member of the team then carefully reviewed each transcript, highlighting all text that appeared to describe a participant's interpretation or description of a microaggression experience. A different color served to represent each taxonomy category (e.g., blue = *assumption of inferiority*). Highlighted text was coded using the predetermined categories. If a response was able to fit into more than one category, members made a note and highlighted with both colors to be able to discuss with the team later. Any text that could not be classified into one of these categories was marked in a distinct color and coded with the label the team member felt captured the essence of the participant's experience. Later, the researchers came to consensus on determining codes for data that could not be classified via the taxonomy.

Once all coding was complete, the researchers determined that they had a large amount of data that was uncoded because it did not represent either (1) a type of microaggressive incident or (2) the message conveyed by the incident—both of which are captured by the gender microaggressions taxonomy that informed the coding scheme. It is common procedure at this stage of analysis to compare the extent to which the data are supportive of the existing framework versus how much represents uncaptured aspects (Hsieh & Shannon, 2005). Team members independently worked to classify the uncoded data into categories and then met as a group to come to consensus on these categories. However, it is beyond the scope of this chapter to present data that was coded in this secondary process. These data represented various forms of reactions to microaggressions and included the subcategories of ignoring microaggressions, allowing microaggressions due to gender roles, minor confrontation, anger, humiliation, and feeling unsafe.

It has been suggested that a directed content-analysis approach can result in an overemphasis on theory that "blinds researchers to contextual aspects of the phenomenon" (Hsieh & Shannon, 2005, p. 1283). For this reason, an audit process was used in the current investigation. The auditor was a female doctoral candidate who has experience with research on women's issues, sexism, and qualitative methodology. The auditor independently reviewed the transcripts, first without codes and then again once all coding was complete. She then discussed these initial categories with the team and raised questions about the uncoded data that were instrumental in aiding the team to assign new operational categories to these data. In this study, the researchers opted not to rigidly adhere to the gender microaggression taxonomy, in order to include reactions to microaggressions as part of the analysis.

RESULTS

Six out of eight taxonomy categories were supported by the data. These themes include sexual objectification, sexist language, second-class citizen, assumption of inferiority, assumption of traditional gender roles, and environmental microaggressions. One original theme, denial of the reality of sexism, and one new theme, leaving gender at the door, represent two underdeveloped categories (i.e., they were supported by data from only one participant in a single group).

SEXUAL OBJECTIFICATION

The theme of sexual objectification refers to behaviors and verbal and nonverbal indicators that reduce a woman to her physical appearance and/or sexuality. Participants in all groups relayed experiences of sexual objectification and discussed feeling like their "body is all men see." An 18-year-old participant in the first focus group spoke of the frequent occurrence of being catcalled: "[At private school] we had to wear these skirts, and every time we passed by, there would be a bunch of guys cracking jokes, and you know, whistling." An 18-year-old Latina participant in the third group relayed a similar incident: "It happens all the time. I mean, like, you know, sometimes just walking down the street, you hear a guy whistling at you or saying 'Oh, hey, you look really cute' or something. 'Let me know your name.'" A 43-year-old woman in the first focus group spoke about being in an elevator with a man who gave her a "leering look." She further commented that "it's a constant thing, and I don't understand why it's still there." This participant also discussed an environmental microaggression that conveyed sexual objectification: Her male co-worker would hang pin-up pictures of women on his wall in the workplace.

In addition to verbal comments and nonverbal gestures such as staring, participants discussed being approached and even touched by strangers in public places. For example, an Asian American participant in the second focus group spoke about an incident on public transportation: "Some stranger guy tried to pick me up on the subway, and that completely creeped me out....I was trying to shoot him down, but he thought I was, like, playing hard to get or something." Other participants spoke about experiences on public transportation as well: "I've had some experiences on the train where you're getting out the door and you suddenly feel someone's hand on your rear end or whatever."

SECOND-CLASS CITIZEN

Second-class citizen refers to incidents that convey to a woman that she does not deserve the same opportunities, benefits, or privileges that are afforded to men. Participants in the second and third focus groups spoke about situations in which they felt like second-class citizens. For example, a 34-year-old woman in the second focus group was discussing differential salaries between men and women at her place of work: "[It's like we're] not as smart or capable and that's why we are not paid as well for the same work." Not being paid for the same level of work may also be considered an environmental microaggression, because it is a systemic issue that conveys the message that women are not as valuable as men. A White woman in the third group relayed her experience of playing on a girls' sports team in high school: "I guess the guys' teams would get, you know, new uniforms every year....They would get new equipment, whereas...the girls' teams, really, we kept the same uniforms for, like, a good five years at a time, and our equipment wouldn't be as good. It would be broken." This participant went on to discuss how she and other members of her team felt devalued and overlooked. Her story was met with several verbal and nonverbal signs of agreement from other participants in the group.

ASSUMPTIONS OF INFERIORITY

Participants in all three focus groups relayed incidents during which men assumed them to be less capable, both physically and mentally. A 20-year-old woman in the third group discussed that she is frequently overlooked when it comes to physical tasks at work: "I mean, my job, I don't necessarily move heavy boxes or anything like that, but a lot of the times, like, the men... they won't...they purposely just won't go ask the girl to do it." Several participants agreed that in their places of work or at school, men are called upon almost exclusively to help with physical tasks such as lifting boxes or technical tasks such as fixing computer equipment. The participants frequently spoke about men's reactions to their participation in women's sports. For example, a Latina woman stated: "I was on the soccer team. ...The guys would sometimes tell us we should stay out of the field because we might break one of our nails and we should instead go take cooking classes." This participant further discussed her feeling that these males were communicating that there is "no point" in women playing sports, because they are not as skilled as their male counterparts. Another participant shared a similar story: "[Often when I played sports, the boys] were definitely like that, which is coming outright and saying, you know, 'We don't really want you here. You really shouldn't be here!'" This participant shared that the girls' teams were treated as less important than the boys' teams, which she attributed to the males' belief that the women were "far less athletically talented."

ASSUMPTIONS OF TRADITIONAL GENDER ROLES

There were many examples from all three focus groups of incidents that involved implicit or explicit messages that women should occupy traditional gender roles such as being "soft and feminine" and caregiving, not using profanity or drinking, and being "domestic." A 21-year-old woman discussed being told that she should neither smoke cigarettes nor frequent a bar by herself: "Not now, but I used to smoke....In Japan, the guys think women shouldn't smoke....So, I went to the bar alone, but this guy said, 'Oh, you can't come to the bar alone, because you are a woman—you have to have somebody to go with you.'" A White woman shared a similar sentiment referring to behaviors that seem to be acceptable for men but that are judged harshly when exemplified by women:

> People expect you to be more polite, more dainty, just because, you know, you are a woman....Guys they are around in public, they curse, they burp, they do this, they do that, but if a woman were to do that, people would be like, "Oh my god, what is she doing? Who does she think she is?" What is acceptable for a man to do in public is totally different than what a woman is expected to do in public.

Other participants spoke about assumptions of domesticity; specifically, they felt expected to cook and clean for men. For example, a 24-year-old woman discussed feeling that she "should prepare a meal for [her] husband." A 19-year-old woman in her group concurred and responded, "Yeah, in my house also, it was always like the woman cooks the meal and cleans the table and the man just doesn't even think about doing that." A Latina woman in the third group shared a similar story: "At home, my stepfather is, like, old-fashioned, and...he's usually lazy and he does not clean. He just throws his stuff around....I mean, but like, me and my sister or my mom do clean up after him....My mom used to always say that a woman has to...clean after her husband." A White woman in the same group responded: "When we were girls, we were always put into this image that we're going to be the mother, we're going to have the kids. We're always with our moms, cooking, learning, you know, dressing up like her, thinking you know what will be the perfect mom. It's already pre-arranged for us."

SEXIST LANGUAGE

Participants in two out of the three groups discussed the use of indirect and direct sexist language. A 43-year-old participant discussed words she had overheard being used in her office to describe women: "They're bimbos, they're stupid, they don't have brains, women in general." This particular use of language seems to be related to the category of *sexual objectification*, as the participant goes on to state, "It was just, like, might as well just be a model, as a model to men with nothing behind it. It's all physical and that's all." A 19-year-old woman shared a similar sentiment about the use of sexist language that also conveys how men and women are held to different standards of behavior: "You know, if a guy has, like, a lot of girls, and they, like, have sex with all the other girls, they're not called sluts or anything like that....'You're a player,' or like, 'Oh! You're the man!' Like, they're cool. And then if a girl does it, it's all pretty different. It's like, 'Oh! You're a slut. You're sleeping with how many guys?'" Her comment was met with various verbal and nonverbal indicators of agreement around the group.

ENVIRONMENTAL MICROAGGRESSIONS

Participants discussed cues in their social context and environment that represented gender microaggressions. As aforementioned, one participant talked about the discomfort she felt when a co-worker hung up pictures of pin-up models in the workplace, and another participant recognized that women do not get paid the same as men for the same type of work. A separate example of an environmental microaggression included a 43-year-old woman who talked about how she felt about seeing so few women in the corporate world. Seeing very few women in a particular field (e.g., banking, business) may send the message that women are less than or not capable of being successful in that arena. Similarly, a 20-year-old woman discussed how she wanted to play on a Little League baseball team as a child but how she assumed she could not, because there were no girls on the team. While no one directly told her that she could not play, the subtle message that she received from her surroundings was that girls were not allowed and/or that girls could not play sports as well as boys.

UNDERDEVELOPED THEMES

Two underdeveloped themes emerged, represented by incidents that were reported by only one participant. One included *denial of the reality of sexism* in which a woman shared how she complained to her boss about a coworker's sexist behavior, and he replied with "Just ignore it. Don't worry about it." A new category, *leaving gender at the door*, was an underdeveloped theme that emerged from the data and was not captured by the taxonomy. It represents incidents that convey to women to keep feminine aspects of their selves out of the given scenario, such as the workplace or a social discussion. The implication seems to be that characteristics and qualities associated with women should be prohibited in some way. For example, the 43-year-old participant noted, "Some [women] conduct their job as a guy would, because that's how they get ahead. That's what they think. Some of them feel that they have to be like one of the guys." Table 9.1 presents each theme with accompanying examples and implied messages.

Table 9.1
Examples of Gender Microaggressions

Theme	Example	Message
Sexual objectification: occurs when a woman is treated as a sexual object	"[At private school] we had to wear these skirts, and every time we passed by, there would be a bunch of guys cracking jokes, and you know, whistling." "Some stranger guy tried to pick me up on the subway, and that completely creeped me out.... I was trying to shoot him down, but he thought I was, like, playing hard to get or something."	Women's value is in their bodies; they are meant to entertain men.
Second-class citizen: occurs when a woman is overlooked and/or when men are given preferential treatment	"[It's like we're] not as smart or capable and that's why we are not paid as well for the same work." A female sports team not getting the same resources or funding as a male sports team	Women's contributions are not as valuable as men's.
Assumptions of inferiority: occurs when a woman is assumed to be less competent than a man (e.g., physically or intellectually)	"I mean, my job, I don't necessarily move heavy boxes or anything like that, but a lot of the times, like, the men...they won't...they purposely just won't go ask the girl to do it." When playing sports, men telling women that they don't want to play with them.	Women are not physically capable.
Assumptions of traditional gender roles: occurs when an individual assumes that a woman should maintain traditional gender roles	"People expect you to be more polite, more dainty, just because, you know, you are a woman.... Guys they are around in public, they curse, they burp, they do this, they do that, but if a woman were to do that, people would be like, 'Oh my God, what is she doing? Who does she think she is?' What is acceptable for a man	Women should be feminine.

	to do in public is totally different than what a woman is expected to do in public."	
	Women are expected to cook and clean in the house, while men are not	Women should be domesticated.
Use of sexist language: occurs when language is used to degrade a woman	"They're bimbos, they're stupid, they don't have brains, women in general."	Women are intellectually inferior.
	"You know, if a guy has, like, a lot of girls, and they, like, have sex with all the other girls, they're not called sluts or anything like that.... 'You're a player,' or like, 'Oh! You're the man!' Like, they're cool. And then if a girl does it, it's all pretty different. It's like, 'Oh! You're a slut. You're sleeping with how many guys?'"	There are different standards for men and women when it comes to sex.
Environmental invalidations: macrolevel aggressions that occur on systemic and environmental level	A male coworker hanging pln-up pictures of women on his wall in the workplace	Men have a right to sexualize women.
	The notion that women do not get paid the same as men for the same type of work	Women are inferior to men.
	The fact that there are so few women in the corporate world	Business is a man's world.

DISCUSSION

The results of this study support and extend the gender microaggression taxonomy put forth by Sue and Capodilupo (2008) and Nadal (2010). Six out of the original eight taxonomy categories were represented in the data: *sexual objectification, sexist language, second-class citizen, assumption of inferiority, assumption of traditional gender roles,* and *environmental microaggressions.* One of the original themes, *denial of the reality of sexism,* was supported by data from only one participant in one focus group; therefore, it was considered an underdeveloped theme. One new theme, *leaving gender at the door,* was also shared only by one participant and as such was considered an underdeveloped theme.

Participants in this study overwhelmingly reported incidents and perceived messages that represented *sexual objectification* and *assumption of traditional gender roles.* This supports previous investigations that suggest that traditional gender role stereotypes (Swim et al., 2001), sexual objectification, (Fredrickson & Roberts, 1997; Kozee et al., 2007; Swim et al., 2001), and unwanted romantic attention and sexual comments (Leaper & Brown, 2008) pervade women's daily experiences. This finding may reflect the idea that popular press and media are heavily saturated with images of the ideal female (both aesthetically and with regard to traditional gender roles; Orbach, 2009), which may shape society's beliefs about women's worth and contributions. In this way, men may feel authorized or supported in their objectifying and demeaning behaviors because they are reinforced by popular media. It is striking that the majority of women (across ages) in this study reported being leered at, "picked up," and even touched by complete strangers—experiences that made them feel "unsafe" and "vulnerable." Other studies indicate that such experiences lead to higher rates of self-objectification (Hill & Fischer, 2008; Kozee et al., 2007), depression, sexual dysfunction, eating disorders, and body image issues (Fredrickson & Roberts, 1997; Hill & Fischer, 2008). Thus, future studies should specifically query the impact and consequences of microaggressions that reflect sexual objectification.

Categories with the least amount of responses were *second-class citizen, environmental microaggressions,* and *denial of the reality of sexism.* It could be suggested that experiences that involve sexual objectification and traditional gender roles represent more obvious forms of sexism, while the other categories represent less obvious forms of sexism. For example, when a woman is treated like a sexual object and/or is told to adhere to traditional gender roles, perhaps she is more able to identify it as a sexist act or statement. Conversely, when a woman is called on less frequently in meetings or classrooms or is told by her boss that men and women are treated equally, she may not (or may be reluctant to) identify the act or statement as sexist. It would be important for future research to understand the degree to which microaggression categories are experienced and interpreted differentially by women.

This study provides support for the idea that gender microaggressions may manifest in three forms: microassaults, microinsults, and microinvalidations. For example, the experience of being catcalled on the street was identified as being a common experience for these women and a conscious act by the men who perpetrate these behaviors. Because these are conscious, they may be considered microassaults. This is further exemplified by participants' experiences of being called "bimbos" or "stupid," which are direct and conscious attacks on women. Microinsults were described when men (1) assumed that women cannot carry heavy boxes, (2) presumed that women would not be good at sports, or (3) assumed that women should cook and clean. The perpetrators in these cases may not be conscious of the sexism in their actions and may not recognize the insulting messages that are sent to the female recipients. Finally, microinvalidations occurred in the few cases involving leaving one's gender at the door or denying the reality of sexism. Because there were very few examples of microinvalidations, future research would be necessary to examine the prevalence of gender micro-invalidations and the impacts that they have on women.

The choice of how to respond (e.g., nonassertive versus assertive) and the psychological process that one undergoes when faced with gender micro-aggressions was not specifically queried in the present investigation; how-ever, some participants did share various reactions to these incidents. For example, some participants ignored the microaggressions and tried not to let the experiences "get to them." Other participants engaged in some minor confrontation (e.g., giving someone "the middle finger" from far away), while others denied that microaggressions existed at all. It has been sug-gested that more assertive methods (e.g., confronting) of responding can serve the function of terminating the behavior or educating the perpetrator about discrimination, while nonassertive methods (i.e., ignoring) can serve to provide self-soothing or comfort (see Swim, Cohen, & Hyers, 1998, for a review). Very few empirical studies have addressed the advantages and disadvantages of different reactions to microaggressions; this is an area for further inquiry. Of note, some of the younger female participants shared that they did not believe that sexism is "as bad as it was in previous generations." There are several potential reasons why participants may have felt this way. Because these participants are younger (and primarily students), they may not have had the opportunity to enter the working world and experience the types of sexism or sexual harassment that occur in the workplace (Klonoff & Landrine, 1995; Swim & Cohen, 1997). Or perhaps sexism has become more subtle, which may lead these participants to have more difficulty identifying it.

Moreover, it is important to examine how feminist identity development may play a role in identifying microaggressions. For example, focus group leaders, observers, and analysts recognized that there were some participants who maintained more feminist ideologies than others. Downing and Roush (1985) proposed a model of feminist identity development that includes a spectrum of stages ranging from passive acceptance (when a woman is oblivious to sexism and/or denies that individual or institutional sexism exists) to active commitment (in which a woman is moved to meaningful and effective action regarding women's issues). Participants who appeared more likely to have higher levels of feminist identity seemed to recognize micro-aggressions more and appeared more likely to understand the psychological impacts that these microaggresssions would have on themselves and on other women. Participants who appeared less likely to have higher levels of feminist identity were those who appeared to be accepting and/or oblivious of sexism in their lives. For example, some participants seemed to allow microaggressions to occur, as demonstrated by one 18-year-old Latina who stated that she allowed men to carry heavy boxes for her. This may be similar to previous literature on benevolent sexism (see Glick & Fiske, 2001) in which some women may desire for men to be chivalrous and to maintain traditional gender roles. So, while benevolent sexism may be viewed as favorable or courteous by some, messages about women's inferiority are sent (consciously or unconsciously) to the women who receive them.

Limitations

The current investigation includes several limitations. First, though we followed saturation guidelines for focus group research (i.e., minimum of three groups run until no new themes emerge; Krueger & Casey, 2008), we believe that generalizability of our findings is limited. Though the sample was racially diverse and included a wide age range, it is important to note that 10 out of 12 participants were students, which may have affected results. For example, both underdeveloped themes, *denial of the reality of sexism* and *leaving gender at the door*, were discussed in the context of the workplace and were only shared by one participant (a 43-year-old woman). It may be that the students in this study, who have limited experience in the working world, have not experienced these kinds of microaggressions based on their social context. Future studies should assess for within-group differences by race, culture, age, social class, sexuality, and working status.

Second, the use of a directed content-analysis approach is an inherent limitation in that we approached the data from an informed position. We took several steps to account for this limitation, including the use of an audit process and the inclusion of open-ended questions in our interview protocol to elicit spontaneous responses. However, we are aware that data from our study remained uncoded because they did not fall within the operational definitions of our coding scheme. A perusal of these data revealed that reactions to microaggressions, both behavioral and emotional, were represented by these data but are not reflected in these results. Future studies should probe reactions to, coping skills for, and the impact of gender microaggressions.

Third, we noted that participants rarely discussed the intersections of their other identities (e.g., race/ethnicity, sexual orientation, and social class) with their gender identities. Given that there were several women of color in the focus groups, we should consider the idea that the interview protocol, the interviewer's and the observer's race, or some other factors prevented women of color from talking about microaggressive experiences that included their race or ethnicity. Other studies on microaggressions (e.g., Sue, Bucceri, et al., 2007) have supported the idea that Asian American women, for example, believe that microaggression incidents during which they feel exoticized are often directed at them because of both their race and gender. Future studies should specifically query the experiences of micro-aggressions across intersections of identities.

CONCLUSION

The current investigation represents a first attempt to empirically validate the gender microaggression taxonomy put forth by several authors (Nadal, 2010; Sue & Capodilupo, 2008). The results of this study indicate that gender microaggressions are a complex phenomenon, experienced more frequently when they reflect sexual objectification and an assumption of traditional gender roles. These categories have emerged and received similar validation in studies of both overt and subtle sexism. Future studies should further investigate the existence of microaggression incidents that may represent more subtle and covert forms of sexism, such as those related to assumptions of inferiority and second-class status. Understanding women's interpretations of and reactions to these events will also be an important step to discovering the impact and consequences of gender microaggressions on women. Given that women are reporting incidents of sexual objectification and assumption of traditional gender roles in high numbers, it is an important next step to understand how these experiences inform their self-perceptions, self-esteem, and self-worth. Further, a deeper understanding of the systemic impact of gender microaggressions is warranted. For example, women in this study felt devalued in the workplace and on sports teams. It is possible that the cumulative effect of these experiences leads women to withdraw from or avoid certain career paths or athletic endeavors, resulting in underrepresentation and an underrealization of women's abilities in these areas.

REFERENCES

Benokraitis, N. V. (1997). *Subtle sexism: Current practice and prospects for change.* Thousand Oaks, CA: Sage.

Downing, N. E., & Roush, K. L. (1985). From passive acceptance to active commitment: A model of feminist identity development for women. *Counseling Psychologist, 13* (4), 695–709.

Fassinger, R. E. (2005). Paradigms, praxis, problems, and promise: Grounded theory in counseling psychology research. *Journal of Counseling Psychology, 52*, 156–166.

Fine, M. (1992). Passion, politics, and power. In M. Fine (Ed.), *Disruptive voices: The possibilities of feminist research* (pp. 205–231). Ann Arbor: University of Michigan Press.

Glick, P., & Fiske, S. T. (2001). An ambivalent alliance: Hostile and benevolent sexism as complementary justifications for gender inequality. *American Psychologist, 56*(2), 109–118.

Hickey, G., & Kipping, C. (1996). Issues in research: A multi-stage approach to the coding of data from open-ended questions. *Nurse Researcher, 4,* 81–91.

Hill, M. S., & Fischer, A. R. (2008). Examining objectification theory: Lesbian and heterosexual women's experiences with sexual- and self-objectification. *Counseling Psychologist, 36,* 745–776.

Hsieh, H.-F., & Shannon, S. E. (2005). Three approaches to qualitative content analysis. *Qualitative Health Research, 15*(9), 1277–1288.

Klonoff, E. A., & Landrine, H. (1995). The Schedule Of Sexist Events: A measure of lifetime and recent sexist discrimination in women's lives. *Psychology of Women Quarterly, 19,* 439–472.

Kozee, H. B., Tylka, T. L., Augustus-Horvath, C. L., and Denchik, A. (2007). Development of psychometric evaluation of the Interpersonal Sexual Objectification Scale. *Psychology of Women Quarterly, 31*(2), 176–189.

Krueger, R. A., & Casey, M. A. (2008). *Focus groups: A practical guide for applied research* (4th ed.). Thousand Oaks, CA: Sage.

Leaper, C., & Brown, C. S. (2008). Perceived experiences with sexism among adolescent girls. *Child Development, 79*(3), 685–704.

Matteson, A. V., & Moradi, B. (2005). Examining the structure of the Schedule of Sexist Events: Replication and extension. *Psychology of Women Quarterly, 29,* 47–57.

Morrow, S. L., & Smith, M. L. (2000). Qualitative research for counseling psychology. In S. D. Brown & R. W. Lent (Eds.), *Handbook of counseling psychology* (pp. 199–230). New York: John Wiley & Sons.

Nadal, K. L. (2008). Preventing racial, ethnic, gender, sexual minority, disability, and religious microaggressions: Recommendations for promoting positive mental health. *Prevention in Counseling Psychology: Theory, Research, Practice and Training, 2*(1), 22–27.

Nadal, K. L. (2010). Gender microaggressions: Implications for mental health. In M. A. Paludi (Ed), *Feminism and Women's Rights Worldwide, Volume 2: Mental and Physical Health* (pp. 155–175). Santa Barbara, CA: Praeger.

Nielsen, L. B. (2002). Subtle, pervasive, harmful: Racist and sexist remarks in public as hate speech. *Journal of Social Issues, 58*(2), 265–280.

Orbach, S. (2009). *Bodies.* New York: Picador.

Sue, D. W., Bucceri, J., Lin, A. I., Nadal, K. L., & Torino, G. C. (2007). Racial microaggressions and the Asian American experience. *Cultural Diversity and Ethnic Minority Psychology, 13,* 72–81.

Sue, D. W. & Capodilupo, C. M. (2008). Racial, gender, and sexual orientation microaggressions: Implications for counseling and psychotherapy. In D. W. Sue & D. Sue (Eds.), *Counseling the culturally diverse: Theory and practice* (5th ed., pp. 105–130). Hoboken, NJ: John Wiley & Sons.

Sue, D. W., Capodilupo, C. M., Torino, G. C., Bucceri, J. M., Holder, A. M. B., Nadal, K. L., & Esquilin, M. (2007). Racial microaggressions in everyday life: Implications for clinical practice. *American Psychologist, 62,* 271–286.

Sue, D.W., Nadal, K.L., Capodilupo, C.M., Torino, G.C., Lin, A., & Rivera, D. (2008). Racial microaggressions against Black Americans: Implications for counseling. *Journal of Counseling and Development, 86*(3), 330–338.

Swim, J. K., & Cohen, L. L. (1997). Overt, covert, and subtle sexism: A comparison between the attitudes toward women and modern sexism scales. *Psychology of Women Quarterly, 21*(1), 103–118.

Swim, J. K., Cohen, L. L., & Hyers, L. L. (1998). Experiencing everyday prejudice and discrimination. In J. K. Swim & C. Stangor (Eds.), *Prejudice: The target's perspective.* San Diego, CA: Academic Press.

Swim, J. K., Hyers, L. L., Cohen, L. L., & Ferguson, M. J. (2001). Everyday sexism: Evidence for its incidence, nature, and psychological impact from three daily diary studies. *Journal of Social Issues, 57*(1), 31–53.

Swim, J. K., Mallett, R., & Stangor, C. (2004). Understanding subtle sexism: Detection and use of sexist language. *Sex Roles, 51*(3–4), 117–128.

Watkins, M. B., Kaplan, S., Brief, A. P., Shull, A., Dietz, J., Mansfield, M.-T., & Cohen, R. (2006). Does it pay to be a sexist? The relationship between modern sexism and career outcomes. *Journal of Vocational Behavior, 69*(3), 524–537.

APPENDIX A: INTERVIEW QUESTIONS

INTRODUCTION

Hi, my name is [interviewer]. And these are [observers]. They will not be participating in today's discussion but will simply observe to catch things that I may miss.

Thank you very much for coming today to participate in this focus group. The purpose of this group is to understand the experiences of subtle discrimination on specific racial groups, ethnic groups, genders, and sexual minority groups. OK, so, I am going to give you a form, which basically states that your participation in this group is entirely voluntary and that you may decline to participate and leave the interview at any time. Please read this sheet carefully before signing it. It discusses potential risks to you as an interviewee as well as the use of audiotaping during this session.

STATEMENT OF CONFIDENTIALITY

Before we start, I encourage you to share your experiences openly and honestly with me. I will be tape-recording this session in an effort to maintain the integrity of our dialogue. However, your identity will remain confidential, and only the researchers will have access to this tape. This discussion is to be considered confidential, and I would hope that you will all respect each other's right to privacy by not repeating any portion of this discussion outside the session. Do you all agree to keep all information confidential?

OPENING QUESTION

1. So, today we're going to be talking about microaggressions. Microaggressions can be defined as brief statements or behaviors that send denigrating and hurtful messages toward different groups. Because of our current politically correct society, many researchers have noticed that sexism is much more subtle than it may have been 10, 20, or 30 years ago. Today, you are all gathered as a group of women, so we will be discussing gender microaggressions.

At this time, I would like you to introduce yourself and tell me about your initial thoughts about microaggressions.

INTERVIEW QUESTIONS

1. Think about a time when you may have been blatantly discriminated against because of your gender. Describe the scenario as best as you can.

    a. How did you react in this situation?

    b. What do you perceive was the message that was being conveyed to you?

    c. How did you feel after the event? Several days after the event? Several months after the event?

3. Think about a time when you may have been subtly discriminated against because of your gender. Describe the scenario as best as you can.

    a. How did you react in this situation?

    b. What do you perceive was the message that was being conveyed to you?

    c. How did you feel after the event? Several days after the event? Several months after the event?

4. Describe a time when a man has made you feel uncomfortable because of your gender.

    a. How did you react in this situation?

    b. What do you perceive was the message that was being conveyed to you?

    c. How did you feel after the event? Several days after the event? Several months after the event?

5. Describe a time in which someone had made a disparaging remark or used derogatory language about your gender.

    a. How did you react in this situation?

    b. What do you perceive was the message that was being conveyed to you?

    c. How did you feel after the event? Several days after the event? Several months after the event?

6. Describe a circumstance in which someone's behavior made you feel uncomfortable, hurt, or devalued because of your gender.

    a. How did you react in this situation?

    b. What do you perceive was the message that was being conveyed to you?

    c. How did you feel after the event? Several days after the event? Several months after the event?

7. Describe a situation where you felt physically or emotionally unsafe because of your gender.

    a. How did you react in this situation?

    b. What do you perceive was the message that was being conveyed to you?

    c. How did you feel after the event? Several days after the event? Several months after the event?

8. Describe a situation where you felt pressured to act a certain way because of your gender.

    a. How did you react in this situation?

    b. What do you perceive was the message that was being conveyed to you?

    c. How did you feel after the event? Several days after the event? Several months after the event?

9. Describe a situation where you felt that someone treated you a certain way because of stereotypes about your gender.

    a. How did you react in this situation?

    b. What do you perceive was the message that was being conveyed to you?

    c. How did you feel after the event? Several days after the event? Several months after the event?

10. Describe a time when you felt that society (through the media, school system, religion, or other institutions) may have sent negative messages about your gender.

    a. How did you react in this situation?

    b. What do you perceive was the message that was being conveyed to you?

11. What impact do these experiences with subtle sexism have on your mental health?

CHAPTER 10

Sexual Orientation and Transgender Microaggressions
Implications for Mental Health and Counseling

KEVIN L. NADAL, DAVID P. RIVERA, and MELISSA J. H. CORPUS

P REJUDICE AND DISCRIMINATION have changed over the decades from a predominantly overt manifestation to a more subtle and covert form (Dovidio & Gaertner, 2000; Essed, 1991; Nadal, 2008; Solórzano, Ceja, & Yosso, 2000; Sue, Capodilupo, et al., 2007). Traditionally, the study on subtle forms of discrimination has focused on issues of race and gender. For example, Dovidio and Gaertner conceptualize "aversive racism" as being "the racial attitudes of many Whites who endorse egalitarian values, who regard themselves as nonprejudiced, but who discriminate in subtle, rationalizable ways" (p. 315). Additionally, a form of subtle discrimination that is believed to be largely responsible for workplace inequities is called "microinequity" and has been applied to sexual minorities, women, and other marginalized populations (Rowe, 1990). In terms of sexual orientation discrimination, Sue and Capodilupo (2008) postulate that sexual minorities also face daily subtle (and not-so-subtle) indignations due to their sexual orientation and refer to these instances as sexual orientation microaggressions. There are differences in the way these forms of contemporary discrimination have been conceptualized and defined; however, there appears to be one component that spans these conceptualizations. Because these forms of contemporary discrimination tend to be subtle and are often unconscious on the part of the aggressor, the phenomenon of "microaggression" appears to be the common denominator in the equation of each of these definitions.

Literature suggests that lesbian, gay, bisexual, and transgender (LGBT) individuals are exposed to overt sexual prejudice, as well as heterosexist/homophobic and transphobic communication and behaviors. Additionally,

217

sexual minorities and transgender individuals are frequently exposed to sexual orientation or transgender microaggressions, or unconscious forms of prejudice and discrimination toward LGBT people. This chapter will offer an overview of the literature pertaining to anti-LGBT phenomena, as well as provide a conceptualization of sexual orientation and transgender microaggressions.

PREVIOUS LITERATURE ON LGBT DISCRIMINATION, HATE CRIMES, AND MICROAGGRESSIONS

In order to understand sexual orientation and transgender microaggressions, it becomes important to recognize various forms of discrimination toward LGBT individuals, including hate crimes and other discriminatory acts that are more conscious and assaultive. A hate crime can be defined as a criminal act in which the victim is targeted because of the actual or perceived race, color, religion, national origin, ethnicity, disability, or sexual orientation (Anti-Defamation League, 2001). Examples of various hate crimes may include physical assaults, hate mail, threatening phone calls, vandalism, fires, and bombings. For LGBT individuals, hate crimes have been made public in the media, particularly with the well-publicized murder of gay college student Matthew Shepard in 1999 (Herek, 2000). However, it is important to recognize that hate crimes based on sexual orientation or transgender identity are often subtle and unreported (Herek, 2000). In fact, one study found that 94 percent of lesbian, gay, and bisexual individuals reported that they have been the victim of at least one hate crime in their lifetime (Herek, Cogan, & Gillis, 2002). Examples of these various hate crimes may include being bullied or physically assaulted at school for being gay, being called a "fag" or "dyke" (especially in a direct and/or assaultive way), or having the home of a gay or lesbian couple vandalized. Although these hate crimes may vary in type and severity, it appears that the majority of LGBT individuals have experienced the distress and trauma of a hate crime in their lifetime.

Hate crimes based on sexual orientation or transgender identity are comparable to race- and sex-related hate crimes commonly illustrated prior to the civil rights movement and contemporary "politically correct" times. For example, it may have been very acceptable to use the "N-word" in public settings, as it was acceptable (and even commonplace) to sexually harass women in the workplace. In these instances, the perpetrator is well aware of her or his actions and aims to enact assaultive, insulting, or hurtful behaviors onto her or his victims. Accordingly, both the perpetrator and victim are aware of the situation, leaving the two parties to react in different ways: the perpetrator feeling powerful and vindicated, while the victim feels frustrated, angry, hurt, depressed, and/or wronged. There are many potential reasons why perpetrators may enact hate crimes onto LGBT individuals, including their discomfort with LGBT people, their own discomfort with themselves, and/or their desire to exert power over another individual. On the contrary, hate crimes toward LGBT individuals may also have more severe psychological consequences than nonbias crimes, including depression, anxiety, post-traumatic stress disorder, and other mental health disparities in victims (Herek & Capitanio, 1999).

While there have been many legal ramifications and penalties for hate crimes in 44 out of 50 states, only 24 states have passed legislation that punishes hate crimes based on sexual orientation (Anti-Defamation League, 2001; Gay, Lesbian, Straight Education Network, 2004). Because less than half of the U.S. states reprimand hate crimes toward LGBT individuals, the U.S. population receives the implicit message that discrimination toward LGBT individuals is acceptable and inconsequential. Accordingly, it is possible that many heterosexual people may consider themselves to be good and open-minded people because they do not murder or physically attack LGBT individuals; however, they may be oblivious to the ways that they harass or insult LGBT individuals (or allow others to) in alternative, indirect ways.

It is also crucial to recognize that hate crimes that are reported based on sexual orientation do not capture the experiences of those who identify as transgender. For example, according to the Federal Bureau of Investigation (2007), there were 1,265 reported antibias incidents toward individuals based on sexual orientation. The number of hate crimes can further be categorized as anti–male homosexual (772 incidents), anti–female homosexual (145 incidents), anti-homosexual (304 incidents), anti-heterosexual (22 incidents), and anti-bisexual (22 incidents). Based on the aforementioned statistics, it is clear that hate crimes committed against transgender individuals are ignored. This trend is also found in the fields of psychology, education, social sciences, and other disciplines; transgender experiences are overlooked and assumed to be similar to lesbian, gay, or bisexual experiences.

Finally, it is necessary to acknowledge that hate crimes based on the intersections of sexual orientation and race may lead to dire consequences. For example, in 2003, a 15-year-old lesbian Black American female named Sakia Gunn was murdered as a result of a hate crime in New Jersey (Smith, 2004). While there were several thousand local individuals (mostly LGBT youth of color) who attended her funeral services, the event is one that is relatively unknown in public discourse. In contrast, the murder of Matthew Shepard, a young White male, received widespread national attention just a few years prior. The tragic death of Sakia Gunn demonstrates that hate crimes committed against individuals who are both racial and sexual minorities may not be nationally publicized as compared to White LGBT individuals.

SEXUAL PREJUDICE AND ANTIGAY HARASSMENT

While it is clear that public opposition to anti-LGBT discrimination has increased in our more accepting society (Herek, 2000), antigay sentiment still exists. For example, the passage of several propositions in 2008 banned same-sex marriage in California, Arizona, and Florida, as well as banned non-married couples (e.g., same-sex couples) from adopting children in Arkansas. Additionally, there are many bodies of work that suggest that individuals may enact prejudice and harass LGBT populations in direct and indirect ways. For example, some authors purport that individuals become prejudiced toward LGBT individuals as early as adolescence, with prejudice increasing during their middle school or junior high school years for both boys and girls, and even more in the high school years for boys (Baker & Fishbein, 1998). However, while prejudice may be defined as the negative thoughts and behaviors that one may hold toward another group, there are many ways that these prejudices may turn into actions. Various authors have defined this type of discrimination toward LGBT individuals as "sexual prejudice," "antigay harassment," "heterosexist harassment," or "sexual stigma."

Sexual prejudice is defined as "all negative attitudes based on sexual orientation, whether the target is homosexual, bisexual, or heterosexual" (Herek, 2000, p. 19). However, given the heterosexist nature of our society, most instances of sexual prejudice are targeted toward nonheterosexual individuals (Herek, 2000). Sexual prejudice can be used to describe heterosexuals' negative attitudes toward (1) homosexual behavior, (2) people with a homosexual or bisexual orientation, and (3) communities of gay, lesbian, and bisexual people. The authors assert that "sexual prejudice" is a preferable term to "homophobia," because many individuals can be heterosexist or enact sexual prejudice without necessarily having a fear of homosexuals or LGBT individuals. For example, a "liberal" may have LGBT friends and/or may be accepting of LGBT persons while unconsciously believing that heterosexuality is the norm, promoting heterosexual values, and/or holding negative stereotypes about LGBT persons.

Antigay harassment may be defined as "verbal or physical behavior that injures, interferes with, or intimidates lesbian women, gay men, and bisexual individuals" (Burn, Kadlec, & Rexer, 2005, p. 24). Antigay harassment is not necessarily direct or intended to be hurtful to LGBT persons; in fact, it is often indirect, taking the form of heterosexist jokes or comments. Many authors have cited that many adolescents (particularly heterosexual males) use words like "faggot" or "queer" as a way of insulting or hurting others (Burn, 2000). Additionally, in contemporary times, young American adolescents also use the word "gay" as an adjective when referring to something as dumb or undesirable (Burn et al., 2005). The message that is conveyed is that it is bad or inferior to be LGBT and that it is desirable, advantageous, and normal to be heterosexual. This type of harassment is usually targeted toward LGBT individuals but can also impact heterosexuals as well. When heterosexuals fail to conform to traditional gender roles, they are labeled as "gay" or a "dyke" and assumed to be homosexual (Friend, 1998); again, these statements imply that being identified as or affiliated with LGBT persons is shameful or unacceptable.

Heterosexist harassment can be defined as "insensitive verbal and symbolic (but nonassaultive) behaviors that convey animosity toward non-heterosexuality" (Silverschanz, Cortina, Konik, & Magley, 2007, p. 179). Authors conceptualize heterosexist harassment as having two forms: personal (or direct) experiences and ambient (or indirect) experiences. Personal experiences are situations where an individual is directly targeted because of her or his sexual orientation (e.g., being called a "dyke" or "queer" as an insult), while ambient experiences include situations where the LGBT individual is indirectly targeted (e.g., someone making offensive jokes about LGBT persons in front of an LGBT individual). The "Workplace Heterosexist Experiences Questionnaire" (WHEQ) assesses heterosexist harassment in the workplace (Waldo, 1999) and includes various items measuring direct and indirect heterosexism. Direct heterosexism aligns with overt sexual prejudice and antigay harassment (e.g., being harassed for being LGBT). However, the WHEQ offers several examples of indirect heterosexism. For example, asking someone "Why aren't you married?" is heterosexist in nature, because it assumes that being married is the norm, that all people have the legal privilege of being married, and that having an opposite-gendered spouse has significant value. Another example includes experiences where others made an LGBT person feel it was necessary to "act straight" (e.g., monitor your speech, dress, or mannerisms). This could be conveyed in a number of ways, including someone telling an LGBT person to dress or speak in more gender-conforming ways.

Sexual stigma refers to "negative regard, inferior status, and relative powerlessness that society collectively accords to any nonheterosexual behavior, identity, relationship, or community" (Herek, 2007, p. 906). There are three ways that sexual stigma can manifest among individuals, groups, and communities. First, enacted stigma is defined as the overt behavioral expression of sexual stigma. This is similar to the old-fashioned heterosexism that is direct and intentional, occurring when individuals perform hate crimes or deliberately use hurtful words to insult an LGBT person. Next, there is felt stigma, where LGBT individuals may modify their behavior in order to avoid difficult and dangerous situations or enacted stigma. For example, an individual may feel uncomfortable coming out in her or his workplace because of the heterosexist language or norms that her or his coworkers use; she or he feels sexual stigma, even if there are not any direct assaultive or insulting messages given to her or him. Finally, there is internalized stigma in which an individual's personal awareness and acceptance of sexual stigma becomes a part of her or his own value system, individualism, and self-concept. For example, a heterosexual individual may be aware of her or his heterosexist biases, while an LGBT individual may recognize the ways that she or he has internalized negative messages about being LGBT.

The different categories of sexual stigmas are also directly related to microaggressions. Enacted sexual stigmas appear to be similar to sexual prejudice and antigay harassment, while felt sexual stigmas seem to be related to microinvalidations or environmental microaggressions. With these felt sexual stigmas, LGBT individuals may not feel comfortable around certain heterosexuals because of messages that she or he may have received from them. Additionally, LGBT individuals may feel dismissed or invalidated in an environment where heterosexuals are celebrated, while LGBT persons feel like they have to remain closeted or invisible. Finally, it appears that internalized sexual stigma relates to the process whereby individuals become aware of heterosexism and understand how to cope with it. This parallels the aforementioned catch-22 process of racial microaggressions, where individuals learn how to pick their battles in responding to microaggressions and learn to cope in different ways by turning to their social networks (e.g., family, peers, or significant others).

Sexual prejudice, antigay harassment, and heterosexist harassment are all interrelated to sexual orientation and transgender microaggressions. When these prejudices influence an individual's behaviors toward LGBT persons, these actions can take the form of microassaults or microinsults, depending on the situation. For example, if someone is called a "faggot" directly, the behavior is overt, intentional, and malicious; however, if two adolescent students are talking to each other and they use the word "faggot" to taunt each other, an LGBT person who overhears this may feel insulted. In these cases, it appears that the intention and the awareness of the behavior can determine how the microaggression is classified. If the behavior is overt, intentional, and malicious, it would be considered a microassault; if the behavior is covert, unintentional, and not malicious, it would be classified as a microinsult.

MODERN HETEROSEXISM AND MODERN HOMONEGATIVITY

Previous literature has examined how racism and sexism have become more subtle, describing how "modern racism" or "modern sexism" has emerged in American society (Sue & Capodilupo, 2008; Swim & Cohen, 1997).

Accordingly, researchers have also utilized the models of modern racism and sexism to understand modern heterosexism (Cowan, Heiple, Marquez, Khatchadourian, & McNevin, 2005; Walls, 2008) or modern homonegativity (Morrison & Morrison, 2002). Conceptualizations of modern heterosexism maintain that heterosexism toward LGBT individuals is covert and less pathologizing of LGBT persons and assert that same-sex-oriented people are marginalized, while heterosexual people are celebrated in society (Walls, 2008). Similarly, definitions of homonegativity include any prejudicial affective or behavioral response directed toward an individual because she or he is (or is perceived to be) homosexual (Cerny & Polyson, 1984; Morrison, Parriag, & Morrison, 1999). Modern heterosexism and modern homonegativity align with theories of microaggressions in that they purport that prejudice and discrimination is less direct and overt. Accordingly, when heterosexuals do not commit any hate crimes toward LGBT people, they may be unaware of the negative impacts that these heterosexist slights have toward LGBT individuals.

Similar to the review of sexual prejudice and antigay harassment, there are many ways that modern heterosexism and modern homonegativity correlate with sexual orientation and transgender microaggressions. First, it appears that there is a spectrum of behaviors that may be labeled as microassaultive, microinsulting, or microinvalidating. For example, changing seats to be further away from a LGBT person would be microinsulting, while creating an environment where someone feels pushed to "stay in the closet" can be considered microinvalidating. Second, the heterosexist and homonegative behaviors may appear to be harmless but may have a cumulative impact on the LGBT recipient of these microaggressions. For example, while it may seem harmless that an individual put more distance between herself or himself and an LGBT person, the message that is conveyed to the LGBT person is that she or he is contagious, disgusting, immoral, deviant, or dangerous, adversely impacting that individual's self-esteem, self-concept, or mental health.

TRANSPHOBIA/GENDERISM

There are very few studies in psychology that examine the discrimination that may occur toward transgender persons. As aforementioned, hate crimes toward transgender persons are not labeled as such and instead are labeled as hate crimes on the basis of sexual orientation. Moreover, while LGBT hate crimes are underreported in general, hate crimes toward transgender persons are even more invisible and are not likely to be publicized to the general society. There are two major terms that are used to describe the discrimination and prejudice that transgender persons may experience: transphobia and genderism. Transphobia can be defined as "an emotional disgust toward individuals who do not conform to society's gender expectations" (Hill & Willoughby, 2005, p. 533), while genderism is "an ideology that reinforces the negative evaluation of gender non-conformity or an incongruence between sex and gender" (Hill & Willoughby, 2005, p. 534). Transphobia may be a parallel term to homophobia in which individuals are fearful of gay, bisexual, and lesbian people, while genderism may be a parallel term to heterosexism, which describes the subtle ways that individuals may be prejudiced toward gay, bisexual, and transgender persons. While our changing society encourages individuals to be less racist, less sexist, and even less heterosexist, it is possible that individuals (heterosexual and even lesbian, gay, or bisexual) may maintain transphobic or genderist views. This may be due to the rigidity of gender roles in U.S. society, particularly with gender role presentation in which men and women are expected to act, behave, dress, and speak in gender-normative ways.

The research on transphobia and genderism are correlated with microaggressions in numerous ways. First, gender-bashing appears to be most similar to microassaults in that the behaviors are intentional and sometimes assaultive. However, transphobia and genderism may be similar to microinsults or microinvalidations in that they represent the types of internal feelings that individuals may have, which may then manifest in discriminatory behaviors toward transgender persons. For example, if an individual believes that cross-dressing or sex-change operations are wrong, then it is possible that this belief may be noticeable in her or his interpersonal interactions with a cross-dresser or transgender person (e.g., noticeably uncomfortable body language and facial expressions). Additionally, because these genderist or transphobic beliefs may be unconscious, individuals may be completely unaware of their prejudices and biases and therefore may even be completely oblivious to their discriminatory actions as well.

PSYCHOLOGICAL IMPACTS OF SEXUAL ORIENTATION AND TRANSGENDER MICROAGGRESSIONS

There have been many studies that have documented the psychological distress that LGBT individuals experience as a result of sexual discrimination. Some authors have cited that the harassment of gays during adolescence can be linked to the exceptionally high rate of suicide among LGBT youth (D'Augelli, 1992). Other authors have examined how LGBT individuals experience "minority stress," or chronic, consistent stress that is related to their stigmatization and marginalization as LGBT people (Meyer, 1995). This minority stress can create hostile and distressing home, work, and social environments, leading to many mental health problems including depression, anxiety, post-traumatic stress, and internalized homophobia (Meyer, 2003). Other studies have examined how experiences of discrimination and stigmatization may lead to lower self-esteem, fears of rejection, and/or consistent hiding or concealing of identities (Burn et al., 2005; Rostosky, Riggle, Gray, & Hatton, 2007). Accordingly, it is important to recognize that while it has been documented that hate crimes or assaultive experiences toward LGBT persons may lead to mental health disparities (Herek & Capitanio, 1999), sexual orientation/ transgender microaggressions and other subtle forms of heterosexism, homonegativity, transphobia, and genderism may lead to several mental health problems as well. Finally, some studies have asserted that much like other minority groups, failing to recognize, cope with, or acknowledge discrimination can lead to negative health consequences for LGBT people, as measured by an increase in sick days, physician visits, and nonprescription drug usage (Huebner & Davis, 2007). So, not only do LGBT persons and other minorities experience mental health disparities due to microaggressions and other forms of discrimination, but they also experience problems with their physical health, which may include everything from a weaker immune system to higher blood pressure (which have been documented in the medical fields to be caused by stress).

Taxonomy of Sexual Orientation and Transgender Microaggressions

There is only one body of work that examines sexual orientation/transgender microaggressions, including categories of microaggressions, examples, and the messages that are conveyed (see Sue & Capodilupo, 2008). While 12 categories of microaggressions are included, only 4 categories can be applied to sexual orientation microaggressions toward gay, lesbian, or bisexual individuals, while the other categories concentrate primarily on race and gender. Additionally, microaggressions toward transgender individuals are not openly addressed or discussed. The four categories include the themes of (1) second-class citizen, (2) traditional gender role prejudicing and stereotyping, (3) use of sexist/heterosexist language, and (4) assumption of abnormality. The theme of "second-class citizen" occurs when a target group receives differential treatment than a dominant group. For example, this may transpire when an LGBT couple is given secondary service to heterosexual couples. The theme of "traditional gender role prejudicing and stereotyping" takes place when individuals assume that others should hold traditional gender roles or stereotypes. An example may include a woman who is assumed to be a lesbian because she does not wear makeup. The theme of "use of sexist/heterosexist language" refers to language that conveys subtle sexism (e.g., writing the pronoun "he" to refer to all people) and heterosexism (e.g., using the word "gay" to convey that something is bad). Finally, the theme of "assumption of abnormality" occurs when it is implied that it is wrong or immoral to be LGBT. For example, this can occur if someone stares in disgust at a gay male couple holding hands or two lesbians displaying affection in public. While these themes of sexual orientation microaggressions demonstrate the examples of actions, behaviors, and statements that can convey denigrating messages toward LGBT individuals, they do not capture the entire experience that LGBT persons may have with microaggressions. Due to the lack of literature concerning the cumulative nature of sexual orientation or transgender microaggressions, it becomes important for psychologists, counselors, and other practitioners to become aware of the spectrum of microaggressions that LGBT individuals may experience in their everyday lives.

On the basis of the previous literature involving microaggressions, sexual prejudice, antigay harassment, sexual stigma, modern heterosexism, modern homonegativity, transphobia, and genderism, this chapter will provide a taxonomy of the major types of sexual orientation and transgender microaggressions that may occur toward lesbian, gay, bisexual, and transgender persons in everyday life and in therapeutic settings. This hypothesis is based on several empirical studies that have revealed that LGBT individuals experience sexual prejudice (see Herek, 2000, for a review), antigay harassment (see Burn et al., 2005, for a review), and sexual stigma (see Herek, 2007, for a review) and are the victims of modern heterosexism (see Morrisson & Morrison, 2002, for a review) and modern homonegativity (see Walls, 2008, for a review). The hypothesis is also derived from research on transgender individuals who are the recipients of transphobia and genderism (see Hill & Willoughby, 2005, for a review).

There are nine proposed themes of sexual orientation and transgender microaggressions that are identified, including (1) use of heterosexist terminology, (2) endorsement of heteronormative culture/behaviors, (3) assumption of universal LGBT experience, (4) exoticization, (5) discomfort/disapproval of LGBT experience, (6) denial of societal heterosexism/transphobia, (7) assumption of sexual pathology/abnormality, (8) denial of individual heterosexism, and (9) environmental macroaggressions. Table 10.1 lists themes, examples of experiences of sexual orientation and transgender microaggressions, and the messages that are directly or indirectly communicated to the recipient.

These themes of sexual orientation and transgender microaggressions align with the previous literature with racial microaggressions (Sue, Capodilupo, et al., 2007) and gender microaggressions (Nadal, 2010) in that (1) many of these microaggressions are unconscious, and the perpetrator may not realize the impact on the recipient; (2) these microaggressions (whether conscious

Table 10.1
Examples of LGBT Microaggressions in Everyday Life

Theme	Example	Message
Use of heterosexist or transphobic terminology: occurs when heterosexist language is used to degrade LGBT persons	A male student is called a "faggot" by his peers; a female is called a "dyke" by her peers.	LGBT persons are bad. You are inferior.
	Someone says "That's so gay" when talking about something negative.	Gay is bad. I have a right to talk negatively about LGBT people.
	An employer refuses to refer to a female-to-male transgender individual as "he."	I don't have to approve your lifestyle.
	A male individual is told to bring his wife to a social function.	Heterosexuality is normal; everything else is not.
Endorsement of heteronormative or gender normative culture/behaviors: occurs when LGBT persons are expected to be or act like heterosexuals	A family member tells an LGBT person, "Please don't act so gay in public settings."	Being gay is bad; you are not allowed to be yourself.
	An individual tells her/his LGBT coworker that being in an open, nonmonogamous romantic relationship is immoral.	Heterosexuality is moral; everything else is not.
	A professor tells her/his students that bisexuality does not exist.	Your experience is not valid.
	An individual tells a transgender or gender-nonconforming person, "I don't even know what to call you."	You are disgusting and worthless.
	Television shows only portray heterosexual or traditionally gendered couples.	Heterosexuality is the norm; everything else is not.
Assumption of universal LGBT experience: occurs when individuals assume that all LGBT persons are the same	Someone says, "You know how gay people are."	You are not an individual.
	An acquaintance asks a gay male if he likes interior designing.	You people are all the same.
	In a classroom discussion about gender, a lesbian student is asked to speak on behalf of all LGBT persons.	You are not an individual.
Exoticization: occurs when LGBT persons are dehumanized or treated like objects	A heterosexual man tells a lesbian couple that he would like to engage in a threesome with them.	You are a sexual object; I have a right to sexualize you.

(continued)

Table 10.1
(Continued)

Theme	Example	Message
	Someone refers to an individual as their "gay friend."	You only have one purpose in my life.
	An individual says, "I love gay people. They're so much fun!"	You are here for my entertainment.
	A stranger asks a transgender person about her/his genitalia.	I have a right to ask you whatever I want.
Discomfort/disapproval of LGBT experience: occurs when LGBT individuals are treated with disrespect or condemnation	A stranger stares at an affectionate LGBT couple in disgust.	You are sickening.
	A roommate moves out of her/his apartment when she/he learns that her/his roommate is gay/lesbian.	You are immoral and/or contagious.
	A religious group holds signs that state "Faggots are going to hell" at a gay funeral or protest.	You are evil. I have a right to tell you what is moral.
	LGBT history is left out of high school history textbooks.	LGBT people do not/should not exist.
Denial of societal heterosexism/transphobia: occurs when individuals deny LGBT persons that heterosexist/homophobic experiences exist	An LGBT person is told by a heterosexual person that she/he is being paranoid when she/he suspects that others are homophobic.	You complain too much.
	Someone tells an LGBT person that she/he didn't get a job because she/he was not qualified, not because of her/his sexual orientation.	You are to blame, not your sexual orientation.
Assumption of sexual pathology/abnormality: occurs when LGBT persons are presumed to be oversexualized and/or sexual deviants	Someone asks an LGBT person if she/he has HIV/AIDS.	You are sexually immoral and deserve to get HIV/AIDS.
	An individual is surprised when she/he hears that an LGBT person is in a monogamous relationship.	LGBT persons are all sexual deviants.
	A parent tries to keep her/his children away from an LGBT person.	LGBT people prey on children.
Denial of individual heterosexism/transphobia: occurs when a heterosexual	Someone says, "I'm not homophobic. I have a gay friend!"	I am incapable of heterosexism.

| denies her/his heterosexist biases or prejudice | An individual is defensive when corrected about her or his misuse of pronouns with a transgender person. | You don't have a right to correct me. |
| | Someone says, "As a person of color, I'm offended that you would imply that I'm homophobic." | Because I belong to another oppressed group, I do not have biases. |

or not) communicate a variety of oppressive messages to the LGBT individuals who receive them; and (3) the various themes of these microaggressions represent the spectrum of microassaults, microinvalidations, and microinsults. However, microaggressions against LGBT persons may differ from racial microaggressions in that (1) it is more acceptable to be blatantly heterosexist/homophobic or genderist/transphobic than it is to be racist or sexist in American society, (2) microassaults would likely be more common toward LGBT persons than they would be toward persons of color in contemporary American society, and (3) religious and family values (that are usually drawn from religious beliefs) may influence one's view of what is considered discriminatory against LGBT persons.

Previous literature can be revisited to support the categories in the taxonomy of sexual orientation and transgender microaggressions in a number of ways.

Category 1, *use of heterosexist or transphobic terminology*, is thoroughly supported by aforementioned literature of antigay harassment that states that the usage of heterosexist and oppressive terminology (e.g., "fag," "dyke," or "queer") may have an impact on individuals' self-esteem and comfort in accepting their sexual identities (Burn et al., 2005). This may even include unintentional language that connotes superiority of heterosexuality to nonheterosexuality. For example, when someone equates the word "normal" to heterosexuality (e.g., "Did you go to a gay bar or a normal bar?"), an LGBT person may feel insulted, hurt, and misunderstood.

Category 2, *endorsement of heteronormative or gender normative culture/ behaviors*, is established from two sources: (1) previous literature on racial microaggressions, which states that dominant groups tend to assume that oppressed groups should adapt their values, beliefs, and communication styles (Sue, Bucceri, Lin, Nadal, & Torino, 2007; Sue, Capodilupo, et al., 2007; Sue et al., 2008); and (2) previous literature on heterocentrism, which assumes that human beings are naturally heterosexual and that heterosexual lifestyles are the normal standard against which those of sexual minority people should be compared in order to be understood and evaluated (Herek, 1998). For example, it has been accepted in the LGBT community that nonmonogamy can be successful and healthy in maintaining romantic relationships. Studies have shown that only one-third of gay males in romantic relationships are exclusively monogamous (Bryant & Demian, 1994; LaSala, 2004). However, for heterosexuals, monogamy is viewed as the only option for successful romantic relationships, and LGBT couples are penalized or deemed immoral if they do not practice monogamy (Shernoff, 2006). Accordingly, many individuals may have biases that might prohibit them from understanding LGBT individuals from a cultural perspective. Additionally, many individuals assume that others are heterosexual instead of assuming that they could be lesbian, gay, or bisexual (Waldo, 1999). This would be invalidating to these individuals, because it is sending a message that heterosexuality is normal and that being lesbian, gay, or bisexual is abnormal (Conley, Calhoun, Evett, & Devine, 2001). Finally, it is assumed that LGBT individuals should conform to gender role norms or else they would be considered different, evil, or immoral. It has been well documented that any individual who deviates from traditional masculine and feminine roles is particularly susceptible to heterosexist discrimination and even violence (Kite & Whitley, 1998). When heterosexuals directly solicit or indirectly convey that LGBT individuals should adhere to traditional roles, they send the message that LGBT identity is abnormal. Moreover, it is communicated that the affirmation of heterosexuality and gender-conforming norms (based on one's birth-sex) is the standard.

Category 3, *assumption of universal LGBT experience*, is based on previous works of microaggressions (Sue, Bucceri, et al., 2007; Sue, Capodilupo, et al., 2007; Sue et al., 2008) and White privilege (McIntosh, 2003), which state that individuals of oppressed groups are often asked to represent or speak on behalf of their entire cultural group. Moreover, the assumption that there is a "correct way" of being LGBT is one that can oppress many subgroups in the LGBT community—particularly LGBT persons of color, bisexuals, and transgender persons, who may have different processes of identity development, "coming out of the closet," or navigating the LGBT community (Nadal & Corpus, in press). Additionally, LGBT persons who do not fit traditional LGBT stereotypes may feel invalidated or frustrated when others assume that they should behave a specific way.

Category 4, *exoticization*, stems from literature on racial microaggressions in which people of color (particularly Asians or Latinos/as) are often deemed "exotic" for being different (Sue, Capodilupo, et al., 2007). This experience occurs for LGBT individuals, who are often viewed as "funny" or "entertainers" (Nadal & Corpus, in press). While this may be viewed as a positive quality, it also sends a message that LGBT people are only accepted if they are utilized for comic relief or amusement. In the media, this phenomenon is often known as "gaysploitation," because gay men and lesbian women are being exploited to entertain heterosexuals as fashion designers and consultants, comedic sexual deviants, or even gay minstrels. While this may mean an increase in LGBT images in the media, some have argued that this exploitation rejects any forward progress in the LGBT movement (Goldblatt, Barr, & Armstrong, 2003). Exoticization may also include sexual exoticization, particularly of lesbians. Some studies have supported that heterosexual men are disapproving of same-sex male relationships but are sexually aroused by and accepting of same-sex female relationships (Kite & Whitley, 1998). Some heterosexual men may even assume that lesbian couples would be interested in engaging in a threesome (or group sex) with them. This would be considered a microaggression, because the lesbian women in these scenarios are being treated as sexual objects and are not being validated for their sexual identities.

Category 5, *discomfort/disapproval of LGBT experience*, is perhaps the most common form of modern heterosexism/homonegativity or genderism in which individuals subtly enact their heterosexist/genderist biases through their behaviors and statements toward LGBT individuals. This is supported in the research of homonegative behaviors (Patel, Long, McCammon, & Wuensch, 1995; Roderick, McCammon, Long, & Alfred, 1998), which measures the active and passive avoidant actions and manners that heterosexuals engage in that promote heterosexism or convey fear of or discomfort with homosexuality. For example, items on the Self Report of Behavior Scale–Revised (SBS-R) assess harmful behavior toward gays or lesbians in a range of settings. One sample item on the SBS-R reads, "I have changed seat locations because I suspected the person sitting next to me was gay" (Patel et al., 1995). Such behavior sends the message that the heterosexual person is uncomfortable or distressed by being around the LGBT person, perhaps out of fear, awkwardness, lack of awareness, or anxiety. Discomfort can also manifest in genderist or transphobic behaviors. The Genderism and Transphobia Scale (GTS) captures the scope of affective, cognitive, and behavioral attitudes toward gender-nonconforming individuals. The three subscales within the GTS particularly target attitudes of gender-bashing, genderism, and transphobia. Furthermore, the GTS also measures a person's likelihood to enact violence toward a "gender-bending" individual. For example, an item in the GTS reads, "If a man wearing makeup and a dress, who also spoke in a high voice, approached my child, I would use physical force to stop him."

Category 6, *denial of heterosexism or transphobia*, is based on previous literature with racial and sexual microaggressions in which individuals of the dominant group emphasize that the oppressed group (e.g., people of color or women) complain too much about race or gender (Nadal, 2010; Sue, Bucceri, et al., 2007; Sue, Capodilupo, et al., 2007). This is exemplified in the literature on modern homonegative attitudes. For example, the Modern

Homonegativity Scale (MHS) is an instrument that captures present-day negative attitudes toward gay men and lesbian women. However, the MHS is unique in that it does not measure perspectives that are not based on ethical or religious reasoning. One item on the MHS reads, "Celebrations such as 'Gay Pride Day' are ridiculous because they assume that an individual's sexual orientation should constitute a source of pride." Another item reads, "If gay men want to be treated like everyone else, then they need to stop making such a fuss about their sexuality/culture" (Morrison & Morrison, 2002). These items reflect the central concepts of this instrument: (1) Gays and lesbians are requesting superfluous and unwarranted changes in society, (2) prejudice and discrimination toward gays and lesbians no longer exist, and (3) emphasizing the importance of sexual orientation prevents gays and lesbians from integrating into mainstream society.

Category 7, *assumption of sexual pathology/abnormality*, is based on the notion that LGBT individuals have often been viewed as sexual deviants or predators (Levitt & Klassen, 1974). In fact, it is common for LGBT persons to be assumed to endorse symptoms of various sexual disorders not only by members of general society but also by mental health professionals. In a recent study of therapist trainees, it was discovered that 92 percent of participants believed that gay men "felt like women" (gender identity disorder), while 57 percent believed that gay men became "aroused by strange objects" (fetishism). Forty-seven percent believed that gay men "sexually enjoyed suffering" (masochism), and 46 percent believed gay men were "sexually attracted to children" (pedophilia; Boysen, Vogel, Madon, & Wester, 2006). Additionally, since the inception of HIV/AIDS in the 1980s, HIV/AIDS has been deemed the "gay plague" or the gay disease (Flowers & Langdridge, 2007). This stigma leads to many societal and personal assumptions that all gay and bisexual men may be infected with the disease, as evidenced by the current ban on gay men from donating blood. Assumptions of sexual pathology are also related to exoticization for lesbian and bisexual women, who are often stereotyped as sexually kinky or "wild." Lesbians are assumed to be interested in unusual sexual acts with anyone, including heterosexual men. Microaggressions in this category can be exemplified in well-intentioned people who ask inappropriate questions about sex, particularly when they would not ask these questions of their heterosexual peers (Conley et al., 2001). These questions can be described as inappropriate questions (e.g., asking strangers or acquaintances about sexuality or personal topics) or prying questions (e.g., asking numerous questions out of curiosity, including "What do you do in bed?" or "Are you a top or a bottom?").

Category 8, *denial of individual heterosexism*, represents heterosexual individuals who invalidate LGBT persons by stating that they could never be heterosexist or homophobic. This is authenticated by research of well-intentioned heterosexuals who unconsciously offend LGBT persons by failing to admit to their own heterosexual biases and assumptions (Conley et al., 2001). For example, when a heterosexual individual states that she or he knows another gay person, when a traditional-gendered person says that she or he has a transgendered coworker, or when an individual points out that she or he is not prejudiced, she or he neglects to understand that her or his heterosexism or transphobia/genderism may negatively influence her or his relationships with LGBT individuals in subtle and/or hurtful ways.

IMPLICATIONS FOR COUNSELING

While sexual orientation and transgender microaggressions are commonly committed by practitioners in the therapeutic realm, there is a paucity of research concerning this topic. Moreover, mental health practitioners may be unaware of communicating a sexual orientation or transgender microaggression toward a client, whether verbally or nonverbally. This is partly due to clinicians' lack of knowledge regarding how microaggressions could manifest during a session with the client. Table 10.2 explores the various ways that microaggressions can occur in therapeutic settings by applying the proposed themes of sexual orientation and transgender microaggressions to potential enactments between therapist and client.

The conspicuous dearth of training and awareness concerning the LGBT population lends itself to therapeutic missteps, where clinicians might mirror and perpetuate the same negative, judgmental societal views of LGBT individuals. For example, during a clinical assessment or intake session, a clinician can unwittingly commit a sexual orientation or transgender microaggression by conceptualizing their client's nonmonogamous relationship as problematic (despite the fact that the client and her or his partner have openly negotiated the boundaries of their nonmonogamous relationship). In this situation, a clinician may view this client's relationship as overly sexualized or maladaptive and inquire more about her or his sexual behavior within the relationship. Although the client may not perceive her or his open relationship as the presenting problem, the clinician may erroneously view this as a significant aspect of the client's "issue." The clinician's inappropriate focus on the nonmonogamous relationship of the client is communicating three microaggressions: (1) endorsement of heterosexist norms, (2) discomfort or disapproval of LGBT experience, and (3) assumption of sexual pathology/abnormality.

Another example of a sexual orientation or transgender microaggression in therapeutic settings might include the language that is used by the therapist and her or his LGBT client. For example, it may be common for therapists to interject the wrong gender pronouns when referring to a

Table 10.2

Examples of LGBT Microaggressions in Therapy and Other Related Settings

Theme	Example	Message
Use of heterosexist terminology: occurs when heterosexist language is used to degrade LGBT persons	During an intake, a therapist asks a female client if she has a husband (without asking if she has a partner or wife).	Heterosexuality is the norm.
	A therapist refers to a male-to-female transgender client as "he."	I don't have to approve your lifestyle.
Endorsement of heteronormative culture/ behaviors: occurs when LGBT persons are expected to be or act like heterosexuals	A therapist subtly encourages her/his client to enter a monogamous relationship.	Heterosexual norms are healthier than LGBT norms.
	A counselor tells her/his LGBT client that she/he should try to fit in better by dressing to her/his gender.	Being gay is bad; you are not allowed to be yourself.
	In the waiting room of a mental health clinic, the magazines all display heterosexual and traditionally gendered couples.	Heterosexuality is the norm; everything else is not.
Assumption of universal LGBT experience: occurs when individuals assume that all LGBT persons are the same	A psychologist mistakenly calls a bisexual person "gay."	Your sexual identity is not important.
	A therapist is surprised when an LGBT client of color tells her/him that she/he has not come out of the closet to her/his family.	There is only one way to be LGBT.
Exoticization: occurs when LGBT persons are dehumanized or treated like objects	A counselor admits to her/his LGBT client that she/he enjoys hearing her/his "wild stories."	You are here for my entertainment.
Discomfort/disapproval of LGBT experience: occurs when LGBT individuals are treated with disrespect or condemnation	A therapist displays uneasiness when an LGBT client talks about sex.	I do not want to know about your lifestyle.
	A therapist never asks a client about her/his dating life.	I do not approve of your lifestyle.
Denial of societal heterosexism/ transphobia: occurs when individuals deny LGBT persons that heterosexist/ homophobic experiences exist	A therapist tells an LGBT client that she/he spends too much time thinking about sexual orientation.	You complain too much.

Table 10.2
(Continued)

Theme	Example	Message
Assumption of sexual pathology/abnormality: occurs when LGBT persons are presumed to be oversexualized and/or sexual deviants	In an intake, a therapist asks an LGBT client an abundant amount of questions about HIV/AIDS.	You are a sexually immoral and deserve to get HIV/AIDS.
Denial of individual heterosexism/ transphobia: occurs when a heterosexual denies her/his heterosexist biases or prejudice	A heterosexual/traditionally gendered therapist says, "Your sexual orientation [or transgender identity] doesn't affect the way that I view you."	I have no biases against LGBT persons and am incapable of heterosexism.

transgender person and/or to refer to or treat a bisexual client as gay or lesbian. In this case, the therapist is enacting several microaggressions, including (1) use of heterosexist language and (2) assumption of universality of the LGBT experience. In some ways, the therapist is even indirectly endorsing a heteronormative behavior, because she or he is not even aware that her or his behavior is mirroring the heterosexist, homophobic, genderist, and transphobic messages that this client experiences on a regular basis.

The aforementioned sexual orientation and transgender microaggressions can have adverse implications, leaving the client feeling a scope of emotions and experiences—feeling hurt, misunderstood, unsupported, rejected, and angry. Previous authors have found that when therapists unknowingly insult or invalidate their clients, rifts in the therapeutic relationship may occur as clients are filtering through past experiences, expectations, needs, and fears of human relationships (Wachtel, 1993). As a result, sexual orientation and transgender microaggressions committed by the clinician jeopardize the therapeutic alliance, as they may epitomize the various types of discrimination the LGBT client experiences daily. So, rather than providing an environment for protection, safety, and space to learn and grow in therapy, the practitioner has created the contrary—confirming an LGBT person's fears that she or he will be stigmatized, judged, and rejected.

The derailment of the therapeutic alliance can be prevented through receiving comprehensive LGBT-affirmative training, which includes but is not limited to extensive self-exploration on attitudes/biases of LGBT individuals, learning about the life experiences of LGBT individuals, knowledge of appropriate referrals, and awareness of events and organizations concerning the LGBT community. One study found that homonegativity decreased in school counselors when the counselor had a gay or lesbian friend (Satcher & Leggett, 2007). This is important, because it supports exposure to LGBT individuals, which can help to decrease one's own heterosexist or transphobic/genderist biases toward LGBT persons.

However, in cases when the sexual orientation or transgender microaggression has already been committed, it is essential for practitioners to take the lead in repairing the therapeutic bond. Clinicians should address the issue immediately and openly admit and apologize for the comments and/or behavior that might have been hurtful to the client. Additionally, the clinician must be amenable to discussing the incident that occurred with the client and encourage the client to express any feelings that they have toward the clinician and/or the incident. Perhaps through the practitioner's ability to initiate a dialogue and exploration, it may demonstrate to the client an intention to rebuild and repair the therapeutic relationship.

It is also important to recognize that sexual orientation and transgender microaggressions can often intersect with racial, ethnic, and gender microaggressions. For example, there are many cultural implications that prevent LGBT individuals, particularly those from racial/ethnic minorities, from "coming out" to their families and friends (Chan, 1992; Conerly, 1996; Green, 1997; Nadal, 2009; Nadal & Corpus, in press). Since the 1970s, numerous models of identity development concerning LGBT individuals invariably label the process of coming out as an imperative developmental stage for LGBT individuals. In many instances, clinicians do not take into account the client's cultural values and the implications of coming out for the client in that particular culture(s). Oftentimes, clinicians can commit sexual orientation and transgender microaggressions through encouraging clients to disclose their sexual orientation to their family and/or community. Clinicians can unwittingly conceptualize their client's behavior (e.g., inability to come out of the closet) as lacking assertiveness or independence. These aforementioned clinical interventions and assessments communicate to the client that the LGBT experience is universal, as well as that it endorses White, American, middle-class values.

In conclusion, this chapter has demonstrated how sexual orientation and transgender microaggressions may exist and manifest in therapeutic relationships. It is necessary for psychologists, counselors, and other practitioners to understand sexual orientation and transgender microaggressions as a way of abiding by the American Psychological Association ethical guidelines in working with culturally diverse clients. Additionally, further research may be helpful in learning more about sexual orientation and transgender microaggressions in order to provide more effective and culturally competent services for LGBT clients. Empirical data will be beneficial in investigating how sexual orientation and transgender microaggressions may have an impact on various mental health disparities, including depression, anxiety, trauma, and self-esteem. Research may also be necessary in exploring how the intersections of other identities with sexual orientation can lead to a unique experience with multiple levels of microaggressions. Finally, it is important for researchers to ensure that in studying microaggressions, they include microaggressions toward bisexual and transgender individuals, two groups that are often marginalized within the LGBT community. By failing to address the needs of bisexuals and transgender persons, many researchers, psychologists, and other practitioners are unconsciously or unintentionally enacting microaggressions toward these two groups.

REFERENCES

Anti-Defamation League. (2001). Hate crime laws. Retrieved October 1, 2008, from http://www.adl.org/99hatecrime/provisions.asp.

Baker, J. G., & Fishbein, H. D. (1998). The development of prejudice towards gays and lesbians by adolescents. *Journal of Homosexuality*, *36*(1), 89–100.

Boysen, G. A., Vogel, D. L., Madon, S., & Wester, S. R. (2006). Mental health stereotypes about gay men. *Sex Roles: A Journal of Research*, *54*(1/2), 69–82.

Bryant, A., & Demian, R. (1994). Relationship characteristics of American gays and lesbians: Findings from a national survey. *Journal of Gay and Lesbian Social Services*, *1*, 101–117.

Burn, S. M. (2000). Heterosexuals' use of "fag" and "queer" to deride one another: A contributor to heterosexism and stigma. *Journal of Homosexuality*, *40*(2), 1–11.

Burn, S. M., Kadlec, K., & Rexer, R. (2005). Effects of subtle heterosexism on gays, lesbians, and bisexuals. *Journal of Homosexuality*, *49*(2), 23–38.

Cerny, J. A., & Polyson, J. (1984). Changing homonegative attitudes. *Journal of Social and Clinical Psychology*, *2*, 366–371.

Chan, C. (1992). Cultural considerations in counseling Asian American lesbians and gay men. In S. Dworkin & F. Gutierrez (Eds.), *Counseling gay men and lesbians* (pp. 115–124). Alexandria, VA: American Association for Counseling and Development.

Conerly, G. (1996). The politics of Black, lesbian, gay, and bisexual identity. In B. Beemyn & M. Eliason (Eds.), *A lesbian, gay, bisexual, and transgender anthology* (pp. 133–145). New York: New York University Press.

Conley, T. D., Calhoun, C., Evett, S. R., & Devine, P. G. (2001). Mistakes that heterosexual people make when trying to appear non-prejudiced: The view from LGB people. *Journal of Homosexuality*, *42*(2), 21–43.

Cowan, G., Heiple, B., Marquez, C., Khatchadourian, D., & McNevin, M. (2005). Heterosexuals' attitudes toward hate crimes and hate speech against gays and lesbians: Old-fashioned and modern heterosexism. *Journal of Homosexuality*, *49*(2), 83–109.

D'Augelli, A. R. (1992). Lesbian and gay male undergraduates' experiences of harassment and fear on campus. *Journal of Interpersonal Violence*, *7*, 383–395.

Dovidio, J. F., & Gaertner, S. L. (2000). Aversive racism and selective decisions: 1989–1999. *Psychological Science, 11*, 315–319.

Essed, P. (1991). *Understanding everyday racism*. Newbury Park, CA: Sage.

Federal Bureau of Investigation. (2007). Incidents, offenses, victims, and known offenders by bias motivation, 2007. Retrieved February 23, 2009, from http://www.fbi.gov/ucr/hc2007/table_01.htm.

Flowers, P., & Langdridge, D. (2007). Offending the other: Deconstructing narratives of deviance and pathology. *British Journal of Social Psychology, 46*(3), 679–690.

Friend, R. A. (1998). Heterosexism, homophobia, and the culture of schooling. In Sue Books (Ed.), *Invisible children; 1; in the society and its schools* (pp. 137–166). Mahwah, NJ: Lawrence Erlbaum.

Gay, Lesbian, Straight Education Network. (2004). *State of the states, 2004: A policy analysis of lesbian, gay, bisexual and transgender (LGBT) safer schools issues*. New York: Author.

Goldblatt, H., Barr, K. L., & Armstrong, J. (2003, August 8). Super queer. *Entertainment Weekly*. Retrieved October 3, 2008, from http://www.ew.com/ew/article/0,,472474,00.html.

Green, B. (1997). Ethnic minority lesbians and gay men: Mental health and treatment issues. In B. Greene (Ed.), *Ethnic and cultural diversity among lesbians and gay men* (pp. 216–239). Thousand Oaks, CA: Sage.

Herek, G. M. (Ed.). (1998). *Stigma and sexual orientation: Understanding prejudice against lesbians, gay men, and bisexuals*. Thousand Oaks, CA: Sage.

Herek, G. M. (2000). The psychology of sexual prejudice. *Current Directions in Psychological Science, 9*, 19–22.

Herek, G. M. (2007). Confronting sexual stigma and prejudice: Theory and practice. *Journal of Social Issues, 63*(4), 905–925.

Herek, G. M., & Capitanio, J. P. (1999). Sex differences in how heterosexuals think about lesbians and gay men: Evidence from survey context effects. *Journal of Sex Research, 36*, 348–360.

Herek, G. M., Cogan, S. C., & Gillis, J. R. (2002). Victim experiences of hate crimes based on sexual orientation. *Journal of Social Issues, 58*, 319–399.

Hill, D. B., & Willoughby, B. L. B. (2005). The development and validation of the Genderism and Transphobia Scale. *Sex Roles, 53*(7/8), 531–544.

Huebner, D. M., & Davis, M. C. (2007). Perceived antigay discrimination and physical health outcomes. *Health Psychology, 26*(5), 627–634.

Kite, M. E., & Whitley, B. E., (1998). Do heterosexual women and men differ in their attitudes toward homosexuality? A conceptual and methodological analysis. In G. M. Herek (Ed.), *Stigma and sexual orientation: Understanding prejudice against lesbians, gay men, and bisexuals* (pp. 39–61). Thousand Oaks, CA: Sage.

LaSala, M. (2004). Extradyadic sex and gay male couples: Comparing monogamous and nonmonogamous relationships. *Families in Society: The Journal of Contemporary Human Services, 85*, 405–412.

Levitt, E. E., & Klassen, A. D. (1974). Public attitudes toward homosexuality: Part of the 1970 national survey by the Institute for Sex Research. *Journal of Homosexuality, 1*, 29–43.

McIntosh, P. (2003). White privilege: Unpacking the invisible knapsack. In S. Plous (Ed.), *Understanding prejudice and discrimination* (pp. 191–196). New York: McGraw-Hill.

Meyer, I. H. (1995). Minority stress and mental health in gay men. *Journal of Health and Social Behavior*, *36*, 38–56.

Meyer, I. H. (2003). Prejudice, social stress, and mental health in lesbian, gay, and bisexual populations: Conceptual issues and research evidence. *Psychological Bulletin*, *129*(5), 674–697.

Morrison, M. A., & Morrison, T. G. (2002). Development and validation of a scale measuring modern prejudice toward gay men and lesbian women. *Journal of Homosexuality*, *43*(2), 15–37.

Morrison, T. G., Parriag, A. V., & Morrison, M. A. (1999). The psychometric properties of the Homonegativity Scale. *Journal of Homosexuality*, *37*(4), 111–126.

Nadal, K. L. (2008). Preventing racial, ethnic, gender, sexual minority, disability, and religious microaggressions: Recommendations for promoting positive mental health. *Prevention in Counseling Psychology: Theory, Research, Practice and Training*, *2*(1), 22–27.

Nadal, K. L. (2009). *Filipino American psychology: A handbook of theory, research, and clinical practice*. Bloomington, IN: Author House.

Nadal, K. L. (2010). Gender microaggressions: Implications for mental health. In M. A. Paludi (Ed.), *Feminism and Women's Rights Worldwide, Volume 2: Mental and Physical Health* (pp. 155–175). Santa Barbara, CA: Praeger.

Nadal, K. L., & Corpus, M. J. H. (in press) Tomboys and baklas: Experiences of lesbian & gay Filipino Americans in higher education. In V. A. Wall & J. Washington (Eds.), *The colors of the rainbow: Lesbian, gay, bisexual and transgender people of color in the academy*. Lanham, MD: University Press of America and the American College Personnel Association.

Patel, S., Long, T. E., McCammon, S. L., & Wuensch, K. L. (1995). Personality and emotional correlates of self-reported anti-gay behaviors. *Journal of Interpersonal Violence*, *10*(3), 354–366.

Roderick, T., McCammon, S. L., Long, T. E., & Alfred, L. J. (1998). Behavioral aspects of homonegativity. *Journal of Homosexuality*, *36*(1), 79–88.

Rostosky, S. S., Riggle, E. D. B., Gray, B. E., & Hatton, R. L. (2007). Minority stress experiences in committed same-sex couple relationships. *Professional Psychology: Research and Practice*, *38*(4), 392–400.

Rowe, M. P. (1990). Barriers to equality: The power of subtle discrimination to maintain unequal opportunity. *Employee Responsibilities and Rights Journal*, *3*(2), 153–163.

Satcher, J., & Leggett, M. (2007). Homonegativity among professional school counselors: An exploratory study. *Professional School Counseling*, *11*(1), 10–16.

Shernoff, M. (2006). Negotiated nonmonogamy and male couples. *Family Process*, *45*(4), 407–417.

Silverschanz, P., Cortina, L. M., Konik, J., & Magley, V. J. (2007). Slurs, snubs, and queer jokes: Incidence and impact of heterosexist harassment in academia. *Sex Roles*, *58*, 179–191.

Smith, S. D. (2004). Sexually underrepresented youth: Understanding gay, lesbian, bisexual, transgendered, and questioning (GLBT-Q) youth. In J. L. Chin (Ed.), *Psychology of prejudice and discrimination: Bias based on gender and sexual orientation* (Vol. 3, pp. 151–199). Westport, CT: Praeger Publishers/Greenwood Publishing Group, Inc.

Solórzano, D., Ceja, M., & Yosso, T. (2000). Critical race theory, racial microaggressions, and campus racial climate: The experiences of African American college students. *Journal of Negro Education, 69*(1/2), 60–73.

Sue, D. W., Bucceri, J. M., Lin, A. I., Nadal, K. L., & Torino, G. C. (2007). Racial microaggressions and the Asian American experience. *Cultural Diversity and Ethnic Minority Psychology, 13*(1), 72–81.

Sue, D. W., & Capodilupo, C. M. (2008). Racial, gender, and sexual orientation microaggressions: Implications for counseling and psychotherapy. In D. W. Sue & D. Sue (Eds.), *Counseling the culturally diverse: Theory and practice* (5th ed., pp. 105–130). Hoboken, NJ: John Wiley & Sons.

Sue, D. W., Capodilupo, C. M., Torino, G. C., Bucceri, J. M., Holder, A. M., Nadal, K. L., & Esquilin, M. (2007). Racial microaggressions in everyday life: Implications for counseling. *American Psychologist, 62*(4), 271–286.

Sue, D. W., Nadal, K. L., Capodilupo, C. M., Lin, A. I., Torino, G. C., & Rivera, D. P. (2008). Racial microaggressions against Black Americans: Implications for counseling. *Journal of Counseling and Development, 86*(3), 330–338.

Swim, J. K., & Cohen, L. L. (1997). Overt, covert, and subtle sexism: A comparison between the attitudes toward women and modern sexism scales. *Psychology of Women Quarterly, 21*(1), 103–118.

Wachtel, P. L. (1993). *Therapeutic communication: Principles and effective practice.* New York: Guilford Press.

Waldo, C. R. (1999). Working in a majority context: A structural model of heterosexism as minority stress in the workplace. *Journal of Counseling Psychology, 46*, 218–232.

Walls, N. E. (2008). Toward a multidimensional understanding of heterosexism: The changing nature of prejudice. *Journal of Homosexuality, 55*(1), 1–51.

CHAPTER 11

Microaggressive Experiences of People with Disabilities

RICHARD M. KELLER and CORINNE E. GALGAY

L IKE MANY MARGINALIZED groups, people with disabilities (PWDs) have endured a long history of violence, oppression, and discrimination. The needs, experiences, hopes, and aspirations of PWDs are relatively unknown, unrecognized, and underestimated (American Psychological Association [APA], 2009). Some believe that discrimination against PWDs is increasing in frequency and intensity, resulting in both physical and psychological harm for this population (Leadership Conference on Civil Rights Education Fund [LCCREF], 2009). Negative attitudes and behaviors against PWDs seem driven by distorted assumptions and beliefs about disability (Wallace, Carter, Nanin, Keller, & Alleyne, 2003). Since it is beyond the scope of this chapter to summarize the historical treatment of PWDs, we recommend some excellent summaries that can be found in the recent publication of the American Psychological Association titled *Draft guidelines for Assessment of and Intervention with Individuals Who Have Disabilities* (APA, 2009) and in reviews by Keller (2004), Wallace et al. (2003), and Snyder and Mitchell (2006). Readers who wish to review a more comprehensive set of resources are directed to seminal works, such as Vash (1981), Goffman (1963), and Zola (1982), and more contemporary writings, such as Braithwaite and Thompson (2000), Fleischer and Zames (2001), Longmore and Umansky (2001), Russell (2002), or the World Institute on Disability web site (http://www.wid.org). Those who would prefer to review a more theoretical perspective of disability are referred to Olkin (1999) and Pfeiffer (2001).

The authors of this chapter would like to make a special acknowledgment to Lisa L. Robinson, Jennifer Zadikow, and Emily E. Merola for their contribution to the research study.

These sources provide overwhelming evidence that ableism exists and remains alive and well today. Ableism is the unique form of discrimination experienced by PWDs based on their disabilities. Its expression favors people without disabilities and maintains that disability in and of itself is a negative concept, state, and experience. Implicit within ableism is an able-centric worldview, which endorses the belief that there is a "normal" manner in which to perceive and/or manipulate stimuli and a "normal" manner of accomplishing tasks of daily living. Disability represents a deviation from these norms. While PWDs may experience similar forms of discrimination as other socially devalued groups, we contend that they may be subjected to unique group-specific manifestations as well. In addition to the spectrum of overt acts of discrimination, another vast set of group-specific, subtle, and insidious negative daily experiences are thrust upon PWDs. How might these subtle forms of discrimination be experienced in the everyday lives of PWDs? Consider the following example experienced by the senior author of this chapter.

I (Richard Keller, a blind man) was attending a meeting with a work group that has met for more than four years. We know each other very well, and my status as a person with a disability is obvious. Often, I provide some insight into experiences of PWDs to the discussion. In this meeting, a new administrator was invited to meet the group. When he was introduced, I assumed he scanned the table looking for familiar or unfamiliar faces. He was offered introductions but declined, taking it upon himself to call out the names of attendees. When he called out "Richard," I had the sense that he extended his hand to shake mine, as I felt a strange shift in the overall mood and energy of the group. Intuitively, I had the distinct impression that someone had said in a stage whisper "He's blind." I then continued to take in the unrest and hesitancy in the group. Was I being paranoid? Surely these trusted and familiar colleagues would not have treated me in such a dismissive manner. Of course, they respect my disability and with our history together are well equipped to ask direct questions or make direct statements. Was I being too sensitive or misreading the situation?

After a brief pause, the meeting continued, and the administrator presented his materials to the group. At the end of the presentation, while expressing our thanks and wishes to continue to be updated, I reached out my hand to the administrator and shook his hand. Later that day, I called one of my most trusted colleagues, who attended the meeting, and asked him about the awkward moment. I indicated that I thought I heard a stage whisper "He's blind." My friend and colleague chuckled and said that the administrator had attempted to shake my hand and when I didn't respond, he was baffled. At that moment, another person did in fact mouth the words

"He's blind," which resulted in the administrator turning bright red. While this was going on, I questioned myself, and afterward, I wondered if I should use this as a teachable moment for my colleagues. Upon reflection, however, I became angry and frustrated, since I had already spent considerable time and effort guiding these folks to a deeper understanding of the disability movement and the disabled perspective. I felt like a failure.

It was helpful to have discussed the situation with my one colleague, and I felt somewhat better afterward. However, as time passed, I remained angry, embarrassed, and disappointed. I wasn't sure what to do. Again, was I making too much of this situation? Certainly my friends and colleagues would not try to hurt me. So, after about two weeks, I called for a special meeting of the same group. I shared my feelings about my perception of the incident. I indicated that I didn't want an apology and that I wasn't sure of what I hoped would be accomplished but wanted to discuss the matter. We went around the table, and each person tried to share their thoughts and feelings about the event. Some of the people around the table seemed to genuinely want to come to a deeper understanding of what happened and what options might they consider moving forward. Others were silent, while still others took a slightly defensive posture. Near the end of the meeting, I asked the group what would have been so difficult in letting me know at the time that the administrator was trying to shake my hand. No one could answer. There was just no response. I left the second meeting with mixed feelings. I am uncertain whether other attendees did as well. Is disability too embarrassing to talk about in public? After spending so much time with my colleagues, do they not know anything about me or my disability? What about my perceptions of my relationship with them, professionally and personally? What do they now think about me? What about the group as a whole?

When I reached out to the administrator, who had also been embarrassed by the event at the meeting, he expressed deep appreciation. I assured him that I had no hard feelings about what had happened between us; rather, I expressed dissatisfaction with my colleagues and disappointment that they were not able to simply provide me the visual information I was missing in the situation. I wanted to assure him that in general, we are more comfortable in discussing disability at this organization. He seemed to walk away with satisfaction and understanding. But this 30-second example can give some idea of how many people can be affected by an unintentional, subtle act of insensitivity toward PWDs.

This example illustrates why it is important to explore the existence of covert expressions of discrimination toward PWDs, which have been called microaggressions and supported by research with other minority groups (Sue, Bucceri, Lin, Nadal, & Torino, 2007; Sue, Capodilupo, & Holder, 2008; Sue, Capodilupo, et al., 2007). Microaggressions are "subtle, stunning, often automatic, and non-verbal exchanges which are 'put downs'" (Pierce, Carew,

Pierce-Gonzalez, & Willis, 1978, p. 66). Racial microaggressions have been defined as "brief and commonplace daily verbal, behavioral, or environmental indignities, whether intentional or unintentional, that communicate hostile, derogatory, or negative racial slights and insults" toward people of color (Sue, Capodilupo, et al., 2007, p. 273). It has been proposed that as classic racism has evolved into a more modern form often referred to as aversive racism, racial microaggressions have developed as a manifestation of this evolution (Sue, Capodilupo, et al., 2007). The changing face of racism has been attributed to less public tolerance for overt displays of prejudice and increasing legislation that prohibits discrimination.

Likewise, since passage of the Americans with Disabilities Act in 1990 and recent amendments in 2008, overt forms of discrimination (ableism) toward PWDs have suffered a similar public decline like racism (Snyder & Mitchell, 2006). The distorted assumptions and beliefs that fuel negative attitudes and behaviors toward PWDs still exist, but they operate in a much more subtle, secretive, and covert manner, often outside the level of awareness of well-intentioned perpetrators. These covert expressions can be called disability microaggressions. To date, there are only anecdotal examples, along with a few more objective and scholarly descriptions of disability microaggressions, that have been described in the literature (Wallace et al., 2003; White & Epston, 1990). What kind of interpersonal complexities exist for both recipient and antagonist when a disability microaggression occurs?

Let us use the preceding example to tease out some of the dynamics, themes, and manifestations of these forms of microaggressions. First, the well-intentioned male colleague who whispered "He's blind" may be operating from an unconscious worldview that PWDs are helpless or of limited cognitive functioning. The impact upon the senior author, after much reflection, was that he was treated like a child. Second, the colleague appears to be vested in avoiding PWDs or wishes that they were invisible. When the senior author attempted to seek out a deeper understanding about the negative experience from others, he encountered defensiveness and in some cases denial. In other words, his experiential reality was being denied and invalidated. Third, it was quite clear that many of his colleagues were uncomfortable with his disability becoming visible and that most chose to ignore the situation. Were it not for the persistence of the senior author, the entire episode would have remained unspoken and out of sight. Indeed, many PWDs often describe how they are ignored and how others prefer not to see or acknowledge them, as well as the extreme discomfort of able-bodied people when PWDs are in their presence.

Little is known about disability microaggressions. How might these subtle disability insults and invalidations make their appearance in interpersonal and environmental encounters? Why do they occur? What forms do they take? How do disability microaggressions play out between perpetrators and targets? Are there emotional and psychological consequences to the targets? What effects do they have on perpetrators? If disability microaggressions are harmful, what steps must be taken to eradicate them? Our research goal was to address these questions.

METHODS

This research used a qualitative method to explore the existence of micro-aggressions directed at PWDs. We sought to identify patterns in the manifes-tations of these microaggressions and to investigate the impact of these experiences on targets. In order to have a stronger opportunity to compare and contrast our work with findings in other microaggression research, we modeled our methodology after the work of Sue and colleagues (2008) with African Americans and Sue, Bucceri, et al. (2007) with Asian Americans. Some adaptations have been made, specifically to maximize the participation of PWDs. A focus group format was chosen, as it provides rich description as well as contextual understanding of how phenomena occur (Sofaer, 1999). In the area of disability research, focus groups have gained popularity, as they provide an open format and flexibility of implementation (Kroll, Barbour, & Harris, 2007). Furthermore, focus groups are particularly useful for popula-tions who typically are bypassed by quantitative studies, and they also provide an opportunity for PWDs to serve as active research partners as opposed to their usual role of research objects (Imrie & Kumar, 1998). Our research aimed to elicit, through supportive social interaction, descriptions of subtle discrimination experienced by PWDs. These descriptions were then analyzed to yield an initial taxonomy of disability microaggressions.

Participants

Ideal focus group size varies from between 4 to 8 (Kitzinger, 1995) to between 6 to 12 (Morgan, 1997). Focus groups with PWDs may be ideally smaller, depending on the nature of the disability and its impact on the length of time needed for participants to hear, understand, process, and respond fully (Barrett & Kirk, 2000; Seymour, Ingleton, Payne, & Beddow, 2003). The length of time for each group can also be balanced to consider potential fatigue, pain, or discomfort experienced by participants with sensory and/or physical disabilities (Barrett & Kirk, 2000; Kroll et al., 2007). Purposive criteria were used to recruit appropriate participants in a similar manner as other research on microaggressions (Sue, Bucceri, et al., 2007; Sue et al., 2008). All participants in the two focus groups had to self-identify as an individual with a disability, agree that ableism exists today in the United States, and agree that discrimination toward PWDs takes both overt and covert forms.

A total of 12 self-identified PWDs were recruited from two organizations specializing in serving this population and were sorted into two focus groups. The sample was comprised of five males and seven females; eight White Americans, two Latin Americans, and two African Americans. Participants reported the following types of disabilities: Three reported sensory (visually impaired), seven reported physical, and two reported multiple (physical/sensory and physical/cognitive) disabilities. Four participants reported their disability to be congenital, and eight reported adventitious disabilities. Five participants reported their disability to be invisible, and seven reported their disability as visible. Ten of the participants were in their forties and fifties, while two participants reported to be in their twenties. Of the sample, nine were working professionals, two were full-time graduate students, and one was unemployed.

RESEARCHERS

The researchers for the study were 12 master's-level graduate students in the Department of Counseling and Clinical Psychology taking a graduate research seminar on PWDs and ableism taught by the senior author at a private university in the eastern United States. Students were required to examine their potential assumptions and biases related to disability issues in order to assure minimal impact on the data collection, analysis, and the overall integrity of the research (Kroll et al., 2007). This was done through extensive reading in disability studies and guided discussions facilitated by the senior author. The research team was comprised of two males and ten females; eight White Americans, one African American, one Latin American, and two Asian Americans (one non-native). Five members of the research team self-identified as PWDs (including the senior author), and eight did not. The senior author is an assistant professor of psychology and education with a Ph.D. in counseling psychology. He has been involved with the disability rights movement for over 20 years. For the past 15 years, he has conducted disability-related research with a focus on social justice, self-disclosure, and life outcomes for PWDs, with particular attention to discrimination, ableism, and solutions to combat their presence.

MEASURES

Two means of collecting data were employed. First, a brief demographic questionnaire seeking information about race, ethnicity, age, gender, employment status, disability type, onset, and visibility was completed by all participants. Only three of the participants required reasonable accommodations to complete this task. Second, a semistructured interview protocol was developed based on an overview of current microaggression research (Sue, Bucceri, et al., 2007; Sue, Capodilupo, et al., 2007; Sue et al., 2008) and a review of the literature on a variety of forms of discrimination and inequity experienced by PWDs (Keller, 2004; Keller & King, 2008). The questions were open-ended in format in order to allow participants to respond in as flexible a manner as possible with real-life experiences and provide detail about the underlying message they attribute to the experience, as well as their perception of the perpetrator's intention. In addition, we hoped to provide an opportunity and an environment permitting participants to describe the impact these experiences have on their lives and the various strategies they use to deal with them. There were no requests for reasonable accommodations for equal participation within the focus groups.

PROCEDURE

Participants were recruited from two organizations that provide services to PWDs. The corresponding receptionist at each organization asked consumers to consider volunteering as they contacted the organization in the course of normal business. A list of potential research participants was compiled and provided to the research team along with contact information. Two focus groups were scheduled, and potential volunteers were contacted to match their availability with the corresponding dates and times. No compensation was provided to participants. Each focus group was approximately one-and-a-half hours in length and took place in a closed private room at each of the organizations. Two members of the research team who identified as individuals with disabilities were selected to facilitate the focus groups. At the beginning of each of the focus groups, a general description of the research was provided to participants, and the facilitators identified themselves as PWDs. We believed it was important for the facilitators to disclose their disability status to engender a supportive atmosphere where participants were more likely to feel comfortable disclosing sensitive, emotionally laden material about their subtle negative experiences surrounding their disability.

The two facilitators rehearsed the script with the research team under the guidance of the senior researcher to ensure maximum fluidity, effective facilitation, and anticipation of difficult dialogues. Participants were advised of their rights and responsibilities. Following, an informed consent was obtained. Both focus groups were audiotaped, and verbatim transcripts were produced, concealing the identities of participants. At the conclusion of each focus group, participants were debriefed and provided with a list of resources about disabilities and potential sources of emotional, psychological, and community support. Once the facilitators were assured of the accuracy of the transcript, the audiotapes were destroyed. In addition, after each focus group, the facilitators engaged in a debriefing session, which was also audiotaped. These transcripts, along with the transcripts of the focus groups, were brought to the research team.

Five members of the research team, including the facilitators, were selected to make up the coding team and reviewed the two focus group transcripts, identifying instances where microaggressions may have taken place. The content surrounding these instances was analyzed qualitatively. The goal of the team was to identify what type of microaggressions PWDs experience, the related theme, and the overall impact of these experiences on participants. Each member of the team analyzed the transcripts individually to conceptually organize the focus group data. The content from the focus group transcripts were then analyzed qualitatively in order to identify and label the microaggressions, locate quintessential examples of each, and catalogue the cognitive and emotional responses of targets, as well as to connect each microaggression to underlying messages received by the target.

The initial conceptualization of the data was presented to the senior author and an advanced doctoral student who comprised the auditing team. The auditing team reviewed the initial work and provided feedback in order to reach consensus on the accuracy of the microaggressions found. The process for establishing consensus was a modified consensual qualitative research (CQR) method for focus groups (Hill, Thompson, & Williams, 1997). Sue, Bucceri, and colleagues (2007) and Sue and colleagues (2008) have suggested this procedure in microaggression research, with the unit of study as the focus group rather than the individual. Once initial consensus was reached between the coding team and the auditing team, individual coding team members were asked to group together, categorize, and label similar microaggressions into domains and to identify the central concept of each domain. The coding team met together again with the goal of reaching consensus on their domains. These findings were brought back to the auditing team for feedback until consensus was reached. The auditing team focused on looking for similarities and differences in each individual's coding, with an eye toward minimizing group thinking and finalizing results and related structure.

RESULTS

Findings from the two focus groups yielded several patterns of microaggressions experienced by the participants based on their disability status. As shown in Table 11.1, these patterns were then broken down into eight

Table 11.1
Examples of Disability Microaggressions in Everyday Life

Theme	Example	Message
Denial of personal identity: occurs when any aspect of a person's identity other than disability is ignored or denied	"I can't believe you are married."	There is no part of your life that is normal or like mine. The only thing I see when I look at you is your disability.
Denial of disability experience: occurs when disability-related experiences are minimized or denied	"Come on now, we all have some disability."	Your thoughts and feelings are probably not real and are certainly not important to me.
Denial of privacy: occurs when personal information is required about a disability	Someone asks what happened to you.	You are not allowed to maintain disability information privately.
Helplessness: occurs when people frantically try to help PWDs	Someone helps you onto a bus or train, even when you need no help.	You can't do anything by yourself because you have a disability.
	Someone feels incapable of rescuing you from your disability.	Having a disability is a catastrophe. I would rather be dead than be you.
Secondary gain: occurs when a person expects to feel good or be praised for doing something for a PWD	"We're going to raise enough money tonight to get Johnny that new wheelchair."	I feel good and get recognition for being nice to you.
Spread effect: occurs when other expectations about a person are assumed to be due to one specific disability	"Those deaf people are retarded."	Your disability invalidates you in all areas of life.
	"Your other senses must be better than mine."	You must be special in some way.
		You're not normal.
		You have "spidey sense."
Infantilization: occurs when a PWD is treated like a child	"Let me do that for you."	You are not really capable. I know better than you how to do this.
Patronization: occurs when a PWD is praised for almost anything	"You people are so inspiring."	You are so special for living with that.

(continued)

Table 11.1
(Continued)

Theme	Example	Message
Second-class citizen: occurs when a PWD's right to equality is denied because they are considered to be bothersome, expensive, and a waste of time, effort, and resources	People work hard not to make eye contact or to physically avoid a PWD.	PWDs are disgusting and should be avoided.
	A person in a wheelchair waits 15 minutes outside a restaurant for access through the kitchen. She then complains to the manager.	Those people expect too much and are so difficult to work with. They have no patience.
	At a staff meeting, the question is raised about improving accessibility to the restaurant, and the official plan is that changes will be made when more PWDs come to eat.	Your rights to equality are not important to me.
Desexualization: occurs when the sexuality and sexual being is denied	"I would never date someone who uses a wheelchair."	PWDs are not my equal, not attractive, and not worthy of being with me.

domains and can be used as a framework for interpreting the microaggression experiences of PWDs.

There were a few microaggression incidents described by participants that could not be classified within the eight domains and/or group consensus could not be reached in order to justify creating additional domains. As a result, these microaggressions were included as auxiliary findings. The remainder of this section provides examples of the eight domains, the underlying messages received by targets, and the likely intent of the perpetrator.

DOMAIN 1: DENIAL OF IDENTITY

This domain was endorsed by both focus groups. This microaggression was found to have two variations.

Denial of Personal Identity   The first variation is when some salient aspect of the target's identity other than their disability is disregarded. This disregarded aspect of their personal identity remains invisible, leading to an overemphasis on their disability. An example of this might be a reaction of surprise about the target's career or some other affiliation. An excerpt from our research follows: "I've spoken at three different schools in the past month, and the thing that I mostly start out with is that people have said, 'What do you like to be called—disabled, handicapped, challenged?' I'm like, just call me Susan; that's all I want to be—just Susan." The underlying message received by the target is that the only important aspect of their identity to the perpetrator is their disability. Membership to other sometimes prized identity statuses is not expected or believed. The target is left feeling that their potential talents, skills, expertise, awards, or memberships are not valued and are discounted.

Denial of Experience   The second variety of this microaggression is the "denial of disability-related experiences." The participants described several expressions of this microaggression. One expression is the denial or minimization of a negative or discriminatory experience. An example follows: "I couldn't tell you how defeated and deflated I felt. The handicapped-accessible room in Rome was not the way it should have been, and I had a really good time in Florence where the room was accessible, and then to have my friends tell me when I got home—this is almost as hurtful—'Well Susan, don't you think you're being a little overly sensitive?'" Targets also describe encounters where the perpetrator indicates that they understand the experience or some part of it, somehow identify with the experience, or know the solution to the situation. These microaggressions serve to invalidate the experiences of discrimination and suggest that PWDs don't face inequities and that ableism doesn't exist, particularly since the passage of the Americans with Disabilities Act: "One guy told me, 'Why don't you just get over it and get some glasses?'" Or, "The other thing I hate is when people come up to me and say 'I know how you feel.' Someone could have the exact same disability as I do and still not know how I feel."

Finally, the last expression of this microaggression is experienced by outright denial of the target's disability. Amazingly, this seems to occur not only for people with invisible disabilities but also for people with obvious visible disabilities: "Because I don't have an outward disability, people don't necessarily believe me. I've had to deal with that all my life, and I've had to give proof." Or, "When I went to public schools in second grade, they denied I was even disabled—which, don't get me wrong, I'm clearly physically disabled; my disabilities aren't hidden, but they denied I was disabled. They sent me to their doctors in the Medical College of Georgia to examine me; the doctors are like, of course you're disabled, what else do you think!"

The underlying message received by the target is that their experience is not important, not real, or not worth acknowledging. The target experiences these microaggressions as conscious or unconscious attempts to deny their negative disability-related experience. This is construed as an effort by the perpetrator to deny individual responsibility or to deny the responsibility of society or the dominant culture for any difficulties that PWDs experience while encountering barriers to equality. In other cases, the perpetrators are construed as attempting to distance themselves from the oppressive dominant culture through an effort to portray understanding or identification in some manner with the target.

DOMAIN 2: DENIAL OF PRIVACY

This domain was also endorsed by both focus groups and is evidenced when the perpetrator demands, explicitly or subtly, personal information from the target. The target experiences the microaggression as often abrupt, without hesitation and consideration for their comfort. These demands seem to transcend appropriate social norms and ignore the impact that levels of intimacy play in the self-disclosure process (Braithwaite, 1991; Chaikin & Derlega, 1974), lacking attention to the impact of differences in communication in public/private settings. An example follows: "In a crowded elevator...everybody is a little bit self-conscious and not talking, and some guy says to me, 'So, what happened to you?' really loud, so everyone in the car hears it." For targets with invisible disabilities, the request may not be for information about their disabilities but rather for them to simply identify themselves as people with disabilities in order to explain why they might do something differently; for example: "People are like 'Just read this,' but I don't want to out myself; I don't think it's my responsibility."

These denials of privacy seem to mirror the literature findings on difficulties between people with and without disabilities in the communication process (Kleck, 1968; Kleck, Ono, & Hastorf, 1966; Thompson, 1982; Wallace et al., 2003). Overwhelmingly, targets attributed the perpetrators' behaviors to be motivated by their own discomfort and ambiguity about disability. Other targets described their belief that this microaggression is a misguided attempt by the perpetrators to improve their interactions with the targets by getting answers to the questions that are pressing on their own minds or by indicating that they are not ableists. However, targets did not see these "well-intentioned" efforts as harmless but as examples of the insensitivity of the perpetrators, their lack of attention to boundaries, and their lack of concern for the cost (Braithwaite, 1985) to the target in losing control of their personal information. The target feels forced to take responsibility for managing the uncomfortable feelings of the perpetrator and to bear the burden of correcting problems brought about by the dominant culture. The underlying message received by the target is that a person with a disability is not entitled to the right of privacy, especially as it relates to their disability.

DOMAIN 3: HELPLESSNESS

Our third domain is perhaps the most complicated in its manifestation and potential impact for both target and perpetrator. The expectation of helplessness was overwhelmingly a universal experience for almost all research participants in both focus groups. Here again, there seems to be more than one expression of the microaggression. Most of the reports we heard centered on the expectation that PWDs need help most of the time. Theoretically, this seems to be related to the low expectations (Hafferty, 1994) of PWDs held by the dominant culture. An example follows: "On any given day, someone will race across the parking lot, and I won't even be looking for help. I'll be putting my chair in my car, and [I hear,] 'Can I help you, can I help you?'"

Another expression of this microaggression appears to be more closely linked to the potential projection of the perpetrator. Research participants described their sense that perpetrators may look at a person with a disability, be reminded of their own mortality, and be forced to consider the possibility of experiencing disability in their lifetime and thus be driven into action of some kind. As a result, participants believed that some perpetrators project a catastrophic representation of disability due to their lack of knowledge and understanding about living with a disability. An example follows: "One of the things that my boyfriend is dealing with right now is that he can't help me; he can't save me from this. Eventually, I will go blind, so that makes him uncomfortable. He can't do anything about it, and he feels he needs to."

The underlying messages received by the targets seem clear. First, the presence of a disability is equal to a state of helplessness in a wide range of settings and tasks. A PWD cannot do anything without help from another person. While targets seemed to acknowledge these misguided offers of assistance to most likely represent a genuine intent to be helpful on the part of the perpetrator, the aggregate impact of continuous unsolicited, unwanted, and unneeded offers of help was reported to be overwhelmingly negative, intense, and long lasting. The second message is that a disability is a catastrophic event that continues throughout one's life. As a result, the time, effort, and resources devoted to rehabilitation, auxiliary-skills training, and adaptive technology are discounted as a source of real improvement in the life of a PWD. Targets interpreted these experiences as evidence of perpetrators' underlying belief that living with a disability is a torturous experience hardly worth enduring. Targets further related these experiences to the recent eugenics movement exemplified through the actions of Dr. Kevorkian, clearly sending the message that it is better to be dead than to be a PWD. Research participants alluded to the "Not Dead Yet" movement ("Ableism," 2009) by the disability rights community in reaction to the eugenics position.

DOMAIN 4: SECONDARY GAIN

This microaggression was found in both groups and occurs when the perpetrator interacts with, relates to, or serves a PWD with the hidden agenda of personally gaining intrinsically or extrinsically for their effort. One variation was described by research participants as an expectation by the perpetrator to be recognized or praised in some way for their interaction with a PWD. An example: "I started kindergarten in 1972; it was one of the few schools that would take me. Later on, it became apparent to me I was sort of a trophy for them. They helped me out; 'Look, aren't we great, look what we did.' They partnered with IBM to make me a keyboard. I didn't want to type; I wanted to be just like everybody else." A second variation described by research participants is the perpetrator's hope to feel better about herself or himself through her or his experience with a PWD. Participants felt that the perpetrator will sometimes compare herself or himself socially to a PWD and offer sympathy to her or him as a response to her or his disability status. At the same time, the perpetrator enhances her or his own sense of self through the comparison. In effect, perpetrators make their own grass greener by viewing someone else's grass as not green, as in: "Many times, you'll become a pity case. 'Oh, that's so terrible, that must be so horrible.' It's extremely demeaning, because they're making it seem like they are better than you are." The underlying message received by targets is that for perpetrators, PWDs represent an opportunity for social exploitation. The yield might be social credit of some sort or enhanced sense of self worth. Participants indicated that genuine interactions of this sort are valued and appreciated. However, they indicated that when they feel the interaction to be less than genuine, they feel used and taken advantage of. Participants discussed social examples such as political campaigns and fund-raising efforts. The development over time of the disfavor that the "Jerry Lewis Telethon" has received from people within the disability rights movement is a classic illustration of this phenomenon ("Telethon 2000," 2000).

DOMAIN 5: SPREAD EFFECT

This microaggression was endorsed by both groups and occurs when an ascription of ability is made due to the presence of a disability. Participants conjectured that the related assumption is that a limitation in one functional area leads to limitations in other functional areas. Participants described interactions that include instances where people speak loudly when communicating with a blind person, as if the blindness has led to limitations in hearing. An example: "I had a women come up to me—I was a kid—and she says, 'Can you talk?' and then I just wanted to say, 'I'm a leprechaun, I'm after me lucky charms.'"

Within this microaggression, participants also discussed instances where they felt that perpetrators ascribed either high or low intelligence to them due to the presence of their disability, as in the following example: "I don't know why at 12 I wasn't diagnosed as legally blind, but through that time, it was just so difficult with my family, because some of the teachers and other people who were trying to help me were saying to tell me that I was mentally retarded, that there was something wrong with the way I was thinking." The underlying message received by the target is that his or her disability predicts functional ability and intelligence in a wide range of areas, usually in the low direction. In this microaggression, the potential impact of the disability is dramatically inflated and extends far beyond the logical nexus between impairment and functional limitation. While both expressions of this microaggression were found to occur more often in the negative direction, they might also predict unusually enhanced cognitive or other abilities. Such distortions, according to participants, have probably led to many of the myths about people with sensory and other disabilities, culminating in extreme expressions such as the *Rain Man* film character and the concept of the idiot savant. Finally, the idea that one disability leads to numerous functional limitations reinforces the overwhelmingly negative perception about disability held by the dominant society in general.

DOMAIN 6: PATRONIZATION

Both groups described these experiences. This microaggression takes place most often when perpetrators speak to or act toward targets as if they were children, a concept commonly referred to as infantilization. An example follows: "I don't look like a normal adult; people may have a hard time taking me seriously and [treat] me more childlike." The underlying message received by targets is first and foremost that PWDs are overall less capable than people without disabilities. The perception of the target is that the perpetrator feels driven to "do it for you," "explain it to you," and "make the decision for you." The target is left with feelings of humiliation and invalidation. Targets experiencing infantilization interpret the perpetrators' conduct to demonstrate equating ability with maturity. As a result, the presence of a disability reduces the perceived maturity of the target. A very different expression of patronization is the false admiration of a PWD. This most often happens when a PWD is praised for almost anything simply because the disability exists, such as in the following example: "I get, 'Oh, you're such an inspiration.' I'm like, for what? Because I get up in the morning?" The underlying message described by participants related to false admiration is that a PWD should be praised or admired for enduring the torturous experience of living with a disability. Targets of this microaggression construed perpetrators' intent to be helpful and positive, however misguided. Participants discussed appreciation for praise when well deserved but not simply for living with a disability.

DOMAIN 7: SECOND-CLASS CITIZENSHIP

This microaggression was almost universally endorsed by participants in both groups and occurs when the rights of PWDs for equal access are construed by perpetrators as unreasonable, unjustified, and bothersome. In each of the three expressions, the perpetrator fails to respect the rights of the target. We have labeled the three expressions as avoidance, burden, and environmental.

The first expression is illustrated through avoidance of a PWD or the lack of recognition of their existence. Here are some examples: "I remember when I was first disabled, they would always ask whoever I was with, 'What does he want to eat?'" Or, "People literally will not look at you. You are there, and they are going by you, and they are looking wherever they want to look so that they don't even have to nod heads with you or even acknowledge your presence."

The second expression suggests that the person with the disability represents a burden and requires too much time, effort, or resources. Here is an example: "When I actually had worked at a job previous to here, it was like, 'Oh, the disabled person.' They had to make a ramp and they had to do all this stuff for me, and I felt like everyone was always looking at me like, 'We're going to have to change because of her.'"

The third expression of this microaggression is environmental in nature and exists due to decisions by the dominant culture to allow structures that prevent equal access for PWDs or provide for separate access. An example follows: "I remember going to a really nice restaurant down in Manhattan. Everybody is eating, the place is full, and I just simply asked, 'Which way to the restroom?' and they were like, 'You need a restroom? Downstairs.' And then they said to me so-matter-of-factly, 'Well, if you cross over, if you go across whatever avenue, you can use the bathroom there,' and I was like, 'Okay, I'll be back by dessert.'"

The overall underlying message received by targets related to all three expressions of this microaggression is that PWDs are likely to be a drain on people without disabilities on an individual, group, and societal basis. Theoretically, the avoidance expression appears to be related to the moral model of disability (Olkin, 1999), where the person with the disability carries a stigma of moral transgression. The underlying related message received by targets is that PWDs are less worthy, and it is better to avoid them. Considering, responding to, and accommodating PWDs is thought to require time, effort, and of course, money. Participants discussed how this may lead to organizational efforts to hold out as long as possible on making legally mandated physical plant changes. The discussion continued to include how this can be further justified by organizations simply resting in a position that no PWDs go there or ask for that. The message targets receive is that their concerns and desire for equal access is only important when the threat of litigation is present.

DOMAIN 8: DESEXUALIZATION

Both groups endorsed this microaggression, which occurs when a PWD is denied as a sexual being. All aspects of the sexuality and sexual identity of the person are ignored or denied, as in the examples that follow: "My looks are so much different than a normal, traditional guy—the big, brawny, model-type guy. I can't fit that, you know, and so women don't see me as someone who is a possible mate or whatever." Or, "I never dated. I didn't date in high school; I didn't go to the prom. I really thought I was going to go to a coed college, but somehow I got talked into by my guidance counselor that I should look into the women's colleges. So, I did; I went to Smith." The underlying message received by targets is that they are not sexual beings and should neither seek nor be sought after as sexual partners. Targets construe perpetrators' motivation to be based on the assumption that PWDs are not capable of sexual activity or desire. Targets further hypothesized that perpetrators' fear of having children with disabilities is an underlying basis for this microaggression.

Auxiliary Findings   We found two underdeveloped domains. The first we call exoticization, which is assigning hypersexualized status to a person based solely on his or her disability. One report indicated that a perpetrator dated disabled individuals only and reflected a romantic interest in the target purely on the basis of the presence of the disability. The second we call spiritual intervention, which is the experience of having a perpetrator stop the target and sometimes "lay hands on" and pray over the target. Both of these experiences were reported to carry with them a depersonalizing characteristic.

DISCUSSION

The purpose of our study was to explore the existence of disability micro-aggressions and to construct an initial taxonomy. We also hoped to begin to understand their dynamics through the underlying messages received by targets and the perceived intentions of perpetrators. Finally, we hoped to collect some of the strategies people use to minimize the impact of these microaggressions. While the eight microaggressions we identified were universally endorsed in both groups, caution needs to be taken in generalizing our results to all PWDs, owing to several factors. First, we only interviewed 12 initial participants. Our sample, while diverse with respect to a variety of disabilities, did not include people with all disabilities; for example, deaf or hard-of-hearing individuals. The sample failed to collect data from participants in a wide range of ages. Whereas most PWDs are unemployed (Bureau of Labor Statistics [BLS], 2009; Office of Disability Employment Policy [ODEP], 2001), our sample contained only one unemployed person. Finally, our sample contained a majority of participants who identify with the disability rights movement, which might not be the case for PWDs in general.

Our study does provide strong evidence that disability microaggressions exist and are harmful to targets and cause psychological pain, sometimes of long endurance. Targets reported reactions of frustration, anger, rage, embarrassment, insult, and invalidation from the continuous stream of microaggressions that they experienced from family, friends, acquaintances, and strangers. Many participants commented that they felt unimportant, invisible, and misunderstood. They described a variety of dilemmas they experienced in reaction to and as a result of the microaggressions. They also described concerns for proposed dilemmas that they anticipate perpetrators experience as well. While we accomplished many of our goals, the area that we understand least at this time deals with the strategies PWDs use to deal with the disability microaggressions. We only have some hints directly from the participants and a hypothesis based on observing the focus groups. Many participants used humor and sarcasm while recounting these experiences. We hypothesize that these techniques serve to diminish or reduce the negative psychological and emotional impact of the microaggression on targets. But our observation during both groups leads us to believe that the group dynamic of universality (Yalom & Leszcz, 2001) might be another key factor that mitigates the harmful effects of microaggressions. In both groups, as we observed participants increasingly identifying with the experiences of other participants and seemingly becoming less isolated in their own experience, the overall energy within the group increased. By the end of the groups, there was a very high level of energy and a sense of group cohesion. Simply relating to the experiences in common with others may have been therapeutic.

In most of the microaggression experiences, participants felt that perpetrators genuinely intended to "do good" or be helpful in some way. However, regardless of the potential intention, the microaggression was experienced negatively and brought along additional psychological wear, as the dubious intention contributed to the processing energy required by targets to work through the event. Participants also described these negative experiences as evidence of the ableist worldview of both perpetrators and the dominant ableist society. Some participants described having their own ableist world-views prior to becoming PWDs, which added to their psychological and emotional discomfort. Participants concluded that the ableist worldview was one that promoted a lack of respect and value for PWDs.

These additional levels of experience and interpretation seem to serve to complicate the microaggression exponentially. The initial level reported in the results section, including the experience's negative emotional/psycho-logical components along with the target's attempts to grapple with what is meant and with the intention of the perpetrator, is certainly complex. Now, add the additional mental and emotional energy expended to test your own reality—asking yourself, did that happen?—and the dilemma grows. Not only is the targets' clear understanding of the experience called into question, but they must grapple with how best to respond while already emotionally aroused and vulnerable. Which choices will be most suitable in a specific situation? How can the target balance their response between self-preservation and educating perpetrators, or at the least, not confirming distorted assumptions or stereotypes? The following interpreta-tion intends to illuminate these complexities within the context of other microaggression research.

We found two microaggressions in common with previous research on racial microaggressions conducted by Sue, Capodilupo, and colleagues (2007); Sue, Bucerri, and colleagues (2007); and Sue and colleagues (2008). The first is second-class citizenship, which seems to be similarly experienced across groups through a denial of rights and respect. One dilemma that PWDs face in relation to this microaggression is that over time, they may collude with it and agree that in fact they do need too much time, effort, and resources. The related feelings might lead PWDs to take effort to limit their interactions with people without disabilities, which can result in increased social isolation. Other expressions of this microaggression may lead to feelings of worthless-ness and reduction in self-esteem. A person is at risk of eventually feeling they are not worthy of social relationships.

Participants conjectured that perpetrators may have a false sense of justifi-cation, with thoughts such as "I wish I could help you, but I really don't have the time or money." It was also believed that perpetrators of the avoidance expression of this microaggression may experience mixed feelings. On the one hand, they feel justified, as if it is their right to choose who they want to talk with or socialize with, and on the other hand, it is possible for them to leave such situations feeling disappointed. After all, it does not cost anything just to say hello. Lastly, the environmental expression of this microaggression may leave perpetrators again feeling falsely justified. Why spend so many resources on so few people? It is just a good business decision.

The second microaggression in common with racial microaggression research we called denial of identity, which seems closely related to findings of denial of individual racism. These microaggressions have a commonality of the perpetrator's denial of the discriminatory experiences of the target. In our domain, this microaggression included, on occasion, the denial of other aspects of the PWDs' identities. The PWD experiences invisibility and invalidation. Among the dilemmas they may face is the possibility that they might question their understanding of the situation and at times blame themselves for the event. They may lose hope or experience a rupture in the relationship with the perpetrator.

Participants thought that perpetrators may move ahead with feelings of discomfort, or they may further misinterpret the thoughts and feelings of the PWD, complicating future encounters with other PWDs. It was conjectured that if perpetrators take the time to process these experiences further, they may also struggle with discomfort, having uncovered their unwitting injury to the PWD and their contribution to the dominant society's oppression.

We also found two microaggressions that are partially related to racial microaggressions. The first was contained in our domain we called spread effect, with a special expression of ascription of intelligence that is closely related to racial microaggression findings. While PWDs most often reported ascription of low intelligence, similar to the findings of Sue and colleagues (2008), a few participants reported ascription of high intelligence, as Sue, Bucceri, and colleagues (2007) found. The dilemma that PWDs face when they experience a spread effect microaggression is that their abilities, talents, and contributions are likely to be underestimated. This is in extreme opposition to their own experience of living with a disability. Targets reported feelings of disappointment and frustration, eventually leading to self-doubt. The true value or sense of accomplishment one derives as a result of an achievement might be reexamined and devalued. According to participants, perpetrators who are confronted while committing this microaggression are likely to challenge the question. They might become defensive and walk away from the interaction with a feeling of disbelief. They certainly may be less likely to reach out to PWDs in the future and may be increasingly hesitant to do so, owing to the unpredictability of PWDs. Participants conjectured that when perpetrators ascribe high intelligence or other ability to PWDs and are challenged, they are likely to react in disbelief or shock. It was postulated that such perpetrators would think thoughts such as "Those people can't even take a compliment."

The second microaggression we called desexualization, which seems to be the polar opposite of the exoticization found by Sue, Bucceri, and colleagues (2007) in Asian American microaggressions. Their commonality is the assignment of a level of sexual desirability based solely on membership to the minority group. Our desexualization microaggression assigns a low level of sexual desirability to PWDs. The dilemma for PWDs is that this microaggression flies in the face of the reality of them as a sexual being. Except for a few cases where unusually poor health is part of the disability, PWDs are likely to experience the same distribution of sexual desire as does the population of people without disabilities. Participants conjecture that their expected available partners are only other PWDs. Related feelings were reported to include embarrassment, frustration, and rejection. Some PWDs who strive to fulfill their desires might experience humiliation and feel hopeless and worthless.

Participants report that perpetrators who are challenged are completely unaware of the harm they are inflicting. If pressed, they might retreat and claim that they are entitled to have their own preferences and desires. They may not be aware of the deep-seated nature of their own ableist beliefs.

Perhaps most interestingly, we found several microaggressions currently unique to PWDs, which we describe in the following sections.

DENIAL OF PRIVACY

The dilemma for the target is whether to provide the information about their disability, and if so, how. People with disabilities are aware of the expectation that they bear the burden of making people without disabilities more comfortable with them. At the same time, PWDs know that always responding to the request for information contributes to their lack of control about their personal information. These dilemmas may lead to feelings of uncertainty or embarrassment and the reliving of the patient role and may be experienced as dehumanizing.

Participants expressed concerns that perpetrators can leave the situation with a variety of confusing dilemmas. If the target responds and provides the disability-related information, the perpetrator may walk away erroneously thinking they have come to know that individual better and with feelings of satisfaction, when in actuality they have insulted the PWD and have again focused on the disability as the only important characteristic of the individual. On the other hand, if the PWD decides not to respond and will not provide the requested information, the perpetrator confirms the stereotypes that PWDs are angry, socially inferior, and possibly uncooperative. The perpetrator also reconfirms that disability is a tabooed subject.

HELPLESSNESS

The major dilemma associated with this microaggression is how to negotiate the complexity of the concept of help and PWDs. People with disabilities facing an overwhelming number of offers of unwanted help may experience frustration, anger, and uncertainty. They also are aware of the expectations of society around their emotion regulation (Olkin, 1999) and do not want to contribute to additional misunderstanding and stereotyping. There are drawbacks to each potential response. If a PWD responds to an unneeded and unsolicited offer of help harshly or by ignoring it, these responses can feed into existing negative stereotypes, such as the unappreciative, angry disabled person. In addition, a PWD who responds abruptly or forcefully realizes that this encounter might contribute to the perpetrator shying away from future encounters with other PWDs. On the other hand, if the PWD chooses or is forced to accept the help, they may feel demoralized, powerless, and submissive. Finally, if the PWD finds herself or himself continuously having to politely decline unsolicited offers of help, they are vulnerable to feeling intolerant of and offended by these offers. The overwhelming passion with which participants described these experiences is indicative of the permeation of the dominant able-centric worldview saturating PWDs with its distorted assumption of their perpetual helplessness. With respect to the notion that they would possibly be better off dead, participants expressed the concern that they could relive feelings that they have already worked through, including internalized and externalized anger or self-doubt.

Participants were especially concerned about the perpetrator leaving the experience questioning the interaction. Here is where it gets complicated. All humans on occasion need some help; PWDs are no exception. However, the notion that one needs help in most situations and across a wide range of domains is damaging to self-esteem. Uncertainty of how best to respond is also psychologically taxing. The solution to this dilemma is not to decrease interactions between people with and without disabilities, nor is it to eliminate offers of help. The solution is to find a situation-specific balance between offering help continuously and not offering help at all.

Perhaps the presentation of a similar situation without the disability factor will allow readers to feel resonance with the dilemma. Place yourself in a restaurant with a relatively new yet intense love interest. The two of you have just sat down, and the attentive waiter brings menus. The waiter indicates that he will return in a few minutes to take your order. The two of you glance at the menus, and then your eyes lock in a loving stare, and all other reality becomes suspended. A few minutes later the waiter returns, and the lovers are embarrassed that they are not yet ready to order. The waiter again indicates that he will return. As you discuss potential meals, you both remember the last weekend trip with those wonderful steaks and again drift into a romantic stupor. The waiter returns and you quickly order dinner. As the waiter leaves, you begin to discuss potential weekend plans similar to that last wonderful trip. Before you know it, dinner arrives. You begin to eat and speak softly but lovingly with each other. The committed waiter returns to ask if you need additional drinks. You respond no. He then comes and asks if you need freshly ground pepper. You again respond in the negative. The dedicated waiter again returns to ask if you want more drinks, and so on. At this point, you begin to question the degree to which the waiter is engaged in your dining experience. Why can't he leave us alone? Is he hitting on my lover? Doesn't he have anything else to do? Am I being paranoid? Is he acting normally? Am I making more of this than is appropriate? It is our hope to help readers understand that it is certainly necessary to engage with a waiter in order to successfully have dinner in a restaurant. However, the level of engagement between you and the waiter can have satisfying or dissatisfying results. The degree to which you can have a satisfying or dissatisfying engagement with the waiter is similar to how a PWD can have a satisfying or dissatisfying experience with a person without a disability offering help.

SECONDARY GAIN

Here again, the interpretation is complex. Certainly there are many people who take up social causes in a genuine manner. Often, these humanitarian efforts lead to improvements in the lives of PWDs. However, there are other groups and individuals who take similar actions, in part for their own self-interest. People with disabilities are aware of this duality between the true altruist and the opportunist. When a PWD encounters the opportunist, they might experience the interaction as a microaggression of secondary gain. The target of such microaggressions feels used, cheap, and like a pawn in the game of social chess. Participants reported that these experiences lead to feelings of disillusionment about people who engage in altruistic acts. A dilemma for PWDs may arise as they begin to question the authenticity of the actions of people without disabilities in general. In addition, participants described damage to their self-esteem and distortions in their social awareness.

Participants felt that the perpetrator may leave the experience temporarily feeling superior or honored by the praise from others congratulating her or him for her or his selfless act. Perpetrators may believe that they are actually engaged in altruistic behavior, owing to their distorted beliefs about disability. According to participants, when they confront such individuals, the response is usually defensiveness or disbelief.

PATRONIZATION

One dilemma that PWDs experience related to this microaggression is how to operate as an adult in a society with an ingrained attitude based on the medical model of disability (Olkin, 1999) that supports a paternalistic view of PWDs and that appears to be impervious to change. As a result, PWDs face the question of why they must earn what seems to be given to others by default. How can they be taken seriously? What steps can they take to be afforded the respect and responsibility adults receive in America? With respect to the other form of patronization, participants reported that continuously receiving false admiration through unjustified praise serves to undermine their belief in themselves and trust in the validity of their accomplishments. This in turn may reduce their future efficacy in similar situations. Participants described feelings of embarrassment, belittlement, and inferiority and were concerned that perpetrators might feel misunderstood. Perpetrators are likely to erroneously assume that they were indeed being nice, giving praise, or expressing concern and had no idea that targets were hurt, offended, and insulted.

CONCLUSION

We join Olkin and Pledger (2003) in strongly encouraging psychologists to expand current multicultural theory to include disability as an equally salient aspect of diversity. Such an expansion would support the development of a unified model of disability identity as well as ableism as its theoretical counterpart. In addition, as we continue to move toward understanding multiple cultural affiliations, the inclusion of disability in the discourse seems vital. Future research on microaggressions should seek to confirm, disconfirm, or extend our findings and to ensure the comprehensiveness and accuracy of the reported domains in this study. We found microaggressions that seem unique to PWDs and others that are in common with microaggressions experienced by other minority groups. We entrust future researchers to consider the possibility that there exists a universe of microaggressions, some of which are population dependent and some of which are not. We strongly encourage the exploration of this universe. In addition, researchers should continue to expand the study of disability-awareness techniques, focusing on the development of more appropriate and effective interventions. This research could contribute to a reduction in the frequency and pervasiveness of microaggressions perpetrated by people without disabilities. Finally, researchers are encouraged to explore interventions that assist PWDs in managing the negative psychological and emotional effects of microaggressions they experience. Many of the participants of our research indicated the mere discussion of these experiences as helpful, most likely due to feelings of universality, which could be a starting point for such research.

REFERENCES

Ableism: An extreme form of racism (2009). Retrieved April 12, 2009, from http://www.notdeadyet.org/docs/ablism.html.

American Psychological Association (APA) (2009). *APA Task Force on guidelines for assessment and treatment of persons with disabilities: Draft guidelines for assessment of and intervention with individuals who have disabilities.* Retrieved June 23, 2009, from http://forms.apa.org/pi/disability.

Americans with Disabilities Act, 42 U.S.C. § 12101 et seq. (1990).

Americans with Disabilities Act Amendments Act of 2008, S. 3406; Public Law 110 325.

Barrett, J., & Kirk, S. (2000). Running focus groups with elderly and disabled elderly participants. *Applied Ergonomics, 31*, 621–629.

Braithwaite, D. (1985, November). *Impression management and redefinition of self by persons with disabilities.* Paper presented at the annual meeting of the Speech Communication Association, Denver, CO.

Braithwaite, D. (1991). "Just how much did that wheelchair cost?" Management of privacy boundaries by persons with disabilities. *Western Journal of Speech Communication, 55*, 254–274.

Braithwaite, D., & Thompson, L. (Eds.). (2000). *Handbook of communication and people with disabilities: Research and application.* Mahwah, NJ: Lawrence Erlbaum.

Bureau of Labor Statistics (BLS) (2009). Labor Force Statistics from the Current Population Survey. In BLS (Ed.), *Labor Force Statistics from the Current Population Survey: New monthly data series on the employment status of people with a disability.* Retrieved August 30, 2009, from http://www.bls.gov/cps/cpsdisability.htm.

Chaikin, A., & Derlega, V. (1974). Variables affecting the appropriateness of self-disclosure. *Journal of Consulting and Clinical Psychology, 4*, 588–593.

Fleischer, D., & Zames, F. (2001). *The disability rights movement: From charity to confrontation.* Philadelphia: Temple University Press.

Goffman, E. (1963). *Stigma: Notes on the management of spoiled identity.* Englewood Cliffs, NJ: Prentice Hall.

Hafferty, F. (1994). Decontextualizing disability in the crime mystery genre: The case of the invisible handicap. *Disability & Society, 8*(2), 185–206.

Hill, C., Thompson, B., & Williams, E. (1997). A guide to conducting consensual qualitative research. *Counseling Psychologist, 25*(4), 517–572.

Imrie, R., & Kumar, M. (1998). Focusing on disability and access built in the environment. *Disability & Society, 13*, 357–374.

Keller, R. (2004). *The relationship between self-disclosure, attributional style, and life outcomes for people with physical disabilities associated with independent living centers in New York State.* Unpublished doctoral dissertation. Teachers College, Columbia University, New York.

Keller, R., & King, J. (2008). Health disparities and people with disabilities. In B. Wallace (Ed.), *Toward equity in health: A new global approach to health disparities* (pp. 447–459). New York: Springer.

Kitzinger, J. (1995). Qualitative research: Introducing focus groups. *British Medical Journal, 311*, 299–302.

Kleck, R. (1968). Physical stigma and nonverbal cues emitted in face-to-face interaction. *Human Relations, 21,* 19–28.

Kleck, R., Ono, H., & Hastorf, A. (1966). The effects of physical deviance upon face-to-face interaction. *Human Relations, 19,* 425–436.

Kroll, T., Barbour, R., & Harris, J. (2007). Using focus groups in disability research. *Qualitative Health Research, 17*(5), 690–698.

Leadership Conference on Civil Rights Education Fund (LCCREF) (2009). *Confronting the new faces of hate: Hate crimes in America.* Retrieved August 27, 2009, from http://www.civilrights.org/publications/hatecrimes/disabilities.html.

Longmore, P., & Umansky, L. (Eds.). (2001). *The new disability history: American perspectives.* New York: New York University Press.

Morgan, D. (1997). *Focus groups as qualitative research* (2nd ed.). Thousand Oaks, CA: Sage.

Office of Disability Employment Policy (ODEP) (2001). *Statistics about people with disabilities and employment.* Retrieved August 30, 2009, from http://www.dol.gov/odep/archives/ek01/stats.htm.

Olkin, R. (1999). *What psychotherapists should know about disability.* New York: Guilford.

Olkin, R., & Pledger, C. (2003). Can disability studies and psychology join hands? *American Psychologist, 58*(4), 296–304.

Pfeiffer, D. (2001). The conceptualization of disability. In S. N. Barnartt & B. M. Altman (Eds.), *Exploring theories and expanding methodologies: Where we are and where we need to go* (Vol. 2, pp. 29–52). New York: Elsevier Science.

Pierce, C., Carew, J., Pierce-Gonzalez, D., & Willis, D. (1978). An experiment in racism: TV commercials. In C. Pierce (Ed.), *Television and education* (pp. 62–88). Beverly Hills, CA: Sage.

Russell, M. (2002). *Beyond ramps: Disability at the end of the social contract.* Monroe, ME: Common Courage Press.

Seymour, J., Ingleton, C., Payne, S., & Beddow, V. (2003). Specialist palliative care: Patients' experiences. *Journal of Advanced Nursing, 44,* 24–33.

Snyder, S., & Mitchell, D. (2006). Eugenics and the racial genome: Politics at the molecular level. *Patterns of Prejudice, 40*(4–5), 399–412.

Sofaer, S. (1999). Qualitative methods: What are they and why use them? *Health Services Research, 34,* 1101–1118.

Sue, D., Bucceri, J., Lin, A., Nadal, K., & Torino, G. (2007). Racial microaggressions and the Asian American experience. *Cultural Diversity and Ethnic Minority Psychology, 13* (1), 72–81.

Sue, D., Capodilupo, C., & Holder, A. (2008). Racial microaggressions in the life experience of Black Americans. *Professional Psychology: Research and Practice, 39*(3), 2329–2336.

Sue, D., Capodilupo, C., Torino, G., Bucceri, J., Holder, A., Nadal, K., & Esquilin, M. (2007). Racial microaggresssions in everyday life: Implications for clinical practice. *American Psychologist, 62*(4), 271–286.

Telethon 2000 (2000). Retrieved April 12, 2009, from http://www.ragged-edge-mag.com/extra/thon2000.htm.

Thompson, T. (1982). Disclosure as a disability-management strategy: A review and conclusions. *Communication Quarterly, 30*, 196–202.

Vash, C. (1981). *The psychology of disability*. New York: Springer Publishing Co.

Wallace, B., Carter, R., Nanin, J., Keller, R., & Alleyne, V. (2003). Identity development for "diverse and different others": Integrating stages of change, motivational interviewing, and identity theories for race, people of color, sexual orientation, and disability. In B. Wallace & R. Carter (Eds.), *Understanding and dealing with violence* (pp. 41–91). Thousand Oaks, CA: Sage.

White, M., & Epston, D. (1990). *Narrative means to therapeutic ends*. New York: Norton.

Yalom, I., & Leszcz, M. (2001). *Theory and practice of group therapy*. Cambridge, MA: Basic Books.

Zola, I. (1982). *Ordinary lives: Voices of disability and disease*. Cambridge, MA: Alperwood Brooks.

CHAPTER 12

Class Dismissed

Making the Case for the Study of Classist Microaggressions

LAURA SMITH and REBECCA M. REDINGTON

Over and over, I came face to face with people's prejudice against me because my family was poor. My best friend all through school told me in the third grade that she couldn't come home and spend the night with me because her daddy said that I was "white trash." I was incredibly hurt and confused by this, though I didn't know what it was about. That's when I first started feeling bad about myself, feeling I had done something wrong. (Stout, 1996, p. 19)

LINDA STOUT'S CHILDHOOD memory coincides with similar stories that might be told about many forms of oppression: that our friends were not allowed to play with us because we were Black, or because we were Jewish, or because we were queer, and that over time, the oppressive attitudes and corresponding microaggressions that enveloped us were internalized in the form of deep, pervasive shame about who we were. But in a nation that has long considered itself to be classless (Zweig, 2000), the idea of classism as a form of oppression is largely unfamiliar. Given that people at the bottom of the economic hierarchy do not constitute a cultural group in the literal sense of the word, does it make sense for multicultural psychologists to study the existence of classist microaggressions?

This chapter will argue that, in fact, everyday life and ordinary language abound with class-based indignities and affronts. These incidents are directly analogous to other forms of racial and cultural microaggressions—the derogatory verbal, behavioral, and environmental messages that are routinely experienced by members of marginalized groups (Sue et al., 2007). These classist microaggressions expose and reinforce a status quo that devalues poor and working-class people based on their social class and that undermines the psychological well-being of people who hold these class memberships (Belle, Doucet, Harris, Miller, & Tan, 2000; Lott & Bullock, 2007). Moreover, classism intersects with other forms of bias to produce situations of double jeopardy for poor women, poor people of color, and members of other oppressed groups (Smith, 2005), with the result that our understanding of the microaggressions experienced by these groups will be deepened when we add class to the analysis.

In this chapter, we hope to present a rationale for the future study of classist microaggressions. The chapter will open with a definition of classism within a social justice framework (Smith, 2008). Next, we will discuss current economic trends that suggest that the time is right for addressing classism in all its forms. We will follow this presentation by illustrating some of the manifestations of classism within society, including the evidence of biased attitudes as offered by social psychologists. Having laid these foundations, we will turn to literature, research, and current events to provide examples of the everyday classist microinsults, microassaults, and microinvalidations that emerge from attitudinal biases.

CLASSISM

The consideration of classist microaggressions first requires specification of the form of oppression that gives rise to them: classism. Social class and classism are controversial notions in and of themselves, since, as noted, some would contend that the United States is a classless society, or at least a society where class is irrelevant (Zweig, 2000). We offer a particular conceptualization of social class and classism that corresponds to one of three "understandings of socioeconomic status and social class-related inequalities" offered by the American Psychological Association (APA) Task Force on Socioeconomic Status (SES; 2006, p. 17). These three approaches were described as (1) *materialist approaches*, or those that correlate differences in SES with differential access to resources, goods, and services ("materials"); (2) *gradient approaches*, or those where status is constructed as a continuum along which relative differences in class position may be considered; and (3) *reproduction of power and privilege*, or approaches that investigate class inequity as a form of sociopolitical dominance by which some groups systematically prosper at the expense of others. Any one of these approaches might be more or less useful within a particular sphere of inquiry, depending on the precise question of interest. Given that our interest relates to the nature of class-based oppression, the third approach mentioned provides an appropriate jumping-off point.

This approach aligns well with a social justice framework for psychological theory and practice, defined by Goodman et al. (2004) as "scholarship and professional action designed to change societal values, structures, policies, and practices, such that disadvantaged groups gain increased access to these tools of self-determination" (p. 795). A social justice framework is predicated on the assumption that systems of privilege and oppression exist in a real (as opposed to a relative) sense, even though disparate individual exceptions to predominant power relations may exist. These broad systems of power relations provide a backdrop for discussions of the circumstances and well- being of members of dominant and subordinated groups. Classism, then, can be positioned alongside (or more accurately, at intersections with) racism, sexism, heterosexism, and ableism as the systematic privileging of people at the top of the economic spectrum at the expense of those at the bottom. Along these lines, Bullock (1995) defined classism as "the oppression of the poor through a network of everyday practices, attitudes, assumptions, behaviors, and institutional rules" (p. 119). This conceptualization was expanded by Lott and Bullock (2007) to incorporate *institutional classism*, through which social institutions function to perpetuate the deprivation and low status of poor people, and *interpersonal classism*, which is characterized by prejudice, stereotyping, and discrimination.

THE NUMBERS DON'T LIE: WHY WE CAN
NO LONGER DISMISS CLASS

The importance of positioning class-based considerations within existing psychological frameworks of identity and bias finds important support from current economic trends. We are living during a period of our nation's history when the gap between the wealthiest Americans and the poorest has widened prodigiously. This trend has been called *economic apartheid* (Collins & Yeskel, 2005), a term that refers to the institutional and social inequities causing increased disparities in wealth distribution in the United States. This gap has not always been so pronounced: In the 30 years following World War II, economic growth was shared among diverse groups of Americans based on annual earnings. In other words, households across all earning brackets (i.e., from the wealthiest to the poorest) experienced an increase in income of approximately 90 to 100 percent during this time. Households with the lowest annual incomes actually saw the most growth, evidencing an increase of over 116 percent (Collins & Yeskel, 2005). This pattern of across-the-board increases meant that the gaps between the wealthiest and poorest Americans remained relatively stable, even shrinking in size at times, during the three decades following the war.

However, this trend shifted dramatically as the 1970s drew to a close. In the next two decades, the average income of the wealthiest 1 percent of households in America would increase by 201 percent, while the average income of the bottom fifth of American households increased by only 9 percent. As the result of these trends, approximately 10 percent of the U.S. population owned 70 percent of all American wealth (such as savings, home equity, consumer goods, stocks, bonds, and real estate) by 2001 (Collins & Yeskel, 2005). This figure means, of course, that 90 percent of the population was left to share the remaining 30 percent. Among this 90 percent of the population, 17.6 percent (or one in six households) had zero or negative wealth—that is, they owed more than they earned. Increasingly, the group at the bottom of the economic spectrum includes people with jobs. In 2003, a quarter of all American workers could be described as working poor; that is, they earned poverty-level wages (Tait, 2005). The consequence of these trends is that the United States has become "the most economically unequal nation in the developed world; it [has] the widest spread in wealth between the haves and the have-nots" (Fischer, Hout, & Stiles, 2006, p. 137).

CLASS INEQUITY AT THE INTERSECTIONS

It is worth noting that as the equity gap has increased among all people in the United States, it intersects with other identities along the way, highlighting the need to consider multiple oppressions associated with race, gender, and class. According to the Survey of Consumer Finances conducted by the Federal Reserve Bank, African Americans constituted 13 percent of the U.S. population in 2001 but owned only 3 percent of the country's assets; for every dollar earned by the average White family in 2001, a Black family earned less than 17 cents (Lui, Robles, Leondar-Wright, Brewer, & Adamson, 2006). A study of economic security among families of color in the United States further underscored these discrepancies, revealing that even African American and Latino families who have attained middle-class status are not financially secure (Wheary, Shapiro, Draut, & Meschede, 2008). Ninety-five percent of African American and 87 percent of Latino middle-class families are without enough assets to cover three-quarters of their living expenses for three months if they were to be without income—both figures well above the national average of 78 percent for all middle-class families. Moreover, according to this study, 68 percent of African American and 56 percent of Latino middle-class households have no financial assets at all and are living from paycheck to paycheck. Incomes for Asians and Whites are more similar, yet disparity exists in their assets and types of employment they hold. For example, Asians are much less likely than Whites to own their own homes and are absent from higher-ranked positions in business and politics (Lui et al., 2006). The racial wealth divide is perhaps most apparent among Native

Americans, who have the highest poverty rates of any American racial or ethnic group at 25.3 percent (United States Census Bureau, 2006).

Gender also intersects with class. Although the gap between earnings for men and women has decreased in recent decades, women still earn only 80 cents for every dollar earned by men (Collins & Yeskel, 2005). This gain in earnings for women is not the net result of increases in women's wages; rather, half the narrowing of the gap is due to decreases in men's earnings. Single-mother families are almost twice as likely as single-father families to live in poverty (Newman, 2004). In general, women are 40 percent more likely to live in poverty than men, and of all adults living in extreme poverty (with incomes less than half the poverty rate), 60 percent are women (Legal Momentum, 2003).

An examination of class with regard to both race and gender reveals still more about these intersections. Employment within the labor market is both race-typed and gender-typed so that individuals' jobs and subsequently their incomes are highly associated with their race and gender (Amott & Matthaei, 2004). For example, while increased experience and seniority in the workplace may be associated with increased wages for workers in general, this finding does not hold true for women across races. African American women have been shown to receive smaller increases in earnings based on experience and seniority than do White women (England, Christopher, & Reid, 1999). Finally, the race/class/gender intersection reveals one of the highest poverty rates in America—just under 40 percent—which corresponds to single African American and Latina mothers (National Poverty Center, 2006).

SEEING CLASSISM

The data just cited paints a picture of a winner-take-all society where the old cliché finds a basis in reality: the rich get richer as the poor get poorer. Furthermore, this data provides a foundation for consideration of a corresponding form of oppression, classism, as defined earlier. Where can we look to see evidence of the operations of classism? In addition to the economic inequities just described, classism is revealed through the analysis of such examples as environmental injustice, through which the communities of poor people and people of color become the waste-dumping grounds for the nation (Bullard, 2000), and in educational inequities, which result in the provision of fewer books, computers, and teachers for public school students in poor communities (Kozol, 2005). Poor people face "elevated rates of threatening and uncontrollable life events, noxious life conditions, marital dissolution, infant mortality, many diseases, violent crime, homicide, accidents, and deaths from all causes" (Belle et al., 2000, p. 1160); at the same time, their access to medical care, the quality of care they receive, and their relationships with their doctors is reduced relative to other citizens (Scott, 2005).The continuing low level of the minimum wage is also part of this picture. The increase in the federal minimum wage to $7.25 (effective as of July 24, 2009) is a step in the right direction, yet it still will not lift low-wage workers and their families out of poverty by providing a living wage. A living wage is considered to be the amount necessary to bring a family of four at least to the poverty line and no farther than 130 percent of the poverty line, that being the maximum that a family can earn and still be eligible for food stamps (Brocht, 2000). In most communities, living wage estimates begin at about $8.85 (Living Wage Resource Center, 2003). As a nation, we seem content to be without a commitment to the provision of a living wage for the low-wage earners who do the everyday necessary work upon which our society depends.

CLASSIST ATTITUDES

Trends like the ones just outlined sketch out a picture of broad societal patterns of inequity that indicate the operation of structural and attitudinal barriers to the detriment of poor and working-class people. Microaggressions, which derive from and perpetuate these attitudes, are often nuanced and perpetuated by people who are unaware that they harbor underlying biases. If researchers have not yet turned their attention to the existence of classist microaggressions specifically, what evidence is there to support such inquiry? The social psychological research contains important clues in this regard. In a straightforward statement that she went on to support with a review of literature, social psychologist Bernice Lott (2002) wrote:

> I propose that a dominant response [to the poor] is that of distancing, that is, separation, exclusion, devaluation, discounting, and designation as "other," and that this response can be identified in both institutional and interpersonal contexts. In social psychological terms, distancing and denigrating responses operationally define discrimination. These, together with stereotypes (i.e., a set of beliefs about a group that are learned early, widely shared, and socially validated) and prejudice (i.e., negative attitudes) constitute classism. (p. 100)

The research that Lott (2002) reviewed included a study by Cozzarelli, Wilkinson, and Tagler (2001), in which respondents assigned traits such as *lazy*, *stupid*, *dirty*, and *immoral* more often to poor people than to middle-class people; in another (Hoyt, 1999), the most common stereotypes listed for poor people were *uneducated*, *lazy*, *dirty*, *drug/alcohol user*, and *criminal*. Lott and Saxon (2002) presented subjects with information about a hypothetical target woman and found that regardless of their ethnicities, working-class target women were more often described as *crude* and *irresponsible* than were middle-class targets, and working-class mothers were judged to be less suitable as potential officers in a parent-teacher organization. Similar results were reported in a study by Landrine (1985), in which participants more frequently labeled lower-class women (Landrine's identification of them) as *confused, dirty, hostile, illogical, impulsive, incoherent, inconsiderate, irresponsible,* and *superstitious* than they did middle-class women. Fiske (2007), a social psychologist and neuroscientist, investigated automatic prejudicial responses to the poor using MRI technology. Photographs of homeless people were among those that reliably elicited brain reactions characteristic of disgust and avoidance. In fact, photographs of the homeless failed completely to activate the brain response that signals the perception of another human being. "These areas simply failed to light up," reported Fiske, "as if people had stumbled on a pile of garbage" (p. 157).

CLASSIST MICROAGGRESSIONS: HIDING IN PLAIN SIGHT

Our case thus far has been that societal trends depict a state of diminished access to resources and opportunities for people at the bottom of the economic spectrum and that research findings document the corresponding existence of prejudicial attitudes toward poor and working-class people. These circumstances point to the existence of systematic classist bias that could theoretically give rise to corresponding classist microaggressions. In this section of the chapter, we will develop this line of thought further: If classist microaggressions exist, what forms might they take? In organizing this discussion, we will follow a typology for the categorization of micro-aggressions proposed by Derald Wing Sue and his colleagues (Sue et al., 2007). Following a description of this typology, we will present examples of microaggressions taken from research, literature, and popular culture.

Sue and colleagues' (2007) typology describes microaggressions as occurring at three levels. First, *microassaults* are explicit derogations that can be verbal or nonverbal and are intended to hurt the victim through name-calling, avoidant behavior, or discriminatory actions. They are largely conscious and deliberate but may not be completely so. A *microinsult* is more subtle and is characterized by verbal or nonverbal communications that demean a person's heritage or identity. Perpetrators of microinsults are frequently unaware of the insulting implications of their behavior, as when Black individuals are congratulated by Whites on their articulate speech. *Microinvalidations* include communications that exclude, negate, or nullify a person's thoughts, feelings, or experiential reality. To illustrate microinvalidations, Sue and colleagues cite Helms's (1992) example of Whites telling Blacks "I don't see color," which functions to invalidate Black individuals' lived experiences of racism. Finally, microaggressions at any of these levels may be interpersonal or environmental.

CLASSIST MICROASSAULTS

The quote that begins this chapter illustrates the outright classist labeling and name-calling that goes almost unchecked in American culture. Labeling includes the use of overtly class-referenced words as modifiers to indicate favorable or unfavorable evaluations, such as describing an object or a person as "classy," "high-class," or a "class act" in a complimentary fashion or describing it as "low-class" or "low-rent" to discredit it. A 2008 posting to an online parenting discussion board queried readers, "What are some nice ways to say a name sounds 'ghetto'?" The author of the posting went on to provide some synonyms of her own, including "low-rent" and "down-market" (Yahoo! Answers, Pregnancy & Parenting, 2008). After describing the television program *Dog the Bounty Hunter* as "low-rent," a *New York Daily News* reviewer supplied the rest of his formula for who might like such a show: "If you think TV has been too highfalutin' lately and you feel the need to slip away for a night on the low road, grab a bag of pork rinds and a case of Rolling Rock and turn on A&E Wednesday night" (Franklin, 2009, ¶ 1).

Although these examples suggest that the use of *low-rent* crosses racial boundaries as a modifier, other forms of classist name-calling refer to specific intersections with different identities. Hartigan (2005) discussed the meanings inherent in the name-calling directed toward poor White Americans, known variously as *White trash, trailer trash, rednecks*, or *hillbillies*. These labels encompass different shades of meaning while typically carrying negative connotations. Although generally derogatory, *redneck* is a label that poor or rural Whites may nevertheless embrace to convey a defiant attitude, as exemplified by Gretchen Wilson in her 2004 country music hit "Redneck Woman": "Some people look down on me, but I don't give a rip/ I'll stand barefooted in my own front yard with a baby on my hip/'Cause I'm a redneck woman/...Let me get a big 'hell yeah' from the redneck girls like me" (Wilson & Rich, 2004). *White trash*, on the other hand, is a label that corresponds to what Hartigan calls the social bottom of the class spectrum and conveys disgust and contempt; the commonly heard adjective *trashy* is derived from this term. *Hillbilly* has regional connotations and encompasses the poignant complexity of Appalachian Mountain heritage: distinct traditions of music, food, art, and love of the land, frequently experienced against a backdrop of abject poverty and social isolation. Used in microassaults, it refers to characteristics such as laziness, superstitiousness, lack of intelligence, and illiteracy in its targets, which are often portrayed to comic effect, as in the 1960s television program *The Beverly Hillbillies*.

Classist microassaults against poor Blacks were notoriously epitomized by President Ronald Reagan's overt labeling of a poor Black mother as a "welfare queen" during his 1976 presidential campaign (*New York Times*, 1976), a characterization that depicted them as lazy, greedy, and promiscuous. Rose (2008) analyzed the ongoing evolution of this microassault, tracing its usage through the following decades into contemporary culture:

> *To drum up support for drastic reductions in public welfare assistance, those who used this term accused economically-limited Black women of manipulating the welfare system by having babies to increase their welfare assistance payments. The label "welfare queen" relied on the already sedimented idea that Black women are sexually deviant and untrustworthy.... This kind of racist and sexist name-calling is pretty similar to what [a well-known hip hop artist] claims about the "bitches and hoes" in his 'hood.... [His] attitude about poor Black women isn't any better than many of the conservatives who attack him. (p. 181–182)*

CLASSIST MICROINSULTS

Through classist microinsults, poor and working-class people receive communications that are more subtle than name-calling but that convey demeaning messages just the same, although their impact may be outside the awareness of the perpetrators. Chaney (1994) wrote of the "cultural dislocation" (p. 173) that she experienced when she left her home in rural Missouri to attend college. Her new peers found many ways to express their low regard for the circumstances of her upbringing: explaining to her that she could not join them for tennis because she did not have the right clothes, resetting the silverware after she left the room, refusing to eat the foods that she cooked, and offering to give her their hand-me-downs. "I would show pictures of my family to friends from more privileged backgrounds," she remembered, "and have them look away, unable to accept my obviously rural/working-class roots (one said that my family looked very 'casual')" (p.174).

Although some of Chaney's college friends may have been aware of looking down on working-class culture, others likely were not and may have even felt that they were being helpful to Chaney in explaining to her what the "right" clothes and the "right" foods were. This is one of the hallmarks of a microaggressive event: Although people on the receiving end may immediately perceive the message as demeaning, the experience can be confusing in that the perpetrator may simultaneously be perceived as not intending any harm, leaving victims to wonder what actually happened and whether they are entitled to their feelings. The situation is further complicated by the fact that people in marginalized groups have internalized the very same biased messages about themselves that privileged people have learned; in other words, they have internalized their own oppression:

> *I began to recognize my cultural invisibility in the world in which I was living, including my invisibility to myself.... I increasingly felt the loss of my home, but was not able to embrace (or fit into) the world in which I was now living. I could no longer speak as easily in public as in the past, as I was unclear any longer who was speaking. (Chaney, 1994, p. 175)*

Other working-class women have described being complimented by middle-class and wealthy people on the wonderful "common sense" that they have. Although the speakers may have perceived themselves as being kind in these moments, working-class recipients can experience such messages as condescending, as Luttrell (1997) explained in her study of American education and social class. The double message here is that by drawing attention to a working-class individual's supposed common sense, people with class privilege set themselves apart in terms of the kind of knowledge and values that *they* possess—the advanced education, formal etiquette, and "cultured" tastes that they associate with class status. Like other aspects of attitudinal bias, these messages are often internalized by working-class individuals themselves, as articulated by one of the participants in Luttrell's study: "I have just never thought about average people like myself being intelligent. People like me have common sense" (Luttrell, 1997, p. 27). This working-class interviewee's comment illustrated the notion that common sense and intelligence do not necessarily coexist; rather, common sense is kind of a homespun runner-up to the intelligence that is associated with formal education and professional careers.

As formal education has become a marker of intelligence among people with class privilege, working-class individuals who have pursued higher education may struggle to understand the meaning of their own advanced degrees (and the congratulations that come with them). Reflecting upon the attainment of her master's degree, Joanna Kadi (1996) described the contradictory feelings that can be experienced by working-class people in higher education:

> *Working-class people traverse the minefield of academia and end up with initials after our names. We get confused. Very confused, because those initials symbolize the separation between rich and poor. Rich people need these degrees to feel smart, to remind themselves they are not a lowly janitor sweeping halls, a lowly cook slopping out lousy cafeteria food...but somehow we end up with them. We get confused. Are we announcing we're smart? But working-class people can't be smart. (p. 52)*

Psychologists and other mental health professionals are of course not immune to classism (or any other kind of bias), and accounts exist by which therapists' microinsults toward their own clients can be glimpsed. Through a series of interviews with working-class women who had been therapy clients, Chalifoux (1996) highlighted therapists' apparent unawareness of their own class values. The study indicated that middle-class therapists tended to offer unrealistic suggestions as to the goals and alternatives that they thought their clients should consider as part of their development. In this way, their clients were made to feel ashamed, as though they were completely responsible for their struggles and should be able to overcome them. Moreover, the women noted the failure of their therapists to understand that their financial situations did not permit them the luxury of all the options that their therapists envisioned for them; one participant wondered why her therapist could not understand that "freedom of choice takes money" (p. 30). In addition, working-class interviewees noted their therapists' discomfort whenever the topic of fees arose. Middle-class people are often taught not to discuss issues regarding money, and therapists' avoidance of this issue was experienced as invalidating by their financially struggling clients.

CLASSIST MICROINVALIDATIONS

Powerful perpetrations of classist microinvalidations—or communications that broadly negate or demean the lived experiences of poor and working-class people—stream into popular culture daily via the media's focus on middle-class and wealthy people. Fashion and lifestyle programming spotlights the wardrobes, dinner parties, and daily activities of wealthy people; issues relevant to them and to middle-class individuals, such as the stock market, comprise the entire programming schedules of cable networks. Simultaneously, we are fed images and narratives evoking our sense that anything is possible and that in this winner-take-all society, we have as good a chance of taking it all as anyone (Frank & Cook, 1996) and should be trying to do so. These narratives appear in news magazine television programs, magazine articles, and reality shows like *American Idol*, *The Apprentice*, and *Top Chef*, which have popularized the notion that anyone can become a star. Collins and Yeskel (2005) asserted that many Americans are so indoctrinated in "rags-to-riches" ways of thinking that they are willing to accept large-scale poverty in exchange for the belief they may one day make it into the tiny, exclusive percentile of the very wealthy.

By contrast, writer Dorothy Allison (1994), who was raised in poverty, observed, "My family's life was not on television, not in books, not even in comic books" (p. 17), and media analyses bear her out. A study of media images of the poor found that on the infrequent occasions that poor people are featured in television programming, it is most often through reality shows that depict them as lazy, promiscuous, abusive of substances, and involved in dysfunctional relationships (Bullock, Wyche, & Williams, 2001). Similar trends can be seen among print media: Most of the articles published in *Newsweek* on welfare recipients and the poor from 1993 to 1995 degraded people living in poverty, specifically demeaning African American and teenage mothers (De Goede, 1996). By depicting women on welfare as neglectful and greedy (even without the overt name-calling mentioned earlier), the media invalidates the reality of poverty and the daily struggles faced by these women and instead presents them as lazy, undeserving, and waiting for a handout.

The feminist scholar and social critic bell hooks (2000) wrote about the invalidating race-class assumptions that she detected among her affluent, predominantly White neighbors. Although, as hooks observed, her neighbors were socially liberal people who valued multiculturalism and who had "at least one Black, Asian, or Hispanic friend" (p. 3), when it came to who actually moved into their neighborhood, another set of attitudes came into play:

> [W]hen it comes to money and class, they want to protect what they have, to perpetuate and reproduce it—they want to have more…. They really believe that all Black people are poor, no matter how many times they laugh at Bill Cosby, salute Colin Powell, mimic Will Smith, dance to Brandy and Whitney Houston, or cheer on Michael Jordan. Yet when the rich Black people come to live where they live, they worry that class does not matter enough, for those Black folks might have some poor relatives, and there goes the neighborhood. (p. 3)

These assumptions reveal a multilayered microinvalidation in that living near Black people is perceived negatively (at least in part) because living near poor people is perceived negatively, and Blackness and poverty are intertwined in mainstream consciousness. Poor people are thus tacitly affirmed as worthy of avoidance, and the existence of Black individuals across the economic spectrum is negated.

Similarly complex microinvalidations are present in cultural representations of working-class people. In an analysis of televised portrayals of the working class from 1946 to 1990, Butsch (2003) concluded that "the working class is not only underrepresented; the few men who are portrayed are buffoons. They are dumb, immature, irresponsible, or lacking in common sense" (p. 575). Working-class female characters, such as the one played by comedian Roseanne Barr on her 1990s television program, may be cited for breaking with stereotyped portrayals of women, but it is often by being sloppy and loud mouthed (Press & Strathman, 1993). Working-class people may be cast in a particularly unfavorable light when they come together to advocate for themselves via labor unions. Union members are often characterized negatively in the media (Leondar-Wright, 2005); many times, racism intertwines with these representations. For example, in 2005, the New York City Transport Workers went on strike against the Metropolitan Transportation Authority during contract negotiations that centered on retirement age, protection of pension and health care benefits, and the safety of workplace conditions. This group of workers, 70 percent of whom were Black, Latino, or Asian, were described by New York's mayor as being selfish and having "thuggishly turned their backs on New York City," a comment that many observers found to have racial overtones (Cardwell, 2005).

These invalidations of working-class people and unions have dovetailed with the near silencing of working-class Americans' voices in the workplace through the dramatic weakening of labor organizations (Zweig, 2000). Whereas 35 percent of the U.S. workforce was unionized in the 1950s, less than 13 percent of the workforce was represented by labor unions in 2003 (Collins & Yeskel, 2005). Labor unions are responsible for some of the most valued parts of our taken-for-granted social contract, such as the outlawing of child labor, the creation of Social Security, and the establishment of workplace safety guidelines. Yet, companies and corporations are working harder than ever to ensure that the presence of labor unions maintains its decline, evoking fear among workers who have expressed interest in unionization. For example, 92 percent of companies force their employees to attend mandatory closed-door, anti-union workshops, and 51 percent threaten to close the plant if a union platform is elected (although only 1 percent actually do so; Bronfenbrenner, 2000).

Classist microinvalidations against working-class people function to support us in looking the other way as the only vehicle by which working people can sit at the table during workplace negotiations is steadily eroded. Workers without the opportunity to organize have none of the resources that command attention from the rest of us and so must live with whatever conditions come their way. They do not own property or control resources, they do not hold political office, they do not represent a powerful demographic to marketers or other trend watchers, and without a union, they do not have a voice. They are simply left to do the work that carries the nation along. We depend upon working-class wage earners all around us; without them, our lives would come to a standstill. Their silencing in the workplace does not seem to be in keeping with democratic ideals that include the belief in an even playing field.

"American Dream" Dialogue as Classist Microinvalidation The ability of mainstream culture to ignore the deteriorating circumstances of poor and

working-class Americans is intimately intertwined with the existence of classist microaggressions: We are distracted from full comprehension of either of these by what is popularly known as the American Dream, which coincides with a type of racial microaggression referred to as the myth of meritocracy (Sue et al., 2007). Inherent in the American Dream is the belief that movement up the economic ladder is possible for anyone—that the opportunity to achieve success in this country is equal for any hard-working citizen from any social starting point. The other side of this coin, of course, is the unspoken assumption that a working-class identity is something from which one should attempt to escape and that people living in poverty are there because they have not pulled sufficiently hard on their own bootstraps, which paves the way for discrimination toward them. Aside from its invalidating implications, the notion of class mobility itself contains a healthy dose of mythology. Citing data indicating that mobility across classes has essentially flattened, the *New York Times* reported survey results in which 40 percent of respondents nevertheless believed that chances to move up in class status had increased over the last 40 years, as opposed to 23 percent who did not (Scott & Leonhardt, 2005). The same survey reported that 46 percent of participants felt that it is easier in the United States to move up from one social class to another than it is in European countries— even though social mobility is actually greater in other countries such as Canada, Norway, Sweden, Denmark, and Germany (Blandin, Gregg, & Machin, 2005).

ON THE HORIZON: A CALL FOR THE STUDY OF CLASSIST MICROAGGRESSIONS

A single chapter such as this can only invite consideration of a topic as broad as classism and its manifestations, and this listing of microaggressions serves to call many others to mind: the ubiquitous wearing of designer logos, which announce the wearer's purchasing power to the world; the stereotyping of unions as corrupt and greedy, even as white-collar corporations like Enron steal millions; the conventional conversation starter, "What do *you* do?" Yet, inviting this consideration of classist microaggressions and thereby encouraging social scientists to contribute their skills toward their elucidation is precisely what we have hoped to accomplish.

We have presented the need for research on classist microaggressions as analogous to the ongoing study of racial and cultural microaggressions. In other words, as a particular kind of racist expression, the concept of micro-aggressions is useful in that it provides an accessible framework and language for racism beyond neo-Nazis and the Ku Klux Klan; it highlights the ordinary, unexamined racism of well-intentioned people that must be addressed if we are ever to realize the full promise symbolized by the election of President Barack Obama. As we watch more Americans sink into poverty (Collins & Yeskel, 2005) and as working people's jobs are exported and their pensions are pillaged (Sklar, Mykyta, & Wefald, 2001), the need to identify and address unexamined societal classism at this level is also profound. By bringing their expertise to bear on the identification of classist microaggressions, social scientists can open new avenues of exploration and understanding of the operation of classism within a broadened social justice agenda.

REFERENCES

Allison, D. (1994). *Skin*. Ithaca, NY: Firebrand.

American Psychological Association (APA) Task Force on Socioeconomic Status (SES). (2006). *Final report*. Retrieved January 23, 2009, from http://www.apa.org/governance/CPM/SES.pdf.

Amott, T., & Matthaei, J. (2004). Race, class, gender, and women's works. In M. L. Andersen & P. H. Collins (Eds.), *Race, class, and gender* (pp. 228–236). Belmont, CA: Wadsworth/Thomson Learning.

Belle, D., Doucet, J., Harris, J., Miller, J., & Tan, E. (2000). Who is rich? Who is happy? *American Psychologist, 55*, 1160–1161.

Blandin, J., Gregg, P., & Machin, S. (2005). *Intergenerational mobility in Europe and North America*. Retrieved March 17, 2000, from http://www.suttontrust.com/reports/IntergenerationalMobility.pdf.

Brocht, C. (2000, November 1). *The forgotten workforce: More than one in 10 federal contract workers earn less than a living wage*. Retrieved June 18, 2000, from http://www.epi.org/publications/entry/briefingpapers_livwage/.

Bronfenbrenner, K. (2000). *Uneasy terrain: The impact of capital mobility on workers, wages, and union organizing*. Retrieved March 17, 2009, from www.digitalcommons.ilr.cornell.edu/cgi/viewcontent.cgi?article=1002&context=reports.

Bullard, R. D. (2000). *Dumping in Dixie: Race, class, and environmental quality*. Boulder, CO: Westview Press.

Bullock, H. E. (1995). Class acts: Middle-class responses to the poor. In B. Lott & D. Maluso (Eds.), *The social psychology of interpersonal discrimination* (pp. 118–159). New York: Guilford Press.

Bullock, H. E., Wyche, K. F., & Williams, W. R. (2001). Media images and the poor. *Journal of Social Issues, 57*, 229–246.

Butsch, R. (2003). Ralph, Fred, Archie, and Homer: Why television keeps re-creating the White male working class buffoon. In G. Dines & J. Humez (Eds.), *Gender, race, and class in media* (pp. 575–585). Thousand Oaks, CA: Sage.

Cardwell, D. (2005, December 22). Race bubbles to the surface in standoff. *New York Times*. Retrieved from http://www.nytimes.com/2005/12/22/nyregion/nyregionspecial3/22race.html?_r=1&scp=2&sq=transit%20strike%20race%20bubbles&st=cse.

Chalifoux, B. (1996). Speaking up: White working class women in therapy. In M. Hill & E. D. Rothblum (Eds.), *Classism and feminist therapy* (pp. 25–34). New York: Haworth Press.

Chaney, K. (1994). Shifting horizons: Navigating a life. In J. Penelope (Ed.), *Coming out of the class closet* (pp. 173–180). Freedom, CA: Crossing Press.

Collins, C., & Yeskel, F. (2005). *Economic apartheid*. New York: New Press.

Cozzarelli, C., Wilkinson, A. V., & Tagler, M. J. (2001). Attitudes toward the poor and attributions for poverty. *Journal of Social Issues, 57*, 207–228.

De Goede, M. (1996). Ideology in the US welfare debate: Neo-liberal representations of poverty. *Discourse and Society, 7*, 317–357.

England, P., Christopher, K., & Reid, L. (1999). Gender, race, ethnicity and wages. In I. Browne (Ed.), *Latinas and African American women at work: Race, gender and economic inequality* (pp. 139–182). New York: Russell Sage Foundation.

Fischer, C. S., Hout, M., & Stiles, J. (2006). What Americans had: Differences in living standards. In C. S. Fischer & M. Hout, *Century of difference: How America changed in the last 100 years* (pp. 137–161). New York: Russell Sage Foundation.

Fiske, S. T. (2007). On prejudice and the brain. *Daedalus, 136*, 156–160.

Frank, R. H., & Cook, P. J. (1996). *The winner-take-all society: Why the few at the top get so much more than the rest of us*. New York: Penguin.

Franklin, D. (2009, February 4). "Dog the Bounty Hunter" and "Exterminators" are low-rent "A&E" picks. *New York Daily News*. Retrieved March 18, 2009, from http://www.nydailynews.com/entertainment/tv/2009/02/04/2009-02-04_dog_the_bounty_hunter_and_exterminators_.html.

Goodman, L. A., Liang, B., Helms, J. E., Latta, R. E., Sparks, E., & Weintraub, S. (2004). Training counseling psychologists as social justice agents: Feminist and multicultural perspectives. *Counseling Psychologist, 32*, 793–837.

Hartigan, J. (2005). *Odd tribes: Toward a cultural analysis of White people*. Durham, NC: Duke University Press.

Helms, J. E. (1992). *A race is a nice thing to have: A guide to being a White person or understanding the White persons in your life*. Topeka, KS: Content Communications.

hooks, b. (2000). *Where we stand: Class matters*. New York: Routledge.

Hoyt, S. K. (1999). Mentoring with class. In A. J. Murrell and F. J. Crosby (Eds.), *Mentoring dilemmas: Developmental relationships within multicultural organizations* (pp. 189–210). Mahwah, NJ: Lawrence Erlbaum.

Kadi, J. (1996). *Thinking class: Sketches from a cultural worker*. Cambridge, MA: South End Press.

Kozol, J. (2005). *The shame of the nation*. New York: Crown.

Landrine, H. (1985). Race × class stereotypes of women. *Sex Roles, 13*, 65–75.

Legal Momentum. (2003). *Reading between the lines: Women's poverty in 2003*. Retrieved from http://www.legalmomentum.org/womeninpoverty.pdf.

Leondar-Wright, B. (2005). *Class matters*. Gabriola Island, BC: New Society.

Living Wage Resource Center. (2003). *Setting a living wage level*. Retrieved June 19, 2009, www.livingwagecampaign.org/index.php?id=1954.

Lott, B. (2002). Cognitive and behavioral distancing from the poor. *American Psychologist, 57*, 100–110.

Lott, B., & Bullock, H. E. (2007). *Psychology and economic injustice*. Washington, DC: APA.

Lott, B., & Saxon, S. (2002). The influence of ethnicity, social class, and context on judgments about U.S. women. *Journal of Social Psychology, 142,* 481–499.

Lui, M., Robles, B., Leondar-Wright, B., Brewer, R., & Adamson, R. (2006). *The color of wealth*. New York: New Press.

Luttrell, W. (1997). *School-smart and mother-wise*. London, England: Routledge.

National Poverty Center (2006). *Poverty in the United States*. Retrieved from http://www.npc.umich.edu/poverty.

New York Times. (1976, February 29). "Welfare Queen" loses her Cadillac limousine. Retrieved March 17, 2009, from http://select.nytimes.com/gst/abstract.html?res=F00612FF3F5F167493CBAB1789D85F 428785F9&scp=1&sq=welfare%20queen%20loses%20her%20cadillac&st=cse.

Newman, K. S. (2004). The invisible poor. In M. L. Andersen & P. H. Collins (Eds.), *Race, class, and gender* (pp. 248–256). Belmont, CA: Wadsworth/Thomson Learning.

Press, A., & Strathman, T. (1993). Work, family and social class in television images of women: Prime-time television and the construction of postfeminism. *Women and Language, 16,* 7–16.

Rose, T. (2008). *The hip-hop wars*. New York: Basic Books.

Scott, J. (2005). Life at the top in America isn't just better, it's longer. In correspondents of the *New York Times* (Eds.), *Class matters* (pp. 27–50). New York: Times Books.

Scott, J., & Leonhardt, D. (2005). Shadowy lines that still divide. In correspondents of the *New York Times* (Eds.), *Class matters* (pp. 1–26). New York: Times Books.

Sklar, H., Mykyta, L., & Wefald, S. (2001). *Raise the floor: Wages and policies that work for all of us*. New York: Ms. Foundation for Women.

Smith, L. (2005). Psychotherapy, classism, and the poor: Conspicuous by their absence. *American Psychologist, 60,* 687–696.

Smith, L. (2008). Positioning classism within psychology's social justice agenda. *Counseling Psychologist, 36,* 895–924.

Stout, L. (1996). *Bridging the class divide*. Boston: Beacon Press.

Sue, D. W., Capodilupo, C. M., Torino, G. C., Bucceri, J. M., Holder, A. M. B., Nadal, K. L., and Esquilin, M. (2007). Racial microaggressions in everyday life: Implications for clinical practice. *American Psychologist, 62,* 271–286.

Tait, V. (2005). *Poor workers' unions*. Chicago: South End Press.

Wheary, J., Shapiro, J. M., Draut, T., & Meschede, T. (2008). *Economic insecurity: The experience of the African-American and Latino middle class*. Retrieved March 18, 2009, from http://iasp.brandeis.edu/pdfs/byathreadlatino.pdf.

Wilson, G., & Rich, J. (2004). "Redneck Woman", performed by Gretchen Wilson, on *Here for the Party* [CD]. New York: Sony BMG Entertainment.

Yahoo! Answers, Pregnancy & Parenting. (April 15, 2008). Baby names. Message posted to http://answers.yahoo.com/dir/;_ylt=AuGgkO7UUgx2uB2F2hdHKm p47hR;_ylv=3?link=list&sid=396547166.

Zweig, M. (2000). *The working class majority*. Ithaca, NY: Cornell University Press.

CHAPTER 13

Religious Microaggressions in the United States

Mental Health Implications for Religious Minority Groups

KEVIN L. NADAL, MARIE-ANNE ISSA, KATIE E. GRIFFIN,
SAHRAN HAMIT, and OLIVER B. LYONS

S THE UNITED STATES moves toward becoming a progressively tolerant society, religious discrimination remains a blight that Americans have yet to overcome. Religious discrimination and persecution can be traced back to as early as the first century when Christians, long regarded by the Romans as a suspicious people, were often blamed for many of society's troubles (Engh, 2006). During the Crusades, disputes over "holy land" amongst Christians, Muslims, and Jews resulted in a death count estimated at two million or more (Engh, 2006). During the Spanish Inquisition, Muslims and Jews were tortured or imprisoned on a daily basis, and in the seventeenth century, separatist Puritans fled to America so they could freely practice their religion (Engh, 2006). Finally, in the early part of the twentieth century, Adolf Hitler rose to power in Germany, resulting in the Holocaust and the genocide of six million Jewish men, women, and children (Sue & Sue, 2008).

While these differing religious conflicts have led to some of the greatest atrocities in human history, contemporary religious discrimination is still a major issue in the United States. The Council on American-Islamic Relations (CAIR, 2008) reported 2,652 cases of civil rights violations against Muslims in America, in which 462 of the cases were of workplace discrimination—an increase of 18 percent from 2006. There were also 141 cases of passenger profiling and 613 cases of hate mail reported toward Muslim persons, with the individuals' ethnicity or religion as the leading cause of the discriminatory act (CAIR, 2008). In the same year, the Anti-Defamation League (ADL, 2008) reported 1,460 anti-Semitic incidents in the United States, with vandalism and harassment accounting for about half of the incidents, respectively.

The Federal Bureau of Investigation (FBI, 2008) also reported 1,477 religious hate crimes in the United States in 2007 including 969 that were anti-Jewish, 115 that were anti-Islamic, 61 that were anti-Catholic, 57 that were anti-Protestant, and 6 that were anti-Atheist/Agnostic. In the same FBI report, the number of race-based hate crimes perpetrated was 4,724 for the year 2007, which is three times the total amount of FBI-reported hate crimes due to religion (FBI, 2008). Also, this number is higher than the combined amount of anti-Semitic incidents reported by the ADL (2008) and the anti-Muslim incidents reported by the CAIR (2008). Despite the higher prevalence of race-based hate crimes, it is important to recognize that an individual's race, ethnicity, and religion are often closely tied together, and it may be hard to know which demographic aspect of the individual was the true cause of the hate crime (e.g., was the hate crime because they were non-White, Arab, or Muslim?). In fact, some reports (e.g., CAIR, 2008) consider religion and ethnicity as the same category when discussing factors that trigger discrimination.

Despite the prevalence of religion-based hate crimes, there has been paucity in the psychology literature regarding religious discrimination. A 2009 search in the PsychINFO database using the term "religious discrimination" resulted in 26 works. This is comparatively lower to a search on the terms "racial discrimination," which resulted in 716 works and in which the combined terms "race" and "discrimination" generated 2,957 publications (retrieved on February 24, 2009). This finding aligns with one report that cited that a search of *social work abstracts* using the keywords "religion," "spirituality," and/or "social justice" produced zero articles that could assist social workers in understanding religion in context of their work (Hodge, 2007c). Clearly, more empirical research regarding religious discrimination is needed, especially in the United States and particularly for other religious minorities and nonreligious groups.

Furthermore, in recent years, there has been an increase in the literature focusing on subtle forms of racial discrimination otherwise known as racial microaggressions (see Nadal, 2008; Sue, Bucceri, Lin, Nadal, & Torino, 2007; Sue, Capodilupo, et al., 2007; Sue, Capodilupo, & Holder, 2008; Sue, Nadal, et al., 2008). Microaggressions are defined as "subtle, stunning, often automatic, and nonverbal exchanges which are 'put downs'" (Pierce, Carew, Pierce-Gonzalez, & Willis, 1978, p. 66) but have evolved to be defined as "brief and commonplace daily verbal, behavioral, or environmental indignities, whether intentional or unintentional, that communicate hostile, derogatory, or negative racial slights and insults toward members of oppressed groups" (Nadal, 2008, p. 23). Examples of racial microaggressions may include asking a Latino/a or Asian American where they were born or telling them that they speak good English. While both may be intended to be a benevolent or neutral question/comment/statement, the indirect and unconscious messages (e.g., "You are a foreigner" or "You are not American") sent to the recipient may potentially cause distress and other psychological problems for the individual who receives these microaggressions on a regular basis.

Because microaggressions are subtle and somewhat automatic, both the perpetrator and the victim may be oblivious to their effects. The perpetrator may not be aware of the microaggressive act or comment, while the victim may not recognize the cumulative nature of these microaggressions and their impact on psychological health (Nadal, 2008; Sue, Capodilupo, et al., 2007). Specifically, one study has discovered that victims of such discrimination report negative feelings toward or reactions to such experiences, including sadness, anger, doubt and frustration; these experiences may result in increased stress levels for victims that may have a lasting impact on their lives (Sue, Nadal, et al., 2008). Another study has revealed that although many participants felt the enactor's intentions were not malevolent and in some cases even meant to be complimentary, the subtle prejudicial comments or acts still left them feeling disturbed, uncomfortable, and alienated (Sue, Bucceri, et al., 2007). Because microaggressions may have subtle or unclear intentions, victims or recipients of these microaggressions may be faced with the decision of how to respond to such acts in conjunction with whether they were just victimized (Sue, et al., 2008).

Because of the damaging nature of racial microaggressions, it has been hypothesized that gender, ethnic, sexual orientation, and religious microaggressions may also exist, with separate themes emerging for each type of microaggression (Nadal, 2008). Using racial microaggressions as a template, the purpose of this chapter is to examine religious microaggressions and the mental health implications for victims of religious and nonreligious minority groups. Some of these religious groups may include Jews, Muslims, Hindus, Sikhs, and Buddhists, while some of these nonreligious groups may include Agnostics (i.e., individuals who believe in a higher being but do not follow a specific religion or practice), Atheists (i.e., individuals who deny the existence of a higher being), and nonreligious/nonpracticing persons (i.e., individuals who do not practice any religion).

Because discrimination of all types has become more covert than overt, it is likely that religious microaggressions do exist and that religious discrimination would follow the pattern of being more subtle than blatant. For example, when a Christian says "Merry Christmas" to a Jewish or Muslim person, she or he is sending the message that Christianity is the norm and that being non-Christian or nonreligious is abnormal, inferior, or even evil (Nadal, 2008). Another example may include an individual of any religious background who stares in fear or suspicion at a Muslim person on an airplane (Nadal, 2008). In this case, the individual is sending the indirect message that she or he believes that all Muslims are terrorists, which may potentially have detrimental mental health impacts on the Muslim individual who may experience such microaggressions on a regular basis. Given these examples, this chapter will present an original taxonomy of specific religious microaggression themes as well as messages that are conveyed. In understanding the ways that religious microaggressions may manifest in educational and clinical settings, counselors, clinicians, and educators can recognize the multifaceted experiences of religiously oppressed individuals and the impact of microaggressions on their psychological health.

LITERATURE REVIEW OF RELIGIOUS DISCRIMINATION

Before reviewing the literature on religious discrimination, it is necessary to highlight the religious demographics of the United States. The majority of Americans identify with a denomination of Christianity (76.5%), with the largest Christian groups being Catholic (24.5%), Baptist (16.3%), nondenominational Christian (6.8%), and Methodist (6.8%; Kosmin, Mayer, & Keysar, 2001). Other major religions in the United States include Judaism (1.3%), Islam (0.5%), Buddhism (0.5%), and Hinduism (0.4%; Kosmin et al., 2001). Fourteen percent of Americans do not identify with any religion, with 13.2 percent identifying as nonreligious, 0.4 percent identifying as Atheist, and 0.5 percent identifying as Agnostic (Kosmin et al., 2001). The number of nonreligious persons has doubled from 1990 to 2001 (Kosmin et al., 2001), suggesting that it may be especially important for counselors/clinicians to become more attentive to the experiences of nonreligious individuals.

Furthermore, in order to understand religious microaggressions, it is crucial to acknowledge that members of virtually every religious group will experience religious persecution, depending on their geographic location (Hertzke, 2004). For example, while Christianity may be the most widespread religion in the United States (Kosmin et al., 2001), Christians are also considered the most widely persecuted religion in other parts of the world (Hertzke, 2004; Marshall, 2000). So, while Christians in the United States may be perceived as White and wealthy, most Christians live in poverty in Asia and Africa and are often oppressed because they are the religious minority in their respective countries (Jenkins, 2002). Accordingly, Christians may be the dominant group in the United States (and therefore the potential enactors of religious microaggressions), whereas they may be the oppressed group in other countries (and thus the potential recipients of religious microaggressions).

Some religious groups have been more prone to religious discrimination in the United States (due to their minority status) and thereby will be the recipients of religious microaggressions. In the United States, the two largest religious groups with the highest prevalence of documented religion-based hate crimes include Jewish and Muslim persons (Uniform Crime Statistics [UCS], 2005). Accordingly, this next section will cover literature involving anti-Semitism, or prejudice and discrimination toward Jews, and Islamophobia, or prejudice and discrimination toward Muslims. This section will also highlight discrimination against other religious groups (e.g., Hindus, Buddhists, and Sikhs) and nonreligious groups (Agnostics, Atheists, and nondenominational persons), who are almost always overlooked or invisible in the discourse on religious discrimination in academic literature. Understanding the history of religious discrimination in the United States is imperative for understanding the religious microaggressions that may occur toward these religious minority groups. Additionally, because of the lack of empirical research on religious discrimination in the United States, this literature review may focus on global religious discrimination in order to highlight the impacts of religious microaggressions (and other forms of religious discrimination) on mental health.

ANTI-SEMITISM AND DISCRIMINATION AGAINST JEWS

There has been some literature that examines the existence of anti-Semitism, or prejudice and discrimination against Jews in the United States (see Marcus, 2007; Simon & Schaler, 2007). One report indicated that out of 1,314 religious-based hate crimes across the United States in one year, 68.5 percent were anti-Jewish (UCS, 2005). However, despite the overwhelming amount of discrimination that Jews may face in the United States, there is very little literature in psychology that discusses their experiences as a cultural or religious group (Sue & Sue, 2008). The Anti-Defamation League ([ADL] 2005) revealed that many Americans still hold many anti-Semitic beliefs, including (1) Jews are more loyal to Israel than to the United States, (2) Jews have too much power in the United States, and (3) Jews were responsible for the death of Jesus Christ. The same report reveals that African Americans and Latinos/as tend to hold the most anti-Semitic attitudes (ADL, 2005), while other reports posit that older White persons with less formal education also have more anti-Semitic feelings than other groups in the United States ("Social Science and the Citizen," 1996).

Despite these reports on anti-Semitic sentiments that exist in the United States, there are few empirical studies that examine the impact of anti-Semitism on mental health. Most studies involving anti-Semitism have been more focused in Europe and the Middle East than in the United States (Kramer, 2006). This may potentially be due to the fact that anti-Semitism has been found to be affected by the emergence of fascism in Europe, the tension in Palestine, and the spread of anti-Semitic motifs in these regions (Kramer, 2006). There have also been reports of growing feelings of anti-Semitism among Middle Eastern people and Muslims, especially after the break of two major events: (1) the Second Intifada in September 2000 (or the second Palestinian rising, in which violence between the Palestinians and the Israelis dramatically increased) and (2) the World Trade Center attacks on September 11, 2001 (Kramer, 2006).

Anti-Semitism has also manifested through the endorsement of stereotypes about Jews. Previous research has identified two kinds of stereotypes toward Jews: benign stereotypes and malevolent stereotypes (Wilson, 1996). Malevolent stereotypes depict Jews as pushy, clannish, ill-mannered, cruel, dishonest, greedy, arrogant, and money-loving, while benign stereotypes depict Jews as financially successful, ambitious, intelligent, loyal to their kin and other Jews, hardworking, and energetic (Wilson, 1996). Utilizing data from the 1990 National Opinion Research Center's General Social Survey, Wilson (1996) found that in some cases, endorsing benign stereotypes of Jews had no relationship with being "pro-Semitic," since around a third of those with benign stereotypes also held blatant anti-Semitic beliefs (e.g., viewing Jews as overly influential).

Finally, one author asserts that Jews are often discriminated (overtly and covertly) in the fields of counseling or psychology, citing that (1) institutions often do not recognize Jewish holidays and/or ignore requests for scheduling changes when Jewish holidays conflict with meetings and other events, and (2) texts on multicultural counseling do not recognize Jews as a cultural group in the same way that other races and ethnicities are acknowledged (Weinrach, 2002). These two examples demonstrate religious microaggressions that may occur toward Jews, which may result in feelings of invalidation, annoyance, sadness, and frustration. Furthermore, because most American counselors and clinicians may be of a Christian background, it is possible that Jewish traditions, values, and identity development may be overlooked or dismissed in counseling and psychotherapy (Sue & Sue, 2008).

ISLAMOPHOBIA AND DISCRIMINATION AGAINST MUSLIMS

After the attacks on September 11, 2001, Americans have gradually associated Islam (and Muslim people) with terrorism and violence (Gottschalk & Greenberg, 2008; Hassouneh & Kulwicki, 2007; Rippy & Newman, 2006). Additionally, Americans (the majority of whom are Christian) have viewed

Islam as having a conflicting set of cultural values from Christianity (Gibbon, 2005). This prejudice and discrimination toward Muslims is often referred to as Islamophobia and has been documented in many Western, European countries (both pre- and post-9/11). For instance, Strabac and Listhaug (2008) used data from the European Values Study (1999–2000) to examine the prevalence of prejudice against Muslims in both Eastern and Western Europe and found that Muslims experience more prejudice than other immigrants. Brown (2006) also revealed that before 9/11, media discourses and narratives about Islam in France and Britain included stereotypes including exoticism, fanaticism, and delinquency, suggesting that Islamophobia existed before the World Trade Center attacks. This notion of pre-9/11 discrimination is further supported by James (2008), who claims that Islamophobia did not begin with 9/11 or the fall of the Shah in Iran but rather has existed throughout history.

Some authors assert that Islamophobia has become more pervasive since 2001 and continues to be on the rise in the United States and across the world. One study purported that Muslims have experienced increased hostility in the United Kingdom post-9/11, mainly through nonphysical forms of abuse (e.g., verbal insults or teasing) and rarely through violent, physical abuse (Sheridan, 2006). Similarly, researchers in Australia reported an increase in Islamophobia post-9/11, particularly in perceptions of Muslims as "terrorist threats" or in being labeled as "alien" or "other" (Dunn, Klocker, & Salabay, 2007). Another study revealed that German participants expected Muslims to be more aggressive than Christians and that Muslims were stereotyped to be more supportive of terrorism. However, when actually surveyed, Muslim participants were no more aggressive than Christians, and they did not endorse attitudes that support terrorism (Fischer, Greitemeyer, & Kastenmuller, 2007). Additionally, in the United States, one study found that Christian participants explicitly (i.e., a survey on attitudes toward Muslims) and implicitly (i.e., latency measures of the Implicit Association Test) preferred Christians as opposed to Muslims (Rowatt, Franklin, & Cotton, 2005), suggesting the negative attitudes that Christians may have toward Muslims. Given that the findings from the American study on Islamophobia (e.g., Rowatt et al., 2005) parallel results from studies from other Westernized countries (e.g., Dunn et al., 2007; Fischer et al., 2007; Sheridan, 2006), it can be argued that Muslims may experience religious microaggressions in the United States and other parts of the world.

This discrimination against Muslims pre- and post-9/11 has manifested through different behaviors and attitudes. In a study of British Muslims, the majority of the participants revealed that they experienced an increase in implicit racism and religious discrimination post-9/11 (Sheridan, 2006). The discrimination was more likely to be in the form of hearing offensive jokes, being stared at, hearing insensitive remarks, and witnessing more offensive stereotypes in the media. Covering data from all 15 European Union member countries, Allen and Nielsen (2002) found that the more it is visually clear that a person identifies with Islam (e.g., a woman wearing a *hijab*), the more likely this person would be attacked (as cited in Sheridan, 2006). These studies suggest that Muslims may experience a spectrum of discrimination, ranging from religious microaggressions (e.g., hearing offensive jokes or insensitive remarks) to hate crimes (e.g., being violently assaulted or attacked).

Although many of these studies on Islamophobia take place in Europe, there are many implications for religious microaggressions in the United States. One author explained the anti-Muslim sentiment in the United States by linking prejudice to religious beliefs and practices as well as perceived out-group threat (Gibbon, 2005). In other words, those who view their own religion as the "true religion" would adopt less favorable attitudes toward other religions. This can be demonstrated through the studies that assert that individuals who attend church more regularly have been found to have more religious prejudice toward other groups (Gibbon, 2005). Furthermore, the same study found that Americans who perceive the existence of realistic threats (e.g., threat to the power, economy, and well-being of the in-group) as well as symbolic threats (e.g., threat to the values, norms, and standards of the in-group) might also harbor anti-Muslim feelings (Gibbon, 2005). These studies of prejudice are important, because religious prejudice may potentially lead to microaggressions in that perpetrators may behave in ways that may reflect their unconscious biases, assumptions, and stereotypes.

Finally, one author reported that regardless of geographic location (e.g., in the United States, Europe, or other non-Muslim regions) or their racial/cultural traits (e.g., whether they are Black, White, or Asian), Muslims are oftentimes stereotyped as a group of fanatical faith (i.e., those who commit terrorism in the name of their religion) while being associated with the current political climate in the Middle East (Brasted, 1997). In addition, the role of the media may contribute to promoting the negative religious stereotypes that are placed on Muslims. Previous studies indicate that the media portrayal of Muslims and the Islamic culture has been biased, since Muslims have been consistently portrayed as terrorists and fanatics (James, 2008). These biases may potentially affect the mental health of Muslims, especially those who are living as minorities in the United States and other Westernized countries. For instance, one study reported that among a sample of Muslim Americans, perceived discrimination was related to increased vigilance and suspicion (Rippy & Newman, 2006), while another study reported that there was a significant positive association between physical health problems (i.e., scoring high on the General

Health Questionnaire) and the reporting of an abusive incident post-9/11 (Sheridan, 2006). These studies suggest that religious microaggressions may lead to psychological problems (e.g., paranoia or anxiety) and problems in physical health (e.g., sleep difficulties).

DISCRIMINATION AGAINST OTHER RELIGIOUS AND NONRELIGIOUS GROUPS

Articles on religious discrimination of other religious groups such as Hindus, Sikhs, Buddhists, and nonreligious groups (e.g., Atheists, Agnostics) are scarce. One study found that most of the words that students who self-identified with a religion use to describe their nonreligious counterparts were negative, including "immoral," "anti-Christian," "self-centered," and "hardheaded" (Harper, 2007). Even though some of these labels were neutral (especially those associated with individualism), the initial reactions the religious students exhibited included choosing more offensive and derogatory words such as "arrogant," "ignorant," and "evil." This study suggests that individuals who strongly identify as religious may possess negative stereotypes toward nonreligious persons, which may potentially lead to religious microaggressions toward these individuals.

One study found that Hindu and Muslim students were often bullied in the United Kingdom due to their religious backgrounds and that members of these two religious minority groups often bullied each other (Eslea & Mukhtar, 2000). This study suggests that being the victim of religious discrimination may lead some to discriminate against others. Perhaps it is possible that individuals who are the victims of microaggressions may in turn become the perpetrators of abuse in their adulthoods. Other religious groups (e.g., Sikhs, Buddhists) have been overlooked in the literature and need to be included in future discourses on religion. Perhaps this may be due to their smaller numbers in the United States or because the discrimination these individuals from religious minority groups experience are confounded by race or ethnicity. For example, Sikhs who experience microaggressions may attribute the discrimination to their race (i.e., South Asian) or ethnicity (i.e., Indian).

Religious/spiritual groups like Wiccans or polytheists (i.e., those who believe in many gods) may also experience religious microaggressions. However, their experiences may be overlooked by psychologists and other practitioners, because general society may stereotype these groups as being nontraditional, bizarre, and satanic (see Harper, 2007). Similarly, nonreligious groups (e.g., Atheists, Agnostics) may also be the targets of religious microaggressions. However, because the United States is a predominantly Christian nation and because society may not recognize these individuals as an organized group, the mental health experiences of nonreligious persons may not be considered, studied, or noticed. Because of the lack of empirical research on these religious or nonreligious groups, it becomes difficult to make solid statements about the impact of religious microaggressions on the mental health of members of these groups.

Although Christians are the majority religion in the United States, there is some literature that suggests that some Christians may be the recipients of religious microaggressions. Hodge (2006) revealed that there are various levels of Christianity and that these levels may lead to differences in experiences of discrimination. In terms of religious prejudice and discrimination toward Christians in the United States, Hodge (2006) found that Evangelical Christian students reported more perceived discrimination than their more liberal Christian counterparts and that those who identify as more religious might experience or perceive more discriminatory behaviors based on religion. Furthermore, this study demonstrated that while Christianity may be the dominant religion in the United States, there may be various negative stereotypes within this group, whereby individuals who are less religious and less conservative may experience less stereotyping or discrimination. Accordingly, it is possible that Christians who are more religious and more conservative may be victims of some forms of religious microaggressions.

Another study purported that Christians had more positive attitudes about other Christians over Muslims; however, these Christian participants' ratings of other Christians became increasingly negative as these participants' religious fundamentalism increased (Rowatt et al., 2005). In other words, while Christians in general may prefer liberal Christians over Muslims, individuals may be less accepting of other Christians when they themselves are more religious or conservative. So, while Hodge (2006) may argue that Evangelical Christians are discriminated against more than their liberal counterparts, Rowatt and colleagues (2005) maintain that Christian fundamentalists may hold more prejudicial attitudes toward liberal Christians. Thus, Christian fundamentalists may be the recipients of religious microaggressions by general society, yet may potentially be the enactors of microaggressions in other situations.

THE MANIFESTATION OF RELIGIOUS MICROAGGRESSIONS

This section will explore the different ways that religious microaggressions manifest and the impact they have on the victims. Given the types of microaggressions that have been empirically supported to occur toward other groups based on race (Sue, Bucceri, et al., 2007; Sue, Capodilupo, & Holder, 2008; Sue, Nadal, et al., 2008), gender (Capodilupo et al., Chapter 9 in this volume), and ability (Keller & Galgay, Chapter 11 in this volume), this section will provide a taxonomy on religious microaggressions that is similar to the

categories and themes of racial microaggressions that were originally conceptualized (see Sue, Capodilupo, et al., 2007). This proposal is derived from the
previous research on microaggressions as well as the existing research involving anti-Semitism, Islamophobia, and other forms of religious discrimination.
Though the psychological research on religious discrimination is limited, these
suggested themes and categories of religious microaggressions are also based
on the current political and social conflicts between religious groups, which
have resulted from historical and contemporary events (e.g., the Holocaust, 9/
11 World Trade Center attacks, Israeli-Palestinian conflicts) and can be
observed in the media and in interpersonal interactions.

Religious microaggressions can be defined as subtle behavioral and verbal
exchanges (both conscious and unconscious) that send denigrating messages
to individuals of various religious groups. As aforementioned, religious
microaggressions may be confounded with racial or ethnic microaggressions
(e.g., an Arab American dressed in Muslim garb who receives substandard
service from a store owner may be receiving such treatment based on her or his
race, ethnicity, or religion). Accordingly, this taxonomy proposes six major
categories of religious microaggressions that are based primarily on religion
and are likely independent of race, ethnicity, or other variables. These six
categories include (1) *endorsing religious stereotypes*, (2) *exoticization*, (3) *pathology of different religious groups*, (4) *assumption of one's own religious identity as the
norm*, (5) *assumption of religious homogeneity*, and (6) *denial of religious prejudice*.
Noted in Table 13.1 are a list of these categories, examples of how these
religious microaggressions may manifest in everyday interactions, and the
messages that are sent to the victim.

Religious microaggressions may also follow the original taxonomy of racial
microaggressions, in which there may be three major types of microaggressions. These classifications of microaggressions are based on the intentions of
the perpetrators, the severity of the act, and the underlying themes of the
messages that are being conveyed (Nadal, 2008; Sue, Capodilupo, et al., 2007).
Religious microassaults are conscious comments or behaviors that are made
to intentionally hurt, derogate, or humiliate an individual of a religious
minority group. For example, insulting a Jewish person by calling her or
him "cheap" may be a conscious slight to perpetuate historical stereotypes
about Jews. Religious microinsults are subtle behaviors that express messages
of dislike, rudeness, and insensitivity. These microinsults are often unconscious, and enactors may be unaware of the impact of these statements
or behaviors on recipients (Nadal, 2008; Sue, Capodilupo, et al., 2007). For
example, a person who stares at someone who is wearing religious garb may
be unaware that their behaviors send indirect yet denigrating messages to the
recipient. Finally, religious microinvalidations are exchanges that negate the
psychological experiences of individuals of religious minority groups (Nadal,

Table 13.1

Examples of Religious Microaggressions

Theme	Example	Message	Subcategories
Endorsing religious stereotypes	Someone angrily yelling to someone that they are a "cheap Jew" (conscious)	You are nothing but a stereotype.	Microassault
	A woman asking to be reseated on a plane because she assumes a Muslim is a terrorist (conscious)	Your religion is evil.	Microinsult
	Asking a nonreligious/Atheist/Agnostic person if she/he believes in witchcraft (unconscious)	Without a religion, you are evil.	Microinsult
Exoticization	An individual asking an incessant amount of questions to a Jewish person about her/his religious practices	I have the right to ask you whatever I want.	Microinsult
	A non-Hindu couple deciding to use Hindu traditions in a wedding ceremony	Your religion is exotic and can be used as a trend.	Microinsult
Pathology of different religious groups	Refusing to serve a Muslim, Sikh, Jewish, or Hindu person in restaurants or stores (conscious)	You do not belong here.	Microassault
	Staring at a Hasidic Jew on the subway or at the airport (unconscious)	Your cultural dress is weird.	Microinsult
	Telling a nonreligious person, "I can't believe you don't believe in a higher power" (conscious)	Your way of thinking is wrong.	Microinvalidation
Assumption of one's own religious identity as normal	Telling an Atheist that they are going to hell (conscious)	Your lack of religion is immoral.	Microassault
	Saying "Merry Christmas" to Jewish, Muslim, Buddhist, Hindu, Sikh, or Atheist/Agnostic persons (unconscious)	Your religious beliefs do not matter. Everyone must celebrate Christianity.	Microinsult
	"In God We Trust" being written on American currency (environmental)	Christianity is the norm.	Microinsult

	Schools celebrating only Christian holidays (environmental)	Christian holidays are the only ones worth celebrating.	Microinsult
Assumption of religious homogeneity	"You're Filipino, so you must be Catholic, too." (unconscious)	You are only allowed to be of a specific religion because of your ethnicity.	Microinsult
	"You can't be Jewish. You have blonde hair." (unconscious)	Everyone in your religion is the same.	Microinsult
	A college professor asking a Hindu student, "Well, how do Hindus feel about this?" during a discussion about religion (unconscious)	You are all the same.	Microinsult
Denial of religious prejudice	"I don't see you based on your religion. I only see you." (unconscious)	Your religious identity doesn't matter.	Microinvalidation
	"I am not anti-Semitic. I have a Jewish friend." (unconscious)	I cannot be prejudiced.	Microinvalidation

2008; Sue, Capodilupo, et al., 2007). For example, a religious individual who tells a nonreligious person to "stop complaining about discrimination" may illustrate a lack of understanding of the nonreligious person's worldview or reality.

Category 1, *endorsing religious stereotypes*, involves a perpetrator stereotyping victims through religiously biased statements and behaviors. By endorsing a stereotype about a religious or nonreligious group, it is implied that the group is inferior and does not deserve to be learned about. For example, blatantly calling a Muslim person a terrorist sends the message that everyone in this religion is involved in terrorist acts or causes harm to others. This type of religious microaggression (which may be categorized as a microassault in that the enactor is conscious of her or his statements/behavior) may result in psychological distress and even physiological symptoms for the victim (Rippy & Newman, 2006; Sheriden, 2006).

The endorsing of religious stereotypes can also take microinsult forms. For example, if a religious or spiritual individual asks a nonreligious person (e.g., Atheist or Agnostic) if they worship the devil or if they practice witchcraft, the message that is sent to the recipient is that nonreligious persons are evil, morally wrong, or abnormal (Nadal, 2008). These stereotypes of nonreligious persons are exemplified by an aforementioned study in which nonreligious persons are described as being "immoral," "anti-Christian," and "self-centered" (see Harper, 2007). Moreover, these types of microaggressions may not be malicious in intent (e.g., the perpetrator may genuinely want to inquire about the individual's spiritual practices); however, the negative messages that are sent to the nonreligious person may impact her or his self-esteem and psychological health.

Category 2, *exoticization*, is a type of microaggression that has been described in previous literature on racial microaggressions (see Sue, Bucceri, et al., 2007). These microaggressions transpire when an individual holds views of other religious groups as "foreign" or "bizarre" and acts accordingly. For example, an individual might ask an incessant number of questions to a member of a religious minority group about her or his religion and respond by exclaiming "Wow" or "That's so weird." This can send the message that the religious minority is strange or different because they do not hold the same religion as the dominant society. Similarly, exoticization can occur when religion is culturally appropriated in the same ways that race and ethnicity are. For example, when individuals practice certain religious customs, traditions, or beliefs as new trends or fads or when individuals wear religious garb as a form of fashion, they send the message that such religions are ones that can be played with, instead of treating them as sacred.

Category 3, *pathology of different religious groups,* refers to the conscious (and sometimes unconscious) belief that there is something wrong or abnormal with someone of a different religion. This may lead to behaviors in which individuals may be punished, judged, or maltreated. This category is derived from previous studies on racial microaggressions that support that individuals are taught that the dominant group's cultural values are the norm (e.g., Sue, Bucceri, et al., 2007; Sue, Nadal, et al., 2008). For example, because the Torah prohibits its followers from speaking or writing the term "God" in Hebrew, some Jewish people have applied that rule to all languages and use the term "G-d" or "G-D" when writing any papers in English (see Russ, 2007). If a teacher or professor does not honor the religious beliefs of their students and punishes them for spelling the word as such, the teacher is sending the message that there is only one "correct" way of doing something and that all the other ways are wrong. This may be considered a microinsult, because the teacher/professor does not recognize her or his biases against the Jewish culture and is unaware of how she or he is being religiously insensitive.

This view of pathology can also occur when employers or teachers/professors do not recognize non-Christian religious holidays and customs that may interfere with one's work schedule. For example, it has been documented that Jewish holidays are often not considered when creating college/university schedules or workplace meetings (Weinrach, 2002). One author cites an example in counseling when a Jewish client asked the therapist to reschedule a session because of Yom Kippur. The therapist became defensive and questioned the schedule change, leaving the client feeling embarrassed, devalued, and unsupported (Langman, 1999). The devaluing of religions can also be exemplified by workplaces or institutions that do not allow or provide space for Muslims or other religious groups to engage in their prayer times throughout their work or school days. While there are environmental elements to these types of microaggressions, the interpersonal interactions between individuals (e.g., an individual who could not change a counseling session due to a Jewish holiday or an individual uncomfortably staring at a Muslim praying at work) exemplify microinsults and microinvalidations.

Pathologizing different groups' values may also occur toward nonreligious groups. For example, after finding out that someone is not religious, it is not uncommon for a religious or spiritual person to then ask that person "How do you not believe in a god?" Whilst it may appear to be a simple question, an indirect message is sent to the recipient that there must be something wrong with the individual and that the norm is to believe in a higher being. This act may be considered to be a microaggression, since the recipient is indirectly told that her or his choice is not legitimate or substantial and that she or he cannot be a good or moral person without believing in something. While this may not be the intention of the speaker, it may cause the recipient to feel judged or misunderstood. This is similar to the experiences of racial micro-aggressions that are described by Asian Americans or African Americans (see Sue, Bucceri, et al., 2007; Sue, Nadal, et al., 2008). Participants of these racial groups reported that they felt as though White cultural values were the norm, that any culture with different values is defective, and that there is a "right" way to behave if one wants to succeed in the world. Similarly, nonreligious people may also internalize the messages that their nonreligious identity is substandard or insufficient.

Perpetrators of religious microaggressions can engage in behaviors that indirectly and unconsciously pathologize a person from a different religious group. Examples may include staring at individuals of various religious groups when they are dressed in their religious garb or showing disgust (verbally or behaviorally) when individuals are burning incense or oils for religious reasons. These actions send a message that cultural dress or religious practices that are not similar to one's own are considered abnormal or uncivilized. Pathologizing religious groups may also be conscious to the individuals who enact them; for example, refusing to serve someone dressed in religious garb at a restaurant may be considered overt and hostile, with the message conveyed that the recipient is a second-class citizen. This type of religious microaggression is similar to research on racial microaggressions, in which individuals are refused service or treated as substandard to individuals of the dominant group (e.g., Sue, Bucceri, et al., 2007; Sue, Nadal, et al., 2008). Because the effects that these racial microaggressions have on their recipients are reported to be deleterious, it is assumed that recipients of religious microaggressions will suffer similar effects.

Category 4, *assumption of one's own religious identity as the norm*, can describe subtle and unconscious behaviors in which individuals presume that others belong to their same religion. Because the United States is a predominantly Christian society, individuals can forget that there are other religions in the world and that not everyone worships in the same way (Nadal, 2008). For example, in the United States, it is common during the month of December for Christmas decorations to be on display in almost all public areas (e.g., stores, restaurants, parks, and workplaces), with radio stations playing Christmas songs and television networks playing several types of Christmas-theme programs. The messages that are sent to non-Christians (which include other religious groups and nonreligious persons) are that Christmas is the norm and that Christianity is the superior religion, while all other holidays and groups are not as important and/or are inferior. Similarly, while statements like "season's greetings" or "happy holidays" are meant to be less religious and are meant to be inclusive of other religious holidays (e.g., Hanukkah,

Kwanzaa, or Eid al-Adha), these statements send the message that it is the norm to celebrate religious holidays in December, leaving nonreligious persons to feel abnormal or stigmatized for not belonging to any religious group. Similarly, saying "God bless you" after another person sneezes may be considered etiquette or a common American behavior. However, one might argue that by saying "God bless you" to someone who is nonreligious and/or expecting them to reciprocate is a microinsult, because the expectation negates an individual's right to religious freedom. Such a microaggression implies the unconscious message that everyone should believe in the power of a monotheistic god.

The use of specific terminology may also convey assumptions of one's own religion as being the norm and/or universal. For example, while a church is a place of worship for Christians, non-Christian persons may attend a synagogue, temple, or mosque. So, asking a Jewish, Muslim, Buddhist, or Hindu person if they go to church is a way of diminishing their religious authenticity and implies that all religions should be like Christianity. Similarly, referring to a rabbi or a shaman as a priest implies that Christianity is the norm and that priest is a standard term for all religious leaders. Using discriminatory language is one factor that can lead to microaggressions in other groups, including women (Nadal, 2010; Sue & Capodilupo, 2008) and lesbian, gay, bisexual, and transgender persons (Nadal, Rivera, & Corpus, Chapter 10 in this volume).

Category 5, *assumption of religious homogeneity*, is characterized by the notion that everyone in a given religious group looks, behaves, and thinks the same. Comments such as "You can't be Jewish, because you're not wearing a yarmulke" or "You are Latino/a, so you must be Catholic" suggest that a person must be or look a particular way to be a part of a religious group. Such behaviors may be considered microinsults, because they assume that there is no individuality among persons of specific religions. The indirect message that is conveyed to recipients is that there is no individuality or uniqueness to one's religion. Assuming that they belong to a homogenous group is a common experience that occurs with other marginalized groups as well, including Asian Americans (Sue, Bucceri, et al., 2007), Black/African Americans (Sue, Nadal, et al., 2008), and lesbian, gay, bisexual, and transgender persons (Nadal et al., 2009).

Following the theme of religious homogeneity, another common experience for religious minorities may include asking someone to be the spokesperson for their entire religious or nonreligious group. Such an act implies that individuals from a specific religious group have had universal experiences and that each person in the group is interchangeable and nondescript. This phenomenon is similar to the theme "assumed universal Black experience," in which a Black/African American person is asked to speak on behalf of the entire race (Sue, Nadal, et al., 2008). Expecting a person from a religious or nonreligious group to speak for his or her group can be viewed as unfair and may evoke stress for the recipient. Perpetrators from dominant religious groups are rarely asked to be representatives of their groups. This form of religious microaggression can be similar in literature on race; for example, McIntosh (2003) reveals that one privilege that Whites have is that they may never be asked to represent their entire group, while people of color may be asked to be spokespersons regularly. Similarly, Christians may never have to be spokespersons, while Jews, Muslims, Hindus, and other religious and nonreligious minority groups may be asked recurrently.

Category 6, *denial of religious prejudices*, transpires when individuals are not aware of their religious biases. Comments such as "I don't see you for your religion" or "We are all the same" takes away from religious identity in the same way that statements like "I am color-blind" are demeaning to people of color (see Sue, Capodilupo, et al., 2007). While the sentiment behind the statement may be admirable, the declaration is likely not true in that all individuals hold conscious and unconscious attitudes, biases, and beliefs that influence the ways that they see the world (Sue & Sue, 2008). Moreover, in denying one's religious biases, an individual is invalidating the religious reality of an individual in which religion (or nonreligion) is a salient part of their lives.

IMPACTS OF RELIGIOUS MICROAGGRESSIONS ON MENTAL HEALTH

Just as other types of discrimination (e.g., racism, sexism, heterosexism, and ableism) can affect the mental health of their victims, religious discrimination can affect the psychological health of those subjected to its application. Being part of a stereotyped group that is often discriminated against and treated as inferior can have detrimental effects that those of dominant groups may not experience. For example, it has been documented that being a victim of racial discrimination can have injurious effects on one's mental health and physical health (e.g., Kessler, Mickelson, & Williams, 1999; Sellers & Shelton, 2003). However, because prejudicial and discriminatory acts have taken less overt and less explicit forms in contemporary times, victims may often feel confused as to whether they actually experienced discrimination and may not recognize the impact on their overall mental health (Sue, Capodilupo, et al., 2007).

It is also hypothesized that victims of religious microaggressions can be affected in many of the same ways as those victims subjected to racial microaggressions. For example, one study revealed that higher scores on a Perceived Religious Discrimination Scale were positively correlated with experiences of religious discrimination and/or hate crimes and that greater incidences of religious discrimination and/or hate crimes were associated with greater stress levels (Rippy & Newman, 2008). Another study found that levels of perceived discrimination in Muslim males were correlated with paranoia, vigilance, mistrust, and suspicion and that increases in paranoia can disturb one's mental health and consequently lead to interference in one's daily functioning (Rippy & Newman, 2006). Finally, a study on Islamophobia revealed that religious discrimination may even lead to physiological symptoms including loss of sleep or headaches (Sheridan, 2006). While these three studies exemplify the physical and psychological effects of religious discrimination, they do not discuss the impact that religious microaggressions may have on their victims. Moreover, these studies focus primarily on Muslims and may not be generalizable to other religious minority groups (e.g., Jews, Hindus, Sikhs, Buddhists, or non-religious persons). Accordingly, more empirical research is necessary to unveil the mental health consequences that religious microaggressions may have on all of those who experience them.

IMPLICATIONS FOR COUNSELING AND PSYCHOTHERAPY

In order to become an ethical and multiculturally competent counselor/clinician, one must develop culturally appropriate knowledge, awareness, and skills about various oppressed groups (Sue & Sue, 2008). Counselors and clinicians can gain knowledge about individuals of various oppressed groups by learning about their individual and group processes in dealing with religious microaggressions (Nadal, 2008). Counselors/clinicians can attain awareness by learning how microaggressions may occur in one's own interpersonal relationships and how they may often become perpetrators or recipients of microaggressions in their everyday lives (Nadal, 2008). Finally, once counselors/clinicians have gained the knowledge and awareness of microaggressions, they can practice various skills of how to confront microaggressions when they transpire in counseling/psychotherapy settings (Nadal, 2008).

In terms of religious microaggressions, it may be important for counselors/clinicians to be aware of how individuals develop discriminatory attitudes on the basis of religion. Some research has shown that religious discrimination is often experienced in educational institutions of various levels—grammar schools, high schools, colleges, and universities (e.g., Gilbert, 2004; Hodge, 2006; Hodge, 2007a; Hodge, 2007b). Therefore, individuals who witness such discrimination, especially in an educational setting, may adopt these attitudes and eventually mimic the discriminatory behavior. Accordingly, educators must be conscious of the types of religious microaggressions that may occur in school systems and must prevent the normalization or acceptance of religious microaggressions in their nascent stages. For example, teachers can prevent students from overtly or covertly insulting a male student who wears a yarmulke by educating students about Judaism and the value of religious diversity.

Religious microaggressions may be perpetuated because of the direct and indirect messages that are conveyed in the media and society in general. Similar to the impact that negative racial stereotypes toward people of color may have on general society (see Pierce et al., 1978), media portrayals of current news and historical events can often reflect a prejudicial attitude toward certain religious groups (e.g., Jews or Muslims) and may subsequently influence individuals' personal beliefs with regard to the target group. For example, research has shown that after the terrorist attacks on September 11, 2001, Muslims reported increases in perceived societal discrimination (Rippy & Newman, 2006) as well as in experiences of both overt and covert inter-personal discrimination (Sheridan, 2006). Because of this, it may be the responsibility of society to reduce the amount of prejudice and stereotyping in the media and to provide opportunities for individuals of various oppressed groups to create positive images on national and global levels.

Counselors and clinicians should be aware that religion may lead to both positive and negative attitudes in themselves. One study revealed that religion can buffer the impact of racial discrimination, citing that African American individuals may turn to religion for social support, particularly when they experience discrimination (Bierman, 2006). Similarly, sharing a common religion can be used to promote ethnic identity, particularly for immigrant communities (Phinney, 1990). Because immigrants may be prone to experiencing unforeseen racial and/or religious microaggressions when they first arrive in the United States, turning to religious communities for social support may be beneficial in their coping skills. Accordingly, religion can be beneficial in promoting positive mental health and increasing self-efficacy.

Conversely, previous literature has purported that religion may also lead to prejudicial attitudes of other cultural groups and may potentially lead to other microaggressions. For example, a study found that Evangelical Christians were more likely to attribute racial inequality to the individual rather than the societal structure, while Catholics and mainline Christians attributed racial inequality to societal problems and not to individuals (Hinojosa & Park, 2004). Other literature has discussed how religion may influence heterosexism and homophobia, particularly given that every major organized religion in the world is opposed to homosexuality in both blatant and indirect ways (Chung & Singh, 2008). Accordingly, religion may also promote discrimination, resulting in the perpetuation of other types of microaggressions.

Finally, it may be important to revisit findings from Eslea and Mukhtar (2000), which cited that students of two religious minority groups often bullied each other and other religious minority groups. Perhaps there is a "cycle of microaggressions" that exists, in which individuals who enact microaggressions onto others may actually be the recipients of microaggressions themselves (e.g., a White woman enacts a racial microaggression because she is the recipient of gender microaggressions; a Black/African American man enacts a gender microaggression because he is the recipient of racial microaggressions). These cycles of microaggressions may be a crucial future direction of research in understanding the etiology of microaggressions (and other forms of discrimination) and may provide a partial rationale of why oppressed individuals may be discriminatory against other oppressed groups.

For example, some studies have revealed a high number of African Americans and Latinos/as who hold prejudicial views against Jews and Muslims (see ADL, 2005; National Conference of Christians and Jews, 1994), while other authors have asserted that people of color tend to be more homophobic/heterosexist than their White American counterparts (Chung & Singh, 2008). Perhaps these individuals develop their prejudices toward other groups as a way to displace the emotional duress they experience from microaggressions and other forms of discrimination. Because these individuals may experience various oppressions in society, they may enact microaggressions (consciously or unconsciously) in order to feel more superior and/or less oppressed. Future research could examine the potential of these cycles of microaggressions in order to understand the psychological processes of being both an enactor and a recipient of microaggressions. Finally, counselors, clinicians, and other mental health practitioners should be aware of how cycles of microaggressions may become perpetuated and should find ways to prevent these cycles from persisting.

REFERENCES

Anti-Defamation League (ADL). (2005). *ADL survey: Anti-Semitism declines slightly in America; 14 percent of Americans hold "strong" anti-Semitic beliefs.* New York: Author. Retrieved February 20, 2009, from http://www.adl.org/PresRele/ASUS_12/4680_12.htm.

Anti-Defamation League (ADL). (2008). *Anti-Semitic incidents decline for the third straight year in U.S., according to annual ADL audit.* New York, NY: Author. Retrieved February 10, 2009, from http://www.adl.org/PresRele/ASUS_12/5246_12.htm.

Bierman, A. (2006). Does religion buffer the effects of discrimination on mental health? Differing effects by race. *Journal for the Scientific Study of Religion*, 45(4), 551–565.

Brasted, H. (1997). The politics of stereotyping: Western images of Islam. *Manushi, 98*, 6–16.

Brown, M. D. (2006). Comparative analysis of mainstream discourses, media narratives and representations of Islam in Britain and France prior to 9/11. *Journal of Muslim Minority Affairs, 26*(3), 297–312.

Chung, Y. B., & Singh, A. A. (2008). Lesbian, gay, bisexual, and transgender Asian Americans. In N. Tewari & A. N. Alvarez (Eds.), *Asian American psychology: Current perspectives* (pp. 233–246). New York: Psychology Press.

Council on American-Islamic Relations (CAIR). (2008). *The status of Muslim civil rights in the United States, 2008*. Washington, DC: Author. Retrieved February 1, 2009, from http://www.cair.com/Portals/0/pdf/civilrights2008.pdf.

Dunn, K. M., Klocker, N., & Salabay, T. (2007). Contemporary racism and Islamaphobia in Australia: Racializing religion. *Ethnicities, 7*(4), 564–589.

Engh, M. J. (2006). *In the name of heaven: 3,000 years of religious persecution.* Amherst, NY: Prometheus Books.

Eslea, M., & Mukhtar, K. (2000). Bullying and racism among Asian schoolchildren in Britain. *Educational Research, 42*(2), 207–217.

Federal Bureau of Investigation (FBI). (2008). *Hate crime statistics, 2007.* Washington, DC: Author. Retrieved February 10, 2009, from http://www.fbi.gov/ucr/hc2007/index.html.

Fischer, P., Greitemeyer, T., & Kastenmuller, A. (2007). What do we think about Muslims? The validity of Westerners' implicit theories about the associations between Muslims' religiosity, religious identity, aggression potential, and attitudes toward terrorism. *Group Processes & Intergroup Relations, 10*(3), 373–382.

Gibbon, J. (2005, August). *Unveiling Islamophobia in the U.S.: Muslim immigrants and their context of reception.* Paper presented at the annual meeting of the American Sociological Association, Philadelphia, PA.

Gilbert, D. (2004). Racial and religious discrimination: The inexorable relationship between schools and the individual. *Intercultural Education, 15*(3), 253–266.

Gottschalk, P., & Greenberg, G. (2008). *Islamophobia: Making Muslims the enemy.* Lanham, MD: Rowman & Littlefield.

Harper, M. (2007). The stereotyping of non-religious people by religious students: Contents and subtypes. *Journal for the Scientific Study of Religion, 46*(4), 539–552.

Hassouneh, D. M., & Kulwicki, A. (2007). Mental health, discrimination, and trauma in Arab Muslim women living in the US: A pilot study. *Religion & Culture, 10*(3), 257–262.

Hertzke, A. D. (2004). *Freeing God's children: The unlikely alliance for global human rights.* Lanham, MD: Rowman & Littlefield.

Hinojosa, V. J., & Park, J. Z. (2004). Religion and the paradox of racial inequality attitudes. *Journal for the Scientific Study of Religion, 43*(2), 229–238.

Hodge, D. R. (2006). Moving toward a more inclusive educational environment? A multi-sample exploration of religious discrimination as seen through the eyes of students from various faith traditions. *Journal of Social Work Education, 42*(2), 249–267.

Hodge, D. R. (2007a). Progressing toward inclusion? Exploring the state of religious diversity. *Social Work Research, 31*(1), 55–61.

Hodge, D. R. (2007b). Religious discrimination and ethical compliance: Exploring perceptions among a professionally affiliated sample of graduate students. *Journal of Religion & Spirituality in Social Work, 26*(2), 91–113.

Hodge, D. R. (2007c). Social justice and people of faith: A transnational perspective. *Social Work, 52*(2), 139–148.

James, E. (2008). Arab culture and Muslim stereotypes. *World and I, 23*(5), 4.

Jenkins, P. (2002). *The next Christendom*. New York: Oxford University Press.

Kessler, R. C., Mickelson, K. D., & Williams, D. R. (1999). The prevalence, distribution, and mental health correlates of perceived discrimination in the United States. *Journal of Health and Social Behavior, 40*, 208–230.

Kosmin, B. A., Mayer, E., & Keysar, A. (2001). *American Religious Identification Survey 2001*. New York: The Graduate Center of the City University of New York.

Kramer, G. (2006). Anti-Semitism in the Muslim world. *Die Welt des Islams, 46*(3), 243–246.

Langman, P. F. (1999). *Jewish issues in multiculturalism: A handbook for educators and clinicians*. Northvale, NJ: Jason Aronson.

Marcus, K. L. (2007). The resurgence of anti-Semitism on American college campuses. *Current Psychology, 26*(3–4), 206–212.

Marshall, P. (2000). *Religious freedom in the world: A global report on freedom and persecution*. Nashville, TN: Broadman & Holman.

McIntosh, P. (2003). White privilege: Unpacking the invisible knapsack. In S. Plous (Ed.), *Understanding prejudice and discrimination* (pp. 191–196). New York: McGraw-Hill.

Nadal, K. L. (2008). Preventing racial, ethnic, gender, sexual minority, disability, and religious microaggressions: Recommendations for promoting positive mental health. *Prevention in Counseling Psychology: Theory, Research, Practice and Training, 2*(1), 22–27.

Nadal, K. L. (2010). Gender microaggressions and women: Implications for therapy. In M. A. Paludi (Ed.), *Feminism and women's rights worldwide, Volume 2: Mental and Physical Health* (pp. 155–175). Westport, CT: Praeger Publishers.

National Conference of Christians and Jews. (1994). *Taking America's pulse: A summary report of the national survey report of intergroup relations*. New York: Author.

Phinney, J. S. (1990). Ethnic identity in adolescents and adults: Review of research. *Psychological Bulletin, 108*(3), 499–514.

Pierce, C., Carew, J., Pierce-Gonzalez, D., & Willis, D. (1978). An experiment in racism: TV commercials. In C. Pierce (Ed.), *Television and education* (pp. 62–88). Beverly Hills, CA: Sage.

Rippy, A. E., & Newman, E. (2006). Perceived religious discrimination and its relationship to anxiety and paranoia among Muslim Americans. *Journal of Muslim Mental Health, 1*, 5–20.

Rippy, A. E., & Newman, E. (2008). Adaptation of a scale of race-related stress for use with Muslim Americans. *Journal of Muslim Mental Health, 3*, 53–68.

Rowatt, W. C., Franklin, L. M., & Cotton, M. (2005). Patterns and personality correlates of implicit and explicit attitudes toward Christians and Muslims. *Journal for the Scientific Study of Religion, 44*(1), 29–43.

Russ, F. (2007). The structural relationships among perceived parenting acceptance-rejection, conceptions of G-D and psychological adjustment in orthodox Jewish students. *Dissertation Abstracts International, Section B: The Sciences and Engineering, 67*(10-B), 6090.

Sellers, R. M., & Shelton, J. M. (2003). The role of racial identity in perceived racial discrimination. *Journal of Personality and Social Psychology, 84*(5), 1079–1092.

Sheridan, L. P. (2006). Islamophobia pre- and post-September 11th, 2001. *Journal of Interpersonal Violence, 21*(3), 317–336.

Simon, R. J., & Schaler, J. A. (2007). Anti-Semitism the world over in the twenty-first century. *Current Psychology, 26*(3–4), 152–182.

Social science and the citizen. (1996, March). *Society 33*(3), 2–5.

Strabac, Z., & Listhaug, O. (2008). Anti-Muslim prejudice in Europe: A multilevel analysis of survey data from 30 countries. *Social Science Research, 37*(1), 268–286.

Sue, D. W., Bucceri, J. M., Lin, A. I., Nadal, K. L., & Torino, G. C. (2007). Racial microaggressions and the Asian American experience. *Cultural Diversity and Ethnic Minority Psychology, 13*(1), 72–81.

Sue, D. W., & Capodilupo, C. M. (2008). Racial, gender, and sexual orientation microaggressions: Implications for counseling and psychotherapy. In D. W. Sue & D. Sue (Eds.), *Counseling the culturally diverse* (5th ed., pp. 105–130). Hoboken, NJ: John Wiley & Sons.

Sue, D. W., Capodilupo, C. M., & Holder, A. M. B. (2008). Racial microaggressions in the life experience of Black Americans. *Professional Psychology: Research and Practice, 39*(3), 329–336.

Sue, D. W., Capodilupo, C. M., Torino, G. C., Bucceri, J. M., Holder, A. M. B., Nadal, K. L., & Esquilin, M. (2007). Racial microaggressions in everyday life: Implications for clinical practice. *American Psychologist, 62*(4), 271–286.

Sue, D. W., Nadal, K. L., Capodilupo, C. M., Lin, A. I., Torino, G. C., & Rivera, D. P. (2008). Racial microaggressions against Black Americans: Implications for counseling. *Journal of Counseling & Development, 86*, 330–338.

Sue, D. W., & Sue, D. (2008). *Counseling the culturally diverse: Theory and practice* (5th ed.). Hoboken, NJ: John Wiley & Sons.

Weinrach, S. G. (2002). The counseling profession's relationship to Jews and the issues that concern them: More than a case of selective awareness. *Journal of Counseling and Development, 80*, 300–314.

Wilson, T. C. (1996). Compliments will get you nowhere: Benign stereotypes, prejudice and anti-Semitism. *Sociological Quarterly, 37*(3), 465–479.

PART IV

MICROAGGRESSION RESEARCH

CHAPTER 14

Microaggression Research

Methodological Review and Recommendations

MICHAEL Y. LAU and CHANTEA D. WILLIAMS

ARLY RESEARCH ON microaggressions can be traced to Pierce (1995) and Pierce, Carew, Pierce-Gonzalez, and Willis (1978), who defined it as the subtle, stunning, and unconscious put-downs of those in inferior status (e.g., people of color) by the group of superior status. In their study of racism and television commercials, Pierce et al. (1978) revealed that Blacks were severely underrepresented as well as misrepresented in the media. Blacks were less likely to be shown in superior or knowledgeable roles, less often displayed in stable families, and more likely to be cast in subservient positions. With more recent research, Sue and his colleagues (Sue, Capodilupo, et al., 2007) have continued to explore and uncover the subtle, covert, and often inadvertent behavioral, verbal, and environmental slights experienced by people of color and other marginalized groups. The recent burgeoning of research on these experiences provides an opportunity to examine the methodological issues associated with studying the phenomenon of microaggressions.

We will first review current microaggression research and the approaches employed. This will provide a basis to explore existing limitations in methodological approaches and point to areas of future development. Next, we provide a framework for understanding the measurement and design issues in future microaggression research. Lastly, we discuss and highlight several recommendations for future research in light of the issues raised in the first two sections of the chapter.

REVIEW OF CURRENT MICROAGGRESSION LITERATURE

By our review, including the contributions to this edited volume, there have been 20 published papers in the recent literature on microaggressions. Of these publications, 10 are nonempirical or theoretical. Of the remaining 10 empirical studies, we found that a majority were qualitative studies. Of the published qualitative studies, two dominant methodological approaches in design and analysis were employed: consensual qualitative research (CQR; Hill et al., 2005; Hill, Thompson, & Williams, 1997) and interpretative phenomenological analysis (IPA; Smith, 2004; Smith & Osborn, 2004). We briefly review these approaches to introduce them to readers less familiar with qualitative methods.

CONSENSUAL QUALITATIVE RESEARCH

Consensual qualitative research is the primary method employed by researchers to analyze data collected for the study of racial microaggressions. Hill et al. (1997) developed CQR to answer the need for a more rigorous method for conducting qualitative research and outlined a process that breaks away from quantitative research approaches (i.e., surveys). The authors purport that researchers using CQR will attain rich, valuable data about the phenomena under investigation through the use of open-ended questions used to guide, and not restrict, the data collection procedure.

Hill and her colleagues (1997, 2005) credit their development of CQR to an integration of several qualitative methods. Consensual qualitative research is consistent with the well-established framework of qualitative methods. Specifically, it allows information pertaining to the phenomena under investigation to flow naturally from the participant, and the researcher is the data collection instrument, encouraging the participant to describe how they understand their experience of the phenomena. Consensual qualitative research (Hill et al., 2005) is strongly influenced by Strauss and Corbin's (1998) grounded theory, Elliott's (1989) comprehensive process analysis, and Giorgi's (1985) phenomenological research approaches.

Originally adopted primarily for psychotherapy process research, CQR has more recently been extensively used in the research of racial microaggressions. Furthermore, within counseling psychology, the approach has been adopted to examine a range of issues such as social class (Blustein et al., 2002; Nelson, Englar-Carlson, Tierney, & Hau, 2006), vocational trajectories (Juntunen et al., 2001; Nutt et al., 1998), and adjustment issues of immigrants (Constantine, Anderson, Berkel, Caldwell, & Utsey, 2005) and international students (Inman, Howard, Beaumont, & Walker, 2007). Beyond counseling psychology, CQR has been utilized to study the subjective experience of compassion fatigue among genetic counselors (Benoit, Veach, & LeRoy, 2007), as well as how childhood leukemia later shapes the adult lives of those who survive the disease (Brown, Pikler, Lavish, Keune, & Hutto, 2008).

INTERPRETATIVE PHENOMENOLOGICAL ANALYSIS

Interpretative phenomenological analysis (IPA) is another qualitative research method that has been employed by researchers studying racial microaggressions. The IPA approach was founded by Dr. Jonathan A. Smith, a health psychology researcher based in the United Kingdom (University of London, Birkbeck, 2009). The theoretical orientation of IPA is established in phenomenology, double hermeneutics, and ideography (Smith & Eatough, 2007). The IPA approach is employed by researchers and psychologists seeking to understand the experience from the subjective perspective of the individual. Hermeneutics pertains to how individuals make sense of their experience. Thus, by employing double hermeneutics, IPA acknowledges that data analysis incorporates the researchers' understanding of how the participant makes sense of his or her experience.

Interpretative phenomenological analysis has been utilized in the field of health psychology to gain a new understanding of individuals' lived experience with medical conditions, such as the daunting reality of living with chronic back pain (Smith & Osborn, 2007) or how living with Huntington's disease affects both the children who are diagnosed and their families (Smith et al., 2006; Brewer et al., 2008). Due to its holistic nature, IPA is an appropriate method for studies in social, clinical, and developmental psychology (Smith, 2004). Several researchers have used IPA to explore and reveal their participants' experiences of feeling anger (Eatough & Smith, 2006a, 2006b; Eatough, Smith, & Shaw, 2008), coping with dementia (Clare, 2002; Pearce, Clare, & Pistrang, 2002; Robinson, Clarke, & Evans, 2005), lived experiences with auditory hallucinations (Knudson & Coyle, 2002), and the clinician's understanding of the patient's struggle with anorexia nervosa (Jarman, Smith, & Walsh, 1997).

LIMITATIONS IN RESEARCH DESIGN AND ANALYSIS IN CURRENT
MICROAGGRESSION RESEARCH

Of the published studies we reviewed, six employed the CQR approach (e.g., Keller & Galgay, Chapter 11 in this volume; Rivera, Forquer, & Rangel, Chapter 3 in this volume; Sue, Bucceri, Lin, Nadal, & Torino, 2007; Sue, Capodilupo, & Holder, 2008; Sue, Lin, Torino, Capodilupo, & Rivera, 2009; Watkins, LaBarrie, & Appio, Chapter 2 in this volume), whereas two employed the IPA approach (e.g., Constantine, Smith, Redington, & Owens, 2008; Constantine & Sue, 2007). Qualitative methods in general, and both CQR and IPA specifically, are suitable in the research of microaggressions for a number of reasons to be discussed later. It is important to note, however, that criticisms often arise when quantitative standards for research are imposed upon qualitative methods. Some have argued that the differences in paradigmatic and epistemological underpinnings between the two methods call for different standards in evaluating the quality and credibility of qualitative methods (Merrick, 1999; Morrow, 2005; Ponterotto, 2005). As such, we review limitations of these qualitative studies only as a way to continue to expand the methodological possibilities when engaging in microaggression research and improving upon the quality and validity of findings from within qualitative research standards.

Current researchers of microaggressions using CQR and IPA have identified a number of methodological and study limitations. First, a majority of existing studies relied on relatively small samples. A number of researchers have acknowledged the generalizability issue that arises from this (Constantine, 2007; Constantine & Sue, 2007; Sue, Bucceri, et al., 2007; Sue, Nadal, et al., 2008). Some samples, although within acceptable ranges for qualitative designs (e.g., 8–10 participants), had issues of sample imbalance of gender and ethnicity (Sue, Bucceri, et al., 2007). Therefore, gender or ethnic nuances in microaggression experiences may not be well captured in a homogenous sample. Related to the difficulty in generalizing findings from a small sample is the nonsampling of the universe of microaggression experiences (Sue, Capodilupo, & Holder, 2008; Sue, Nadal, et al., 2008). In part due to overall limited sampling of participants and the selection of a particular set of interview questions used, it is likely that this contributes to limited sampling of all possible microaggression experiences. Consistent with recommendations made elsewhere (Hill et al., 2005), we urge future researchers to balance heterogeneity of sample with the number of participants employed. If participants are relatively dissimilar from each other, then a larger sample would be necessary to achieve consistency in the experiences uncovered. Qualitative findings lend themselves more easily to interpretation and have more circumscribed implications when the context (e.g., homogeneity of the background and experiences of participants) of the data is clear and evident (Patton, 2002).

A second methodological limitation of existing microaggression studies is the selective recruitment of participants. In a study on racial microaggressions of Black Americans (Sue, Capodilupo, & Holder, 2008), for example, inclusion criteria for the 13 participants involved participant agreement that subtle racism and discrimination exists in the United States. In another study of Black counseling and counseling psychology faculty (Constantine et al., 2008), purposive criterion procedures (Patton, 1990) were used to select participants who believe that subtle racism currently exists in the United States and that they have had personal experiences within academia. From a traditional scientific perspective, such sampling methods are problematic, because they do not allow for the possibility of uncovering the experiences of participants who do not already believe in the existence of subtle racism. From a qualitative methodology perspective, however, researchers are able to explore deeply the experiences only by gathering data from those who are knowledgeable and who have had recent experiences related to microaggressions. We suggest that future research using qualitative methods continue to be more explicit about sampling criteria and strategies (Patton, 2002), as they correspond differently to original purposes of the study. For example, a sampling of the microaggression experiences of Asian or Asian Americans who do or do not believe that subtle racism exists will address very different research questions.

Third, all of the studies reliant on qualitative methodology encounter the possible criticism of the interpretive biases in the data analytic phase of the study. In studies using IPA, for example, one researcher is often the only person involved in the primary analysis and interpretation of the transcripts (e.g., Constantine et al., 2008). For both IPA and CQR, checks and balances are implemented to rule out or take into consideration possible intrusion of personal biases in the interpretation process. In an IPA study, the primary author openly acknowledged possible personal biases prior to data collection and during data analysis relied on external review of the emerging themes by an independent auditor (Constantine et al., 2008). With CQR, a team approach involving multiple researchers who openly discuss their personal biases and attempt to reach consensus during the analysis process and the use of external auditors further minimize the criticism of subjectivity in arriving at the results found (Hill et al., 1997). Some have suggested that an honest reporting of how researcher biases and expectations influenced the results be reported in the discussion section of the study (Hill et al., 2005). We further suggest that future researchers consider the possibility of involving participants in checking data recording and interpretations, either to minimize biases or to deepen the voices of the participants in the interpretive process (Morrow, 2005). On a related note, most of the recent studies have examined and analyzed transcribed data (e.g., video or audio recordings). As such, a number of researchers have acknowledged the possible limitations resulting from not being able to fully appreciate the experiences shared because verbal inflections or emphases are not captured in the transcripts (Constantine et al., 2008; Constantine & Sue, 2007). Given the focus of qualitative methods on the adequacy and context of the data gathered (Morrow, 2005), future research should consider expanding the sphere of data generation. For example, by conducting both individual and focus group interviews, the richness of the data and understanding of the contextual qualities of the experiences are greatly enhanced.

Fourth, the breadth and depth of the microaggression experiences uncovered through the interviews are in part dependent on the questions formulated and the skills and experience of the interviewer. Interview protocols for many of the studies were generated by examining the literature on related topics (e.g., aversive racism, implicit and explicit stereotyping, and racism experiences of ethnic minorities) and were carried out in an open-ended and semistructured manner. Although set questions were used to guide the interviews, interviewers were allowed to stray from the script and probe and explore topics consistent with the overall trajectory of the interviews. Most of the interviewers were graduate students and postdoctoral researchers with counseling backgrounds. Nevertheless, possible biases of the interviewers and interindividual differences may be potential criticisms for the particular results found in each study.

Lastly, all studies in recent microaggressions literature have relied on retrospective recall of the experiences of participants through surveys or group/individual interviews. The concern for possible inadvertent biases or inaccuracies in retrospective recall is understandable. Looking at coping strategies following potentially stressful life events, Stone and colleagues (1998) found that retrospective reporting resulted in overreporting of behavioral coping and underreporting of cognitive coping when compared to momentary reports (i.e., prompted reporting when randomly paged by a beeper). Also, it has been noted that reconstruction of coping strategies may be influenced by culturally prescribed norms and ideals (Tweed & DeLongis, 2006). As such, it is possible for actual coping strategies to differ from retrospective recall by participants interviewed. Nevertheless, it is important to acknowledge that understanding the gravity of culturally sanctioned ways of coping is legitimately a research question of interest to microaggressions researchers and that reconstructed memories of coping may themselves be very telling of the nature of the stressful event/incident and/or subsequent coping strategies (Tweed & DeLongis, 2006). Qualitative researchers interested in ensuring recall that is phenomenologically and temporally more immediate to a microaggression incident can consider alternative methods of measurement covered in the next section (e.g., use of diaries).

METHODOLOGICAL CONSIDERATIONS FOR FUTURE RESEARCH

In light of the aforementioned limitations, we consider measurement and research design issues relevant for future researchers. Our goal in this section is to broaden measurement methods for capturing microaggression-related variables and to guide researchers in making important research design decisions. In doing so, we hope that future researchers can better design studies to meet demands made by practical, conceptual, and research question factors.

Methods of Measurement

Participant self-reports gathered through interviews is the primary mode of data generation in current microaggression research. Given the focus on the subjective experiences in the everyday lives of those affected by these subtle and often inadvertent acts of racism, self-reports provide the kind of information that reveals the phenomenology of these private experiences. As research in this area expands and progresses, broadening beyond self-reports will benefit our understanding of microaggressions. For example, rather than rely on the self-report of microaggression experiences, researchers could directly observe the effects of microaggressions in a real-life setting. Expanding on the operational forms of measurement has been attempted in the stress and coping research literature (McGrath, 1970) and we consider them here in the context of microaggression research.

As shown in Table 14.1 (Beehr & McGrath, 1996), we present a framework for exploring how measurements of microaggressions can be broadened and diversified by examining both the operational forms of measurement and the system level of measure in future microaggressions research. Operational forms of measurement concern the method of measurement. The four forms considered are (1) subjective reports, which include diaries, questionnaires/surveys, and interviews; (2) observations, which involve direct observation of targeted events or behaviors; (3) trace measures, which are residual evidence of targeted events or behaviors; and (4) archival records, which are documents or records of targeted events or behaviors.

System levels of measure are somewhat arbitrary categories of the target or focus of what is being measured. The four levels of measure examined here are (1) physiological (e.g., neurological or biological targets), (2) psychological (e.g., emotional or cognitive targets), (3) task performance or action (e.g., cognitive assessments or vocational task performance), and (4) interpersonal behavior (e.g., quality of relationships or interpersonal interactions). The levels are not necessarily independent; for example, measuring the effect that microaggressions have on work performance would clearly involve measuring the psychological effects as well. Table 14.1, however, provides a framework and an opportunity for future researchers to consider diversifying and expanding ways of measuring microaggressions and associated variables of interest.

It is practically not possible to examine each cell extensively in Table 14.1; nor do we propose that measures pertinent to microaggressions research are conceivable for every cell in the table. Instead, we highlight a few to demonstrate how measurement of variables related to microaggressions can be broadened and invite future researchers to consider measurements relevant to their conceptual hypotheses or research questions. Current

Table 14.1

Measures of Microaggression Experiences

System Level of Measure	Operational Forms of Measurement			
	Subjective Reports	Observations	Trace Measures	Archival Records
Physiological	Questionnaires, interviews about physiological or behavioral reactions (e.g., self-report physiological responses)	Direct observation of physiological or behavioral reactions (e.g., heart rate, galvanic skin response)	Biochemical analyses of physiological reactions (e.g., cortisol or T-cells)	Medical records (e.g., number of physician visits)
Psychological	Questionnaires, interviews about psychological reactions (e.g., emotional or cognitive responses)	Direct observation of psychological reactions (e.g., brain scans)	Evidence of psychological reactions (e.g., private journals)	Records of psychological functioning or reactions (e.g., number of therapy treatments or length of therapy treatment)
Task performance or action	Questionnaires, interviews about task performance or action (e.g., work effectiveness)	Direct observation of task performance or action (e.g., work tasks or problem-solving tasks)	Evidence of task performance or action (e.g., class attendance)	Records of task performance or action (e.g., job performance evaluation)
Interpersonal behavior	Questionnaires, interviews about interpersonal relationships (e.g., help-seeking behavior, conflict resolution)	Direct observation of interpersonal actions (e.g., level of friendliness)	Evidence of interpersonal actions (e.g., attendance at group meetings)	Records of interpersonal actions (e.g., clinical supervisor observation record)

Note. Adapted from Beehr and McGrath (1996).

research has primarily relied on subjective reports of microaggression experiences. Through individual or group interviews, participants report subjective experiences that have occurred in the past. For example, Latinos/as (Rivera et al., Chapter 3 in this volume) and Blacks (Sue, Nadal, et al., 2008; Watkins et al., Chapter 2 in this volume) frequently report that they are perceived to be intellectual inferiors and are met with surprise or skepticism regarding their professional and educational attainment. Also, the current literature focuses mostly on psychological, task performance or action, and interpersonal behaviors when eliciting recalls of microaggression experiences. For example, Asian Americans have recalled often being asked where they are from and complimented for their English fluency, actions that are based on a belief that all Asians are foreign-born. Such interactions leave the participants feeling insulted and uncomfortable (Sue, Bucceri, et al., 2007).

In considering expanding methods of measuring microaggressions, future researchers should consider the opportunities to examine the phenomenon from other operational and system levels of measurement. It is likely, for example, that the experiences of microaggressions by individuals in their everyday lives involve both psychological and physiological reactions. With the advent of brain imaging technology, researchers interested in the psychological reactions to microaggressions can also examine psychological process at the neural level (e.g., Derks, Inzlicht, & Kang, 2008) through functional magnetic resonance imaging (fMRI) and electroencephalography (EEG). The emergent area of social cognitive neuroscience (Ochsner & Lieberman, 2001) has the potential of shaping a more integrated and holistic view of microaggression experiences. Similarly, encouraging future research to also measure physiological reactions (e.g., stress reactions observed through galvanic skin response, level of cortisol level in body, or immune system responses; Cacioppo, Tassinary, & Bernston, 2000) to microaggressions will better elucidate the underlying physiological processes that interact with the psychological and behavioral processes that researchers observe and measure (Bruning & Frew, 1987; Harrell, Hall, & Taliaferro, 2003; Merritt, Bennett, Williams, Edwards, & Sollers, 2006; Richman, Bennett, Pek, Siegler, & Williams, 2007; Taylor et al., 2008; Utsey & Hook, 2007).

Archival records are other operational forms of measurement not frequently employed in current microaggressions research. Archival records may be more reliable sources of information if accuracy of subjective report is a concern for future researchers. For example, in an experimental study looking at the positive health consequences of writing about the emotional aspects of a traumatic experience, researchers found that students at a university made fewer visits to the health center during the six months following the writing experience than students who wrote about a trivial event (Pennebaker & Beall, 1986). The measurement of the effects of micro-aggressions using archival records may originate from other sources. For example, depending on the research question, length of medical or psycho-therapy treatment, academic absenteeism, and psychotherapy dropout rate are potentially relevant outcome measures.

It would be apparent to readers that the measurement issues discussed so far fit primarily within a quantitative methodology paradigm. Measurement methods have also been elaborated from within qualitative paradigms (Patton, 2002). Madill and Gough (2008), for example, discussed five categories of qualitative data collection method: (1) collaborative, (2) inter-view, (3) naturally occurring, (4) observational, and (5) structured. Interview and structured methods are similar to subjective reports in Table 14.1. Current microaggressions research using CQR and IPA methodologies rely on both individual interview and focus group formats. Structured methods resemble traditional quantitative methods but generally prompt more open and rich qualitative responses. Rivera and colleagues (Chapter 3 in this volume), for example, posed open questions to their participants through e-mail. Naturally occurring methods are analogous to archival records in Table 14.1. Researchers can explore the expressions of microaggressions from a variety of existing sources. For example, qualitative content analyses (Hsieh & Shannon, 2005; Potter & Levine-Donnerstein, 1999) of biographical and literary works or historical documents could potentially provide rich infor-mation about microaggressions expressed in the natural narratives of these authors' lives. Also, with the advent of the Internet, online social network-ing, and online blogging practices, the opportunity to take advantage of research on electronic archival data could uncover interesting findings not as easily revealed in interviews or more structured methods (Evans, Elford, & Wiggins, 2008).

The qualitative equivalent of observational methods in Table 14.1 focuses on the immersion into and observation of natural and qualitatively rich participant environments. Microaggressions have already been reported in a number of naturalistic contexts (e.g., classrooms; Sue et al., 2009) that lend themselves easily to intense observational methods (e.g., ethnography). Given the subtle and interactional nature of microaggressions, qualitative observations provide a contextually rich method for understanding such experiences occurring in natural settings. Lastly, collaborative methods are somewhat unique to qualitative perspectives (Ponterrotto, 2005) in that the traditional boundaries between the researcher and participants are blurred through active conceptualization and/or execution of a research project by both parties. Participatory action research (Kidd & Krall, 2005) is a representative example of such an approach.

RESEARCH DESIGN ISSUES

Measurement issues concern what instrument or tool researchers use to capture and represent microaggression experiences. These decisions cannot be made without a commitment to an overall approach of research design. We consider three broad methodological decisions: quantitative versus qualitative, cross-sectional/retrospective versus longitudinal, and experimental versus correlational/observational designs. It is our stance that decisions to adopt one approach over another should be guided by theoretical and practical considerations, the research question, and an understanding of the relative strengths and limitations of each design in the context of studying microaggressions. Although we discuss these three approaches separately, it is instructive to point out that they are overlapping; that is to say that any number or combination of the three decisions can apply to a single study. For example, although most of the qualitative work conducted with microaggressions has been cross-sectional/retrospective, qualitative methods can also be designed as longitudinal. Furthermore, such a study can either be designed as experimental or correlational.

Quantitative versus Qualitative   The earlier review of current microaggression research revealed that a majority have employed qualitative approaches in both data collection and analysis. Despite the positivistic and quantitative emphasis of mainstream psychological research, qualitative approaches have gradually been adopted in greater frequency in recent decades (Madill & Gough, 2008; Rennie, Watson, & Monteiro, 2002). Counseling psychology, in particular, has been advocating for greater consideration of qualitative approaches (e.g., Hoshmand, 1989; Howard, 2003; Neimeyer & Resnikoff, 1982; Polkinghorne, 1988). Within counseling psychology, where a majority of the recent work on microaggressions has been conducted, the interest in qualitative methods has resulted in a number of recent special issues on the topic in important counseling psychology journals such as the *Journal of Counseling Psychology* (Haverkamp, Morrow, & Ponterotto, 2005) and *The Counseling Psychologist* (Carter & Morrow, 2007a, 2007b). Many have commented that the shift in welcoming qualitative approaches is a reaction to the narrow philosophical commitments to empiricism and positivism in science (Madill & Gough, 2008; Morrow, 2007; Ponterotto, 2005). The necessary limitations of these traditional commitments of psychological science are addressed by turning to qualitative methods.

Within the context of microaggressions as a phenomenon not yet well understood, the strengths inherent in CQR and IPA are particularly fitting in giving voice to these experiences. Grounded more in a naturalistic epistemological position, qualitative methods are suited to exploring microaggressions because of (1) the privileging of description over explanation, (2) the representation of subjective experiences through the eyes of the participants, (3) the conceptualization of the meaning of experiences and behaviors as contextual and complex, (4) the viewing of the scientific process as unfolding working hypotheses rather than immutable facts, and (5) the emphasis of concepts and theories to emerge from the data rather than imposing prior structures on the data (Henwood & Pidgeon, 1992). By using qualitative research methods, rich descriptions have emerged of microaggressions experienced by people with a marginalized identity (e.g., race/ethnicity, gender, sexual orientation, disability, socioeconomic status). Research on the experiences of Latinos/as with racial microaggressions found that while the themes in the taxonomy proposed by Sue et al. (2009) were supported (e.g., ascription of intelligence, second-class citizen), themes specific to their ethnicity emerged as well (Rivera et al., Chapter 3 in this volume; Sue, Bucceri, et al., 2007). For example, under the domain of characteristics of speech, many of the participants recall being harassed for using Spanish or because they spoke with an accent, which implied to the participants that even their speech ought to resemble White Americans. Furthermore, a domain of assumed attributes about Latinos/as emerged as well. Specifically, the participants describe how negative stereotypes about their culture are conveyed in subtle messages, such as being told that all Latinos/as look alike or being labeled an incorrect ethnicity (Rivera et al., Chapter 3 in this volume). In the current research on gender microaggression, female participants described their daily experiences with sexual objectification (Capodilupo et al., Chapter 9 in this volume). For example, verbal manifestations of sexual objectification such as catcalls and remarks about their physical appearance were described by many participants in the study. In addition, a participant gave a glimpse into her personal experiences with subtle sexism and provided a candid account of being told that she wasn't wanted on the soccer field with the other players (all males). In both of these examples, it is evident that the rich description of subjective experiences is privileged over an objective account or explanation of microaggression experiences. Such contextual and phenomenological richness of research data is either preempted by or extremely restricted with quantitative approaches.

The methodological limitations previously explored have largely been a function of the adoption of qualitative designs used in current microaggression research. Due to the in-depth and rich exploration of qualitative data, collecting data from large numbers of participants can be impractical. As mentioned earlier, this raises a number of criticisms regarding the validity and generalizability of the phenomenon. Defenders of qualitative methodologies have argued that because of differences in the fundamental assumptions and goals of qualitative versus quantitative methods, it is not appropriate to hold qualitative methods to the same set of quality criteria (e.g., Merrick, 1999; Morrow, 2005). Nevertheless, future research could adopt quantitative methods as a way of validating existing qualitative findings. Also, the generalizability of the findings can be enhanced by demonstrating that they apply to a wider range of individuals with diverse backgrounds (e.g., social class, gender, etc.). By sampling larger numbers of individuals, the range of microaggression experiences can also be better represented in the findings.

Use of more conventional quantitative methods is beginning to surface in the microaggression literature. Constantine (2007) is one of the first to approach the study of microaggressions from a quantitative perspective. With a sample of African American clients, she developed a 10-item, 3-point Likert-type Racial Microaggressions in Counseling Scale that measures subjective perceptions of occurrence and impact of racial microaggressions experiences in a counseling dyad. Among her findings, Constantine found that greater perception of racial microaggressions is negatively associated with therapeutic alliance and counseling satisfaction ratings of White therapists. One of the strengths of quantitative designs is the ability to test hypothesized relationships amongst the variables of interest. In the case of the Constantine study, qualitative methods would not have easily provided the mechanism to understand what important variables (e.g., therapy outcome and perception of counselor competence) perceptions of microaggressions could lead to in counseling dyads. A large number of analytic models are available to examine simple and more complex quantitative designs. Causal inferences of these targeted relationships can be better supported when quantitative designs are also experimental designs (see more in the following text). Researchers operating from within positivist or postpositivist paradigms (Ponterotto, 2005) can argue that subjectivity introduced in data collection (e.g., unstructured, open-ended individual interviews) and data analysis (e.g., individual or group analysis teams) is minimized or completely ruled out with traditional quantitative designs. At the same time, quantitative studies are by design restricted in targeting a small set of predetermined variables of research interest. Consequently, unique and contextually rich experiences cannot emerge from the data collection process.

Lastly, as more quantitative studies are conducted on microaggressions, issues of assessing for traditional standards of validity and reliability become more relevant. In particular, the cultural validity of microaggressions research deserves serious consideration. In the stress and coping literature, some have alerted to the importance of attending to issues of language and construct equivalence when working with certain multicultural and cross-cultural samples (Sanchez, Spector, & Cooper, 2006). As demonstrated by the diversity of populations studied in this edited book, there is increasing interest in understanding the microaggression experiences of populations not residing in the U.S. context. The exploration of microaggressions in an international context or with U.S. immigrants who are non-native speakers, for example, points to the importance of being sensitive to these measurement issues. Researchers interested in quantitative issues in studying cultural variables can turn to a number of resources for guidance (e.g., Ember, 2009; Quintana, Troyano, & Taylor, 2001; Van de Vijver & Leung, 1997).

Cross-Sectional/Retrospective Versus Longitudinal   The core of the recent literature on microaggressions has uncovered a wealth of rich data on the experiences of racial/ethnic minority and other marginalized groups. As mentioned before, these self-reports have been within cross-sectional and retrospective research designs. Participants share their experiences at one time point and rely on retrospective recall in reconstructing these experiences. Additionally, the narratives generated from interviews allow researchers to understand participants' present attitudes, opinions, beliefs and/or behaviors regarding experiences of microaggressions. In making meaning of these experiences, participants are able to share the *current* or *past* impact on their lives.

Potential concerns raised earlier with retrospective recall can limit our understanding of the findings from recent studies. In particular, one of the main limitations is the likelihood that accuracy of recalls is compromised. However, it can also be argued that understanding microaggressions is more than getting an "accurate" or "truthful" report of the relevant experiences. Rather, as Sue and his colleagues have pointed out (Sue, Capodilupo, et al., 2007), one of the defining features of microaggressions is the clash of experience between the perpetrator and the target. Consequently, there is no single correct recall, but rather, the subjective indeterminacy of that experience is important to record and understand.

In contrast to cross-sectional/retrospective designs, future researchers may consider longitudinal designs. In longitudinal studies, data is gathered over time and pragmatically often requires more resources to conduct than cross-sectional/retrospective studies. There are a number of advantages to examining participants over time. One of the primary advantages is that information about process or change can be more effectively understood. Additionally, recall of microaggressions may be more "fresh" if multiple data collection time points that are temporally closer to the actual incident are gathered. Recording more immediate reactions and the subsequent processes can highlight the development of coping strategies and venues (Sue, Capodilupo, et al., 2007). Here, as with the previous section on measurement issues, we suggest that future researchers broadly consider possible operational forms for collecting data over time. Use of pagers and daily diaries (e.g., experience sampling method; Csikszentmihalyi & Larson, 1987) are possible self-report methods, whereas in vivo observations or coding of taped therapy sessions are possible observation methods.

More recent developments in computer technology have led to the ability of researchers to more immediately sample daily experiences through the use of handheld-sized computers for prompting and experience-reporting purposes. The ability of these methods to capture phenomenologically immediate experiences and situational/temporal changes warrants consideration by future researchers interested in longitudinal designs (Chang, Tugade, & Asakawa, 2006). Whereas current microaggressions researchers acknowledge restricted sampling of microaggression experiences as a limitation in their studies, longitudinal designs broaden the opportunity to capture experiences and events that are not recalled in cross-sectional/retrospective measurement methods.

We strongly believe that qualitative studies should and will play an important role in generating knowledge about microaggressions. Some of the limitations addressed earlier with current qualitative designs can be addressed by considering methodological decisions at the measurement and design level. For example, whereas problems with retrospective recall are a potential limitation, qualitative studies that gather data longitudinally may address that limitation. An example of this is borrowed from the counseling supervision literature. Interpersonal process recall (Kagan, 1965; Kagan & Kagan, 1991) is a method that involves participants reviewing a taped interaction (e.g., therapy/supervision session or vignette of microaggression) with a counselor or researcher who guides them through the process of explicating internal processes during the reviewing of the taped interaction. Review of these interactions can occur over time (e.g., over the course of a training program) such that changes can be qualitatively traced and analyzed. When conducting quantitative studies, methods for longitudinal designs and analysis are abundant (Bijleveld & Van der Kamp, 1998; Collins & Sayer, 2001; Singer & Willet, 2003). For example, Brown and his colleagues (2000) recently found that explicit racial discriminatory experiences at one time point is associated with greater psychological distress one to two years later. Whether from quantitative versus qualitative or experimental versus observational/correlational perspectives, incorporating longitudinal designs into future research will help address a number of research questions that it is not currently possible to address with cross-sectional/retrospective designs.

Experimental versus Observational/Correlational   Lastly, we consider designing studies that are experimental versus observational/correlational. Current microaggression research all falls under observational/correlational designs. With observational/correlational designs, the central design difference with experimental approaches is the lack of random assignment into controlled and narrowly prespecified experimental conditions. In the classic example of treatment efficacy studies, half of the participants are randomly assigned to a treatment condition and the other half to a control condition. Differences found in an outcome measure between the two groups can be attributed solely to the experimental variable manipulated (i.e., presence/absence of treatment). The ability to convincingly draw causal inferences from results is one of the strengths of experiments. Observational/correlational designs, on the other hand, measure variables of interest as they exist. Whether microaggression experiences are uncovered through qualitative interviews or assessed through quantitative measures (e.g., scales), the causal relationship amongst variables of interest cannot be logically inferred in the absence of experimental manipulation.

In observational/correlational studies that are primarily exploratory or inductive in nature, researchers are able to consider a wide range of data by working from the bottom up. Qualitative methodologies, including the ones employed by current microaggressions research, generally fall under this category. This is necessary, given the focus of many qualitative approaches in describing/co-creating but not preemptively explaining experiences under observation (Henwood & Pidgeon, 1992). Observational/correlational designs are also appropriate when variables of interest, for ethical or pragmatic reasons, cannot or should not be manipulated. The harmful and detrimental effects of microaggressions and other subtle forms of discrimination on the health and psychological well-being of individuals is undeniable (Dovidio, Gaertner, Kawakami, & Hodson, 2002; Krieger, 1999; Salvatore & Shelton, 2007; Williams, Neighbors, & Jackson, 2008). Therefore, the experimental manipulation to induce microaggression experiences would raise ethical issues that render observational/correlational designs a more defensible approach.

Experimental designs focus primarily on a targeted set of variables that are manipulated in a controlled way. Although direct experimental manipulation of certain variables (e.g., microaggression assault) may be ethically indefensible, there are nevertheless research questions that can be addressed within experimental designs. For example, the use of vignettes as experimental stimuli is common in a number of social science research areas (e.g., social psychology; Alexander & Becker, 1978; Finch, 1987). Vignettes can elicit perceptions, opinions, beliefs, and attitudes from participants, either through quantitative or qualitative measures. In desiring to understand how participants perceive or react to microaggressions presented in a hypothetical stimulus, researchers may gather qualitative data through individual interviews or focus groups. Alternatively, from an experimental design perspective, variables of interest may be manipulated within the vignettes, and quantitative measures of associated variables may be examined. For example, future researchers may be interested in individual differences (e.g., racial identity) that affect the perceptions of microaggressions under varying situational manipulations (e.g., the perpetrator is of the same or other race). The validity of these vignettes, representing forms of microaggressions particular to targeted populations, can be increased by using qualitative data from existing studies in the development process.

Finally, another experimental area that may be effective in the future study of microaggressions is priming and automacity research (Bargh & Chartrand, 2000). Both types of research are interested in the hidden and passive mediation of internal mental states between social environment and psychological processes and responses. For example, there is broad support for the effect of stereotype activation on behaviors and psychological processes (Wheeler & Petty, 2001). In seminal studies on stereotype threat (Steele, 1997; Steele & Aronson, 1995), researchers primed participants to activate unconscious stereotypes and found that this resulted in decreased performance on cognitive academic tasks. Similarly, in studies on social exclusion (complex processes that lead to individuals/groups feeling excluded or rejected by significant others), researchers have found that experimental manipulation of social exclusion led to a number of negative psychological, interpersonal, and health consequences (Hutchison, Abrams, & Christian, 2007). Microaggressions are known to occur in subtle, unintentional, and often unconscious ways (Dovidio et al., 2002; Sue, Capodilupo, et al., 2007). Priming and automacity research methods offer techniques and designs for addressing the difficulty in directly measuring and manipulating these internal processes.

CONCLUSION AND RECOMMENDATIONS

Decisions about measurement and design issues should be guided by practical, theoretical, and research question factors. Overarching these factors is a consideration and explication of the research paradigm that one originates (Madill & Gough, 2008; Ponterotto, 2005). Consequently, one of the first steps in developing a research project is to explicate the purpose and research questions in light of these paradigmatic assumptions (Haverkamp & Young, 2007). Consistent with the theme that we have developed, we encourage future researchers to broadly consider a diversity of paradigms and methodological approaches covered in this chapter in developing future research studies. In particular, we suggest that openness to alternative paradigms and methodological approaches ameliorates limitations and restrictions inherent in all research studies.

With this in mind, we provide a few broad recommendations that tie together more specific recommendations we have outlined throughout the chapter:

1. Broaden ways to measure microaggressions-related variables (e.g., Table 14.1). We encourage researchers to think of these variables from a number of perspectives that include that of the target, perpetrator, and potential observers. Furthermore, researchers should focus not only on the *experience* of microaggressions but also on *coping* and *management* processes as well.
2. Entertain moderating and mediating variables in understanding microaggression processes. In particular, because research in this area will necessarily involve marginalized groups, the consideration of important cultural variables (e.g., racial/ethnic identity, immigration status, language) and the complexities of intersecting marginalized identities (e.g., Black female) should be entertained.
3. Consider mixed-methods approaches (Hanson, Creswell, Clark, Petska, & Creswell, 2005) in addition to qualitative and quantitative approaches to address the complex, layered, and contextual ways that microaggressions are experienced and perpetrated. We believe that this will elucidate both the universal and unique aspects of microaggressions in the lives of diverse marginalized groups.
4. In taking a social justice stance (Morrow, 2007; Vera & Speight, 2003) on the understanding of microaggressions, embrace research paradigms that transform the research process into proactive social change. Participatory action research (Kidd & Krall, 2005), for example, has the potential to let the voices of those we study influence all stages of the research process.
5. Pursue continuous training and professional development in research methods and design issues. This would include keeping up with advances in methodologies and analytic techniques and with perspectives in ensuring reliability, validity, quality, and trustworthiness of researching findings.

REFERENCES

Alexander, C. S., & Becker, H. J. (1978). The use of vignettes in survey research. *Public Opinion Quarterly, 42,* 93–104.

Bargh, J. A., & Chartrand, T. L. (2000). The mind in the middle: A practical guide to priming and automacity research. In H. T. Reis & C. M. Judd (Eds.), *Handbook of research methods in social and personality psychology* (pp. 253–285). New York: Cambridge University Press.

Beehr, T. A., & McGrath, J. E. (1996). The methodology of research and coping: Conceptual, strategic, and operational-level issues. In M. Zeidner & N. S. Endler (Eds.), *Handbook of coping: Theory, research, applications* (pp. 65–82). New York: John Wiley & Sons.

Benoit, L. G., Veach, P. M., & LeRoy, B. S. (2007). When you care enough to do your very best: Genetic counselor experiences of compassion fatigue. *Journal of Genetic Counseling, 16*(3), 299–312.

Bijleveld, C. C. J. H., & Van der Kamp, T. (1998). *Longitudinal data analysis: Designs, models, and methods.* Newbury Park, CA: Sage.

Blustein, D. L., Chaves, A. P., Diemer, M. A., Gallagher, L. A., Marshall, K. G., Sirin, S., & Bhati, K. S. (2002). Voices of the forgotten half: The role of social class in the school-to-work transition. *Journal of Counseling Psychology, 49*(3), 311–323.

Brewer, H. M., Eatough, V., Smith, J. A., Stanley, C. A., Glendinning, N. W., & Quarrell, O. W. J. (2008). The impact of juvenile Huntington's disease on the family: The case of a rare childhood condition. *Journal of Health Psychology, 13*(1), 5–16.

Brown, C., Pikler, V. I., Lavish, L. A., Keune, K. M., & Hutto, C. J. (2008). Surviving childhood leukemia: Career, family, and future expectations. *Qualitative Health Research, 18*(1), 19–30.

Brown, T. N., Williams, D. R., Jackson, J. S., Neighbors, H. W., Torres, M., Sellers, S. L., & Brown, K. T. (2000). "Being Black and feeling blue": The mental health consequences of racial discrimination. *Race & Society, 2*, 117–131.

Bruning, N. S., & Frew, D. R. (1987). Effects of exercise, relaxation, and management skills training on physiological stress indicators: A field experiment. *Journal of Applied Psychology, 72*(4), 515–521.

Cacioppo, J. T., Tassinary, L. G., & Bernston, G. G. (Eds.). (2000). *Handbook of psychophysiology.* New York: Cambridge University Press.

Carter, R. T., & Morrow, S. L. (Eds.). (2007a). Qualitative issues in analyses in counseling psychology: Part III [Special issue]. *Counseling Psychologist 35*(2).

Carter, R. T., & Morrow, S. L. (Eds.). (2007b). Qualitative issues in analyses in counseling psychology: Part IV [Special issue]. *Counseling Psychologist 35*(3).

Chang, E. C., Tugade, M. M., & Asakawa, K. (2006). Stress and coping among Asian Americans: Lazarus and Folkman's model and beyond. In P. T. P. Wong & L. C. J. Wong (Eds.), *Handbook of multicultural perspectives of stress and coping* (pp. 439–455). New York: Springer.

Clare, L. (2002). Developing awareness about awareness in early-stage dementia: The role of psychosocial factors. *Dementia, 1*(3), 295–312.

Collins, L. M., & Sayer, A. (Eds.). (2001). *New methods for the analysis of change.* Washington, DC: American Psychological Association (APA).

Constantine, M. G. (2007). Racial microaggressions against African American clients in cross-racial counseling relationships. *Journal of Counseling Psychology, 54*, 1–16.

Constantine, M. G., Anderson, G. M., Berkel, L. A., Caldwell, L. D., & Utsey, S. O. (2005). Examining the cultural adjustment experiences of African international college students: A qualitative analysis. *Journal of Counseling Psychology, 52*, 57–66.

Constantine, M. G., Smith, L., Redington, R. M., & Owens, D. (2008). Racial micro-aggressions against Black counseling and counseling psychology faculty: A central challenge in the multicultural counseling movement. *Journal of Counseling and Development, 86,* 348–355.

Constantine, M. G., & Sue, D. W. (2007). Perceptions of racial microaggressions among Black supervisees in cross-racial dyads. *Journal of Counseling Psychology, 54*(2), 142–153.

Csikszentmihalyi, M., & Larson, R. (1987). Validity and reliability of experience-sampling method. *Journal of Nervous and Mental Diseases, 175,* 526–536.

Derks, B., Inzlicht, M., & Kang, S. (2008). The neuroscience of stigma and stereotype threat. *Group Processes & Intergroup Relations, 11,* 163–181.

Dovidio, J. F., Gaertner, S. L., Kawakami, K., & Hodson, G. (2002). Why can't we all just get along? Interpersonal biases and interracial distrust. *Cultural Diversity and Ethnic Minority Psychology, 8,* 88–102.

Eatough, V., & Smith, J. A. (2006a). I feel like a scrambled egg in my head: An idiographic case study of meaning making and anger using interpretative phenomenological analysis. *Psychology & Psychotherapy: Theory, Research & Practice, 79,* 115–135.

Eatough, V., & Smith, J. A. (2006b). I was like a wild person: Understanding feelings of anger using interpretative phenomenological analysis. *British Journal of Psychology, 97,* 483–498.

Eatough, V., Smith, J. A., & Shaw, R. (2008). Women, anger, and aggression: An inter-pretative phenomenological analysis. *Journal of Interpersonal Violence, 23,* 1767–1799.

Elliott, R. (1989). Comprehensive process analysis: Understanding the change process in significant therapy events. In M. J. Packer & R. B. Addison (Eds.), *Entering the circle: Hermeneutic investigations in psychology* (pp. 165–184). Albany: State University of New York (SUNY) Press.

Ember, C. (2009). *Cross-cultural research methods* (2nd ed.). Lanham, MD: Rowman and Littlefield.

Evans, A., Elford, J., & Wiggins, D. (2008). Using the Internet for qualitative research. In C. Willig & W. Stainton-Rogers (Eds.), *The Sage handbook of qualitative research in psychology* (pp. 315–333). Los Angeles, CA: Sage.

Finch, J. (1987). The vignette technique in survey research. *Sociology, 21,* 105–114.

Hanson, W. E., Creswell, J. W., Clark, V. L. P., Petska, K. S., & Creswell, J. D. (2005). Mixed methods research designs in counseling psychology. *Journal of Counseling Psychology, 52,* 224–235.

Harrell, J. P., Hall, S., & Taliaferro, J. (2003). Physiological responses to racism and discrimination: An assessment of the evidence. *American Journal of Public Health, 9,* 243–248.

Haverkamp, B. E., Morrow, S. L., & Ponterotto, J. G. (Eds.). (2005). Knowledge in context: Qualitative methods in counseling psychology research [Special issue]. *Journal of Counseling Psychology 52*(2).

Haverkamp, B. E., & Young, R. A. (2007). Paradigms, purpose, and the role of the literature: Formulating a rationale for qualitative investigations. *Counseling Psychologist, 35,* 265–294.

Henwood, K. L., & Pidgeon, N. F. (1992). Qualitative research psychological theorizing. *British Journal of Psychology, 83*, 97–111.

Hill, C. E., Knox, S., Thompson, B. J., Williams, E. N., Hess, S. A., & Ladany, N. (2005). Consensual qualitative research: An update. *Journal of Counseling Psychology, 52*(2), 196–205.

Hill, C. E., Thompson, B. J., & Williams, E. N. (1997). A guide to conducting consensual qualitative research. *Counseling Psychologist, 25*(4), 517–572.

Hoshmand, L. T. (1989). Alternative research paradigms: A review and teaching proposal. *Counseling Psychologist, 17*, 3–79.

Howard, G. S. (2003). A philosophy of science for cross-cultural psychology. In D. B. Pope-Davis, H. L. K. Coleman, W. M. Liu, & R. L. Toporek (Eds.), *Handbook of multicultural competencies in counseling and psychology* (pp. 72–89). Thousand Oaks, CA: Sage.

Hsieh, H., & Shannon, S. E. (2005). Three approaches to qualitative content analysis. *Qualitative Health Research, 15*, 1277–1288.

Hutchison, P., Abrams, D., & Christian, J. (2007). The social psychology of exclusion. In D. Abrams, J. Christian, & D. Gordon (Eds.), *Multidisciplinary handbook of social exclusion research* (pp. 29–57). Chichester, England: John Wiley & Sons.

Inman, A. G., Howard, E. E., Beaumont, R. L., & Walker, J. A. (2007). Cultural transmission: Influence of contextual factors in Asian Indian immigrant parents' experiences. *Journal of Counseling Psychology, 54*, 93–100.

Jarman, M., Smith, J. A., & Walsh, S. (1997). The psychological battle for control: A qualitative study of healthcare professionals' understandings of the treatment of anorexia nervosa. *Journal of Community and Applied Social Psychology, 7*, 137–152.

Juntunen, C. L., Barraclough, D. J., Broneck, C. L., Seibel, G. A., Winrow, S. A., & Morin, P. M. (2001). American Indian perspectives on the career journey. *Journal of Counseling Psychology, 48*, 274–285.

Kagan, N. (1965). *Interpersonal process recall*. East Lansing, MI: Bureau of Educational Research Services, College of Education.

Kagan, N., & Kagan, H. (1991). Interpersonal process recall. In P. W. Dowrick (Ed.), *A practical guide to using video in the behavioral sciences* (pp. 221–230). New York: John Wiley & Sons.

Kidd, S. A., & Krall, M. J. (2005). Practicing participatory action research. *Journal of Counseling Psychology, 52*, 187–195.

Knudson, B., & Coyle, A. (2002). The experience of hearing voices: An interpretative phenomenological analysis. *Existential Analysis, 13*(1), 117–134.

Krieger, N. (1999). Embodying inequality: A review of concepts, measures, and methods for studying health consequences of discrimination. *International Journal of Health Services, 29*, 295–352.

Madill, A., & Gough, B. (2008). Qualitative research and its place in psychological science. *Psychological Methods, 13*, 254–271.

McGrath, J. E. (1970). *Social and psychological factors in stress*. New York: Holt, Rinehart & Winston.

Merrick, E. (1999). An exploration of quality in qualitative research: Are "reliability" and "validity" relevant? In M. Kopala & L. A. Suzuki (Eds.), *Using qualitative methods in psychology* (pp. 25–36). Thousand Oaks, CA: Sage.

Merritt, M. M., Bennett, G. G., Williams, R. B., Edwards, C. L., & Sollers, J. J. (2006). Perceived racism and cardiovascular reactivity and recovery to personally relevant stress. *Health Psychology, 25*(3), 364–369.

Morrow, S. L. (2005). Quality and trustworthiness in qualitative research in counseling psychology. *Journal of Counseling Psychology, 52,* 250–260.

Morrow, S. L. (2007). Qualitative research in counseling psychology: Conceptual foundations. *Counseling Psychologist, 35,* 209–235.

Neimeyer, G., & Resnikoff, A. (1982). Qualitative strategies in counseling research. *Counseling Psychologist, 10,* 75–85.

Nelson, M. L., Englar-Carlson, M., Tierney, S. C., & Hau, J. M. (2006). Class jumping into academia: Multiple identities for counseling academics. *Journal of Counseling Psychology, 53*(1), 1–14.

Ochsner, K. N., & Lieberman, M. D. (2001). The emergence of social cognitive neuroscience. *American Psychologist, 56,* 717–734.

Patton, M. Q. (1990). *Qualitative evaluation and research methods* (2nd ed.). Thousand Oaks, CA: Sage.

Patton, M. Q. (2002). *Qualitative research and evaluation methods* (3rd ed.). Thousand Oaks, CA: Sage.

Pearce, A., Clare, L., & Pistrang, N. (2002). Managing sense of self: Coping in the early stages of Alzheimer's disease. *Dementia, 1*(2), 173–192.

Pennebaker, J. W., & Beall, S. K. (1986). Confronting a traumatic event: Toward an understanding of inhibition and disease. *Journal of Abnormal Psychology, 95,* 274–281.

Pierce, C. (1995). Stress analogs of racism and sexism: Terrorism, torture, and disaster. In C. Willie, P. Rieker, B. Kramer, & B. Brown (Eds.), *Mental health, racism, and sexism* (pp. 277–293). Pittsburgh, PA: University of Pittsburgh Press.

Pierce, C., Carew, J., Pierce-Gonzalez, D., & Willis, D. (1978). An experiment in racism: TV commercials. In C. Pierce (Ed.), *Television and education* (pp. 62–88). Beverly Hills, CA: Sage.

Polkinghorne, D. E. (1988). *Narrative knowing and the human sciences.* Albany: SUNY Press.

Ponterotto, J. G. (2005). Qualitative research in counseling psychology: A primer on research paradigms and philosophy of science. *Journal of Counseling Psychology, 52,* 126–136.

Potter, W. J., & Levine-Donnerstein, D. (1999). Rethinking validity and reliability in content analysis. *Journal of Applied Communication Research, 27,* 258–284.

Quintana, S. M., Troyano, N., & Taylor, G. (2001). Cultural validity and inherent challenges in quantitative methods for multicultural research. In J. G. Ponterotto, M. J. Casas, L. A. Suzuki, & C. M. Alexander (Eds.), *Handbook of multicultural counseling* (2nd ed., pp. 604–631). Thousand Oaks, CA: Sage.

Rennie, D. L., Watson, K. D., & Monteiro, A. M. (2002). The rise of qualitative research in psychology. *Canadian Psychology, 43,* 170–190.

Richman, L. S., Bennett, G. G., Pek, J., Siegler, I., & Williams, R. B. (2007). Discrimination, dispositions, and cardiovascular responses to stress. *Health Psychology*, *26*(6), 675–683.

Robinson, L., Clarke, L., & Evans, K. (2005). Making sense of dementia and adjusting to loss: Psychological reactions to a diagnosis of dementia in couples. *Aging & Mental Health*, *9*(4), 337–347.

Salvatore, J., & Shelton, J. N. (2007). Cognitive costs of exposure to racial prejudice. *Psychological Science*, *18*, 810–815.

Sanchez, J. I., Spector, P. E., & Cooper, C. L. (2006). Frequently ignored methodological issues in cross-cultural stress research. In P. T. P. Wong & L. C. J. Wong (Eds.), *Handbook of multicultural perspectives of stress and coping* (pp. 187–201). New York: Springer.

Singer, J. D., & Willet, J. B. (2003). *Applied longitudinal data analysis: Modeling change and event occurrence*. New York: Oxford University Press.

Smith, J. A. (2004). Reflecting on the development of interpretative phenomenological analysis and its contributions to qualitative research in psychology. *Qualitative Research in Psychology*, *1*, 39–54.

Smith, J. A., Brewer, H. M., Eatough, V., Stanley, C. A., Glendinning, N. W., & Quarrell, O. W. J. (2006). The personal experience of juvenile Huntington's disease: An interpretative phenomenological analysis of parents' accounts of the primary features of a rare genetic condition. *Clinical Genetics*, *69*(6), 486–496.

Smith, J. A., & Eatough, V. (2007). Interpretative phenomenological analysis. In E. Lyons & A. Coyle (Eds.), *Analysing qualitative data in psychology* (pp. 35–50). London, England: Sage.

Smith, J. A., & Osborn, M. (2004). Interpretative phenomenological analysis. In G. M. Breakwell (Ed.), *Doing social psychology research* (pp. 229–254). Leicester, England: British Psychological Society.

Smith, J. A., & Osborn, M. (2007). Pain as an assault on the self: An interpretative phenomenological analysis on the psychological impact of chronic benign low back pain. *Psychology & Health*, *22*(5), 517–534.

Strauss, A., & Corbin, J. (1998). *Basics of qualitative research: Grounded theory procedures and techniques* (2nd ed.). Thousand Oaks, CA: Sage.

Sue, D. W., Bucceri, J., Lin, A. I., Nadal, K. L., & Torino, G. (2007). Racial microaggressions and the Asian American experience. *Cultural Diversity and Ethnic Minority Psychology*, *13*, 72–81.

Sue, D. W., Capodilupo, C. M., & Holder, A. (2008). Microaggressions in the life experience of Black Americans. *Professional Psychology: Research and Practice*, *39*, 329–336.

Sue, D. W., Capodilupo, C. M., Torino, G., Bucceri, J. M., Nadal, K., & Esquilin, M. E. (2007). Racial microaggressions in everyday life: Implications for clinical practice. *American Psychologist*, *62*, 271–286.

Sue, D. W., Lin, A. I., Torino, G. C., Capodilupo, C. M., & Rivera, D. P. (2009). Racial microaggression and difficult dialogues on race in the classroom. *Cultural Diversity and Ethnic Minority Psychology*, *15*, 183–190.

Sue, D. W., Nadal, K. L., Capodilupo, C. M., Lin, A. I., Torino, G. C., & Rivera, D. P. (2008). Racial microaggressions against Black Americans: Implications for counseling. *Journal for Counseling and Development*, *86*, 330–338.

Taylor, S. E., Burklund, L. J., Eisenberger, N. I., Hilmert, C. J., Lieberman, M. D., & Lehman, B. J. (2008). Neural bases of moderation of cortisol stress responses by psychosocial resources. *Journal of Personality and Social Psychology*, *95*, 197–211.

Tweed, R. G., & DeLongis, A. (2006). Problems and strategies when using rating scales in cross-cultural coping research. In P. T. P. Wong & L. C. J. Wong (Eds.), *Handbook of multicultural perspectives of stress and coping* (pp. 203–221). New York: Springer.

University of London, Birkbeck. (2009). Department of Psychological Sciences in the School of Science: Dr. Jonathan A. Smith. Retrieved March 14, 2009, from the University of London, Birkbeck web site: http://7/www.bbk.ac.uk/psyc/staff/academic/jsmith.

Utsey, S. O., & Hook, J. N. (2007). Heart rate variability as a physiological moderator of the relationship between race-related stress and psychological distress in African Americans. *Cultural Diversity and Ethnic Minority Psychology*, *13*, 250–253.

Van de Vijver, F. J. R., & Leung, K. (1997). *Methods and data analysis for cross-cultural research*. Thousand Oaks, CA: Sage.

Vera, E. M., & Speight, S. L. (2003). Multicultural competence, social justice, and counseling psychology: Expanding our roles. *Counseling Psychologist*, *31*, 253–272.

Wheeler, S. C., & Petty, R. E. (2001). The effects of stereotype activation on behavior: A review of possible mechanisms. *Psychological Bulletin*, *127*, 797–826.

Williams, D. R., Neighbors, H. W., & Jackson, J. S. (2008). Racial/ethnic discrimination and health: Findings from community studies. *American Journal of Public Health*, *93*, 200–208.

About the Contributors

Lauren M. Appio is a doctoral student in counseling psychology at Teachers College, Columbia University. Her areas of interest include cultural competence, intersections of identity, and socially just research methodology and clinical practice.

Bushra Aryan is a doctoral candidate in higher education at the Morgridge College of Education, University of Denver. Her major research interests include women of color in the academy, critical race feminism, and access and equity for underrepresented students in higher education.

Christina M. Capodilupo is an assistant professor in the Graduate Institute of Professional Psychology at the University of Hartford. Her areas of interest include the etiology of eating disorders for women of color, the impact of idealized media images on women's body image, and everyday experiences of racism and sexism.

Lindsay Corman is pursuing her doctorate in the Clinical Child Psychology Program at the University of West Virginia. Her research interests include forensic interviewing, jurors' views toward victims of sexual assault, and the impact of race on the perception of eyewitnesses.

Melissa J. H. Corpus is a doctoral candidate in the Counseling Psychology Program at Teachers College, Columbia University. She is an adjunct faculty member at Kingsborough Community College, City University of New York. Her research interests include examining the intersections of identities, such as sexual orientation, race/ethnicity, and gender.

Erin E. Forquer is currently a doctoral student in the Counseling Psychology Program at Teachers College. Her research interests include racial identity development and sexual orientation discrimination.

Corinne E. Galgay received her master's of education in psychological counseling at Teachers College, Columbia University. She currently works as the career counselor in the Career Services Office at Teachers College. Her research interests focus on disability discrimination, the impact of microaggressions on mental health, and the relationship between trauma and psychopathology.

Katie E. Griffin is a master's student in forensic psychology at John Jay College of Criminal Justice, City University of New York. Her research interests include microaggressions and mental health, as well as hate crimes and associated legislation.

Fernando Guzman is assistant provost for multicultural faculty recruitment and retention and an adjunct assistant professor in the Graduate School of Professional Psychology at the University of Denver.

Sahran Hamit received her master's in forensic mental health counseling from John Jay College of Criminal Justice, City University of New York. Her research interests include the development of juvenile delinquent behavior, alternatives to incarceration for youth, and the effects of discrimination on mental health and behavior.

Jill S. Hill is an assistant professor in the Department of Counseling and Clinical Psychology at Teachers College, Columbia University. Her areas of interest include culturally competent approaches to psychological assessment and clinical interventions with Indigenous groups; examination of disparities in mental health service availability, accessibility, delivery, and utilization that adversely affect Indigenous peoples; and ethical and culturally valid approaches to research.

Marie-Anne Issa is a doctoral candidate in forensic psychology at John Jay College of Criminal Justice. She received her master of arts in psychology from the American University of Beirut, Lebanon, and a master of arts in forensic psychology from John Jay College of Criminal Justice, City University of New York. Her research interests include psychopathy, juvenile   justice, violence, forensic assessment, stereotypes and prejudice, and cross-cultural issues.

Marc P. Johnston is a doctoral student in the Higher Education and Organizational Change Program at University of California, Los Angeles. His major research interests focus on diversity issues in higher education, especially related to multiracial college students.

Richard M. Keller is an assistant professor of psychology and education at Teachers College, Columbia University, and director of the Office of Access and Services for Individuals with Disabilities at Teachers College. His scholarly interests focus on social justice, disability, employment and people with disabilities, self-disclosure, and microaggressions. Dr. Keller is a person who lives with a disability and has been involved with the disability rights movement for the past 20 years.

Rachel H. Kim is a doctoral student in counseling psychology at Teachers College, Columbia University. Her research interests include the impact of microaggressions, experience of international students, multicultural competence, and intersectionality of multiple identities.

Suah Kim is a doctoral student in counseling psychology at Teachers College, Columbia University. Her areas of interest include ethnic minority and women's mental health issues, as well as feminist theory and multicultural competence in therapy, supervision, and training.

Theressa L. LaBarrie is a doctoral student in clinical psychology at DePaul University. She obtained her master's degree in psychology and education at Teachers College, Columbia University, and her interests include multicultural competence and the development of culturally sensitive evidence-based assessments and interventions.

Michael Y. Lau is an assistant professor of psychology and education at Teachers College, Columbia University. His major research interests include philosophical and theoretical issues in psychology, research methodology, and Asian/Asian American psychology.

Annie I. Lin is a doctoral candidate in counseling psychology at Teachers College, Columbia University. Her major research interests include racism, acculturation, and Asian American issues.

Oliver B. Lyons holds a master's degree in forensic psychology from John Jay College of Criminal Justice, City University of New York. His areas of interest include the etiology of juvenile conduct problems, noninstitutionalized psychopathy, and the contribution of everyday discrimination to mental illness and antisocial behavior.

Fernand Lubuguin is an assistant professor in the Graduate School of Professional Psychology at the University of Denver. He is also the director of diversity and multicultural training and the director of the Professional Psychology Clinic.

Kevin L. Nadal is an assistant professor of mental health counseling and psychology at John Jay College of Criminal Justice, City University of New York. He has published several works focusing on Filipino American, ethnic minority, and LGBTQ issues in the fields of psychology and education.

Rebecca Rangel is a doctoral student in counseling psychology at Teachers College, Columbia University. Her major interest area involves cultural competence with a focus on working with monolingual Spanish speakers and Latino immigrant populations.

Rebecca M. Redington is a doctoral candidate in the Counseling Psychology Program at Teachers College, Columbia University. She received her master's of science in child development from Tufts University. Her research interests include counselors' perceptions of interracial families and parent-child relations in nontraditional families, including those formed through transracial and international adoptions.

David P. Rivera is a doctoral candidate in counseling psychology at Teachers College, Columbia University. His research interests include issues impacting the marginalization and health of people of color and sexual minorities.

Laura Smith is an assistant professor of psychology and education at Teachers College, Columbia University. Her research interests include social class, poverty, participatory action research, and the development of socially just community-based psychological practice.

Jesus Trevino is associate provost for multicultural excellence with the Center for Multicultural Excellence at the University of Denver.

Nicole L. Watkins is a doctoral candidate in counseling psychology at Teachers College, Columbia University. Her academic and professional emphases include clinical multicultural competence, factors that promote resilience among marginalized populations, student development, psychological assessment, and the intersections of race, gender, social class, and sexual orientation.

Alexa Weinberg is a doctoral student in clinical psychology at the Florida Institute of Technology. Her areas of research/interest include sex offender recidivism, negative maladaptive behaviors, and subtle sexism.

Chantea D. Williams is a doctoral student in counseling psychology at Teachers College, Columbia University. Her areas of interest include racism and multicultural competency, research, and education.

Microaggressions
and Marginality

Author Index

Subject Index